South Asia

Directed and Designed by Hans Hoefer
Produced and Edited by Geoffrey Eu
Featuring photographers of the Apa Photo Agency

APA PUBLICATIONS

THE INSIGHT GUIDES SERIES RECEIVED SPECIAL AWARDS
FOR EXCELLENCE FROM THE PACIFIC AREA TRAVEL
ASSOCIATION.

SOUTH ASIA
First Edition (Reprint)

© **1988 APA PUBLICATIONS (HK) LTD**
Printed in Singapore by APA Press Pte. Ltd.
Colour Separation in Singapore by Colourscan Pte Ltd

APA PUBLICATIONS

Publisher: Hans Johannes Hoefer
General Manager: Henry Lee
Marketing Director: Aileen Lau
Editorial Director: Geoffrey Eu
Editorial Manager: Vivien Kim
Editorial Consultants: Adam Liptak (North America)
Brian Bell (Europe)
Heinz Vestner (German Editions)

Project Editors

Helen Abbott, Diana Ackland, Mohamed Amin, Ravindralal Anthonis, Roy Bailet,
Louisa Cambell, Jon Carroll, Hillary Cunningham, John Eames, Janie Freeburg,
Bikram Grewal, Virginia Hopkins, Samuel Israel, Jay Itzkowitz, Phil Jaratt, Tracy
Johnson, Ben Kalb, Wilhelm Klein, Saul Lockhart, Sylvia Mayuga, Gordon
MaLauchlan, Kal Müller, Eric Oey, Daniel P. Reid, Kim Robinson, Ronn Ronck,
Robert Seidenberg, Rolf Steinberg, Sriyani Tidball, Lisa Van Gruisen, Merin
Wexler.

Contributing Writers

A.D. Aird, Ruth Armstrong, T. Terence Barrow, F. Lisa Beebe, Bruce Berger, Dor
Bahadur Bista, Clinton V. Black, Star Black, Frena Bloomfield, John Borthwick,
Roger Boschman, Tom Brosnahan, Jerry Carroll, Tom Chaffin, Nedra Chung,
Tom Cole, Orman Day, Kunda Dixit, Richard Erdoes, Guillermo Gar-Oropeza,
Ted Giannoulas, Barbara Gloudon, Harka Gurung, Sharifah Hamzah, Willard A.
Hanna, Elizabeth Hawley, Sir Edmund Hillary, Tony Hillerman, Jerry Hopkins,
Peter Hutton, Neil Jameson, Michael King, Michele Kort, Thomas Lucey,
Leonard Lueras, Michael E. Macmillan, Derek Maitland, Buddy Mays, Craig
McGregor, Reinhold Messner, Julie Michaels, M.R. Priya Rangsit, Al Read,
Elizabeth V. Reyes, Victor Stafford Reid, Harry Rolnick, E.R. Sarachandra, Uli
Schmetzer, Ilsa Sharp, Norman Sibley, Peter Spiro, Harold Stephens, Keith
Stevens, Michael Stone, Desmond Tate, Colin Taylor, Deanna L. Thompson,
Randy Udall, James Wade, Mallika Wanigasundara, William Warren, Cynthia
Wee, Tony Wheeler, Linda White, H. Taft Wireback, Alfred A. Yuson, Paul Zach.

Contributing Photographers

Carole Allen, Ping Amarand, Tony Arruza, Marcello Bertinetti, Alberto Cassio,
Pat Canova, Alain Compost, Ray Cranbourne, Alian Evrard, Ricardo Ferro, Lee
Foster, Manfred Gottschalk, Werner Hahn, Dallas and John Heaton, Brent
Hesselyn, Hans Hoefer, Luca Invernizzi, Ingo Jezierski, Wilhelm Klein, Dennis
Lane, Max Lawrence, Lyle Lawson, Philip Little, Guy Marche, Antonio Martinelli,
David Messent, Ben Nakayama, Vautier de Nanxe, Kal Müller, Günter
Pfannmüller, Van Philips, Ronni Pinsler, Fitz Prenzel, G.P. Reichelt, Dan
Rocovits, David Ryan, Frank Salmoiraghi, Thomas Schollhammer, Blair Seitz,
David Stahl, Bill Wassman, Rendo Yap, Hisham Youssef.
While contributions to Insight Guides are very welcome, the publisher cannot
assume responsibility for the care and return of unsolicited manuscripts or
photographs. Return postage and/or a self-addressed envelope must accom-
pany unsolicited material if it is to be returned. Please address all editorial
contributions to Apa Publications, P.O. Box 219, Orchard Point Post Office,
Singapore 9123.

Editori SRL. Via Ganaceto 121, 41100 Modena, Italy. **Jamaica:** Novelty Trading
Co., P.O. Box 80, 53 Hanover Street, Kingston, Jamaica. **Japan:** Charles E.
Tuttle Co. Inc., 2-6 Suido 1-Chome, Bunkyo-ku, Tokyo 112, Japan. **Kenya:**
Camerapix Publishers International Ltd., P.O. Box 45048, Nairobi, Kenya.
Korea: Kyobo Book Centre Co., Ltd., P.O. Box Kwang Hwa Moon 1 658, Seoul,
Korea. **Philippines:** National Book Store, 701 Rizal Avenue, Manila, Philippines.
Singapore: MPH Distributors (S) Pte. Ltd., 601 Sims Drive #03-21 Pan-I
Warehouse and Office Complex, S'pore 1438, Singapore. **Switzerland:** M.P.A.
Agencies-Import SA, CH. du Croset 9, CH-1024, Ecublens, Switzerland. **Tai-
wan:** Caves Books Ltd., 103 Chungshan N. Road, Sec. 2, Taipei, Taiwan,
Republic of China. **Thailand:** Asia Books Co. Ltd., 5 Sukhumvit Road Soi 61,
P.O. Box 11-40, Bangkok 10110, Thailand. **United Kingdom, Ireland and
Europe (others):** Harrap Ltd., 19-23 Ludgate Hill, London EC4M 7PD, England,
United Kingdom. **Mainland United States and Canada:** Graphic Arts Center
Publishing, 3019 N.W. Yeon, P.O. Box 10306, Portland OR 97210, U.S.A. (The
Pacific Northwest title only); Prentice Hall Press, Gulf & Western Building, One
Gulf & Western Plaza, New York, NY 10023, U.S.A. (all other titles).

French editions: Editions Gallimard, 5 rue Sébastien-Bottin, F-75007 Paris,
France. **German editions:** Nelles Verlag GmbH, Schleissheirner Str. 371b,
8000 Munich 45, West Germany **Italian editions:** Zanfi Editori SLR. Via
Ganaceto 121 41100 Modena, Italy. **Portuguese editions:** Cedibra Editora
Brasileira Ltda, Rua Leonidia, 2-Rio de Janeiro, Brazil.

Advertising and Special Sales Representatives

Advertising carried in Insight Guides gives readers direct access to quality
merchandise and travel-related services. These advertisements are inserted in
the Guide in Brief section of each book. Advertisers are requested to contact their
nearest representatives, listed below.
Special sales, for promotion purposes within the international travel industry and
for educational purposes, are also available. The advertising representatives
listed here also handle special sales. Alternatively, interested parties can contact
Apa Publications, P.O. Box 219, Orchard Point Post Office, Singapore 9123.

Australia and New Zealand: Harve and Gullifer Pty. Ltd. 1 Fawkner St. Kilda
3181, Australia. Tel: (3) 525 3422; Tlx: 523259; Fax: (89) 4312837.
Canada: The Pacific Rim Agency, 6900 Cote Saint Luc Road, Suite 303,
Montreal, Quebec, Canada H4V 2Y9. Tel: (514) 9311299; Tlx: 0525134 MTL;
Fax: (514) 8615571.
Hawaii: HawaiianLMedia Sales; 1750 Kalakaua Ave., Suite 3-243, Honolulu,
Hawaii 96826, U.S.A. Tel: (808) 9464483.
Hong Kong: C Cheney & Associates, 17th Floor, D'Aguilar Place, 1-30 D'Aguilar
Street, Central, Hong Kong. Tel: 5-213671; Tlx: 63079 CCAL HX.
India and Nepal, Pakistan and Bangladesh: Universal Media, CHA 2/718, 719
Kantipath, Lazimpat, Kathmandu-2, Nepal. Tel: 412911/414502; Tlx: 2229 KAJI
NP ATTN MEDIA.
Indonesia: Media Investment Services, Setiabudi Bldg. 2, 4th Floor, Suite 407,
Jl. Hr. Rasuna Said, Kuningan, Jakarta Selatan 12920, Indonesia. Tel: 5782723/
5782752; Tlx: 62418 MEDIANETIA; Mata Graphic Design, Batujimbar, Sanur,
Bali, Indonesia. Tel: (0361) 8073. (for Bali only)
Korea: Kaya Ad Inc., Rm. 402 Kunshin Annex B/D, 251-1 Dohwa Dong, Mapo-
Ku, Seoul, Korea (121). Tel: (2) 7196906; Tlx: K 32144 KAYAAD; Fax: (2)
7199816.
Philippines: Torres Media Sales Inc., 21 Warbler St., Greenmeadows 1,
Murphy, Quezon City, Metro Manila, Philippines. Tel: 722-02-43; Tlx: 23312 RHP
PH.
Taiwan: Cheney Tan & Van Associates, 7th Floor, 10 Alley 4, Lane 545 Tun Hua
South Road, Taipei, Taiwan. Tel: (2) 7002963; Tlx: 11491 FOROSAN; Fax: (2)
3821270.
Thailand: Cheney, Tan & Van Outrive, 17th Floor Rajapark Bldg., 163 Asoke
Rd., Bangkok 10110, Thailand. Tel: 2583244/2583259; Tlx: 20666 RAJAPAK
TH.
Singapore and Malaysia: Cheney Tan Associates, 1 Goldhill Plaza, #02-01,
Newton Rd., Singapore 1130, Singapore. Tel: 2549522; Tlx: RS 35983 CTAL.
Sri Lanka: Spectrum Lanka Advertising Ltd., 56 1/2 Ward Place, Colombo 7, Sri
Lanka. Tel: 5984648/596227; Tlx: 21439 SPECTRM CE.
U.K., Ireland and Europe: Brian Taplin Associates, 32 Fishery Road, Boxmoor,
Hemel Hempstead, Herts HP 1ND, U.K. Tel: (2)215635; Tlx: 825454 CHARMAN.

Distributors:

Australia and New Zealand: Prentice Hall of Australia, 7 Grosvenor Place,
Brookvale, NSW 2100, Australia. **Benelux:** Utigeverij Cambium, Naarderstraat
11, 1251 AW Laren, The Netherlands. **Brazil and Portugal:** Cedibra Editora
Brasileira Ltda, Rua Leonidia, 2-Rio de Janeiro, Brazil. **Denmark:** Copenhagen
Book Centre Aps, Roskildeveji 338, DK-2630 Tastrup, Denmark. **Germany:** RV
Reise-und Verkehrsuerlag Gmbh, Neumarkter Strasse 18, 8000 Munchen 80,
West Germany. **Hawaii:** Pacific Trade Group Inc., P.O. Box 1227, Kailua, Oahu,
Hawaii 96734, U.S.A. **Hong Kong:** Far East Media Ltd., Vita Tower, 7th Floor,
Block B, 29 Wong Chuk Hang Road, Hong Kong. **India and Nepal:** India Book
Distributors, 107/108 Arcadia Building, 195 Narima Point, Bombay-400-021,
India. **Indonesia:** Java Books, Box 55 J.K.C.P., Jakarta, Indonesia. **Israel:**
Steimatzky Ltd., P.O. Box 628, Tel Aviv 61006, Israel (Israel title only). **Italy:** Zanfi

APA PHOTO AGENCY PTE. LTD.

The Apa Photo Agency is S.E. Asia's leading stock photo archive, representing
the work of professional photographers from all over the world. More than
150,000 original color transparencies are available for advertising, editorial and
educational uses. We are linked with Tony Stone Worldwide, one of Europe's
leading stock agencies, and their associate offices around the world:
Singapore: Apa Photo Agency Pte. Ltd., P.O. Box 219, Orchard Point Post
Office, Singapore 9123, Singapore. **London:** Tony Stone Worldwide, 28 Finch-
ley Rd., St. John's Wood, London NW8 6ES, England. **North America &
Canada:** Masterfile Inc., 415 Yonge St., Suite 200, Toronto M5B 2E7, Canada.
Paris: Fotogram-Stone Agence Photographique, 45 rue de Richelieu, 75001
Paris, France. **Barcelona:** Fototec Torre Dels Pardais, 7 Barcelona 08026,
Spain. **Johannesburg:** Color Library (Pty.) Ltd., P.O. Box 1659, Johannesburg,
SOuth Africa 2000. **Sydney:** The Photographic Library of Australia Pty. Ltd., 7
Ridge Street, North Sydney, New South Wales 2050, Australia. **Tokyo:** Orion
Press, 55-1 Kanda Jimbocho, Chiyoda-ku, Tokyo 101, Japan.

The Indian subcontinent seems to hold an irresistible attraction for Apa Publications and its series of Insight Guides. In recent years, the region has spawned various titles, including guides to *India, Rajasthan, Nepal, Sri Lanka* and the first in the *Great Adventure* series, *Indian Wildlife*. More titles featuring the region are currently on the drawing board. It seemed only logical to package the subcontinent into a single, compact volume, sort of a highlight guide.

Insight Guide: South Asia represents the second compilation of Asian countries in the *Grand Tour* format, following *East Asia*, published in 1987. While India, Nepal, Bhutan, Tibet, Pakistan, Sri Lanka and Bangladesh by themselves provide material enough for a whole series of books, the idea (or selective reasoning, given the space constraints) behind *South Asia* was to focus on the better known sites of each destination, presenting potential travelers with a limited but well-rounded choice of places to visit and things to do. This book will be especially useful for first-time visitors or those who intend to cover several countries during a single regional trip.

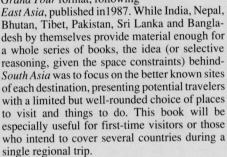

Hoefer

Eu

Apa founder/publisher **Hans Hoefer** is an old Asia hand, having first arrived in Indonesia from his native Germany in 1969, when he developed *Bali*, the first of the *Insight Guides*. *Bali's* in-depth text and superb photography, coupled with an innovative page layout and exciting graphic approach, elevated the guidebook concept to a whole new art form, setting the standard for a new generation of travel guides. These fundamental features have been developed further, but in essence they remain at the core of *Insight Guides*. Hoefer established a base in Singapore in the 1970s, and he continues to travel extensively from there. Under his creative direction, the series has expanded to over 50 titles and achieved global recognition.

Editorial Director **Geoffrey Eu**, who got his feet wet as project editor of the *East Asia* book, again found it his task to assemble writers and photographers and seeing *South Asia* through to completion. This former newspaper reporter from Singapore gained some insight into the business of travel during earlier, carefree days in the School of Travel Industry Management at the University of Hawaii. Later, he developed a deeper understanding of the relationship between business and travel at Northwestern University's Medill School of Journalism, where he learned one of the important maxim's in life, "Have credit card, will travel."

The search for suitable writers to handle each of *South Asia's* destinations led, naturally enough, to some familiar names. **Lisa Van Gruisen**, who wrote the section on Nepal, had previously produced *Insight Guide: Nepal*. The English-born Van Gruisen, who has been living in Nepal for some 15 years, has a background in art history. Her early career took her to New York as an art dealer and later to Ireland to conserve Georgian architecture and to coordinate a book on Irish painting. She has also worked for a London magazine and researched a film on Marco Polo in Iran and Turkey. During her Southeast and South Asian wanderings, she arrived for two weeks of trekking in Nepal in 1974—and has been there ever since. Her experience in art preservation has been transferred to concern for Nepal's cultural heritage and the conservation of the country's rich wildlife and natural environment. Van Gruisen has a Tibetan husband from Kham and one son.

John Sanday was trained at the Royal West of England School of Architecture and first came to Asia with UNESCO to prepare the masterplan for the conservation of the cultural heritage of the Kathmandu Valley. He was a key figure in helping to get *Insight Guide: Nepal* off the ground. Considered to be one of the leading experts of conservation and restoration in Asia, Sanday now works throughout the region from his Kathmandu-based office, John Sanday Consultants International. In addition to writing and providing several photos for the *South Asia* section on Bangladesh, Sanday is also a consultant to the government of there, where he is supervizing a plan to restore the country's cultural heritage. He has edited a book on monuments of Bangladesh and is now planning a more comprehensive *Insight Guide* to the country.

Ravindralal Anthonis is another who has renewed acquaintances with Apa. The Colombo-based writer photographer played a prominent role in *Insight Guide: Sri Lanka*, writing and editing several articles in addition to contributing many excellent photographs. Although he manages the family trading business, his greatest love is wildlife photography, a hobby which has taken him to evry remote corner of his island home.

Anthonis' articles and photographs have appeared in newspapers and magazines both in Sri Lanka and overseas. His favored topics are history and archaeology, and he also retains a keen interest in the sport of badminton, having been a three-time national champion in the 1970s.

Shalini Saran is a Delhi-based writer and photographer who has been widely published in travel and art magazines. Her specialty lies in places of historical interest (of which there is no shortage in India), peoples, crafts and lifestyles. Her writing and photographic contributions to *Insight Guide: Rajasthan* have established her as a knowledgeable and talented writer and photographer.

Francoise Pommaret-Imaeda continues the trend of the 'twin threat' writer-photographer. She wrote the section on Bhutan and has photo selections of both Bhutan and Tibet. Pommaret-Imaeda was born in France and spent her childhood in the Congo. Asia had long held an attraction for her. Her first venture was to Nepal in 1973 and she has been a tour leader of cultural groups for over a decade. She obtained her doctorate in Tibetology from Paris, but since 1981, has been resident in Bhutan, where she works for the Department of Tourism. She is the co-author of *Bhutan: A Kingdom of the Eastern Himalayas* and is currently working on a history of Bhutan for the Education Department. Pommaret-Imaeda is married to a fellow Tibetologist who is employed by the National Library of Bhutan.

Victor Chan became interested in Tibet after meeting the Dalai Lama in 1969. Having trained as a particle physicist in Canada and the US, he decided instead to travel and participate in a number of entrepreneurial projects, including magazine publishing and the food and beverage business. A current resident of Kathmandu, he has lived in the Canaries, Denmark, North Africa and Afghanistan. Chan has made numerous trips to Tibet to research the *Tibet Handbook*, a monumental volume on Tibet's sacred places and trek routes. He has traversed some 25,000 miles within the region on various modes of transportation, including foot, horse, yak, coracle, truck, bus and mountain bike. That extensive research came in handy while writing the section on Tibet.

Irish-born **Isobel Shaw**, who wrote the section on Pakistan, has been following her husband around the world for over 25 years, living in Tanzania, the US, Indonesia and Pakistan. Armed with a Master's in Anthropology and English from Cambridge (Mass.), Shaw has made full use of her various postings by pursuing a career in freelance journalism. She is co-author of *Spotlight Indonesia* and *A Traveller's Guide to Pakistan*. Now settled in Geneva, the Shaws still travel widely and visit Pakistan frequently.

The pictures in *South Asia* represent the work of various international photographers, many of whom have been longtime collaborators with *Insight Guides*. Their magnificent images have helped in no small way to establish Insight Guides' deserved reputation as the best travel series around. **Bill Wassman**, for example, has been a regular feature since he amazed readers of the *Nepal* guide with his stunningly beautiful portraits of the country.

Lyle Lawson is another regular who has made a significant contribution to *South Asia*. Her extensive photo coverage of the entire subcontinent is an indication of the tireless dedication to

Van Gruisen   Sanday   Anthonis

Pommaret-Imaeda   Chan   Shaw

her task that is the hallmark of this globe-trotting American. Lawson is now based in England, but more often than not, she can be counted on to be clicking away in some remote corner of the world.

Other well-known Apa contributors include **Luca Invernizzi, Paul Van Riel, Wilhelm Klein, Simon Hughes, Hermann Maier, Jean Kugler, W. D. Andreae, John Borthwick, Ashvin Gatha, Marcus Brooke, R. Ian Lloyd, G. P. Reichelt, Alain Evrard, Dallas and John Heaton, Tom Tidball, Nik Wheeler, K. Debnicki, A. Cassio, Philip Little, David Messent, Michael Gebicki** and **Toby Sinclair.**

There are also several illustrious debutants in this book. **Tom Owen Edmunds**, whose work is featured in the section on Bhutan, is an England-based wildlife specialist whose photos have been published all over the world. His current projects include a major commission for BBC Publications on great journeys of the world and his soon-to-be-published book, *Bhutan: Dreams of the Peaceful Dragon*.

Craig Lovell is another photographer who has been widely published. His pictures in the Tibet section show why. Other impressive newcomers to *Insight Guides* include **Salman Rashid, Rob Stratton, Jimmy Holmes, Andy Black, Ian MacWilliam, John Noble, K. Masherbrum, Maggie Mosey Payne, G. Lawrie, Pierre-Antoine Donnet, Heldur J. Netocny, Voja** and Bangkok-based **"Shrimp."**

The daunting task of contacting various photographers and culling material from existing stock fell to **Sylvia Muttom**, manager of the Apa Photo Agency in Singapore. Muttom has developed the admirable capacity to sift through hundreds of potential shots in a jiffy before coming

Plus computers and the latest software available in the fast-evolving and highly competitive field of desktop publishing. As the system develops, the goal is for subsequent titles to be generated entirely by Apa's team of writers, field editors and in-house staff, from writing first drafts to publishing the finished book.

South Asia also signals a new-look section of practical travel information, previously called the Guide in Brief. The newly-named Travel Tips, which appear at the end of each country section, introduces a tighter, more compact three-column format, increased graphics and bigger size text. It represents a beginning in a continually evolving process as we at Apa make the effort to keep up with technological advances in the publishing world. Stay tuned.

—Apa Publications

Wassman   *Lawson*   *Owen Edmunds*

Muttom   *Kim*

up with just the right one for a particular page. Her "big play" ability made photo selection an enjoyable process.

For the umpteenth time, Apa Editorial Manager **Vivien Kim's** timely advice and clear-headed demeanor proved to be the glue that held the project together, solving editorial and production problems as they cropped up (and paying the bills on time!). Copy Editor **Ng Swee San** was an invaluable help in getting *South Asia* to the presses on time. Her help in various phases of the editorial process was much appreciated. Other members of Apa's editorial department, including **Karen Goh, Eileen Lim** and **Audrey Simon**, provided their usual reliable assistance whenever it was required. **Lim Peng Yam** drew most of the maps, while **Richard Yong** and **Sulinko Teo** coordinated all the artwork.

Finally, thanks go to **Ronald Harris**, president of Hemphill/Harris Travel Corporation in California. *South Asia* is the second *Insight Guide* he has collaborated on. May there be many more.

While *South Asia* has familiar names and does go over some familiar *Insight Guide* territory, it is in other respects a milestone title. It is the first book to benefit from Apa's commitment to move into desktop publishing. In an effort to streamline the in-house editorial process, all manuscripts were stored on disk, edited and flowed into standardized page layouts using Apple Macintosh

TABLE OF CONTENTS

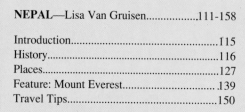

TABLE OF CONTENTS

OTHER INSIGHT GUIDES TITLES

COUNTRY/REGION

ASIA
Bali
Burma
Hong Kong
India
Indonesia
Korea
Malaysia
Nepal
Philippines
Rajasthan
Singapore
Sri Lanka
Taiwan
Thailand
Turkey

PACIFIC
Hawaii
New Zealand

NORTH AMERICA
Alaska
American Southwest
Northern California
Southern California
Florida
Mexico
New England
New York State
The Pacific Northwest
The Rockies
Texas

SOUTH AMERICA
Brazil
Argentina

CARIBBEAN
Bahamas
Barbados
Jamaica
Puerto Rico
Trinidad and Tobago

EUROPE
Channel Islands
France
Germany
Great Britain
Greece
Ireland
Italy
Portugal
Scotland
Spain

MIDDLE EAST
Egypt
Israel

AFRICA
Kenya

GRAND TOURS
Australia
California
Canada
Continental Europe
Crossing America
East Asia
South Asia

GREAT ADVENTURE
Indian Wildlife

CITYGUIDES
Bangkok
Berlin
Buenos Aires
Dublin
Istanbul
Lisbon
London
Paris
Rio de Janeiro
Rome
San Francisco
Venice
Vienna

A NEW TRAVEL FRONTIER

Adventure travel is going places. As the 21st century approaches and the prospects of really "getting away from it all" begin to fade, more and more jaded travelers looking for that adrenalin fix are heading for one of the great new frontiers—South Asia and Tibet. Seasoned trailblazers are certainly familar with the delights of India and Sri Lanka, but not many have jeeped across Pakistan's Karakoram Highway, gone trekking in the kingdom of Bhutan, climbed Nepal's mountains or journeyed across Tibet in a four-wheel drive vehicle.

Few regions in the world can compare with the stunning diversity offered by the South Asian and Tibetan landscape. Certain areas are still inaccessible, but there is enough to satisfy even the most intrepid explorer—the monasteries of Tibet, the river deltas of Bangladesh, the lush hills of Sri Lanka, the ancient cities of Pakistan and the myriad attractions of India, which is both the geographic and cultural heart of the region.

And what a rich culture it is. Based on religious heritage alone, South Asia has been the breeding ground for many of the world's great religions, including Buddhism, Islam and Hinduism. The importance of religion is underlined by the vast number of monuments, ancient and modern, found throughout the region.

Any list of man-made monuments would be bound to include Agra's incomparable Taj Mahal, Kathmandu's super *stupa*—Swayambhunath, the magnificent cave frescoes of Sigiriya and the ancient city of Moen-jodaro.

Mother nature has been equally dramatic. The peaks of alpine Asia, including the Himalayas, the Tibetan Highlands and the Karakoram Range, make up some of the highest mountains in the world. Mount Everest, of course, is the jewel in the crown. Further south, in the jungles, plains and deserts of peninsular India, the air may be less rarified but the scenery no less spectacular.

Insight Guide: South Asia opens the doors to these and many more marvels, incorporating sites, stories and sensations from India, Nepal, Bhutan, Tibet, Pakistan, Sri Lanka and Bangladesh.

> *....so it is in traveling, a man must carry knowledge with him if he would bring home knowledge.*
>
> —Samuel Johnson (1778).

Insight Guides were not available in the 18th century, but we take pleasure in the fact that present-day travelers to the Indian subcontinent can now carry that knowledge, so valued by Mr. Johnson, in the form of *Insight Guide: South Asia.*

Preceding pages: the Kandy Perahera pays homage to the Tooth Relic; the eyes have it: regal Rajasthani ladies; a Buddhist welcome to Bhutan; Tibetan tribesman; mountain man from Hunza; one of the many faces of Nepal.

EMPIRE DU MOGOL

Cet Empire est d'une fort grande étendue. Cette vaste contrée connue sous le nom d'Inde a reçu son nom du fleuve Indus qui l'arrose. Elle est bornée au nord par la gr. Tartarie au Levant par la Chine, au couchant par la Perse et au midi par la Mer qui porte son nom.

L'air y est généralement chaud et le Terroir fertile en ris en millet en fruits excellents comme Figues, Grenades &c et toutes sortes d'épiceries, il produit aussy beaucoup de coton, don on fait de très belles Toiles. On y voit des animaux qu'on ne trouve point ailleurs. On y trouve des mines d'or d'argent, de Diamans &c.

Les Indiens sont ordin. de teint basanné, ils sont fort bien faits et robustes mais ils aiment l'oisiveté et sont fort passionnés pour les femmes. Ils sont divisés en 3 ordres à scavoir, les Brames qui sont les Prêtres idolâtres, les Rebitos ou gens de guerre qui se disent descendus des anciens Rois, et les Bantians qui sont les marchands.

L'année des Indiens est l'année. Ils sont idolâtres et Mahometans. Les uns et les autres sont très cruels dans leurs Enfers qui sont de certains devots errans qui pratiq. des austerités incroyables. On en voit qui passe plusieurs années sans se coucher mais en s'appuiant seulem. sur une corde suspendue. D'autres tiennt leurs bras élevés au Ciel si longtems qu'ils ne leur est plus possible de les abaisser quand ils le veulent. Et malgré ces mortifications ils sont extrêmement méprisés.

L'Empire du gr. Mogol est un des plus gr. de l'Asie. On lui donne 480 L. du midi au nord et 860 dans sa plus gr. largeur du Levant en couchant. Ses principales rivières sont l'Inde et le Gange qui ont leur source au Mt. Imaus.

Le gr. Mogol est un des plus puissans et des plus riches princes de l'Asie. Il est le maître de toutes les Terres de son Empire et il en dispose comme il lui plaît aussi bien que de la vie de ses sujets. Ses forces militaires sont fort considérables outre les troupes qui sont rég. dans les différentes Prov. et les troupes ordin. que les Rajas princes tributaires sont obligés de fournir, formant une armée de 500000 de Cavalerie sans l'infanterie tout ce.

Le gr. Mogol donne tous les jours audience publique. Il rend lui même la justice dans la capitale ou il réside et les gouverneurs et Chefs d'ordre en font de même dans l'étendue de leur Jurisdiction.

Les peuples Indiens se partagent en deux sortes, les naturels du pays et les Mogols originaires de Tartarie qui s'emp. de l'Inde sous le fameux Prince Genghiskan dans le XIII.e siècle. Il n'y a presque de fixe pour la succession au Trône ce qui occasionne souvent de grands troubles.

On divise actuellement les États du Mogol en 39 Gouvernemens scavoir Cachemire, Ayoud, Varal, Patna, Bengale, Conduh, Orixa, Balagate, Tatonga, Baglana, Guzarat, Tata, Moultan, Caboul, Lahor, Dely, Agra, Asmer, Malva, et Balabar.

Le Gouvern. de Cachemire est un pays fort agréable, fertile. C'est un peuple, et est environné de M. qui le mettent à couvert des insultes de leurs voisins. Ekbor Empereur Mogol s'en rendit maître vers la fin du XVI. siècle. Les habitans du pays passent pour les plus ingénieux et les plus spirituels des peuples de l'Inde. Sa c. Nikias est cap.t est une gr. ville et se voir bien bâtie. L'air y est bon et les eaux excellentes quoy que l'air y soit froid.

Le Gouv. d'Ayoud renf. le R. de Nagracut et de Bankinch. Les Indiens vont en pelerinage à Nigracut cap.t de ce gouvernement.

Le G. de Varal compr. les anciens Roy. de Piton de Gor de Siba et de Kandouna. Le gouv. de Patna comp. les Roy. de Patna Bakar Jesnat et Udossa. Le pays est fertile. Patna sa cap. est gr. et très marchande. On y fabriq. de belles Toiles peintes. Elle est défendue par un château. Les autres villes de ce gouv. sont Benares ville marchande et bien bâtie. C'est l'endroit où les Bramins ont une Univers. que appr. leur Theologie &c.

Le Gouv. de Bengale a eu autr. ses rois particuliers. Le gr. Mogol l'unit à son domaine vers le milieu du XVI. siècle. Sa ville de Decan de France du Lev au couchant et 200 du midi au nord. La fertilité et ce. y attirent beaucoup d'étrangers. On entre des Toiles très fines des mousselines & le pays produit de la soie du ris du sucre du poivre &c. Bengale sa cap.t est située dans une belle plaine. Les autres villes sont Kinkie autr. cap.t de ce pays, où le cap.t d'une Province du R. de Bengale, ou y fait un gr. comm. Chandernagor comptoir François & Chincurat, gr. ville commerçante. Dacca gr. ville ou les anglois et les Holandois font un comm. considérable. On en tire les plus belles broderies des Indes en or et en argent et on. y.

Le gouv. de Conduh est un des plus gr. et des plus riches des États du Mogol. Il compr. les Royaumes de Candish et de Berar dont la partie sept. de la Prov. d'Orixa Brampour est la capitale de ce gouv. c'est une gr. ville bâtie sur un terrain inégal. Le château renferme le Palais du Roy. Le R. de Berar a Chapour pour capitale.

Au sept. Mal. cap.t du R. de Balagate qui après de 200 L. du midi au nord et 120 dans sa plus gr. largeur a donné son nom au Gouv. d'Auroy. Cette ville est marchande et bien peuplée, le terrain y est excellent.

Le Gouv. de Tatinga est arrosé au Nord Est au sud Ouest par la Rivière de Guanga. Beder en est la capitale.

Le Gouv. de Baglana renferme le R. de Decan qui a eu ses vice-rois particul. ses habitans s'aplic. aux arts et au commerce Andanagor en est la cap.t.

Le Gouv. de Guzarat est une des plus agréables Provinces de l'Indoustan. ses campagnes sont fertiles et agréables, à cause de la quantité de Ris-rie qui les arrosent. On y recueille beaucoup de coton et d'opium, ses princi.

de Tipra d'Arasan d'Ava et de Pegu. Les R. d'Asem et de Tipra sont peu connus. On en tire beaucoup de laque chandara et Marbagan en sont les cap.s. Le R. d'Arasan est fort fertile et très peuplé. Arasan sa cap.t est gr. et très riche. Le Palais du Roy renferme des rubis immenses. Le R. d'Ava est d'une gr. étendue. L'air y est doux et le peuple fort humain. Ava sa cap.t est une gr. ville très peuplée. Le Palais du Roy est magnifique. Les franqu. rubailles du Royaume de Pegu sont la Porcelaine. La Mine la plus abondant en pierres precieuses. Pegu. cap.t située sur la Rivière de ce nom. Les vues sont fort commerçantes. On dit que les Peguans sont fort courageux.

La partie méridionale de cette Presqu'ile renferme le R. de Tanjaour et le R. de Maduré. La ville de Maduré en rend. du R. de Maduré. Le R. de Maissour est aussi considérable. Le Raja de Maissour tient sa cour à Maissour. La Presqu'ile est divisée en deux parties, mais cela ne convient plus auj. aux divers tributaires du Roi dont Malaca a un seul été le cap.t aux Hollandois.

Map labels: CHINE · SIFANS · Hoan Ho · Kian Ho · Koan Ho · INDOSTAN · R. D'ASHAM · Chamdara · R. D'AVA · Roy. d'Ava · Santa · BRAMAS · Prom · MIEN · R. DE TONQUIN · Kesho · Hai nan I. · Kuang Tcheu · R. DE LAO · R. DE PEGU · Pegu · R. DE SIAM · Bas Siam · COCHINCHINE · R. DE CAMBOJA · Golfe de Siam · Mergui · Tanasserim · L. d'Andaman · Nicobar · MALACCA · D. de Malaca · I. de Sumatra · Pahang · Sincapura

110 · 115 · 120

Les princip. Villes sont Cambeya Cap.le du Royaume de ce nom cerne de périt ville des Indes. Amadabad, cap.le de la Prov. du Guzarat, grande ville bien peuplée et fort commerçante, la place dite du Roi a 1600 pieds de long, et 800 de largeur, Les Hollandois et les Anglois y ont des comptoirs. Surate est la Ville la plus marchande de toute l'Asie son comm.ce consiste en étoffes de soie, de coton, et l'Or en épiceries et en drogues, perles, et Diamans, Outre les Provençois, les Anglois, et les Hollandois, qui y sont un comm.ce considerable, on y trouve des marchands de toutes les autres nations. Diu cap.le de l'isle de ce nom &c.

Le Gouv.t de Tatta est composé les Roy.es de Tatta de Soret et de Buker. Tatta cap. Les Portugais par leur commerce et l'industrie de ses habitans ont rendu cette ville celebre.

Le Gouv.t de Multan renf. les R.es de Moultan et de Kgbacan Moultan est la Capitale. Le Gouv.t de Caboul quoique peu fertile, est riche à cause de sa situation avantageuse pour le commerce. Caboul est une gr.de ville bien fortifiée.

Le Gouv.t de Lahor renf. à R.es Attock Bakrock, le pays des Hendowns est la bas. Cette provin.ce est une des plus fertiles des Indes. Lahor en est la cap.le on y voit un palais R.al où les Mogols rend.t autrefois.

Les Gouv.ts de Dely et d'Agra ont pour cap.le des villes celebres Agra est la capi.le de l'Empire du gr. Mogol cost une gr.de ville bien peuplée qui passe pour la plus considerable de l'orient. On y voit le magnifique palais du gr. Mogol, et une avenue qui va d'Agra à Dely qui a 4000 villes. L'Angleterre de longueur. Dely étoit autre la cap.le du Lindoustan, le Mogol y réside encore quelquefois pendant l'été, elle est gr.de et bien fortifiée.

Les Gouv.ts d'Asmer, Malwa et habat.ys sont peu considerables. Jagernat dans la Prov.ce d'Orixa est une pagode fort frequentée des Indiens idolatres cest où reside le gr. Prêtre des Bramins.

PRESQU'ISLE DE L'INDE en deçà du Gange.

Cette Presqu'Isle est située sous la Zone Torride, ses habitans different peu de ceux de l'Indoustan. Elle renf. plusieurs etats dont les principaux sont le R.e de Visapour de la côte de Carnate. Les Europeens y ont diff. erens comptoirs. Le R.e de Visapour a env. 150 L. detendue du midi au Nord et ne dans ça plus gr. largeur ses princip. places sont Damijn, belle ville où les Portugais ont garnison son port est défendu par un fort Baijtin app. aussi aux Portugais elle est gr.de et bien batie. Bombain est une dans l'Isle de ce nom app. aux Anglois qui y ont un Gouverneur son port est fort bon. Dabul qui a été ruinée par les guerres elle app. aux Anglois. Visapour cap.le du Roy. de ce nom est une gr.de ville le roy y faisoit sa residence Il y fait un gr. commerce de riz et de pierres precieuses. Goa qui est une des villes les plus celebres des Indes est située dans une Isle qui a 9 L. de circuit elle app. aux Portugais cette ville est riche et marchande et son port est le plus beau de l'Asie des chaleurs y sont excessives les maisons en sont bien baties les titres de l'Archevêque du Vicero et du gr. Inquisiteur sont fort beaux. Raolconde est celebre par sa mine de Diamans qui est une des plus estimée de l'Asie.

La côte de Canara fournit beaucoup de riz, de poivre on y eleve aussi du bétail les peuples qui l'habit.sont payens et Mahom.ce les gr. princip. sont les principautez de Canara Bardel Batecala et Onar dont les Cap.les sont Cananor port les Hollandois y ont un de leurs establiss.ts Baliour à 7 ou 6 L. de la côte Batecala et Onar port et place forte.

La côte de Malabar est fertile en épiceries en coton et en cocos &c. ce pays est peuplé, fertile et cultivé, les habitans sont payens ou idolatres les principaux états sont les R.es de Calicut de Cochin et de Travancor. Calicut port et cap.le est une gr.de ville mal batie Mahé près de Calicut app. aux françois ils en ont un petit fort de pierre. Cochin cap.le une des plus belles de la presqu'isle après Goa les Holl.s y ont garnison, le Roy est leur tributaire. Le Roy de Travancor est tribu.re de celui de Mallure et son R.e est devenu celebre par ses Mils.ns de St. Xavier. Caralan en est la cap.le et Tim gapatan app. aux Hollandois.

La côte de Coromandel com.ce à la porte orientale de la presqu'isle et renf. de principaux états qui sont les R.es de Mallure Maijfur Tanjaor Genji Carnate Balagate &c. L'etat de Mallure est gouverné par un R.al les Europeens y ont important.tes comptoirs Le R.e à Mahé, sont imperisbal le l.as et à midi sont le gr.e territoire. Le Roy Mallure Cap.le où le Roy fait sa résidence à Tranikapah, y renf. autrefois les chaleurs y sont excessives. L'etat de Maijsor à Sering y escouvrir cap.re est un pays peu connu.

La côte de la Pecherie dépend de la principauté de Mestine ou la s.e est donnée ce nom à cause de la perte qu'on y fait très-bon. Le R.e de Tanjaor est un des meilleurs pays de l'Inde Moris le roi est tributaire du Mogol. Negapatan est la Cap.le de l'etat de ce pays situé sur un...

Presqu'Isle de l'Inde au dela du Gange.

Cette presqu'Isle est située entre le 2.e et le 27.e degré de latit. Sa côte en occid.t en occidentale et en orientale. La partie Sep. renf. les R.es d'Asem...

INDIA: MAJESTIC DIVERSITY

India can perplex the first-time visitor, for there are few countries that offer such a range of experience. Diversity is intrinsic to her being. The people, the landscape, religions and castes, philosophy and culture, architecture and cuisine, occupations and preoccupations are all as varied as the land is vast. Folk, tribal and classical cultures coexist, as do 21st-century ideas with medieval attitudes and age-old lifestyles. As a highly evolved civilization, India has offered invaluable perspectives; as a nation she is still young. She ranks 10th among industrialized countries even as an ancient mythology permeates her psyche. Hundreds of gods are enthusiastically worshipped, yet the Supreme Reality has been keenly perceived. Fourteen languages are spoken and over 200 dialects. Extremes exist here, if anywhere, and while the contradictions are myriad, their explanations are often more startling.

This diversity is the pulse of India. It creates a texture, alive and enduring. It can make one doubt all certitudes and dwell upon the meaning and purpose of life. The perennial associations with the Orient are here—the exotica, the palaces and forts, the remnants of royalty, the heat, dust and crowds, even the elephant on the highway. But the essence of India's beauty, her Indianness as it were, is contained in the texture of life here. It can be sensed by one who comes without preconceived ideas, who resists the tendency to constantly measure against a known reality, and who is willing to look beyond the apparent chaos.

The subcontinent is demarcated by the desert, mountains and sea. Nature has not withheld her bounty and, imbued with mythological associations, bears a sacred dimension as well. Geographical factors have to a large extent determined the course of history. In the last 3,500 years India has harbored waves of alien influences, especially from Central Asia and Europe. Some survive in a quaint and whimsical manner, others entered the mainstream while simultaneously retaining a part of their identity. But the richest and the finest were absorbed and assimilated, resulting in a synthesis which was profoundly creative.

Today, India has emerged as the world's largest democracy. She is in the throes of change, generated equally by her specific historical and cultural context, by a burgeoning population and the pressures of a shrinking globe. It is not easy to understand India, for she does not reveal herself instantly or entirely. But it is not impossible either. And once the curiosity is awakened it cannot be readily subdued. Once the seed of interest takes root, it craves to be nourished. This has been the experience of travelers throughout the centuries.

Preceding pages: 18th-century French map shows the South Asian perspective; palace mural of a royal hunt, Jodhpur; boatman steering serenely past the Taj Mahal. Left, Kashmiri maiden.

To understand the complexities of present day India it is necessay, first, to turn to the past. The confines of a brief historical outline, however, allow mere mention of some of the myriad influences that generated these complexities. If the focus is on outstanding dynastic powers, it must also be realized that caste structures, agrarian patterns and mercantile activites point to continual change at other levels, too. Some of the factors which determined change were topography, ecology, manpower, social divisions and religion.

The Harappan Culture: In the 1920s, archaeologists discovered the remains of a civiliza-

Indus River eventually destroyed the cities. The civilization had practically vanished by the time the Aryans came.

The Vedic Age: Aryan tribes, originating from northeast Iran and the region near the Caspian Sea, started migrating to India around 1500 B.C. The following millenium is loosely referred to as the Vedic Age after the four *Vedas,* the Sanskrit texts comprising hymns that were composed in that era. The *Rig Veda,* imbued with a sense of awe and wonder, is not only the earliest Hindu scripture, it is also the earliest literary source from which historians have reconstructed

tion in the Indus Valley, dating to 2500 B.C. It not only predated the acknowledged beginnings of Indian history by a thousand years, it also proved to be a highly sophisticated urban civilization. The major sites were Mohenjodaro and Harappa (now both in Pakistan), with ample evidence of being planned cities where a clear social stratification prevailed. There was also evidence of agricultural surplus, the knowledge of metals, and trade with Sumer (Iraq). Once the script on the numerous seals that were found is deciphered, some of the mysteries of this civilization will be unveiled. Since then, other sites related to the Indus Valley culture have been identified in Rajasthan, Punjab and Gujarat, and the civilization is referred to as the Harappan Culture. Ecological changes and the periodic flooding of the

Aryan life and institutions.

The Aryans were pastoralists; cattle-breeding was their mainstay and cattle the most valuable commodity. The word *gavishti,* which means "to search for cows" eventually became synonymous with fighting. Beef-eating was taboo, except on special occasions. Perhaps the uniquely Indian veneration for the cow has its roots in the Aryan lifestyle.

The Aryans gradually realized the potential of the fertile plains they inhabited. The discovery of iron in 1000 B.C. facilitated the clearing of forests for farming and in course of time nomadic pastoralism gave way to an agrarian economy. The ox-drawn plow was—and still is—the main agricultural implement. Tribes settled in different parts of northwest India and since they were often at war with one another, the tribal chief was essentially a military leader. His position eventually became hereditary though tribal assemblies kept his power in check.

The foundation of the caste system was laid when the Aryans, perhaps in an effort to retain their identity, treated the Dasas, the original—and dark-skinned—inhabitants of the land, as beyond the social pale. *Varna,* the original word for caste, meant color. In course of time four major castes emerged and they were initially concerned with work specialization. The priests were the *Brahmins,* the warriors were the *Ksha-*

fire, were worshipped. Sanskrit was the language of the Aryans. A script evolved only around 700 B.C. To begin with, the *Vedas,* believed to have been composed by divinely inspired sages, were handed down orally and the system of chanting reveals a highly developed knowledge of sound.

It was an age when a spirit of enquiry prevailed, when the beginnings of the religious tradition known as Hinduism took root. The idea of the transmigration of the soul was vaguely emerging, later to develop into the doctrine of *Karma* (action) whereby actions in one's previous life determined one's situation in the present life. *Dharma,*

triyas, the agriculturalists were the *Vaishyas* and the menial workers, *Shudras.* Within this overall framework a vast network of subcastes emerged. Though intimately connected with occupation, it eventually came to be birth and not work which determined caste. (The caste system, which has often assumed ugly proportions, continues to burden the Indian social structure.)

The earliest religious ideas of the Aryans were those of primitive animism where the incomprehensible forces of nature were invested with divinity. The sun, wind, water and especially,

Left, relief sculpture at Mahabalipuram. Above, ancient sandstone Buddha from the Mathura Museum.

which can at best be translated as the natural law of society, was for maintaining the social order and together with *Karma,* facilitated the enforcement of caste laws. The *Upanishads* (800 B.C. to 400 B.C.) are dialogues between teachers and disciples and emerged as a reaction to declining values that over-emphasized the importance of ritual, and made the *Brahmins,* who conducted these rituals, the dominant class. Regarded as a continuation of the *Vedas,* the *Upanishads* refine the monistic trend with keen perception. Many of the later systems of thought evolved from the metaphysical subtleties of the *Upanishads.*

The Aryans made a significant contribution to the evolution of Indian society. They cleared the land for agriculture; they laid the foundations of social institutions and a religion that have survived for over 2,000 years. And Sanskrit is the source of many languages spoken in India today.

While the caste structure initially provided a practical framework for the functioning of society, it grew to be increasingly oppressive. By the sixth century B.C. agricultural expansion had led to an uneven distribution of wealth. In the midst of this prevalent misery two thinkers, Mahavir and the Buddha (both *Kshatriyas,* and the founders of Jainism and Buddhism, respectively) meditated separately upon the cause of suffering and the way to end it. Their answers were simple—a moderate, non-violent and truthful life would free one from desire, and consequently, suffering. Their teachings appealed instantly to the socially downtrodden, not only because they were communicated in commonly spoken languages, but also for their simplicity, their rational

Kalinga (Orissa). He conquered Kalinga but the brutality of that war made him eventually turn to Buddhism. During his reign Buddhism spread even beyond the boundaries of the subcontinent, not merely as a religion but as a social and intellectual movement as well, influencing many aspects of society. Though himself a practicing Buddhist, Ashoka did not attack Brahmanism. The idea of *Dhamma* (Universal Law or Righteousness) which he spread through edicts and inscriptions, aimed, above all, at creating an attitude of social responsibility and its principles, as such, were acceptable to people of any religious sect.

The Mauryan economy was predominantly agrarian. Land revenue was the accepted, and secure, source of income. The efficient centralized bureaucracy also facilitated the functioning

undertone and their complete rejection of caste. Buddhism and Jainism, both essentially atheistic, posed a threat to Brahmanical orthodoxy. Jainism remained confined to India, but Buddhism eventually spread throughout Asia and for many, even today, India is the land of the Buddha. Some of the finest painting, sculpture and architecture emerged from Buddhist and Jain traditions.

The First Empire: The concept of landownership was initially non-existent in Aryan society, but as it took hold, tribal settlements grew into kingdoms and republics. The first empire was that of Magadha, created by the Maurya Dynasty, with its capital at Pataliputra near Patna. Its greatest ruler was Emperor Ashoka (269 B.C. to 232 B.C.). Ashoka inherited an empire that encompassed almost the entire subcontinent, except for

of various craft guilds and consequently, trade.

India's brief contact with the Hellenic civilization occured with the invasion of Alexander of Macedon in 327 B.C. A century later the disintegration of the Mauryan empire paved the way for invaders from Central Asia—the Bactrian Greeks, the Parthians, Shakas and Kushanas established kingdoms in the north and northwest. They were eventually absorbed in the Indian mainstream, some adopting Buddhism. Interestingly, Buddhist sculpture dating to this era and area and known as Gandhara art, bears a distinct Greek influence.

The Gupta Age: The fourth century A.D. witnessed the emergence of the Gupta empire which, though not as large as Mauryan, lasted 200 years. Under the patronage of the Gupta kings there was a powerful, non-violent resurgence of orthodox Hinduism. The Vedic deities had lost their importance to Brahma, Vishnu and Shiva, who became the predominant gods in the Hindu pantheon. Rama and Krishna, both incarnations of Vishnu, were particularly appealing. The two great epic poems, the *Mahabharata* and the *Ramayana,* composed some centuries earlier, were now considered a part of sacred literature. Both epics have permeated the Indian psyche. They continue to fire the imagination through dance forms and theater, classical and folk, through storytellers and itinerant performers. Recently, a TV serial on the *Ramayana* proved to be extraordinarily popular.

By the fifth century A.D., the *Puranas* were completed. These are the historical tradition as recorded by the brahmins, from the creation of the universe to the geneaology of dynasties. While sacrifice was still an important part of ritual, the image became the center of worship, and inspired a tradition of excellence in sculpture. The caste system, however, grew more rigid, defining even a group of "untouchables" whose very sight was sufficient to pollute the upper castes. Later, to solve the problem of expanding agricultural land and labor scarcity, some of the lower castes were deprived of the right to own land.

The Gupta age is referred to as the classical age, for it was a period of intense activity in the fields of literature, fine arts and science, in particular mathematics and astronomy. Theater, prose and poetry received lavish patronage. Kalidasa lived in the Gupta court; he is considered the most outstanding writer of classical Sanskrit, and *Shakuntalam* is his best known play. The exuberant frescoes in the Ajanta caves also date to this era. Formal education was offered at brahmanical institutions and Buddhist monasteries, and Nalanda emerged as the foremost center of learning.

The Huns invaded the northwest at this time, and a number of Central Asian tribes and people came with them and settled in the region of Rajasthan. Fa Hsien the Chinese Buddhist pilgrim who came to India in search of manuscripts, records the general prosperity and well-being of the people in the Gupta empire.

South India: At the turn of the last century

B.C., south India moved from pre-history into history. Literary records, in particular the 2,000 *Sangam* poems composed at assemblies, reflect contemporary events. Peninsular India, unlike the northern plain, was less conducive to vast empires. Smaller kingdoms were rather the pattern and these were constantly at war with one another. There is evidence of trade with Rome and Southeast Asia. Christianity came to India with the arrival of St. Thomas in Kerala in 52 A.D. It was a time, too, when there was a significant emergence of Tamil culture.

The crystallization of Tamil culture, which set the classical pattern in south India, took place between the ninth and the 13th centuries, particularly under the rule of the Chola kings. Highly evolved standards were set in social institutions,

Opposite page: Shiva mural at Varanasi, left, and right, the Lion Capital, emblem of the Indian government. Above, a flute-playing Krishna and wife Badha.

architecture, religion and fine arts, in particular, dance, music and sculpture, and these came to dominate patterns of living in the south. Many of these standards have been maintained to this day.

The Sultanate: North India, in the meanwhile, comprised several regional states, each concerned with local rather than countrywide matters. But at the beginning of the 13th century an event of immense significance took place and it altered the course of Indian history. Another wave of invaders from Central Asia came through the northwestern passes, but this time they founded an independent state with their capital at Delhi. And, more important, they brought their religion—Islam. The Sultanate, as the kingdom was called, lasted 320 years and was ruled by six dynasties. While it was generally acknowledged that the Turkish rulers were the dominant politi-

done in cash. This gave rise to a vigorous urban culture, to markets and to a more sophisticated style of living which in turn promoted trade and crafts. An unusually varied and live tradition of crafts evolved, and skills were handed down from father to son. The Persian wheel, the spinning wheel, paper and gunpowder were introduced, as were new styles in architecture.

The disintegration of the Sultanate began in the second quarter of the 14th century, during the reign of Muhammad bin Tughlaq. The Vijayanagar and Bahmani kingdoms emerged as independent powers in its southern limits. The chaos generated by a diminishing 'empire' paved the way for the devastation wrought by Timur's invasion in 1398.

The Mughal Empire: In 1526 Zahiruddin Mohammed Babur, a descendant of Timur and

cal power, it took time to grasp the extent to which their presence would modify cultural patterns.

The Turkish nobility stayed aloof from the local population. But assimilation did take place, especially among artisans and cultivators who eventually formed the bulk of the converts. The teachings of the Sufis, the mystics of Islam, appealed to Hindus and Muslims. The doctrine of union with God through love of God bore resemblance to the teachings of Bhakti saints. The Sufis, regarded as heretics by orthodox Muslims, were far more effective in spreading the word of Islam than the often aggressive rulers.

The Sultanate had a centralized and highly organized revenue system, though the officials merely collected the revenue; they had no right over the land. In course of time collection was

Genghis Khan, invaded India, defeated the last Lodi sultan and established the Mughal Empire. His reign was too shortlived to consolidate his gains. His son Humayun lacked sufficient determination to do so. But Akbar, who ascended the throne in 1556 at the tender age of 13, proved to be an outstanding monarch, of the same caliber as Ashoka and one who is recalled to this day for his wisdom and statesmanship.

He realized the importance of ruling as an Indian, of establishing local roots, not only because he was a shrewd politician but also because he was genuinely tolerant. The Rajputs, longtime enemies of the Muslims, became his allies through matrimonial alliances and through warfare. For the first time, Hindus were given high official posts. Having extended his imperial sway over a large part of the subcontinent, Akbar made a genuine effort to govern it properly. An efficient bureaucratic framework was evolved and each official was given a military rank, depending on his responsibilities. Land was classified on the basis of productivity and the peasant was aware of his liability. Akbar also abolished discriminatory taxes paid by Hindus.

Akbar had an insatiable curiosity about religions and metaphysics. Though he was illiterate, he had prolonged discussions with representatives of various religious sects, including Christians and Zoroastrians. He patronized the writing of history, and artists illustrated these manuscripts. An extraordinary fusion of Hindu and Islamic cultures took place under his keen interest and perhaps it was epitomized in his court at Fatehpur Sikri.

throne after much bitterness and bloodshed. A puritan at heart and a devout Muslim, he was driven by religious zeal to impose austere measures and to establish an 'Islamic' state. He reigned for 50 years. At the time of his death, in 1707, the empire was already beset with problems, and it steadily diminished thereafter. The later Mughal emperors were weaklings, unable to prevent nobles from setting up regional states, such as those of Hyderabad, Awadh and Bengal. Nor could they suppress rebellions which also resulted in the emergence of the Maratha Empire in the Deccan and the Afghan Rohilla state in Uttar Pradesh.

In the 17th century the Marathas had emerged as a formidable fighting force under the leadership of Shivaji. They raised impenetrable forts and received 'protection money' as insurance

INDIAN STATE CARRIAGE.   T 3572.

Akbar's son Jehangir, and grandson Shah Jahan, had none of his dynamism, nor were their ways tempered with wisdom. But the empire they inherited was secure and stable. It allowed them to indulge—as only emperors could—in cultural pursuits. This was aided by the fact that a large percentage of the revenue was controlled by an exceedingly small number of nobles. The finest Mughal miniature paintings date to Jehangir's reign. Shah Jahan is immortalized in the splendid buildings he raised, particularly the Taj Mahal.

Shah Jahan's son Aurangzeb ascended the

Left, portraits of a former sultan of Delhi and a Maharaja of Kashmir. Above, the only way to travel!

against their deadly raids. By the third quarter of the 18th century they had vast areas under direct or indirect rule, and complete manipulation over the Mughal emperor.

In the 18th century north India suffered further under three attacks—the first by the Iranian ruler Nadir Shah in 1739. He ordered the massacre of several thousand citizens of Delhi and plundered the capital. The Koh-i-Noor diamond and the Peacock Throne, encrusted with jewels, were part of the loot he took back. The Afghans attacked twice. On the second instance in 1761 their army defeated the Marathas, and put an end to the dream of a Maratha Empire.

17th-Century India: Seventeenth-century India emerges as being prosperous and dynamic. The economy continued to be essentially agrarian but the benefits of trade and money reached even the villages. Urban settlements flourished; there were over 3,000 towns, some of which compared favorably with London and Rome.

Significant regional development took place, particularly in language and literature. Urdu, Hindi, Gujarati, Bengali and Marathi became fully evolved languages, each with its own literature. The country harbored diverse religious elements. The population was still predominantly Hindu. Among the Muslims there were Shia and Sunni. The Jains had settled in western India. There were Christians, especially in Kerala, and a small number of Jews and Zoroastrians. Buddhism had vanished from India, but a new religious sect emerged—the Sikhs. The sect was founded by Guru Nanak who, influenced by Hinduism and Islam, denounced caste and

and Denmark. Their traders bought mainly textiles and indigo and paid for their purchases in gold and silver.

These trading companies established warehouses or 'factories' in several towns, and soon maintained small armies. By the 18th century the French and the British were the only European competitors in the Indian market. The political situation of the declining Mughal Empire was such that they were able to offer their services to rival states and thus give vent to their own rivalry. After a series of wars the French were ousted. Only the British remained, and they remained to rule.

The British Raj: By 1765 the British had gained a firm foothold in Bengal, taken charge of the revenue of the state and paid for their purchases from its coffers. This, coupled with the

preached devotion to God and the word of the *Guru* (teacher). He was the first of 10 *Gurus*, two of whom were executed by the Mughals. It was in self-defence that Sikhism was transformed into a militant religion by the last *Guru* in the early-18th century. Considering the communal problem that currently plagues India, it is interesting to note that only one instance of communal rioting is known to have occured in five-and-a-half centuries in medieval India.

It was also a time when India attracted European travelers and, as the land of spices and textiles, traders as well. The Portuguese had already settled in Goa in the early-16th century, and became successful pirates. In the 17th century, East India Companies were floated by the governments of England, France, the Netherlands

rampant corruption of Company officials, drained Bengal of its legendary wealth. To gain local support they devised the "Permanent Settlement," creating a class of "landed aristocracy" that paid revenues to the state and in exchange owned land permanently. The peasants bore the burden of merciless exploitation by this class; the British gained firm allies. The settlement became applicable to territories under the Company's administration. These continued to grow, unchecked by the British Parliament which had vested interests. By 1857 the area under British control had grown to an empire.

Drastic changes took place in the 19th century. The peasant was already burdened beyond proportion. Then, the import of finished textiles from India posed a threat to the British textile industry.

At first heavy duties and fines were imposed on Indian goods. Later, raw material was imported, the processing was done in Britain and the finished goods sold in the Indian market. This not only meant the loss of skills for Indian artisans, it also ruined them and the economy. The lack of patronage had a devastating effect on crafts. It is only since independence that a concerted effort has been made to revive a shattered tradition. Industrialization poses a threat but craftsmen are being encouraged to relearn skills, and clients are gradually becoming aware of the beauty of handmade objects.

To facilitate administration and the collection of raw materials, transport and communications were developed. Civil administration was separated from the army and police. The idea of equality before the law was introduced, together

with western education through the English medium, in Calcutta in 1835. The British also made an effort to put an end to traditional practices such as *sati* and female infanticide. Some of these measures received the support of Indian social reformers and intellectuals who, exposed to the western tradition, were able to compare it with their own. Western ideas began to influence a small section of Indian society— the educated urban elite.

Growing resentment against British rule was expressed in the Rebellion of 1857. It began in

Left, a friendly game of 18th-century chess. Above, Rajiv Gandhi makes the rounds at an official ceremony.

Meerut and spread over north and central India under the determined leadership of some extraordinary persons. The hapless Mughal emperor, who still lived in the Red Fort, emerged as its symbol. The British succeeded in crushing the rebellion; the emperor was exiled to Burma, his sons were executed and the rebels brutally punished. In 1858, power was transferred from the Company to the Crown, represented by the viceroy. The army was strengthened and Indians were excluded from all offices of consequence.

However, the seed of political consciousness had taken root, even though sections of the population remained loyal to the British. In 1885 the Indian National Congress was formed. Realizing the threat of a united Indian people, the British began to maneuver a rift between Hindus and Muslims. In 1905, they partitioned Bengal, East Bengal being predominantly Muslim. This sparked the flame of protest, which became widespread. The British countered protest with repression. And their aim to 'divide and rule' succeeded. In 1906 the All India Muslim League was formed.

The arrival of M K Gandhi in 1915 changed the face of the national movement. He advocated moral protest against oppression in the form of peaceful "civil disobedience," and under his leadership the movement became increasingly broadbased. By 1929, a younger generation of leaders, people like Jawaharlal Nehru, joined the movement, and Congress demanded an independent India. After a brief lapse the civil disobedience movement gained momentum. Indians were not appeased with the niggardly concessions granted by the Crown.

The British policy of 'divide and rule' culminated in the establishment of separate electorates for Hindus and Muslims. By 1940, the Muslim League had voiced its demand for the separate nation of Pakistan.

India became independent on August 15 1947, but the devastating tragedy of partition loomed behind the euphoria. Free India adopted a federal constitution to contain its diversity and the states were later redefined according to linguistic and ethnic divisions.

In the last 40 years India has made significant progress. She has emerged as a powerful democracy and overcome political crises. But her path is not yet smooth; her resilience is still on trial. Deep-rooted traditions—whether social, religious or cultural—are being relentlessly confronted with modern ideas, for better and for worse. Sometimes the result is incongruous, even bizarre. But a new identity is emerging, whether in the arts, 'new wave' cinema, literature, lifestyles, social norms, economic patterns or in the field of science. At this crucial moment of transition, the Indian situation is more dynamic then it has ever been.

Empire-Building: Delhi is India's capital, a sprawling metropolis that spreads on both sides of the **Jamuna River**, and stretches 25 miles (40 km) from one end to the other, accommodating some 4.5 million people and engulfing a many layered past. It is a fine entry point for travelers because of its central location, and because it offers a glimpse of India's diversity.

As an administrative and commercial center Delhi has attracted people from all parts of the country. Delhi is the bastion of bureaucracy, the cultural capital and a venue for national and international events. It has excellent museums, shopping malls and restaurants, and innumerable ancient monuments.

Delhi has been the epicenter of successive medieval empires whose monarchs established new 'cities' to proclaim their might. Seven such cities acknowledged by historians are scattered over Delhi; of these only the last is still 'alive'. Recent excavations at the **Purana Qila** revealed that the site was probably inhabited around the third century B.C., and legend locates the Indra-prastha of the *Mahabharata* not far away.

Historically, Delhi dates to the eighth-century **Dhillika**, established by Tomar Rajputs whose 16th ruler built the first city **Lal Kot**, in 1060 A.D. In the early-12th century, the Chauhans of Ajmer conquered Lal Kot, enlarged the fortifications and named the area **Qila Rai Pithora**. However, their reign was shortlived; in 1192 Muhammad of Ghor stormed through the north-western passes and defeated Prithviraj Chauhan. Prithviraj was the last Hindu ruler of Delhi till the British left in 1947.

Qila Rai Pithora was occupied by Qut-buddin Aibak, a general of Muhammad Ghor who established the independent Slave Dynasty (1206-1290). Some of Delhi's finest monuments date to this era.

The Slave kings were displaced by the Khaljis (1290-1320) and in 1302 Alauddin Khalji built **Siri**, the second city of Delhi. Practically nothing remains of Siri, but travelers recorded the splendors of its Palace of 1000 Pillars. The ascendancy of the Tughlaqs in 1320 was accompanied by much bloodshed. The founder, Ghiyasuddin (1321-1325) established the third city, **Tughlaqabad**. Muhammad bin Tughlaq established the fourth city, **Jahanpanah**, between Siri and Qila Rai Pithora, and Firuz Shah Tughlaq (1351-1388) raised the fifth, **Firuzabad**, the remains of which rest silently behind the busy artery of **Bahadur Shah Zafar Marg**. In 1398 Delhi reeled under the onslaught of Timur's army and for a century thereafter, during the reigns of the Sayyids and Lodis (1414-1526), growth was stagnant.

Babur laid the foundation of the Mughal Empire in 1526 and his son Humayun created Delhi's sixth city, Dinpanah. Its citadel is today known as Purana Qila. Sher Shah Suri, an Afghan who temporarily ousted the Mughals, made several additions to Humayun's city, material for which is known to have been brought from Siri. Humayun's grandson Shah Jahan (1628-1658) shifted the Mughal capital from Agra and created Delhi's seventh city, Shahjahanabad, with its magnificent Red Fort and Jama Masjid. Alive and bustling, it is today known as **Old Delhi** and is one of the most interesting parts of the city. Shahjahanabad remained the capital of Mughal India till 1857, though from the last years of the 18th century the emperors were mere puppets in the hands of the British.

On December 12 1911, at an imperial durbar held for King George V and Queen Mary, it was announced that the headquar-

Left, exponent of the Bharata Natyam dance style. Right, rugs are a hot tourist item.

ters of the British administration in India would move to Delhi. For this purpose, a new city was to be built, "conceived with spaciousness and care so that the new creation may be in every way worthy of this ancient and beautiful city." Edwin Lutyens and Herbert Baker were appointed architects. They traveled through the country studying ancient monuments, and eventually designed buildings that incorporated eastern and western stylistic elements, and were placed amidst sprawling gardens and tree-lined avenues. New Delhi, capital of British India, was inaugurated in January 1931. It was above all an imperial city, a symbol of power accentuated by the Rajpath axis and the Viceregal Lodge (now **Rashtrapati Bhavan**, the President's Estate) atop Raisina Hill. Neither architects nor planners had visualized the extents to which the city has grown, and continues to grow.

City Tour: There are certain landmarks in Delhi that should not be missed. One can start at the southern extremity, with the early Islamic monuments in the **Qutb** area, where Qila Rai Pithora once stood. The 12th-century **Quwwat ul Islam** (Might of Islam) **Mosque** was built by Qutbuddin Aibak, using material from a Hindu temple,

as is evident in the sculpted pillars of the cloisters. What remains of the prayer hall is an arched screen with beautiful Koranic inscriptions.

The adjacent **Qutb Minar,** a victory tower begun by Qutbuddin is one of the most beautiful Islamic monuments in India. The **tomb of Iltutmish** the Slave king, and the **Alai Darwaza** of the Khalji era are among other notable monuments in this area. There is also an **Iron Pillar,** dating to the fifth century A.D., that continues to puzzle metallurgists because it has remained rust-free.

The massive fortifications of **Tughlaqabad** were raised to intimidate Mongol invaders. The fort is deserted and barren, though the **tomb of Ghiyasuddin** is a fine specimen of Tughlaq architecture.

The 16th-century **Lodi tombs** are surrounded by one of the finest gardens in Delhi, the **Lodi Gardens,** once known as Lady Willingdon Park. The octagonal **tomb of Sikandar Lodi** and the **Bara Gumbad Mosque** with its tiles and incised inscriptions are characteristic of the age. Adjacent to the Lodi Gardens is the **tomb of Safdarjang,** viceroy of Awadh in the 18th century. It is the last example of the garden tomb, "the last flicker in the lamp of Mughal

Geometric lines of the Jantar Mantar, one of several 18th-century observatories built by Jai Singh.

architecture in Delhi."

Purana Qila manifests the emergence of Mughal architecture, and there is a beautiful **mosque** and **pavilion** within. **Humayun's tomb** (1565) was built by his widow Haji Begum and designed by the Persian architect Misak Mirza Ghiyas. It is a forerunner of the Taj Mahal and one of the finest garden tombs. Bahadur Shah Zafar, the last Mughal emperor, surrendered to the British within its precincts.

The 14th-century citadel of **Firuz Shah Kotla** has an **Ashokan pillar;** also a **mosque** where Timur is believed to have prayed. The **Red Fort** in Shahjahanabad once epitomized the splendor of the Mughal court. To some extent this can be recreated in the imagination while walking through the **Halls of Public and Private Audience, the Pearl Mosque, the Royal Baths, the Rang Mahal** and the **Khwabgah,** set near the **Hayat Baksh** garden. This was the palace of the Peacock Throne, and the scented Stream of Paradise that flowed through the emperor's apartments, masterpieces of an emperor who created some of the finest building in marble the world has ever seen.

Jama Masjid (1656) is a magnificent mosque rising above an esplanade in the heart of the walled city, one of the most densely populated localities in the world. Some 90 percent of Delhi's Muslims live in the walled city and some of them are descendants of those who served the Mughals. This is an area where many medieval traditions linger.

Chandni Chowk (the moonlit square) was also part of the original plan of Shahjahanabad and lies between the Red Fort and the **Fatehpuri Mosque.** It is the largest trading center in north India, a teeming hub of activity that retains the scars and embellishments of some three-and-a-half centuries.

North of Shahjahanabad was once the British locality, the Civil Lines with bungalows and offices. **St. James's Church** (1824), **Metcalfe House** (1855) where the British Resident lived, and the old **Viceregal Lodge,** now a part of **Delhi University,** are some of the relics of that era.

West of Purana Qila are some important landmarks of **New Delhi**—the **India Gate,** a World War I Memorial, the 340-room **Rashtrapati Bhavan, Parliament House,** the **National Museum** and **Jaipur House, the Gallery of Modern Art.** (Other interesting museums include the **Crafts Museum** and **Rural India Complex** in Pragati Maidan, and the **Rail Museum** situated in

The 13th-century Qutb Minar monument, built by pre-Mughal Delhi sultans.

FEASTING AT THE BUKHARA

There is no dearth of restaurants in Delhi, and the speciality of this city is Mughal cuisine. Something that simply should not be missed is a meal at the Bukhara, in the Maurya Sheraton Hotel. The restaurant specializes in cuisine of the Northwest Frontier, the mountainous region that spans Mardan, Peshawar, Bannu, Kohat and Waziristan, peopled by hardy, nomadic Pathans. In keeping with the nomadic lifestyle, simplicity is the essence of their cuisine.

More than 10 years ago Madan Lal Jaiswal, Master Chef at the Bukhara, explored the remote interiors of the Frontier to learn about time-tested Pathan delicacies, and there is no doubt that he brought back the best recipes. "The secret of Pathan cooking," he says, "lies in the excellent quality of the meat and the

the counter but made in the traditional manner with fine clay, bound by animal hair and wheat husk and strengthened with a wash of salt and water.

Chicken *tikka* and chicken *tandoori*, crisp on the outside and succulent within; *sheikh kabab*, lamb or *burra kabab;* Sikandari *raan* and fish *tikka*, tender and subtly flavored—these are among the delicious fare that emerges from the *tandoors* of the Bukhara. The *kabab* is the epitome of Pathan cuisine, and James Spain, an American writer who spent time in the Frontier region, writes: "It is easy enough to describe the *kabab* as ground meat mixed with spices. To convey an impression of the flavor is as difficult as it is to describe the spirit of the East."

The only option is to taste the meat—with a range of *tandoori* breads offered at the Bukhara. The bread is baked by patting the dough against the wall of the *tandoor*. There are plain *rotis*, flavored *naans* and *parathas* stuffed with minced meat or cottage cheese.

chicken, just a light touch of spices, a sprinkling of *shahi zeera*—black cumin seed—and the lack of fussy sauces or curries which can drown the flavor of the meat." Jaiswal and his assistants have grasped the secret to perfection and even after a decade the food at the Bukhara is of unsurpassed excellence.

It is cooked in a *tandoor*, a hollow, barrel-shaped clay oven indispensible, and perfectly suited, to nomadic needs. At the restaurant the *tandoors* are built into

The Bukhara shatters the myth about Pathan food being totally non-vegetarian. Jaiswal found not only a variety in vegetarian cuisine, but as one who believes in experimentation, has contributed to it as well. *Paneer tikka,* cottage cheese marinated like chicken and cooked on the skewer and *tandoori* vegetable salad are among his creations.

The decor of the Bukhara is simple; and you are invited to eat with your fingers, the traditional and best way for this cuisine.

Bukhara chefs whipping up something savory.

Chanakyapuri.)

Connaught Place is still the most important commercial center in New Delhi. The **Central Cottage Industries Emporium** in Janpath is an excellent place to shop; so are the various **state emporia** along the nearby **Baba Kharak Singh Marg.** It is also very interesting to stroll along **Janpath,** where among a variety of stalls are those of the Tibetan refugees, selling an assortmentt of curios and jewelry.

Mughal Splendor: Uttar Pradesh, or UP, is India's most densely populated state. It includes the Himalayas in the north but most of UP lies in the fertile Gangetic plain. This region has been a part of empires since ancient times with Mathura, Kanauj, Jaunpur and Agra as successive epicenters. It is associated with the rise of Buddhism and Jainism; it has a rich Islamic heritage; while Hindu pilgrimage centers such as Ayodhya, Allahabad, Hardwar and Varanasi are integral to religion and mythology. Between the Mughal era and the Raj the area was ruled by the Nawabs of Awadh and Afghan Rohillas. In more recent times UP has produced many eminent politicians. **Lucknow** is the capital, though **Agra** and **Varanasi** are its most fascinating cities.

In the mid-15th century the Afghan ruler Sikandar Lodi established his capital near Agra. Within a century it became the Mughal capital. Three outstanding emperors—Akbar, Jehangir and Shah Jahan—whose reigns spanned the transition from aggression to the ease of security, ruled from here over an immense and powerful empire. The opulence of the Mughal court is legendary. It was an age of refinement when, in art and architecture particularly, Hindu and Islamic traditions merged in unique perfection. Time has changed the face of Agra but the palaces and mausoleums of that era survive, like frozen moments of an enchanted hour.

In 1566 Akbar built the **Agra Fort** on the south bank of the Jamuna. Its immense gateways and solid ramparts of red sandstone are characteristic of his style. The palaces he built within were mostly demolished and replaced by his grandson Shah Jahan. However, the **Jehangiri Mahal** survives, its sandstone facades finely carved. Shah Jahan, with whom building was a passion, raised the paradise-like marble palaces for his beloved queen Mumtaz Mahal (who is buried in the Taj Mahal). The Khas Mahal, as these palaces were called, include the exquisite **Musammam Burj** or Jasmine Tower, richly inlaid with precious

Colorful kites on show in a Delhi sidestreet.

stones; and the glass-encrusted **Sheesh Mahal,** where the glow of a single candle was illumined in a thousand reflections.

Ironically, Shah Jahan spent his last days in the Jasmine Tower, a hapless prisoner in the hands of his son Aurangzeb. The **Moti Masjid** or Pearl Mosque and the **Diwan-i-Am** and **Diwan-i-Khas** (the Halls of Public and Private Audience) were his other outstanding additions, beautiful in totality as well as in the minutest detail. The fort was eventually garrisoned by the British. Like other monuments in Agra, much of the gold, silver and precious stones were lost to pillaging Jats in the 18th century.

On the opposite bank two miles (three km) downstream is the marble mausoleum of Mirza Ghiyas Beg, styled **Itmad ud Daula** or Pillar of the State by Jehangir. Mirza's daughter Nur Jahan married Jehangir and the mausoleum was completed under her patronage in 1628. This 'jewelled casket' has a smooth surface of marble profusely inlaid with jasper, lapis lazuli, onyx, topaz and cornelian.

The **Taj Mahal,** mausoleum for the Empress Mumtaz Mahal, was begun in 1632. It took 20,000 laborers 22 years to complete. The architect remains unknown but was most likely a Turk, Ustad Isa Afandi. The finest carvers, stonemasons and engineers were summoned from Lahore, Delhi, Turkey and Persia. Only one, Amanat Khan Shirazi, master calligrapher from Persia, left his signature on the monument. The marble was brought from Makrana in Rajasthan, the precious and semi-precious stones from all parts of India, the Indian Ocean, Afghanistan, China, Tibet and Baghdad.

Perfection is the essence of the Taj Mahal; restrained ornamentation has lent a matchless beauty, the symmetry of its form and setting an eloquent harmony, the play of light on the marble an ethereal luminosity. It is at once simple and exotic, chaste and sensuous, immense and fragile.

The only asymmetrical feature is the cenotaph of Shah Jahan, hurriedly buried by Aurangzeb in the octagonal hall below the central dome. It is no less beautiful, however, and it lies within the exquisite marble latticed screen. The real graves are in a crypt below.

Sikandra, 7.5 miles (12 km) from Agra, goes back in time. Akbar is buried here in a mausoleum he designed but which Jehangir altered considerably. The cenotaph is in a white marble courtyard atop three storeys of sandstone, the actual tomb in an austere

Akbar's mausoleum at Sikandra.

crypt. At Sikandra, the ornamentation consists of colorful expanses of geometric mosaics set against red sandstones. The impressive gateway, with its four marble minarets, is visible from a long distance.

Fatehpur Sikri lies 23 miles (37 km) southwest of Agra. Akbar built it in 1571 to honor Sheikh Salim Chishti, the Sufi saint who prophesied the birth of his sons. The city spread over the ridge above Sikri village where the saint dwelt. It was eventually encompassed by a six-mile (10-km) wall. The scale of its splendor is revealed in simple statistics—for instance, 6,000 elephants and 30,000 horses were maintained here. The imperial residence and the Jama Masjid crowned the ridge. For 14 years this was the exclusive core of the empire and the court was alive with a concentration of intellectuals and creative talent—artists and calligraphers, poets, musicians, theologians, generals and financiers, all of extraordinary calibre.

Most of the city is in ruins. Only the imperial residence remains, and the mosque. The red sandstone palaces are in such a perfect state of preservation it seems as if Akbar left yesterday. The sprawling palaces include the **Halls of Public and Private Audience**, the **treasury**, the astrologer's kiosk, the **Turkish Sultana's palace**, the **Khwabgah** (Akbar's bedroom, with an ingenious cooling system) and the **Harim Sara**, with the palaces of Queen Jodha Bai and Maryam Makani. Towering above all this is the **Panch Mahal**, the five-storey wind tower.

At the western extremity of the ridge is the **Jama Masjid**. The **Buland Darwaza**, the immense gateway, commemorating Akbar's victory in Gujarat, rises on the southern periphery of the courtyard. Sheikh Salim Chishti lies buried near the mosque. His wish-fulfilling marble shrine glows like a solitary pearl in the red sandstone setting. The perforated screens that enclose the corridors are of unsurpassed beauty. In 1585 Akbar moved his court to Lahore; by 1610, travelers who passed through Fatehpur Sikri noted that the city was deserted. Only the palaces were maintained for emperors who made periodic visits to the shrine.

The tradition of marble inlay and fretwork lingers in Agra, and there still are mastercraftsmen who create fine objects. The stones used for inlay are however, mostly synthetic. Incidently, Agra also has the largest shoe industry in the world.

Pilgrim Center: "Benares (Varanasi) is older than history, older than tradition, older

even than legend, and it looks twice as old as all of them put together," wrote Mark Twain. By 600 B.C. **Varanasi** was already a place of pilgrimage for Hindus, for whom it holds the promise of ultimate liberation, and a center for learning. It has enjoyed a continuous tradition for 2,500 years, attracting pilgrims from farflung corners of India.

Varanasi is one of the most crowded cities in India. The **Ganga** flows to its east; on the north and northwest it is bound by the **Varuna River** and to the south by the **Asi River**—hence the name Varanasi. But even more, Varanasi is bound by a traditional sacred geography. Politically it has been of little significance. The belief is that Shiva reigns supreme in Varanasi, so when Raja Chait Singh founded a state here in 1725 he built his palace across the river, in nearby **Ramnagar.**

Shiva reigns as Vishwanath, Lord of the Universe. Varanasi is known by many names, each revealing a unique aspect of its mythological associations. Among these is Kashi, City of Light, for it enshrines the supreme Linga of Light. It is also Mahashamshana, the great cremation ground, where fires have not ceased to burn for over 2,000 years. People come to Varanasi to die, and funeral processions are a common sight.

With a temple—and there is literally one at every turn and corner—dedicated to almost every god and goddess, Varanasi is a microcosm of the Hindu world, and its sanctity is enriched by the Ganga, worshipped here incessantly as goddess and mother. Legend says that when Ganga reached Varanasi she was so captivated by the city that she lost her way and began flowing northwards again, momentarily. Pilgrims circumambulate a set path, visiting several temples, holy tanks and walls enroute. The **Vishwanath Temple** near Dasashwamedha Ghat is the most important shrine. It was first built in 490 A.D., but destroyed several times by fanatics. The present structure dates to 1777 and was built by Rani Ahilyabi of Indore. (Among the temples open to non-Hindus are the **Tulsi Manas Mandir,** where Tulsidas wrote the Hindi version of the *Ramayana*, the **Durga Temple** and the **Sankat Mochan Hanuman Temple.**) An essential ritual is a dip in the Ganga where ancestor worship is performed and in whose waters there is no distinction of class or caste. Catering to the needs of pilgrims is a source of livelihood for thousands of persons in Varanasi.

The city's waterfront is a dramatic sight, viewed with ease from a boat. The scene is

Temples abound at Varanasi.

best at dawn, when the first rays of the sun bring to light the magnificent three-mile (five-km) sweep of 70 *ghats* (stepped embankments). Over the centuries rulers of various states like Jaipur, Gwalior, Udaipur, Mysore, Nepal and Bundi, built palaces and *ghats* for their convenience and temples to express their devotion. There are also several *ashrams* along the *ghats* and homes for widows. Aurangzeb's **mosque** pierces the skyline. Not far from it is Raja Jai Singh's 18th-century **observatory.**

The *ghats* are teeming with people, absorbed in sacred and mundane activities. For some it is daily fare, for others the fulfilment of a long-cherished dream. **Dasashwamedha Ghat** is the most frequented, rather picturesque with its swaying matted umbrellas under which *ghatias*, who are not full-fledged priests, assist in the performance of a few simple rituals.

The labyrinthine lanes of Varanasi are fascinating. The city still has two big universities. Within the campus of the **Benares Hindu University** is the **Bharat Kala Bhavan Museum** with a rich collection of Mughal miniatures and brocade textiles. Since 600 B.C. Varanasi has been famous for its silk, a fabric associated with ritual, ceremony and celebration. Large localities

like Madanpura are occupied almost wholly by weavers, and more than 30 percent of the population is involved in the trade. Silk stores abound, and the man selling *sarees* from a tiny shop in **Kunj Galli** will be far richer than he appears.

The **Ramnagar Palace** across the river, wears a deserted look though it is still a royal residence. The remnants of pomp and pageantry are housed in a compact museum. However, during the months preceding the Dussehra festival in October, Ramnagar steals the show from Varanasi. For, every evening a scene from the *Ramayana* is elaborately enacted, with the Maharaja presiding over the celebrations.

About six miles (10 km) north of Varanasi is **Sarnath**, a tranquil world apart. Here, in the **Deer Park,** the Buddha preached his first sermon. The remains include a **monastery**, the huge **Dhamek Stupa** (500 A.D.) and an **Ashokan pillar.** There is also the modern **Mahabodhi Society Temple.** Sarnath, which was at its peak in the sixth and seventh centuries A.D., is a major Buddhist pilgrimage center. There is a fine **Archaeological Museum** which has the Lion Capital of Ashoka and stone sculptures dating to Mauryan, Kushan and Gupta eras.

Giving the lowdown on high-tech.

HIMALAYAN SPLENDOR

Himalaya means "abode of snow." The Himalayan ranges extend 1,500 miles (2,400 km) from southeast to northwest, separating India from China. They are 248 miles (400 km) wide with a mean elevation of 19,800 feet (6,000 meters) at the central axial range. **Nanda Devi** (25,796 feet/7,817 meters) is the highest peak in India.

The lifestyle and occupations of mountain dwellers remained largely unchanged over the centuries, and various cultural expressions endured in quiet seclusion. Among the arts, painting especially flourished in some hill kingdoms in the 18th and 19th centuries.

The scenic splendor of this region has an ethereal quality, more so after the heat and dust of the plains. In the early years of the last century, several 'summer resorts' were developed by the British, who made these hitherto remote regions accessible by road and rail. They came upon suitable locations accidentally, often in the pursuit of game. **Darjeeling** became the summer capital for the headquarters in Calcutta. When the government moved to Delhi, **Shimla** took over. **Nainital**, **Mussourie, Dalhousie** and **Ranikhat**, to name a few "hill stations, " grew into little English hamlets in the mountains. Even today one finds red-roofed cottages covered with creepers, stone churches, the inevitable Mall and names like Violet Bank, Sleepy Hollow and Wolly's Folly. The summer months came to be known as 'The Season,' a time when the British revelled in parties, balls and amateur dramatics, but perhaps most of all in the weather. Lord Lytton, viceroy (1876-1880), records his delight: "The afternoon was rainy, and the road muddy, but such beautiful *English* rain; such delicious *English* mud ..."

The Himalayas span the states of Jammu and Kashmir, Himachal Pradesh, Uttar Pradesh, Sikkim and West Bengal. Of these, Kashmir is the most popular with tourists.

Hamlets in the Hills: Jammu is the railhead for **Kashmir**. It is 189 miles (305 km) from Srinagar and linked to it by air and road. Jammu and Kashmir were merged into one state under the Dogra Maharaja Gulab Singh in 1832. Jammu is of little interest except for the **Dogra Art Gallery** which has over 600 miniatures of the Basohli and Kangra schools.

The Mughal emperors described Ka-shmir in a single word—paradise. And indeed, this high altitude valley surrounded by snowcapped peaks is one of the most beautiful places in India. The air is crisp and clean, there are streams and meadows and forests and in summer the valley is resplendant with fruit laden trees, rice fields and magnificent *chinar* trees (the oriental plane).

Srinagar (5,230 feet/1585 meters) is the capital, and linked by air to Delhi, Chandigarh, Amritsar, Jammu and Leh. It is believed to have been founded by Ashoka in the third century B.C. though the present site belongs to a later date. Hindu kings ruled here till 1331; thereafter it was taken over by Muslims whose most renowned ruler was Zain al Abidin (1421-1472). Crafts, in particular, flourished under his patronage. The Mughals conquered Kashmir and are immortalized there in the splendid gardens they laid in and around Srinagar. In 1819 the Sikhs overthrew the last Muslim ruler and they were later replaced by the Dogras.

Srinagar spreads on both sides of the Jhelum River, with seven original bridges spanning it. Water is a way of life in this city. Srinagar is synonymous with *shikaras* (hand paddled water-taxis) and houseboats.

Preceding pages: cene from a dream— Srinagar's Dal Lake. Left, dressed to thrill in Ladakh. Right, rice terraces in Kashmir.

Houseboats were developed by the British towards the end of the 19th century as a result of the Maharaja of Kashmir's refusal to permit non-Kashmiris to own land in his state. It is believed that a merchant whose shop burnt down shifted his goods onto a boat over which he later built a wooden shelter. This triggered the idea of a houseboat and the merchant soon took to boatbuilding. The British bought these houseboats which enabled them to possess permanent retreats in Kashmir without violating the Maharaja's stipulation. Today these houseboats, moored along **Dal Lake** and **Nagin Lake**, are let out to tourists, and cater to all budgets. Some are managed by hotel chains, and have luxuriously appointed rooms and sun decks. The lakes are famous for lotus gardens and floating vegetable patches built on rafts. *Shikara*-borne vendors row past the houseboats selling flowers, curios and carpets. Dal Lake has facilities for swimming, waterskiing and surfboard riding. It is linked by a causeway to the smaller, cleaner Nagin Lake.

Srinagar has fine Mughal gardens which are symmetrically planned, terraced, with fountains and water channels. The **Chashma Shahi** garden was laid by Shah Jahan in 1632. The nearby **Pari Mahal** was once a Buddhist monastery, later converted by Shah Jahan's son Dara Shikoh into a center of learning. **Nishat**, the garden of bliss on the shores of Dal Lake, has a magnificent view of the snowcapped **Pir Panjal** range west of the valley. It was created in 1633 by Asaf Khan, brother of Nur Jahan. The **Shalimar Garden** is more famous for its association with Jehangir, who planned it for his Empress Nur Jahan. There is a sound and light show in this garden from May to October.

One of the oldest mosques in Srinagar is that of **Shah Hamadan,** on the banks of the Jhelum. It is made of wood and has fine *papier mache* work on its walls and ceilings. The **Hazratbal Mosque** is specially revered for it enshrines a hair of the Prophet. The **Jama Masjid** (1402) originally built by Sikandar Shah, was enlarged by his son Zain al Abidin. It has been destroyed several times by fire and the present structure dates to the time of Maharaja Pratap Singh.

The **Hari Parbat fort**, surrounded by almond orchards, and the **Shankaracharya Hill** afford fine views of the valley.

Kashmir is famous for its silk and wool carpets. These are worked in looms and knotted by hand to the chant of a color caller. Carpet weaving was begun here in the 15th

A breathtaking Himalayan sunset.

century, and received special impetus under Jehangir, in whose time the Governor of Kashmir returned from Persia with craftsmen and tools. The average weaver can make between 10,000 and 14,000 knots a day. Hand embroidered woollen shawls, and Pashmina and the exclusive *shahtoosh* shawls are a speciality of this region. Kashmir is also known for its carved walnut wood artifacts, felt rugs, crewel embroidery work and *papier mache*.

It is the only place in the world, apart from Spain, where saffron grows. The *wazwan* is an elaborate feast where numerous meat dishes are eaten with rice.

Pahalgam (7,244 feet/2,195 meters), 56 miles (90 km) northeast of Srinagar is a forested retreat at the junction of the Lidder and Seshnag streams. The streams abound in trout and fishing is possible if a permit is obtained in Srinagar. Pahalgam is the base for a three-day, 22-mile (35-km) trek to the **Kolahoi glacier** (10,560/3,200 meters).

Gulmarg (8,755 feet/2,653 meters) is 32 miles (52 km) southwest of Srinagar. The name means 'meadow of flowers'. It has a fine view of the Himalayas, an 18-hole golf course and is also the top ski resort in India (December to April). Several day treks are possible from Gulmarg.

Out of this World: Entering **Ladakh** through the **Zoji La Pass** (11,550 feet/3,500 meters) is like stepping into another world, one that has a stark, barren grandeur. In a geophysical sense the visitor has left India for Tibet. The Dogra conquest brought Ladakh into the Indian orbit, but till 1959 the Lamas continued to look to Lhasa for religious inspiration. Ladakh is one of very few places where Tibetan Buddhism continues to be practiced in a manner that has not changed in the last 1,000 years. The population, however, does include the Balti Shia Muslims and animist Dards.

Leh (11,350 feet/3,440 meters), the main town, rests in the valley of the Indus at the trijunction of the historic Silk Route from China to West Asia and the plains of India.

Acclimatization takes a day. Ladakh has several monasteries and the architecture is such that the buildings seem to grow out of the rocky mountainsides. These monasteries have a wealth of idols, painted scrolls, frescoes, silverware and carvings. **Shey**, **Thikse** and **Hemis** are the monasteries closest to Leh. Hemis has a colorful three-day festival in June. The **Alchi Monastery**, which has exceptionally good wall paintings, is one-and-a-half hour's drive from Leh. The Ladakhis are a gentle people who

Rugged Thikse Monastery, Ladakh.

enjoy archery, dancing and polo, and *chang*, a mildly alcoholic drink made from fermented barley (also popular in Bhutan). The women are exotically attired with coral, silver and turquoise jewelery.

Himachal Pradesh: Though less frequented by tourists, Himachal Pradesh is no less beautiful than Kashmir, and offers splendid trekking opportunities.

Shimla (6,930 feet/2,100 meters) the capital spreads over a seven-mile- (12-km-long) ridge, and has recently been linked by air. It is also linked by rail from **Kalka**. The train runs on a narrow guage (2.5 feet) and in the course of the 58-mile (96-km) journey traverses 107 tunnels and numerous arched viaducts.

Shimla was 'discovered' by Le Rose in 1819 when he came upon a thickly wooded place dedicated to the Goddess Shamla. Though population has taken its toll, relics of the Raj survive. Shimla offers riding, golf and ice skating. Winter sports are popular at **Kufri** and **Narkanda**. The season is from end-December to end-February.

Kangra Valley, with an abundance of ancient temples, has its headquarters at **Dharamsala**. This hill station is known as 'Little Lhasa' for its large Tibetan settlement in **Mcleodganj**. It is also the base for

the government in exile of His Holiness the Dalai Lama and there are Buddhist temples as well as a **Tibetan library and medical center**. Dharamsala affords a grandstand view of the magnificent **Dhauladhar Range** (19,800 feet/6,000 meters).

Kulu, Valley of the Gods, stretches for 50 miles (80 km) along the upper reaches of the deep Beas gorge, and leads to the **Rohtang Pass**, entrance to the predominantly Buddhist **Lahaul** and **Spiti** valleys. There are shrines, old castles, temples and hot springs en route, and the area is abundant in fruit. **Manali** is an excellent base for treks to **Chandrakhani** (seven days), **Chandratal** (11 days), **Deo Tibba** (seven days) and **Solang Valley** (seven days), the last offering winter sports as well. Kulu (linked by air) is known for its Dussehra festival which takes place in October, when local deities are brought down from mountaintop shrines in colorful, decorated palanquins.

UP Hills: The Himalayas also span the **Garhwal** and **Kumaon** districts of Uttar Pradesh. While **Nainital**, **Mussourie** and **Landsdowne** are popular tourist resorts, this area has shrines of immense significance to Hindus, as well as the sources of the Ganga and Jamuna at **Gangotri** and **Yamnotri. Hardwar**, where the Ganga

High summer pastures near Mcleodganj, on the Dhauladhar Range.

descends to the plains is one of India's sacred cities. There are fine views of the Nanda Devi, Nanda Kot, Trishul and Bandar Poonch peaks from these hills.

The Kumaon region specially comes to life in the writings of Jim Corbett. The **Corbett National Park** is a 50-square-mile (125-square-km) wildlife sanctuary in the Kumaon foothills near **Ramnagar**, giving refuge to tigers, elephants, leopards, deer and bears.

West Bengal: Darjeeling (7,042 feet/ 2,134 meters) is the premier hill station of West Bengal and synonymous the world over with tea, which the British planted in 1840. It derives its name from a Buddhist monastery, Dorjeling, "the place of the thunderbolt." The monastery was destroyed by Nepalis in the 19th century.

Darjeeling is an abrupt change from the plains and Calcutta. The population is Nepali, Lepcha, Tibetan and Bhutia. There is no pollution or crowds, and life goes on at an easy pace. Darjeeling is also famous for its 'toy train', the **Darjeeling Himalayan Railway** established in 1882. The two-foot guage is still used, and the oldest existing engine, the *Mountaineer,* dates to 1892. The train loops and climbs for 53 miles (86 km) from **New Jalpaiguri,** taking seven hours to complete the journey, which features spectacular Himalayan vistas. **Ghoom** (8,045 feet/2,438 meters) has a well known monastery and is the highest railway station in the world. From Ghoom the train winds down 1,000 feet (300 meters) to Darjeeling. There is also a road from **Bagdogra airport** near **Siliguri** and one can reach Darjeeling in three hours. Rail and road pass through dense tropical forests, tea gardens, terraced rice fields and pines."

Kanchanjunga (28,000 feet/8,500 meters) "the five treasure houses of the great snows," is the third highest peak in the world and about 50 miles (80 km) from Darjeeling as the crow flies. On a clear day the view is beautiful and is more so from **Tiger Hill,** at sunrise.

As with most hill stations, Darjeeling has a busy **Mall;** there are some interesting antique stores. The town retains an old world charm, and the **Planters Club** (where visitors can stay on a daily basis) dates from the time of the Raj. Tenzing Norgay, who with Edmund Hillary climbed Everest in 1952, belonged to Darjeeling, and the **Indian Mountaineering Institute** has since trained several mountaineers. Darjeeling also has a tiny racecourse, a zoo and botanical gardens.

Locals of Kulu Valley, Himachal Pradesh.

COLORFUL WEST

Rajasthan: Rugged forts tower defensively atop the oldest mountains in the world and fine palaces yield their delicate images on still waters. Thousands of peasants surge towards a sacred site brimming with color and anticipation. On the dunes, the song of a lone shepherd pierces the primeval silence. Royalty lingers, even as it succumbs to the present. Nomadic tribes drift into crowded cities and traditional craftsmen seek new clients. This is **Rajasthan,** the "abode of Kings." The land of a hardy people who are descendants of a quaint mixture of races, whose kings were accorded *Kshatriya* status and geneologies which linked them to solar and lunar gods. A land of heros who prized honor above life, and queens and princesses who preferred death by fire to the enemy's harem. It is a land where for centuries an extraordinary vitality has defied the environment, a vitality variously manifested against the bleak and harsh terrain to inspire both awe and delight.

The Rajputs rose to political power in the ninth and 10th centuries A.D., establishing themselves as local kings in various parts of western and central India over an area comprising the Thar desert, semi-arid terrain and the Aravalli Ranges. Fiercely resisting Muslim domination, they were frequently at war with one another, too. In all there were 36 clans with the Maharana of Udaipur as the acknowledged head.

It was Akbar who eventually succeeded in subduing the Rajputs—with warfare, but more enduringly with matrimonial alliances. Jodhpur and Amber sent the first princesses to the Mughals, and in course of time Rajput generals were at the forefront of imperial campaigns. When the Mughal empire declined the Rajput rulers reasserted themselves, but had soon to submit to the British, who allowed them nominal powers. At the time of Independence the State of Rajasthan was created from 23 princely states.

Jaipur, the capital of Rajasthan, is also one of its most interesting cities. It was established in 1728 by Raja Jai Singh II, in the sprawling plains seven miles (11 km) from Amber. Along with the chief architect Vidyadhar, Jai Singh gave India her first "planned" city. Though the pressures of population are telling on its charms, the old city is still the nerve center of Jaipur. To discern order within its present chaos may seem impossible, but from the heights of the **Nahargarh Fort** the plan is clearly visible. The old city is divided into squares, the regal spaciousness of the City Palace giving way to markets and residences patterned in a grid and contained within crenellated walls that once marked the boundary. Only a few of the seven imposing gateways remain. The buildings are characterized by balconies, tiny windows, cupolas, courtyards and arched entrances. The city was given a wash of pink for the visit of Prince Albert in 1876 and the color has since been maintained. In the original plan the wide main streets were lined with bazaars, the uniformity even specifying the number of shops on either side, the layout of the houses and their entrances through the side lanes. Areas were allocated according to professions, and this type of zoning remains even today. Dyers, stone carvers, jewelers, hand block printers, to mention a few, have inhabited the same localities for 250 years. Jai Singh made it abligatory for nobles to build houses near the city. These miniature palaces have all been engulfed by modern Jaipur and many of them are now hotels. Vaishnav and Jain temples were also built and one is never far from flower sellers and the sound of temple

Preceding pages: Fairground posing in Rajasthan. Left, peacock door of the City Palace in Jaipur.

bells. When Nadir Shah, the Persian adventurer, invaded Delhi in 1739 traders, jewelers and bankers fled to the relative haven of Jaipur. So from its very inception Jaipur became a center of commerce and religion. Today it is one of the fastest growing cities in India. It is the largest emerald cutting center in the world and is renowned for its enamelled jewelry and precious stones. Extraordinarily rich in craft, Jaipur is also famous for its hand block prints, tie and dye fabrics, blue pottery, puppets and miniatures. Young entrepreneurs have excelled in adapting ancient skills to modern designs, making the city a shopper's paradise. Necessity has caused heirlooms to be turned into merchandise and there are numerous antique stores, specializing in objects from Gujarat and Rajasthan. Observing life around the bazaar of the old city is an unforgettable experience.

Restoring miniature paintings is no small task.

Part of the **City Palace** is still the residence of the ex-Maharaja, but enough of it has been converted into a **museum** that affords a vivid glimpse of a bygone era. It also has a fine selection of textiles, arms, carpets, paintings and regal accessories. Near the museum is the **Jantar Mantar,** the largest stone observatory in the world. Legend says that the innocent questions of a young girl inspired Jai Singh to build his observatories (the other four are at Delhi, Mathura, Ujjain and Varanasi). Completed in 1727, the huge instruments at the Jaiur observatory resemble 20th century sculptures. Their accuracy is remarkable and they are consulted by *pandits* ("wise men") even today.

The nearby Hawa Mahal or **Palace of Wind** was built by Maharaja Pratap Singh in the late-18th century. This quaint five-storey structure resembles a stage set. It has several hundred windows fitted with perforated screens and topped with cupolas.

Across the Ajmer Road, between the Ajmeri and Sanganeri Gates are the famous **Ram Niwas Gardens,** laid out by Maharaja Ram Singh II in 1868. The **zoo** is here; also the **museum** and **Albert Hall,** whose foundation was laid by Prince Albert. The museum has a varied collection that includes coins, photographs, paintings of the rulers of Amber and Jaipur, frescoes and Egyptian antiquities. Ram Singh also built the grand **Rambagh Palace** as a billiard retreat. It is now a luxury hotel.

Amber Fort was the original seat of the rulers of Jaipur and its expansive splendor is reminiscent of one of the most illustrious ruling houses of Rajputana. "I am able to

compare nothing with Amber," wrote Bishop Herber in the 19th century. There is a motor road to the top but visitors can also go on elephant back. Within the fort, the earlier palaces built by Raja Man Singh (c. 1589-1614) are stark by comparison to those built by Mirza Raja Jai Singh and Jai Singh II. In the short span of a few decades the Mughal influence permeated the Rajput court and is evident in the splendid and ornate halls of audiences, residential palaces and gardens. Behind the fort are the eerie remains of a ruined city. The ramparts of Amber are linked to the higher, rugged **Jaigarh Fort,** recently opened to the public. Closer to Jaipur, **Nahargarh Fort** was built by later Maharajas as a resort for queens. It is particularly pleasant to visit at night. There is a restaurant in the palace, though meals must be ordered in advance. The cenotaphs of the Maharajas at **Gaitore** are also worth a visit.

Romantic State: Udaipur has the air of a tranquil pleasure resort where scenic beauty has been utilized to perfection. The city was founded by Maharana Udai Singh in the 1560s after the third sack of Chittor, the original capital of Mewar. Built around lakes and surrounded by gentle hills Udaipur is considered one of the most romantic places in India. Its recorded history goes back to 728 A.D. The Udaipur Maharana was the last of the Rajput kings to submit to the Mughals, and later, under the British, earned the distinction of the highest gun salute.

There are three lakes—**Pichola, Fateh Sagar** and **Udai Sagar.** Pichola, on the shores of which are the palace and the old city, has two islands. On one is the **Jag Mandir,** a palace begun by Maharana Karan Singh but named after Maharana Jagat Singh (1628-1652). As Prince Khurram, Shah Jahan stayed here in 1623 when he was rebelling against his father Jehangir. The other island has the enormous **Jag Niwas Lake Palace,** built in 1754 by Maharana Jagat Singh II. It has been converted into a luxury hotel. Sunset is a specially beautiful hour on the lake, from where one gets a splendid view of the City Palace.

Founded by Maharana Udai Singh the **City Palace** is the largest palace complex in Rajasthan. Though successive Maharanas made numerous additions it has retained an architectual unity. A major portion of the palace is now a museum. **Mor Chowk** is known for its peacock mosaics; **Ruby Palace** for its glass and porcelain figures; **Krishna Vilas** for its miniatures; **Chini**

Lady of the Lake, Udaipur.

60

Mahal for its tile work; **Moti Mahal** for its mirror work. Outside the City Palace is the **Jagdish Temple** (1651), enshrining Vishnu as Lord of the World. As with most places in Rajasthan, the bazaar in the old city is fascinating. Udaipur is especially renowned for *lahariya bandhani,* a tie and dye method that patterns waves of color. It is most often worked on delicate muslin. *Pichwai,* temple hangings, are also painted by numerous craftsmen.

Chittorgarh, a massive fort and capital of Mewar from the seventh to the 16th centuries, is 55 miles (112 km) from Udaipur. The immense citadel crowns a 594-foot-(180-meter-) high hill, and covers an area of 700 acres (280 hectares). Chittor is associated with extraordinary incidents of heroism. It was sacked three times—by Alauddin Khalji in 1303, by the Sultan of Gujrat in 1535 and by Akbar in 1567. On the second occasion, 13,000 women committed *Jauhar* (voluntary collective immolation) and 32,000 warriors rode out to certain death. There are several palaces, a victory tower visible from miles away, a tower of fame and many temples including one where Mirabai, the 16th century mystic, worshipped.

Jaisalmer: Eight hundred years ago,

masons crafted an awesome citadel in golden yellow sandstone on the lonely sands of the Thar Desert. Caravans on the Silk Route and from West Asia found hospitality there, and it was called **Jaisalmer**, the Oasis of Jaisal. Lord Krishna, head of the Yadav clan, had prophesied that a remote descendant would raise his capital here. In 1156 Rawal Jaisal, a Bhatti Rajput, shifted his capital from **Lodurva** and built the fort. Warring neighbors wondered at the magnificence of the new capital and the power of the man who subdued more then just the tyranny of the desert. Today it is like a "living museum" for though a new city has grown beyond the massive bastions a quarter of the population of Jaisalmer still lives within the fort, in a maze-like area of streets, squares, markets and houses with finely carved facades. The variety of spaces does not cease to surprise the visitor. There are Jain temples (12th to 15th centuries) and *havelis,* homes of the wealthy, with carvings of outstanding and sophisticated craftsmanship. Among these elaborate *havelis* are the five-storey **Patwa Haveli,** the 300-year-old **haveli of Salim Singh,** one of the prime ministers, and the **Nathmalji Haveli,** built in the 19th century by two architect brothers. All three have been declared national

The desert citadel of Jaisalmer.

treasures. The **Gyan Bhandar Jain Library** has an impressive collection of old Jain manuscripts.

At **Aakaal,** 10.5 miles (17 km) from Jaisalmer on the Barmer road, are the fossils of a 180 million-year-old forest. Sand dunes and expansive desertscapes can be seen 25 miles (40 km) from Jaisalmer. There are also monuments at the erstwhile capital of **Lodurva**, 10 miles (16 km) away. Jaisalmer is at the western extremity of the desert, but it is linked by road, rail and air and a visit is immensely rewarding.

Jodhpur: The Rathors established themselves in hot and arid Marwar in the 13th century but it was only in 1459 that Rao Jodha founded Jodhpur fort, six miles (10 km) from the old capital at Mandore. The **Mehrangarh Fort** now overlooks the sprawling, bustling city 400 feet (120 meters) below. The palaces within have finely worked exteriors. Some rather lavish interiors have been maintained as part of a museum which also has a rich collection of miniatures, musical instruments, royal palanquins, *howdahs* and cradles. A prized possession is a unique, exquisitely elegant royal tent, embroidered with gold, dating to the 17th century. On the way to the fort is **Jaswant Thada,** a beautiful marble memorial, near which the Maharajas of Jodhpur are cremated.

On another hill, right across the city is the **Umaid Bhawan Palace.** A famine relief project, constructed between 1929 and 1942, this 347-room palace is built of interlocked sandstone blocks. It was the private residence (one of the largest in the world) of Maharaja Umaid Singh. While part of the palace is still occupied by the erstwhile royal family, the rest has been converted into a gracious luxury hotel that affords a taste of regal living. It is set on a 26-acre (10-hectare) plot with beautiful gardens. The hotel organizes village safaris as well as splendid open-air dinners on the ramparts of Mehrangarh Fort where guests are entertained by *Langas* and *Manganiyars*—folk musicians of the desert. Jodhpur is known for its lacquerware and embroidered leather shoes.

Mount Abu, situated at 4,026 feet (1,220 meters), is the summer resort of the desert. It is worth a visit for those who are particularly interested in temples. The marble **Dilwara Jain Temples** here date from the 11th to the 13th centuries, and are renowned for their carvings.

The **Keoladeo Ghana Bird Sanctuary** at Bharatpur on the Agra-Jaipur road is the

Havelis are homes for those who have it all.

largest in Asia. Between October and February it attracts a wide variety of migratory birds, including the Siberian Crane. A wildlife sanctuary—with tigers—is situated at the foot of **Ranthambore Fort,** eight miles (13 km) from **Sawai Madhopur.**

Rajasthan abounds in colorful fairs and festivals. The most spectacular of these is the Pushkar Mela. **Pushkar** is a sleepy temple town, nine miles (14 km) from **Ajmer.** But a week-long camel fair culminating on the full moon in November transforms the place. Thousands of peasants come in their finery. It is a unique experience and a visual feast.

Gujarat: The history of **Gujarat** dates to the Harappan culture. The state derives its name from the immigrant tribe of Gujjars who came through the northwestern passes in the first century A.D. As a coastal state it has encountered widespread influences, and it retains a rich diversity of ethnic cultures. Maritime trade engendered a remarkable business acumen in its people, a faculty enhanced by the fact that trade is one of the few options open to Jains. Today, Gujarati businessmen prosper in all parts of the world.

The state encompasses the salt marshes of Kutch, semi-arid peninsular Saurashtra and the lush coastal plains, and there is an abundance of cotton and groundnut. Surat, the first British commercial outpost, was famous for its silk and brocade, and the wealth of Gujarat attracted several conquerors. Gujarati men—and women—are a most unique blend of the traditional and the progressive.

Gandhidham is the capital, but **Ahmedabad**, on the banks of the **Sabarmati River**, best affords an experience of Gujarat. Its origins can be traced to the 11th century ruined township of Karnavati. In 1411, Sultan Ahmed Shah I rebuilt the city, named after him. Sir Thomas Roe, envoy from the court of James I, described it as "a goodly city, as large as London, the handsomest town in Hindustan, perhaps the world." Today, it is the second largest city in western India and the foremost center for design and textiles. The cotton industry was patronized by medieval rulers, and the first mill was established in 1859.

Four bridges over the Sarbarmati connect the comparatively modern localities with the old city, where **Manek Chowk** is the hub of activity. Impressive gateways mark the periphery of the once-walled city, that continues to be a fascinating maze of alleys, *pols* and *chowks*, where generations of

craftsmen and traders have pursued their professions. Particularly interesting are the immense wooden facades of temples and houses, some outstanding examples of which are the **Dwarkanathji Vaishnav Mandir**, near Raipur Chakla; **Harkore Sethani ni Haveli**, opposite Doshivada ni Pol, and the **Swaminarayan Mandir** on Swaminarayan Road. The skill of the wood carvers was as finely expressed in traditional furniture and transformed even the most functional household articles into aesthetic objects. The markets in the old city abound in a variety of textiles including block prints and tie and dye, and shawls, rugs, brass and silverware. Much of the carved wood, as well as traditional embroidered textiles from the villages have found their way into antique stores in (and beyond) Ahmedabad, making it a collector's paradise. A kite festival that takes place in the old city on January 14 is a colorful event that generates much excitement.

Ahmedabad is rich in Indo-Saracenic architecture, particularly mosques. Ahmed Shah raised the **Juma Masjid** in 1724 and it is considered one of the finest in India. The **Sidi Sayyid Mosque**, built by his Abyssinian slave, is on Relief Road. Once a part of the old citadel, this mosque is internation-

ally renowned for its exquisite stone tracery. The **Rani Sipri Mosque** (1514) near Astodia Darwaza was built by a queen of Sultan Mahmud Begada. Delicate as a gem, it is also known as the Masjid e Nagina.

The **Sarkhej Monuments**, a royal retreat for pleasure and repose, are five miles (eight km) from the city. Created in the mid-15th century, they comprise an elegant complex of a mosque, palace, pavilion and tombs, rising above the stepped embankment of a reservoir connected with the Sabarmati. The saint, Ahmed Khattu Ganj Baksh is buried there; so are Mahmud Shah Begada and his queen. Another interesting site is the polygonal **Kankaria Lake**, an artificial lake constructed in 1451. It has an island garden with a summer palace, once frequented by the Mughal emperor Jehangir and his queen. A zoo and park are nearby.

The finest example of a unique architectural feature of medieval Gujarat lies 12 miles (19 km) north of the city. This is the 15th-century **Adalaj Vav** step well. Step wells are cool subterranean retreats, with profusely carved pavilions, shrines and sacred niches all the way down to the reservoir and well. They are remarkable equally for their beauty and ingenuity.

Rich Jain businessmen have built numer-

Kids of Kutch— portraits taken in the 1960s

ous temples in the city. The most famous is the carved marble **Hutheesing Temple** (1850) outside Delhi Gate.

Ahmedabad's museums afford a taste of the innately aesthetic traditions of Gujarat, and its rich ethnic culture. Topping the list is the **Calico Museum of Textiles** in **Shahibag**, the Sarabhai family estate. It is acknowledged to be among the best in the world and its splendid collection is supplemented by a vast reference library and publications program. The adjoining **Pichwai** (temple hangings) **Museum** is also excellent. The **Shreyas Folk Art Museum** at **Ambavadi** and the **Gujarat Tribal Museum** at **Gujarat Vidyapith** reveal the colorful world of tribes in Kutch and Saurashtra, in particular their intricate hand embroidery on textile and leather, of which there are exquisite examples. The **Institute of Indology** at **Gujarat University** is known for its Jain manuscripts. The **NC Mehta Museum** at **Sanskar Kendra** has a fine collection of miniatures. **Vichaar**, the Utensils Museum, has an enormous array of traditional brass, bronze and metalware. Adjacent to it is the popular open-air **Vishalla Restaurant**, where a typical Gujarati meal is served in a rural setting that is enlivened by folk entertainers.

Gurjari, on Ashram Road, and scattered private boutiques, are among fancier shopping centers for the handcrafted objects of Gujarat. Ahmedabad can boast of some fine modern architecture, as evidenced by the **Indian Institute of Management**, and the **National Institute of Design**, India's foremost design center.

Ahmedabad is also Mahatma Gandhi's city. In 1915, he set up a retreat a few miles up the Sabarmati. This was **Hriday Kunj**, his Satyagraha Ashram, integral to the freedom moment. The Ashram and the **Gandhi Memorial Museum** should be seen.

Excursions: A magnificently carved sun temple at **Modhera**, 66 miles (106 km) northwest of Ahmedabad, dates to 1026 A.D. Built by Bhimdev Solanki, it was one of the temples attacked by Mahmud Ghazni.

Palitana, 155 miles (250 km) southwest of Ahmedabad, is the most important Jain pilgrimage center. Here, 863 temples, built over a span of 800 years, crown the peaks of Shatrunjay Hill. Steps lead to the top, and after sunset the area is entirely deserted. **Bhavnagar**, 35 miles (56 km) away, is a convenient base for visiting these temples. For the wildlife enthusiast, **Sasangir**, 136 miles (220 km) from Bhavnagar, is the last preserve of the Asiatic lion.

Fabric being dried after being dyed.

CENTRAL INDIA

Maharashtra: Most of **Maharashtra** stands on the Deccan Plateau and includes the picturesque Western Ghats. It formed the core of the Maratha empire which, under the leadership of Chattrapati Shivaji Maharaj posed an enormous threat to the British. Rugged impregnable forts built by Shivaji are scattered throughout the state. Shivaji is still revered here and a political party demanding "Mumbai for the Maharashtrians" is named after him. Maharashtra is an economically important state. It has produced some of the finest writers, philosophers and freedom fighters. **Bombay** is the capital, but it is only partially representative of the state.

When the Portuguese acquired Bombay in 1534 it consisted of seven swampy islands. In 1661 these became part of the dowry of Catherine of Braganza when she married Charles II of England. Four years later the British leased Bombay to the East India Company for the princely annual rent of £10 in gold. Gerald Aungier, Governor of Bombay, said, "It is a city which, by God's assistance, is intended to be built." And he proceeded to do just that. By the early-18th century, Bombay, with its excellent natural harbor, had become the headquarters of the western coast and the main shipbuilding yard. The city derives its name from the goddess Mumbai Devi who was enshrined by the Kolis, the aboriginal fisherfolk of Bombay. There is an ongoing campaign to rename Bombay after Mumbai.

A century of land reclamation joined the islands into the promonotory it is. Its second phase of development was initiated by Sir Bartle Frere, governor from 1862 to 1867. The first railway line was laid, the cotton industry flourished and numerous Victorian Gothic public buildings, offices and educational institutions were raised. The promise of commercial success attracted Jews, Parsis and Gujaratis, as Maharashtrians as well, and each community has retained an indentity even as it merged in the melting pot.

Today, Bombay is India's commercial capital, contributing 25 percent of the industrial output, 45 percent of the income tax and handling 50 percent of its maritime trade. Pressure on property prices has made desireable areas like Nariman Point as expensive as Manhattan.

Bombay is also the biggest film city in the world, with all the inevitable accompanying glitter. The population is over eight million and the sight of humanity spewing out of Victoria Terminus and Churchgate Station each morning makes one believe that only "God's assistance" will keep the city functioning. Bombay is synonymous with suburban trains packed like sardines, with bumper-to-bumper traffic, with an expressive *lingua franca* all its own, with the unique lunch box delivery system, with exclusive stores and endless pavement bazaars, relentless monsoons and soothing seascapes, quaint Irani cafes and restaurants to suit every purse and palate, with sailors and smugglers and underworld dons, with entrepreneurs, "yuppies," business magnates and the jet set. Bombay swings till the early hours of the morning, its pace of life quite apart.

The **Gateway of India** is Bombay's landmark. Designed by George Wittet, it was built to commemorate the visit of King George V and Queen Mary in 1911. It overlooks the harbor channel, which can also be seen from the nearby and renowned **Taj Mahal Hotel**.

Victoria Terminus, and opposite, the **Municipal Corporation Office**, are fine examples of Victorian Gothic architecture

Preceding pages: Imaginative temple sculpture at Khajuraho. Left, the Gothic inspired Victoria Terminus.

characteristic of Bombay. Both buildings were designed by Frederick William Stevens. Flora Fountain (now **Hutatma Chowk**) built in honor of Sir Bartle Frere is in the heart of the business center and close to shopping malls, art galleries and the **Prince of Wales Museum**. Opened in 1914, the museum is among the best in India and has a particularly rich collection of miniature paintings, ancient sculptures and jade. The **Royal Asiatic Society** near Horniman Circle is housed in the 1833 **Town Hall** and has a vast library and interesting statues. The **Bombay Natural History Society**, which has done remarkable work under the guidance of renowned ornithologist, the late Dr. Salim Ali, also has a fine library. The **National Center for Performing Arts**, at the southern tip of Marine Drive is an active cultural center.

Marine Drive, a lively promenade, is especially beautiful at night. The crescent of lights has earned it the sobriquet of the Queen's Necklace. At the northern end of Marine Drive is **Chowpatty Beach**, unsuitable for swimming but crowded, in the evening, with foodstalls selling *pau bhaji, bhelpuri* and *kulfi* ice cream. The **Tarporewala Aquarium** is also on Marine Drive.

Bombay's **Hanging Gardens** (1881) are laid out on top of a series of reservoirs on the exclusive **Malabar Hill**. The **Mahalakshmi Temple** enshrines the much-propitiated goddess of wealth; the **racecourse** is nearby and further north the **Haji Ali Mosque**, built on a tidal island.

While **Juhu Beach** is more a funfair ground, swimming is recommended further away at **Marve Manori** and **Madh Island**. Highrise Bombay still has old-style houses with woodwork, ornate balconies and tiled roofs, adding a quaint charm to the concrete jungle. There are many at **Bandra**, a suburb with a large Christian population.

About six miles (nine km) northeast from Bombay harbor are the **Elephanta Caves**, easily accessible by frequent launch services from the **Apollo Bunder Jetty**. Originally called Gharapuri, the island was named Elephanta by the Portuguese who found a sculpted stone elephant (which is now in the **Victoria Zoo and Gardens**, Byculla). There are four rock-cut cave temples at Elephanta, dating to between 450 A.D. and 750 A.D. The immense Trimourti, depicting Shiva as Creator, Preserver and Destroyer is profoundly beautiful, as are the reliefs. A visit is very rewarding.

Ajanta and Ellora: Aurangabad, 230 miles (370 km) from Bombay, and linked by

Time out for some quiet reading.

air, is a convenient base for visiting Ajanta and Ellora. It is named after Aurangzeb, whose queen lies buried in the **Bibi Ka Maqbara**, a mausoleum that unsuccessfully attempts to imitate the Taj Mahal. There are also a few Buddhist caves, dating to the sixth and seventh centuries A.D.

The most famous Buddhist cave cluster is found at **Ajanta**, 64 miles (103 km) from Aurangabad. Between the second and eighth centuries A.D. monks enlarged natural caves in the steep face of the gorge formed by the Waghore River. Of the 29 caves, 24 were *chaityas* or prayer halls, and five were monasteries. These "wondrous caverns of light" remain an unparalleled aesthetic achievement. There are some sculptures but the caves are particularly renowned for tempera paintings. These depict extravagant court scenes, incidents from the Buddha's earlier lives and, most beautifully, *Bodhisattvas,* all in sensous earth colors. There are fine paintings in Cave 16; the best, that of the dying princess, is in Cave 17. The important caves are 1, 2, 9, 10, 16, 17, 19, 21 and 26. (It is advisable to carry a light.) After the decline of Buddhism these caves lay deserted and forgotten, until they were accidentally discovered by a British hunting party in 1819.

Ellora, 16 miles (25 km) from Aurangabad was associated with Buddhism, Hinduism and Jainism between the third and the 13th centuries A.D. Here, the most spectacular example of a rock-cut temple was hewn in the eighth century during the reign of a Rashtrakuta king. The monolithic **Kailashnath Temple** marks the transition from the rock cut to the free-standing temple; 70,000 square feet of rock weighing over 200,000 tons was excavated over a 60-year period to create this temple, which stands open to the sky. The masons worked from top downwards and no other material was added. Symbolizing Shiva's abode in Mount Kailash, the temple is imbued with mythological images.

All but one of the Buddhist caves at Ellora are monasteries. Some are two and three storeys high with ornate pillars and horse-shoe shaped entrances. Cave 9, a *Chaitya*, has a tranquil image of a seated Buddha before a 30-foot-(nine-meter-) high *stupa*. The light falls in such a way as to illumine the statue.

Coastal State: Goa, India's smallest and newest state nestles in the Konkan coast. In 1510 Alfonso de Albuquerque wrested it from Sultan Yusuf Ali Shah, founding a colony that lasted with the Por-

tuguese till 1961, when it was reabsorbed into the Indian Union.

Goa has a 62-mile (100-km) coastline, with estuaries and headlands interspersing "crescents of firm white sands," those famous sun-drenched beaches. The land abounds in mango, coconut and cashew; the sea affords an endless feast.

The Portuguese were traders and proselytizers. They have left a unique and indelible stamp, though everything Goan is not Portuguese. The people of the Konkan coast began to pray in Latin, it was said, but the *mando*, a love song, continued to be sung in Konkani.

Panaji (Panjim) became the capital in 1843. It was once the "cultured habitat of the boulevardier." Panaji still has numerous walks and promenades, *tavernas* (bars) and cafes; life ambles on at an even pace. The **Church of The Immaculate Conception** (1541) and the **Secretariat**, onetime residence of the Portuguese Viceroy are some of its outstanding buildings. The old residential area of **Fontainhas** is especially interesting.

The original capital was **Old Goa,** *(Goa Doirada)*, a few miles upstream from Panaji. It is famous for **Sé Cathedral**, the largest in Asia; but more for the **Basilica of Born Jesus**, where the remains of St. Francis Xavier are enshrined. This "Apostle of the East" came to Goa in 1542; he died in 1552, traveling in the Far East, and his remains were brought to Goa in 1554. The grand Duke of Tuscany donated a marble tomb and the silversmiths of Goa fashioned a silver casket that contains the coffin. A periodic exposition attracts thousands of devotees, for whom Goa is synonymous with the saint.

Feasts and processions, which combine gaiety and religious fervor, are associated with churches and saints. Of late there is an explosion of revelry during a three-day carnival before Lent.

Goa's major towns—**Maragao, Marmagao** and **Vasco da Gama**, line the coast. The quiet verdant villages are marked by lime washed churches, many of which date to the 16th and 17th centuries. Also typically Goan are villas with verandahs, patios, ornate balconies, stained glass and opaque window panes of oyster shell. Many houses still have Chinese porcelain, richly carved furniture and chandeliers.

Among the finest beaches of Goa are, north of Panaji, **Sinquerim, Calangute** and **Candolim**; **Vagator** and **Anjuna** are secluded. Around Marmagao and further

south are **Dona Paulo**, **Bogmalo**, and the largest beach, **Colva. Siridao** is a shell collector's heaven, while **Betul** has the best mussels, brought onshore by expert divers.

There is food aplenty to please the palate. Seafood apart, there are such Goan delicacies as *sarpatel,* a pork dish, spicy *vindaloo* and of course *feni,* a heady local brew made from cashew or coconut. No wonder the British governors of Bombay vied with the Parsi elite to acquire Goan cooks ....

Madhya Pradesh: Surrounded by seven states, **Madhya Pradesh** lies in the very heart of India. It encompasses river valleys, ravines, dense forests, hill ranges and a part of the Deccan plateau. **Bastar,** a tribal area and India's largest district, is in Madhya Pradesh.

At the northern tip of the state is **Gwalior**, where one of India's most splendid forts crowns an isolated outcrop that towers above the sprawling city. This "pearl in the necklace of the castles of Hind" has its origins in legend. Gwalipa, a sage who dwelt on this hill once cured a prince of leprosy. In gratitude, the prince fortified the hill. Its strategic location made it the stronghold of several dynasties, each of which added fortifications. Its hour of glory was under the Rajput Tomar Raja Man Singh

(1486-1516). Politician, warrior, musician, literateur and aesthete, he covered the immense facade with yellow, green and blue tiles, and built the beautiful **Man Mandir Palace** and the **Gujari Mahal** at the foot of the hill. Within the precincts of this enormous fort are the **Teli ka Mandir** and the **Sas Bahu Temples** with profuse carvings, and ruins of several palaces and stepwells. Gigantic statues of Jain saints have been excavated along the face of the **Urwahi Gorge**, through which the road leads to the top.

Khajuraho, a remote village, is on the international tourist map, famed for its sculpted temples. Between 950 A.D. and 1050 A.D., 85 temples were built under the patronage of the Chandella Rajputs who claim descent from the lunar races. Of these, 22 have survived. The sculptures that ornament the facades of the temples are renowned for their uninhibited expression of the erotic, but in fact the entire spectrum of life in those days is portrayed with beauty and sensitivity, and even a touch of humor. In the face of such exuberant carvings, the total architectural merit of these soaring structures is often overlooked. The **Kandariya Mahadev Temple**, enshrining a Shiva *lingam,* is the largest and most typical

Left, priests in Old Goa and right, fisherman at Calangute.

and has a profusion of carved gods and goddesses, celestial nymphs and blissful lovers. Other important temples include the **Chausant Yogini**, dedicated to Kali; the **Chitragupta** and the **Lakshmana** temples. The **Matangeshwar Temple** dedicated to Shiva is still in use. All these temples belong to the western group. In the eastern group there is a Jain temple as well as three Hindu ones. Those grouped in the southern part of the village belong to the last phase and the decline in skills is evident. In March, Khajuraho becomes the venue of a dance festival, where artistes perform at the entrance of the Kandariya Mahadev Temple. Khajuraho is conveniently linked by air.

Bhopal, set around a lake, is the picturesque capital of Madhya Pradesh. (It was recently the scene of one of the world's worst industrial disasters.) The foundations of the city were laid in the first half of the 18th century by the Afghan Dost Mohammad Khan. The city grew between 1812 and 1926, when it was ruled by a succession of Begums. The **Shamla** and **Idgah hills** afford a panoramic view of the city. Bhopal has some interesting mosques, in particular the **Taj ul Masjid** and the **Jama Masjid**. At the entrance to the *chowk,* in the heart of the walled city are the **Sadar Manzil** and **Sha-**ukat Mahal**, designed by a Frenchman for the royal family. The **Bharat Kala Bhavan**, a prestigious center for the performing and visual arts, has a fine tribal museum.

Sanchi lies 28 miles (46 km) from Bhopal, on a quiet hill. There are eight *stupas* and pillars dating to the Ashokan era. It is from here that Ashoka's son left for Ceylon to propogate Buddhism. Once a seat of learning with a nunnery and monastery, Sanchi is a popular place of pilgrimage for Buddhists.

The **Great Stupa** at Sanchi, begun by Ashoka, is the oldest stone structure in India. The circumambulatory path and the *stupa* can be approached through four finely carved gateways, that were created by the ivory workers guild from **Vidisha**. The carvings narrate scenes from the Buddha's life. They were done at a time when the Buddha was still portrayed through symbols. Thus, the lotus is symbolic of his birth; the tree, of enlightenment; the wheel, of the first sermon; the footprint and throne, of his presence. On the eastern gateway are scenes of the Buddha leaving home; on the western, the incarnations of the Buddha; on the northern, the miracles of the Buddha; and on the southern, the story of his birth. There is also an **Archaeological Museum** at Sanchi.

EASTERN GLIMPSES

Bihar was once the land of numerous *vihara*, Buddhist monasteries, hence the name. The Buddha lived here, which makes it of special significance to the traveler with an interest in Buddhism. The Ganga and its tributaries water the state, which is bordered in the north by Nepal. Bihar contains 40 percent of India's mineral wealth and an industrial zone has emerged in the southeast of the state.

Patna, the capital, is on the confluence of the Sone and the Ganga, and linked by air and road to Nepal. Over 2,000 years ago it was renowned as Pataliputra. Modern Patna dates to the 16th century, to Sher Shah Suri who temporarily ousted the Mughal Emperor Humayan. **Sher Shah's mosque**, built in 1545 is a landmark in the skyline; his fort houses a museum. Nearby is **Harmandir**, an important Sikh shrine. The **Khuda Baksh Oriental Library** is in the once-fashionable locality of Bankipore. It was set up in 1888 from the private collection of the Patna lawyer after whom it is named. It has rare and valuable Arabic and Persian books and manuscripts. Other places of interest include the **Patna Museum**; the **Gulzaribagh printing press**, once an East India Company factory with remnants of that era; and the **Golghar**, the 18th-century granary which affords a fine view of the city.

At **Kumrahar**, four miles (six km) south of Patna, are the ruins of **Pataliputra** (600 B.C. to 600 A.D.). Megasthenes, Greek ambassador to the Mauryan court in the third century B.C. wrote that the magnificent palaces here surpassed any royal residence he had seen. Among the ruins are ramparts, wooden beams and sandstone pillars. Patna forms a convenient base for the Buddhist trail.

Heart of Buddhism: Bodhgaya lies 117 miles (188 km) south of Patna. Gautama Buddha attained enlightenment here, under the Bodhi tree, 2,500 years ago. Locally known as *pipal* (*ficus religiosa*), this particular tree is said to have grown from the original. A stone slab, the *Vajrasana* or **Diamond Throne,** marks the sacred spot below the tree. Bodhgaya is the center of the Buddhist world and Tibetans believe it will survive all destruction. The most revered shrine is the **Mahabodhi Temple,** with a gilded image of the Buddha and profuse depictions of his life. There are Burmese, Thai, Chinese, Japanese and Ti-

betan temples and monasteries here. The Tibetan *gompa* has a large Dharma Chakra and a worship hall lavishly ornamented with frescoes. There are also *chaityas* (prayer halls) and monasteries commemorating sacred incidents associated with the Buddha. Bodhgaya receives a constant flow of pilgrims.

Gaya is nine miles (15 km) away, on the Patna road. It is held sacred by the Hindus as a place where sins are absolved.

At **Nalanda**, 56 miles (90 km) southeast of Patna lie the ruins of the foremost Buddhist monastery and educational center of the ancient world. It was already a place of learning at the time of Buddha and Mahavira and both taught here. A regular university was established in the fifth century A.D. Endowed by beneficent kings it flourished till the 12th century. It had a rich library and at its finest hour several thousand students and teachers. Huien Tsang studied and taught here for several years. Students, many of whom came from southeast Asia and China, worked for 10 years. Those who wished to be ordained stayed longer. Apart from the scriptures they were instructed in a wide range of disciplines including medicine, logic and prose composition. Educational and residential facilities

Preceding pages: Sacred footprints at Bodhgaya Left, Calcutta sunrise.

were free of cost. The destruction of this fine university by the Turks practically ended Buddhist education in India. Excavations have revealed nine levels of remains which include temples, monasteries, dormitories, *stupas,* stairways and lecture halls as well as objects that are housed in the **Archaeological Museum**. Nalanda now has an International Center for Buddhist Studies.

Rajgir, nine miles (15 km) from Nalanda, has several sites associated with the Buddha. The first Buddhist Council was held here after the Mahaparinirvana of the Lord. **Vaishali**, 35 miles (56 km) north of Patna, and birthplace of Mahavira, is also where the Buddha preached his last sermon.

"Oh, Calcutta!": Bengal once included Bihar, Assam and Orissa and what is now Bangladesh. Its wealth attracted successive dynasties, as well as traders who came from all parts of the world for textiles, indigo and saltpeter. **Calcutta** was the capital of British India till 1911, and after Independence became the capital of West Bengal.

In 1690, Job Charnok of the East India Company acquired three villages, Kalikata, Govindapur and Sutanati, along the Hooghly River. Kalikata was fortified in 1707, but proved to be vulnerable when attacked by the Nawab of Bengal. He con-

fined 146 British residents in a tiny room; only 33 survivors emerged the next day from the "Black Hole of Calcutta." Robert Clive eventually usurped power and became Governor of Bengal in 1757. When Clive left three years later and half a million pounds richer, he was (compared to the fortunes the other officials had amassed) "astonished at his own moderation."

Fort William, nucleus of the city, was rebuilt in 1773 and became the headquarters of British administration in India. Calcutta prospered in the following decades while the British lifestyle grew increasingly European. The city also became home to the newly created, pro-British landed "aristocracy," an Indian urban elite. In the 19th century, Calcutta witnessed the Bengali Renaissance spearheaded by men like Raja Rammohan Roy and Ishwar Chandra Vidyasagar, who sought to imbibe the best of tradition and modernity. As a result, Calcutta became the heart of a sophisticated Bengali culture that nurtured persons like Rabindranath Tagore. The flame of nationalism also spread from here and the Partition of Bengal by the British in 1905 was an attempt to subdue it.

Today Calcutta is the bastion of a leftist government and a business center. Jute, its

main industry, is controlled by commercial barons. The city has survived the flood of refugees at Independence and more recently during the Bangladesh crisis. The population exceeds nine million; the congestion is staggering. But it is a city with a soul. Theater is the epitome of its cultural life; renowned film makers and writers are associated with it. It is a city "much discussed, much misunderstood and fiercely defended, claimed alike by poet, revolutionary and industrialist." A city which, with some courage and more determination, must be experienced.

Fort William can be viewed from the outside but the adjacent 1.2-square-mile **Maidan**, the "firing space" maintained by the British, is the heart—and lungs—of Calcutta. The **Hooghly River** flows to its west. An interesting medley of activities unfold at the Maidan at dawn, and continue well into the night.

As its southern end is the **Victoria Memorial**, conceived by Lord Curzon as a museum to highlight British India culture. His request for donations of money and art objects was generously heeded and the memorial was inaugurated in 1921 by the Prince of Wales (later Duke of Windsor). It contains Victorian memorabilia and many exhibits that highlight the Empire at its peak.

The nearby **Racecourse** was opened in 1819 and encircles the **Polo Grounds**. East of Victoria Memorial is **St. Paul's Cathedral**, consecrated in 1847. This fine church has two Florentine frescoes, a reredos in alabaster and stained glass by Burne Jones. The adjacent **Birla Planetarium** is the best in India. Not far away is the **Academy of Fine Arts** with a collection of Tagore memorabilia and modern Bengali art.

South Calcutta is mainly residential but the **Zoo**, opened in 1876, is here. So is the prestigious **National Library**, largest in the country with over eight million books. As Belvedere House it was the residence of the Governor of Bengal.

Kalighat, the shrine of the patron goddess of Calcutta, is situated in a middle-class locality once covered by dense forests. It is a very ancient temple, and was associated with fearsome bloody rituals. The Hooghly, then known as the Adiganga, flowed by the temple and merchant ships waited to propitiate the goddess. In 1776, Colonel Tolly drained the dry riverbed and the canal was named after him. Although goats are beheaded every day, ritual sacrifice to the dreaded goddess occurs twice

19th-century view of the Esplanade

annually. The present temple structure dates to 1810. Southeast of Kalighat is the **Rabindra Sarovar,** a pleasant lake near which are the **Birla Academy of Art** (modern painting and sculpture) and the **Ramakrishna Mission Institute of Culture.** The **Tollygunje Club** (golf, tennis, squash) typifies a British Indian culture that lingers in Calcutta. Opened in 1815 it was the one-time residence of the Maharaja of Mysore. Membership may be obtained on a daily basis.

The eastern end of the Maidan is bounded by the **Esplanade** and the busy thoroughfare of **Chowringhee.** The **Indian Museum** is located here and considered among the best in Asia. North of the Maidan is **Raj Bhawan,** one time residence of the Viceroy and now of the Governor of West Bengal. It was built by Lord Wellesley in 1805 and modelled on Keddleston Hall, Derbyshire. It contains rare works of art. Nearby are the **Assembly Hall,** the **Town Hall** and the **High Court,** the latter built in 1872 in the Gothic style of Ypres.

St. John's Church (Council House Street), consecrated in 1787, is where Job Charnok lies buried. There is also a monument to the "Black Hole" victims.

Writers' Building is on **Dalhousie Square** (renamed **BBD Bag**). It was the headquarters of the East India Company, whose officials were called writers, and is now used by the government. The original Fort William is where the GPO stands. Calcutta's commercial houses further north bear an unmistakable Victorian stamp.

Bustling bazaars surround **Tiretta,** the area north of BBD Bag. It formed the heart of the Chinese settlement till the 1962 war with China. About 30,000 Chinese remain, and **Bentinck Street** still abounds in excellent shoemakers. The Chinese came to Calcutta in the early-19th century and it is from here that they migrated to major cities in India, and are associated with hairdressing, shoemaking, dentistry and restaurants.

North of Tiretta are several places of worship; the massive red sandstone **Nakhoda Mosque** (1926), the **Jewish Synagogue,** the **Parsi agiary,** a **Sikh temple** and the **Armenian Church of Our Lady of Nazareth.**

Jorasankho, further north, is *the* locality of the landed "aristocracy." Tagore's house is on **Darpanarain Street,** adjacent to which is the **Rabindra Bharati Center**, a cultural rendezvous for Indian dance, music, art and theater. Nearby is the **Marble Palace** built in 1835 by Raja Mullick.

Morning ritual in the Hoogly River.

Though partially occupied by descendants it houses a quaint collection that includes works by Houdon and Rubens.

The **Ashutosh Museum,** which also has a fine selection of Bengali folk art, is in **Calcutta University** (1871). On Sundays and holidays a fascinating second-hand book bazaar springs up on the pavements of **College Road.**

Park Street, behind Chowringhee, was once the European residential area. It now has hotels, restaurants and shops. The **Asiatic Society and Museum** is here and its founder Sir William Jones lies buried in the **South Park Street Cemetery.** The **Netaji Museum** (Lala Lajpat Road) and the **Birla Industrial and Technological Museum** (Gurusaday Road) are not far from here.

At the southern end of Calcutta's riverfront is **Garden Reach Road,** which leads to the ferry crossing for the **Botanical Gardens.** Sir William Jones, also a connoisseur of flora, conceived the idea of a garden with rare botanical species. Inaugurated in 1787, the garden sprawls over 272 acres (110 hectares). Despite its 12,000 species of flora the major attraction remains a Banyan tree, the largest known in India. It is over 200 years old and its decayed main trunk has been removed. But it thrives, with 1,125

aerial roots reaching the ground, covering a circumference of 1,367 feet (412 meters).

Further up the river is Calcutta's **Strand,** adjacent to the Maidan and a popular meeting point. It is the scene of frenzied activity on the last of the 10-day Durga festival in October. Elaborate images of the goddess, created by craftsmen of the **Kumarthuli** locality are brought to the various *ghats* (embankments) for immersion. Howrah Bridge (renamed **Rabindra Setu**) is further upstream. The cantilever bridge links Calcutta to **Howrah** and is notorious for its traffic jams at peak hours. Beneath the chaos, congestion and decay is Calcutta's showpiece—its spanking new metro system which, in the face of gargantuan odds, is running superbly.

Orissa: The ancient Kalinga, now called **Orissa**, is predominantly rural, with paddy fields and coconut and cashew plantations. Tribal groups inhabit its hilly interiors. Ashoka's bloody victory over Kalinga in 260 B.C. eventually made him turn to Buddhism. Kalinga later reasserted itself under a Jain king. Traders from here are known to have colonized parts of Burma and Java. Between the second and 12th centuries A.D. two Hindu dynasties, the Kesari and the Ganga, flourished. They were patrons of art

Chariot wheel at the Sun Temple in Konarak.

and literature, and of architecture and sculpture epitomized in monumental temples. The Mughals conquered the area in the 16th century, followed by the British in 1803.

The few temples that remain of the Kesari and the Ganga eras are superb examples of the sophisticated level of temple architecture in medieval India, in which the sanctuary, topped by a spire, in preceded by porches, a dancing hall and a hall of offering. These are interconnected within but discernable as distinct entities from outside, and enriched with carvings that depict all aspects of the human, natural and mythological worlds. These temples, unlike the south Indian counterparts, were not centers of civic and corporate life.

Bhuvaneshwara has been the capital of Orissa since 1956. It is dominated by the immense **Lingaraj Temple,** built by the Kesaris around 1090 A.D., and dedicated to Shiva as Tribhuvaneshwara, Lord of the Three Worlds. It is beside the **Bindu Sagar** tank, said to contain sacred waters from all parts of India. A thousand temples once surrounded the lake; today there are about 50. These include fine temples dedicated to Parvati and Vishnu as Ananta Vasudeva. The Lingaraj temple is an important venue for the Shivratri festival. (Non-Hindus cannot go in but there is a viewing platform.)

Other temples worth seeing are the **Parasurameshwara,** dating to the seventh century; the **Rajarani, Vaitul Deul** and the **Brahmeshwara,** the last a miniature version of the Lingaraj complex. **Mukteshwara** temple is renowned for its fine sculpture. Hindu, Buddhist and Jain influences, and a lively folk art tradition make the **Orissa State Museum,** the **Handicrafts Museum** and the **Tribal Research Bureau** rich repositories of artifacts.

At **Udaygiri,** three miles (five km) from Bhuvaneshwara, are some second century Buddhist caves. A little further are the Jain Cave temples of **Khandagiri** with relief carvings and a massive figure of Mahavira. **Dhaulagiri,** five miles (eight km) south of Bhuvaneshwara and site of the Kalinga battle, has an **Ashokan edict** and the **Shanti Stupa,** the White Pagoda of Peace built by Japanese Buddhists.

Konarak, 40 miles (64 km) from Bhuvaneshwara, is renowned for the spectacular **Sun Temple** built by Narasimha Deva Ganga in the 13th century. The architect, Sabai Santra, conceived the temple as a chariot for Surya, the sun god, resting on 24 wheels and drawn by seven horses. The wheels symbolize the division of time, the horses colors of the prism. It took 1,200 workers over 12 years to complete the masterpiece which has three images of Surya illuminated by rays at dawn, moon and sunset. The sculptural ornamentation is as profuse, and beautiful as Khajuraho, depicting amorous, devotional and mundane images. Much of it is vividly reflected in the classical dance form of *Odissi,* once performed as part of worship in Orissan temples.

Puri, 22 miles (35 km) from Konarak and 37 miles (60 km) from Bhuvaneshwara, is one of four major Hindu pilgrimage centers. The presiding deity at the 12th-century **Jagannath Temple** built by Chodaganga is Krishna as Jagannath, Lord of the Universe, with his brother Balabhadra and sister Subhadra. (Non-Hindus can observe temple activities from the Raghunandan Library.) The Rath Yatra festival in June/July draws thousands of devotees. In commemoration of Krishna's journey from Gokul to Vrindavan, the deities are taken out in procession in immense wooden chariots. Earlier, people are known to have sacrificed themselves under the wheels of the moving chariot, hence the word "juggernaut."

Puri has a fine beach but rough waters. The **South Eastern Railway Hotel** offers old world charm and excellent cuisine.

Heading off with the day's catch at Puri beach.

SOUTHERN STATES

Andhra Pradesh: Much of **Andhra Pradesh** spreads over the Deccan Plateau. The culture of this region has a Dravidian base though Aryan influences were absorbed and continue to find expression. Of the southern areas it was the most exposed to Islam, and in the 18th century **Hyderabad** replaced Delhi as the center of Muslim India.

Golconda, source of the Koh-i-Noor diamond, was the capital of the Qutb Shahi Dynasty, founded in 1512. In 1591 the fourth ruler, Muhammed Quli Qutb Shah created a new capital seven miles (11 km) away and named it Hyderabad after his Queen Hyder Mahal. He graced this walled city with fine buildings; among them are the **Charminar**, a massive arch topped with four minarets commemorating the end of the plague in 1593, and the **Jama Masjid** (1598). He began the construction of the enormous **Mecca Masjid** in 1614, but it was completed in 1687 by which time Golconda was annexed by the Mughal Emperor Aurangzeb. (The tombs of the Nizams of Hyderabad are in an enclosure near the mosque.) After Aurangzeb's death, his Viceroy Asaf Jah proclaimed himself Nizam of Hyderabad in 1725. He ruled over a vast and independent kingdom with Hyderabad as its epicenter. The city gradually became synonymous with refinement, culture and enormous wealth. Turks, Somalis, Afghans, Abyssinians and Persians attempted to make their fortunes in its flourishing court.

Hyderabad spread to both sides of the River Musi, south of **Hosainsagar**, a reservoir which separates it from the twin city of **Secunderabad** where the British Resident once lived.

The sixth Nizam, Mahboob Ali Khan, enthroned in 1869, maintained the most lavish and exotic court. He was one of the richest men in the world; also one of the most eccentric. His laundry went to Paris; his wardrobe occupied two floors of an entire wing of the palace. The stories are numerous and bizarre. Among those who enjoyed his extravagant entertainment were Archduke Ferdinand of Austria (whose assassination triggered the First World War) and the ill-fated Nicholas, future Tzar of Russia. Raja Deen Dayal, appointed court photographer in 1884, vividly docu-

Preceding pages: Kathakali dancers of Kerala. Left, his business is going to pot.

84

mented the events at court.

Mahboob Ali's prime minister built the **Falaknuma Palace**—now a museum—whose architecture has evoked extreme response. Three shops in Europe were emptied to decorate its gilded interiors. The Nizam himself lived there for a while. Equally famous is the **Salarjung Museum,** created from a private collection begun in 1876 by General Salarjung I and augmented over three generations to include 35,000 exhibits.

Osman Ali Khan, far more restrained, founded the **Osmania University**, a center for Persian, Arabic and Urdu studies. Mir Bakht Ali was the last Nizam, during whose time Hyderabad was merged with the Telegu-speaking areas of Madras state to form Andhra Pradesh.

Banjara Hills was developed by the nobility and is now prime real estate. The Banjaras lived here once, a migrant gypsy tribe whose caravans were used by medieval armies for supplies. Modern communication has forced them to adopt other means of livelihood around the city. Their exotically attired women are easily identifiable.

There are fascinating bazaars around the Charminar. Andhra is known for its *ikat* and hand-worked *kalamkari* textiles, *bidriware*

or silver inlaid in bell metal and its lacquerware. However, Hyderabad, long since an eminent jewel market, is especially famous for pearls and the merchants are concentrated on **Patherghatty Road**.

Hyderabadi cuisine is distinct and renowned. *Haleem, nahari* and *kachi biriyani* are some of the delicacies which must be tasted. So must the traditional, subtle vegetarian cuisine of Andhra. The area also abounds in vineyards that produce fine, seedless grapes.

Golconda Fort, now almost a part of Hyderabad, is surrounded by battlements of masonry. Most of the remains date to the Qutb Shahis, though the origins of this fort go back to ancient Hindu dynasties. Half a day is necessary to explore the fort.

Tamil Nadu: Traditional art, culture, religion and society are a living reality in **Tamil Nadu**. In the early centuries A.D. the Aryan pattern was assimilated with Dravidian culture; institutions were established and have been vigorously maintained. This region, especially under the Pallava and Chola Kings, made a substantial contribution to the development of Indian civilization. **Madras**, the capital, affords a good introduction to this culture. It bears its British legacy with grace, and also sports

The Shiva Temple at Mylapore.

modern phenomena such as celebrity public office bearers.

Over the course of four centuries, Madras has grown from a nondescript fishing village on the Coromandel Coast to the fourth largest city in the country. It was fortified by the British in 1650 and **Fort St. George** now has the **Secretariat and Legislative Assembly. St. Mary's Church,** consecrated in 1680, is the oldest Anglican church in the East. Robert Clive, Governor of Madras (and later of Bengal) was married here in 1753. There is a museum with an interesting section on China. **St. George's Cathedral** and **St. Andrew's Kirk** are also beautiful churches, while the **San Thome Church** on **St. Thomas Mount,** where the saint was martyred, enshrines his remains. The ancient Shiva temple is in the traditional **Mylapore** locality. Madras has an eight mile (13 km) long **Marina Beach,** the **Guindy Deer Park** and the **Snake Park**. The **State Government Museum,** opened in 1846, has a specially fine gallery of Chola bronzes. **Kalakshetra** is a prestigious academy of music and dance; **Cholamandalam** is an artists' village en route to **Mahabalipuram.**

Temple Towns: The temple is the heart of Tamiliam culture, the center of all social, religious and creative activity, and integral to daily life. A poet likened a "village without a temple to a man without a soul." The importance of the temple was such that the town grew around it, contained in concentric walls.

The elaborate rituals of worship included music and dance. A variety of craftsmen were needed to cater to the temple, but the bronze casters and silk weavers are especially renowned. Scale apart, the south Indian temple is different from its northern counterpart in architectural details. The *vimana*, the tower rising above the sanctuary, consists of several receding pyramidal storeys. The gateways have towers called *gopurams*; while 1,000 pillared halls within the precincts are also characteristic. Of considerable splendor, these temples make interesting observation points to study the culture of the area.

Mahabalipuram is 34 miles (55 km) on the coastal road from Madras, and has one of the earliest examples of temple art in south India. It was ruled by the Pallavas in the seventh century A.D., at which time it was also a famous port. There is an abundance of carved monuments, five monolithic shrines named after the heros of the *Mahabharata* and the beautiful **Shore Temple** dedicated

Madurai's Sri Meenakshi temple, dedicated to the fish eyed goddess.

to Shiva, Parvati and Skanda.

Kanchipuram, 43 miles (70 km) from Madras is one of India's seven sacred cities, and famous for its silk. It was the capital of Pallava and Chola Kings between the seventh and 13th centuries A.D. There are more than 150 temples, the most famous being the **Kailashnath Temple** (725 A.D.) dedicated to Shiva.

The Cholas ruled from 907 A.D. to 1310 A.D. Their most imposing temple is the **Brihadeswara**, built in **Thanjavur** (Tanjore) by Rajaraja I in the 10th Century. It is called the **Devalaya Chakravartin**, the emperor among temples. The granite temple has a *vimana* rising to 216 feet (65 meters) on the top of which is an 80-ton *shikhara*. It was raised to that height by an inclined plane that started four miles (six km) away. There is also an enormous *Nandi*, the bull, which is Shiva's mount.

Next to the temple is a 200-year-old church built by the Danish-German missionary, Schwartz, who was a personal friend of the Maratha king Serfogee. Tanjore has an 18th-century palace and an excellent art gallery. The city is also famous for inlay in copper, and more so for its paintings, portraits of gods and goddesses made on wood, against a background of gold leaf that never tarnishes and illumined with small pearls and semi-precious stones. Tanjore is also an important center for Carnatic music and Bharata Natyam dance.

Chidambaram, believed to be the venue of the Cosmic Dance of Shiva, has a magnificent Chola Temple spread over 32 acres (13 hectares). Here Shiva, as Natraj, king of dance, manifests creative energy. Chidambaram has a 1,000-pillared hall.

Srirangam, near **Tiruchirapalli**, enshrines Vishnu in an enormous temple town complex contained within seven concentric walls. Additions to this temple were made up to the 18th century.

Madurai, home of Meenakshi, the fish-eyed goddess, has a thriving temple dedicated to her. Here, the *gopurams* tower to such a height, and are so profusely carved that they dwarf even the *vimana*.

Rameshwaram is on an island on the sea route to Sri Lanka. This temple was built to commemorate the place where Rama prayed to Shiva on his way to Lanka. The pillared corridors of this temple, measuring a mile on each side, are the largest in the world.

Karnataka: The varied terrain of **Karnataka** includes the lush coastal plain, the spice-laden, forested Western Ghat and the

dry Deccan Plateau. The area was ruled by several dynasties, Hindu and Muslim. Outstanding among these were the Hindu rulers of the kingdom of Vijayanagar (1336-1565). This is also the land of Tipu Sultan, one of the most formidable enemies the British faced.

Bangalore, the capital, dates to 1537 when a petty chieftan Kempa Gowda built a mud fort. Today it is one of the fastest growing cities in India, a commercial and industrial center, at the forefront of science and technology. Renowned for its salubrious climate, splendid gardens, flowering trees and the horse racing season, the city retains its British legacy alongside the traditional flavor.

Mysore city, capital of the erstwhile Mysore state, is far more interesting for the tourist. The Wodeyars (the word is derived from the Kannada *odeya*, meaning Lord or Master) were feudatories of the Vijayanagar Empire and established an independent kingdom in the 14th century. They ruled Mysore till 1759, when their power was shattered by the rebel soldier Hyder Ali, who declared himself king. In 1782 Hyder Ali was succeeded by his son Tipu Sultan, the "Tiger of Mysore." Tipu was a tough enemy of the British and died fighting them

in 1799. His territory came under the British who eventually restored the Mysore Maharaja with full powers in 1881. Mysore witnessed extraordinary progress in the following decades. Several palaces were also built. The most imposing of these is the Indo-Saracenic **Mysore Palace**, home of the Wodeyar rulers. A major portion of it was rebuilt in 1897 after the havoc caused by a fire. The walls of the **Durbar Hall** are covered with paintings by famous artists of the day, such as Raja and Ravi Varma. The **Amba Vilasa**, the smaller, private durbar, has a carved teak ceiling, 58 bronze pillars, silver doors and a floor inlaid with gems. The **Lalitha Mahal** has been converted into a hotel; so has the **Rajendra Villas Palace** atop Chamundi Hill from where one gets a panoramic view of the city. The **Jagamohan Palace** near the Mysore Palace was a royal residence that now houses the **Chamarajendra Art Gallery** and a museum created from the Maharaja's collection.

On the Bangalore Road, nine miles (15 km) from Mysore is **Srirangapatnam**, the one-time capital of Tipu Sultan. His summer palace, the **Daria Daulat** (Splendor of the River) was built in 1784. It is made of teak and entirely covered with frescoes and murals. His **mausoleum** is nearby, and the

Medieval ruins at Hampi.

88

fort has dungeons, ramparts, a mosque and the Sri Ranganathaswamy temple. There are also some drawings by employees of the East India Company depicting Tipu's last battle.

Mysore is the city of jasmine, silk, sandalwood and incense, and ivory carving. The **Cauvery Arts and Crafts Emporium** has a full array of handicrafts.

Hampi was once the capital of the Vijayanagar Empire, founded in 1336 by two Telegu princes Harihar and Bukka. It was at its peak between 1509 and 1529 under Krishnadeva Raja who ruled over practically the whole of peninsular India. Travelers have recorded that the city, with a population of half a million, was larger than Rome. There were magnificent palaces and temples, the state was administered efficiently, creative pursuits were encouraged and a rich culture thrived. Vijayanagar was sacked in 1565 after the battle of Talikota and Hampi ceased to be of importance. In 1900 a British civil servant-turned-archaeologist studied the neglected, deserted site and wrote about it in *A Forgotten Empire*.

Situated on undulating terrain beside the **Tungabhadra River**, Hampi covers an area of 13 square miles (33 square km). There are royal palaces, harems and carved towering temples. It was originally surrounded by seven concentric walls of defence. The 15th-century **Virupaksha Temple** has an 11-storey carved *gopuram*, and ornate pillared halls. Devaraya II (1422-1426) built the Vithala Temple dedicated to Vishnu. Its large stone chariot brings to mind the Konark Sun Temple. The **Hazara Rama Temple** depicts scenes from the *Ramayana*. There is also a water reservoir, each section of which is labelled, and an old stone bridge. Hampi has a haunting beauty. It lies on the outskirts of **Hospet**, which is well-connected by rail and road.

Karnataka is considered the "cradle of temple architecture" and there are several ancient temples at **Badami, Aihole, Halebid** and **Belur**.

Coastal Beauty: Kerala claims its origins in myth. Its narrow, fertile coastal strip, some 372 miles (600 km) long, is washed by the Arabian Sea. The aerial view is of verdant expanse, an immense mosaic of varying greens set amidst sinuous waterways and hamlets and encroaching cities. The coconut-fringed coast gives way to emerald rice fields, banana and pepper plantations, and in the higher reaches of the Ghats, to rubber, cashew, cardamom, cloves and tea. As the spice coast of India, it

Ancient emple site t Badami.

has attracted seafarers since the time of the Babylonians. Jews came here 2,000 years ago; the Syrian Christians, converted by St. Thomas in 52 A.D. are among the oldest Christians in the world; Arab traders frequented Kerala and one of the oldest mosques in India is at Kodungallur; the Chinese have left their mark on the fishing nets of Cochin; the Portuguese brought Latin liturgy, while Protestantism came with the Dutch and British.

All these influences have merged harmoniously with the traditional culture that evolved during the Kulasekhara period (800 A.D. to 1100 A.D.) which witnessed the predominence of Hinduism. Shankaracharya, the ninth-century philosopher who spearheaded the Hindu renaissance, was from here. It was also an era when the many beautiful temples of Kerala were built, and art and dance forms were perfected.

The abundance of nature is balanced by a restrained beauty in traditional architecture and dress. But in dance and theater, originally a part of worship, the imagination knows no bounds. *Kathakali*, a dance drama which draws its inspiration from the *Ramayana* and *Mahabharata* is the most spectacular of the performing arts.

The present state of Kerala was created in 1956 by merging Travancore, Cochin and the Malayalam-speaking areas of Malabar. In 1957 it became the first place in the world to elect a Communist government. Kerala has the highest literacy rate in India (70 percent) and the lowest birth rate (24 percent). It is politically active and has introduced significant labor and land reforms. But alongside the red flags of protest and prestigious institutions of scientific research and development, religion remains intrinsic to daily life. Everywhere, there are temples, rituals, flowers and coconuts.

Trivandrum is the capital and derives its name from the deity of Anantha Padmanabhaswamy, enshrined in the main temple. The city became important in the 18th century when the celebrated Raja Marthanda Varma shifted his capital from Padmanabhapuram. The **Napier Museum**, with its quaint mix of architectural elements, is a good introduction to some aspects of the state. It is near the **Zoo and Botanical Gardens**, established in 1859 on an eight-acre plot. Kathakali performances can be seen at Trivandrum. The state is known for its wood and ivory carvings, bell metal lamps and vessels, Kathakali masks and coir carpets.

Kovalam, 10 miles (16 km) from Trivan-

The museum a Trivandrum.

drum, is one of the finest beach resorts in India. It has facilities for water sports and a ride on a catamaran can be fun. There is a fishing village at the far end of the bay, good seafood and plenty of refreshing coconut water.

Padmanabhapuram, 33 miles (53 km) from Trivandrum on the Cape Road, is actually in Tamil Nadu. This palace, seat of the Travancore rulers, is in the finest traditions of Kerala architecture, which makes extensive use of wood and is more akin, in fact, to that of the monsoon lands of Southeast Asia. Wood has rarely been used as beautifully; the palace is aesthetic to the smallest detail and is unlike any other in India. There are also some murals of exceptional quality.

Cochin is the commercial hub of Kerala, a town of great historical importance. A mosaic of myriad influences makes its one of the more quaint towns in India. Because of its fine natural harbor, it is also known as the Queen of the Arabian Sea. The backwaters, an area of intense beauty, extend east and south of Cochin. The man-made **Willingdon Island** links Cochin to mainland **Ernakulam**, a few miles and a world apart.

All the historical sites are in Cochin, around **Fort Cochin** and **Mattancherry**.

The Chinese cantilever fishing nets are suspended like giant webs along the tip of Fort Cochin. They were introduced by traders from the court of Kublai Khan. The **Church of St. Francis**, built by Portuguese Franciscan Friars in 1503, is the oldest church constructed by Europeans on Indian soil. Vasco da Gama, who died in 1524, was buried here but his body was later removed. There is an ancient Register here, with entries in Portuguese, Dutch and English. Adjacent to the remains of Fort Cochin are some Portuguese and Dutch-styled houses, which, along with street names and signboards, make the area look like a blend of "medieval Portugal, Holland and English countryside." Fort Cochin also has the **Basilica of Santa Cruz.**

The **Dutch Palace** in Mattancherry was built by the Portuguese in 1557 and presented to the Raja of Cochin. It was subsequently renovated by the Dutch in 1663. It houses a museum, while some rooms of the palace are covered with exuberant murals depicting incidents from the *Puranas* and *Ramayana.*

The **Jewish Synagogue**, built in 1568, is the oldest in the Commonwealth. The Jews moved here from Cranganore in the 11th century and this part of Mattancherry is known as **Jew Town**. The pungent aroma of spices fills the air, for exporters' godowns are in Jew Town. Today, there are only 30 Jews left in Cochin, and they are all elderly. There has been no rabbi in living memory. The synagogue is well-maintained; it has the great scrolls of the Old Testament and the floor is covered with hand-painted tiles that came from Canton in the 18th century.

The **Bolghatty Palace** on the palm-fringed **Bolghatty Island** was built in 1774 and is now a hotel. The airport is on Willingdon Island, which also has the **Malabar Hotel,** excellent for seafood.

A backwaters trip is organized from Cochin. The more adventurous traveler is recommended a ferry crossing on **Vembanad Lake,** between **Kottayam** (42 miles/ 68 km from Cochin) and **Alleppey** (39 miles/63 km from Cochin). For the still more adventurous, it is possible to hire a launch from Kottayam and do a day trip to the real backwater islands. It is an unforgettable experience, well worth the effort. **Thekkady,** 50 miles (80 km) from Kottayam, is a 310 square-mile (775 square-km) wildlife sanctuary around **Periyar Lake** and is famed for its collection of elephants. View the wildlife from the comfort of your launch, or make use of a selection of lodges and huts.

DESTINATION INDIA

GETTING THERE

By Air : Most visitors arrive in India by air at one of the four major international airports: Indira Gandhi International Airport (Delhi), Sahar (Bombay), Dum (Calcutta), and Meenambakam (Madras). All are well served by 50 international airlines operating more than 170 flights a week. The choice of entry point depends on the scope of the itinerary. A large number of tourists land in Delhi.

Other international airports include Trivandrum in Kerala, which caters mainly to the needs of Indians working in West Asia, particularly the Gulf states, and Dabolim in Goa, intended primarily for the handling of charges. Expansion and rebuilding programs, in various stages of completion, are gradually improving passenger facilities and handling, and immigration and customs formalities are completed fairly rapidly. Licensed porters are available and can be helpful in guiding you in the right direction for transport to town. All four international airports have luggage facilities and dormitories. Some offer restrooms as well, and Delhi has a duty-free shop.

Special bus services operate from all airports to city terminals with stops at major hotels. Convenient shuttle buses are also run for their guests by some hotels. Taxis are available, but opt only for the black vehicles with yellow tops, as these are licensed and have a fixed fare system. Although licensed taxis are metered, it is advisable to check the sample fare listing to major stops in the city prominently displayed at all airports.

By Sea: Although India is not a regular cruise stop, several passenger lines and freighters offering excellent accommodation and food do call at Bombay, Calcutta and Madras. Among the more prominent are: American President Lines, British India Steam Navigation Company, Eastern Shipping Corporation, Lloyd Triestino, Messageries Maritimes and Scindia Steam Navigation Company. Periodic cruises between India and the Far East are also operated.

Overland: The overland route from the west through France, Germany, Yugoslavia, Bulgaria, Turkey, Iran and Pakistan is currently inadvisable due to the political instability in neighboring countries. As and when conditions improve this could once again be an exciting entry for the adventurous. Major motoring organizations would be the best sources for detailed and up-to-date information..

Visas: A valid national passport (ensure its validity covers the entire period of your trip), tourist or transit visas, and an entry permit for non-tourists are required for most foreign nationals, including Commonwealth citizens. Visas must be procured from Indian embassies or consultates, or British embassies in countries where there is no Indian representation. This should be done before departure as none will be issued on arrival. Applications can be handled personally or by mail, but allow extra time for the latter.

A tourist visa is valid for only six months from the date of issue and permits a stay of three months, extendable on application for another three months. A transit visa is valid for only three months and permits a maximum stay of 15 days. Tourist visas are valid for triple entry to simplify visits to neighboring countries. Applications for extension of the period of stay permitted under a visa should be made to the Foreigners Registration Offices in New Delhi, Bombay, Calcutta or Madras, or to the Superintendent of Police in District Headquarter towns.

Special permission and in some cases visa endorsements are necessary for visits to the Andaman and Nicobar Islands, the Lakshadweep Islands, and the northern districts of West Bengal (Darjeeling, Cooch Behar, Malda, Jalpaiguri and West Dinajpur). Overland travel to Nepal and

Bhutan also require prior permission.

Check for further details when applying for your visa.

Health: Only visitors arriving from Africa and South America are required to have an International Health Certificate with record of a valid yellow fever inoculation (validity is for 10 years). Remember immunity is effective only 10 days after vaccination.

No other vaccination certificate is required, but for personal protection the whole range of inoculations is recommended—cholera, typhoid, and tetanus. Do consult your doctor for advice on gama globulin shots to boost immunity to hepatitis and for suggestions on anti-malaria pills.

A personal medical kit to take care of minor ailments is useful to have along. Antiemetic and anti-diarrhoeal medication, a broad spectrum antibiotic, something for throat infections and allergies and aspirins would be a good idea. Also include bandaids, and antiseptic cream, an insect repellant and water purification tablets. Salt pills to combat heat exhaustion are particularly necessary if your visit is in summer.

Never drink unboiled or unfiltered water. When in doubt, stick to a soda, mineral water, or aerated drinks of standard brands. In smaller towns avoid factory ice as this is often made with unboiled water. All food should be cooked and eaten hot. Avoid salads and always peel fruits.

Money: All encashments of traveler's checks and exchange of foreign currency must either be recorded on the currency declaration form or receipts kept, as hotel bills, airline tickets etc., can be paid for in local currency only against proof of legal conversion. These will also be necessary for reconversion of any balance of Indian currency left unspent on departure. Visitors leaving after a stay of 90 days or more will have to produce proof of encashment of traveler's checks or exchange of currency for income tax exemption, and to show that they have been self-supporting.

Indian currency is based on the decimal system, with 100 paise to the rupee. Coins are in denominations of 5, 10, 20, 25 and 50 paise. One and two rupee coins are also in use. Notes are in one, two, five, 10, 20, 50, 100 and the rarer 1,000 rupee denominations. Indian rupees may not be brought in or taken out of the country. Exchange rates fluctuate against all currencies. As we go to press, the exchange rate is around Rs 12 per US dollar and Rs 17 per Pound Sterling.

Major credit cards are accepted in the larger hotels, restaurants and shops. Although traveler's checks and cash can get you a better (and illegal) rate of exchange in small establishments, it is best to deal with banks and licensed money changers. Since encashing traveler's checks could take time, it is advisable to change amounts adequate to cover a few days' needs at a time.

Customs: Most international airports have red and green channels. Tourists seldom have any trouble. Occasionally, customs officials ask to see one suitcase at random and take a quick check. Prohibited articles include certain dangerous drugs, live plants, gold and silver bullion and coins not in current use. Firearms require possession licenses (valid for six months), issued by Indian Embassies or Consulates abroad, or on arrival in India, by a District Magistrate. For further details, check with the issuing authority.

Duty-free imports include 200 cigarettes (or 50 cigars), 0.95 liters of alcohol, a camera with five rolls of film and a reasonable amount of personal effects, including binoculars, a portable typewriter, sound recording instruments and so on. Professional equipment and high-value articles must be declared or listed on arrival on the TBRE form with a written undertaking to re-export them. Both the list and the articles must be produced on departure. As this is sometimes a lengthy process, allow extra time, both on arrival and at departure. For unaccompanied baggage or baggage misplaced by the airline, make sure you get a landing certificate from customs, to expedite location.

To avoid last-minute departure problems, remember that the export of antiques (over 100 years old), all animal products, and jewelry valued at over Rs 2,000 (in the case of gold) is banned. When in doubt about the age of semi-antiques, contact the office of the Archaeological Survey of India in Delhi, Bombay, Calcutta, Madras or Srinagar.

Currency Declaration forms for amounts in excess of US$1,000 must be completed at customs on arrival.

Departure: Remember to reconfirm your reservations for departure well in advance to avoid any last-minute difficulties. Security checks can be intensive and time consuming, so allow two hours for check-in. An airport/seaport tax of Rs. 100 per person (even in the case of infants) is charged on departure and must be paid prior to check in. *Ensure that your out-bound carrier is endorsed on the tax receipt.* For visitors with Entry Permits, exit endorsements are necessary from the office where they were registered. Should a stay exceed 90 days an income tax exemption certificate must be obtained from the Foreign Section of the Income Tax Department in Delhi, Bombay, Calcutta or Madras.

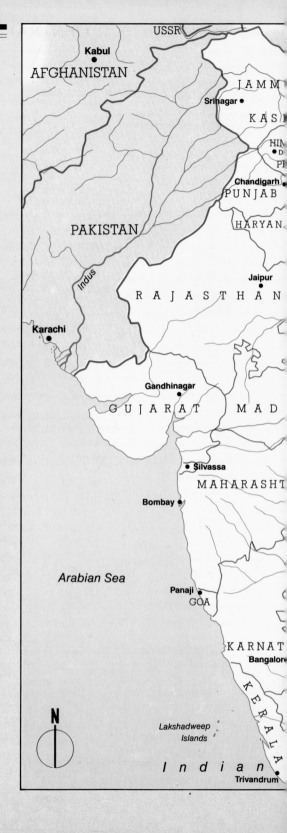

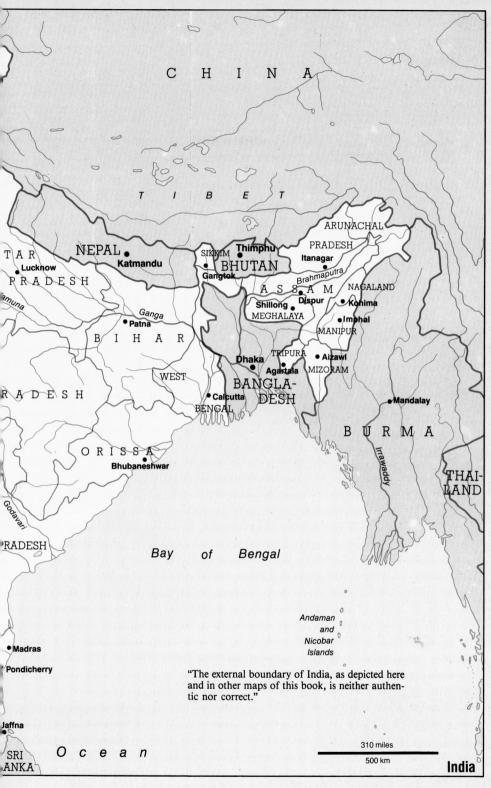

C H I N A

T I B E T

ARUNACHAL
PRADESH

T A R
PRADESH

NEPAL

Lucknow

SIKKIM   Thimphu
        BHUTAN
Katmandu
        Gangtok

Itanagar

Brahmaputra

A S S A M

NAGALAND

amuna

Ganga

Patna

B I H A R

Shillong
MEGHALAYA

Dispur

Kohima

Imphal
MANIPUR

WEST

RADESH

Dhaka

Calcutta

BENGAL

TRIPURA
Agartala

BANGLA-
DESH

Aizawl
MIZORAM

Mandalay

O R I S S A

Bhubaneshwar

B U R M A

Irrawaddy

THAI-
LAND

Godavari

RADESH

Bay   of   Bengal

Madras

Pondicherry

Andaman
and
Nicobar
Islands

"The external boundary of India, as depicted here
and in other maps of this book, is neither authentic nor correct."

Jaffna

O c e a n

SRI
LANKA

310 miles

500 km

India

95

INSIDE INDIA

Government: The Indian Union is a federation comprising 25 States and seven Union Territories. Each State, and some Union Territories, has its own Legislative Assembly and government, headed by a Chief Minister. The Central (federal) government is headed by a Prime Minister and Council of Minsters (Cabinet) responsible to the two houses of Parliament: the *Lok Sabha* (the Council of the People) which is directly elected by the people on the basis of adult franchise; and the *Rajya Sabha* (the Council of States), an indirectly elected body, with functions somewhat like those of the British House of Lords. The President and Vice-President are elected by an electoral college which consists of Members of Parliament and Members of the State Legislatures.

Elections are normally held every five years but can, in certain situations, be called earlier. India has had eight general elections since independence in 1947.

Economy: With a well-developed, democratic political and administrative structure, a large skilled labor force and an adequate communications system, India has made considerable progress since independence.. Despite the agrarian bias of its economy, industry has grown enormously, placing India among the top 20 industrial nations of the world. Its relatively low level of exports is partly due to the large volume of domestic consumption. The per capita national income of about US$260 in 1984/85, although meager in comparison with the rest of the world, is a considerable improvement over 1947. In the area of production of foodgrains particularly, the advance has been spectacular—once a chronically deficit area, India can now export foodgrains.

Time: Despite its size, India has a uniform time zone all over the country. Indian Standard Time is 5.5 hours ahead of Greenwich Mean Time and 9.5 hours ahead of US Eastern Standard Time.

Specific international time differences are listed below:

Delhi/India	12 noon today
Bonn	7:30 am today
Paris	7:30 am today
London	6:30 am today
New York	1:.30 am today
San Francisco	10:30 pm yesterday
Hawaii	8:30 pm yesterday
Sydney	4:30 pm today
Tokyo	3:30 pm today

Climate: When talking about a country of such tremendous size and geographical diversity as India, it is difficult to make a general statement concerning the climate. It ranges from the eternal snows of the Himalaya and the temperate conditions along the coasts, to the continental climate of inland areas. Besides that, there are many regional and seasonal variations.

October to March is the cool season and therefore the best time of the year to visit. On the whole, the weather is beautifully predictable in winter, with blue skies and bright sunshine in most areas. Some parts of the south and the east see a brief spell of rain from the northeast monsoon, while snow and sleet make the extreme northern areas very cold andoften inaccessible.

Summer, from April to June, is hot and dry in most of the country, and humid along the coasts. Kashmir and the hill stations of Himachal and Uttar Pradesh are particularly lovely at this time of the year. The South West Monsoon begins to set in along the western coast towards the end of May, bringing welcome respite from the heat, and varying amounts of rain, as they move across the rest of the country through June and July and withdraw by late September. North Eastern India has particularly heavy rain during this season, and is one of the world's wettest regions.

What to Wear: Plan your wardrobe according to your itinerary and the season of your visit. In winter a sweater, preferably two, one light and one heavy, as well as a jacket or an *anorak* are necessary, especially in the north where daily temperature differentials can be quite wide. Lighter clothing would be adequate in the south and along the coast. Cottons are ideal for summer. Avoid synthetics. Casuals in natural fibers are inexpensive in India, so bring only essentials and leave plenty of room in your suitcase for acquisitions. Comfortable footwear, sneakers for winter and sandals for summer, make walking on rough or uneven surfaces easier.

Etiquette: Removing one's shoes before entering temples, mosques or *gurdwaras* is essential. Overshoes are provided in some places at a nominal cost and stockinged feet are usually permissible. Avoid taking leather goods of any kind into temples as these could be taken exception to. Photography is prohibited inside most places of worship. Make sure you obtain permission before using a camera. Visitors are usually welcome to look around at their leisure and can sometimes stay during religious rituals. For visits to places of worship, modest clothing, rather than brief skirts and skimpy tops or shorts, would be appropriate. A small contribution to the donation box is customary.

The *namaste*, the greeting with folded hands, is the Indian form of greeting and its use will be appreciated though men, especially in the cities, will not hesitate and will even offer to shake hands with you if you are a man. A handshake would even be appreciated as a gesture of special friendliness. Most Indian women would hesitate to shake hands with men, whether Indian or foreign, and no offence is meant. Most would also be somewhat taken aback at the easy informality of interaction between the sexes common in the West.

In private homes visitors are received as honored guests and your unfamiliarity with Indian ways will be accepted and understood. Should you be tempted to eat with your fingers, remember to use only your right hand.

Tipping: There is no harm expressing your appreciation with a small tip. Depending on services rendered and the type of establishment, this could range from Rs 2 to Rs 10. In restaurants, the tip is customarily 10 percent to 15 percent of the bill. Leading hotels add a 10 percent service surcharge and tipping in such places is therefore optional. Although tipping taxis and three-wheelers is not an established norm, it would not be unappreciated. Here again, 10 percent of the fare or leaving the change if substantial would be adequate. Porters at railway stations would expect around Rs 3 a bag. At airports, a rupee per bag in addition to the fee charged by the airport authority, though not essential, would be welcome.

If you have been a house guest, please check with your host whether he has any objection to your tipping any of his domestic helpers (e.g. a chauffeur who may have driven you around) before doing so.

Weights and Measures: The metric system is uniformly used all over India for weight and for measure. Precious metals, especially gold, are often sold by the traditional *tola*, which is equivalent to 11.5g. Gems are weighed in carats (0.2g). Financial outlays and population are often expressed in *lakhs* (one hundred thousand) and crores (one hundred lakhs or ten million units).

Electricity: India is on a 220-volt, 50-cycle system. Most larger hotels provide step-down transformers to provide voltage suited to your electrical appliances. Check with the bell-boy or at the information desk.

Business Hours: Central Government offices now work a five-day week, from 9 a.m. to 6 p.m., Monday through Friday.

Post Offices are open from 10 a.m. to 4.30 p.m. on weekdays, and only till 12 noon on Saturdays. Here again, in most larger cities, the Central Post Office works till 6.30 p.m. on weekdays and 4.30 p.m. on Saturdays. On Sundays, they are open only up to 12 noon. Major telegraph offices are open all 24 hours.

Shops are usually open from 10 a.m. to 7 p.m. Some close for lunch. Although Sunday is the official holiday, different localities have staggered days off so that there are always some shopping areas open. Most restaurants are open till 11 p.m. with some nightclubs and discotheques closing very much later. Hotel coffee shops are often open round the clock.

Banking: Business hours of all foreign banks and nationalized Indian banks (of which the State Bank is the largest) are from 10 a.m. to 2 p.m., Monday through Friday, and from 10 a.m. to 12 p.m. on Saturdays. Some banks operate evening branches, while others remain open on Sundays, closing on another day of the week. All banks close on national holidays and on June 30 and December 31. Outward remittance, which goes through the Reserve Bank of India, is a difficult and lengthy process, and is best avoided. However, should you require additional money while you are in India, have it remitted through a draft or mail transfer. Remember to keep all receipts.

Religion: There are few towns in India, even among those of medium size, that are without a church and a mosque, though you may not always get one of your particular denomination. There are *gurdwaras* in major towns all over the country and Hindu temples everywhere. There are a number of synagogues in Bombay, two in Calcutta, and one each in New Delhi and Pune. Your hotel will give you more information as to the kind of religious institution you are seeking.

Postal Services: Mail services in India are generally good. The rate for inland letters is 60 paise for the first 10 g and 20 p for every additional 10 g. Inland letter forms cost 35 p each and a plain post-card 15 p. Picture post-cards and post-cards with printed matter require 30 p stamps. For foreign destinations, airmail letters require stamps of Rs 6.50 depending on the destination, for the first 10 g. Aerograms cost Rs 5 each for all countries and airmail postcards must carry stamps worth Rs 4.

It is advisable to personally affix high-denomination stamps to a letter and to hand it over the counter at a post office for immediate franking instead of posting it in a letter box. Sending parcels abroad is a complicated and time-consuming process. Either bear with the excess baggage problem or get government emporia to ship your shopping home. Do not rely on other shops.

Poste restante facilities are reliable. To avoid difficulties, make sure that your surname is written in capitals and underlined.

Domestic telegrams up to 10 words cost Rs 3.50 and every additional word 50 p. Express telegrams cost roughly double but are worthwhile if the matter is important and urgent. Foreign telegrams are of two categories—the ordinary at Rs 2.50 per word and the L.T. (Letter telegram) which takes longer, and has a flat rate of Rs 27.50 for a maximum of 21 words. Departmental telegraph offices remain open for 24 hours, while those combined with post offices close by the evening.

Telephone and Telex: Overloaded exchanges can make calls a frustrating business. Long-distance calls can in many cases be dialed direct, or booked through the domestic trunk operation. Demand services available to certain places, are faster but more expensive. Lightning calls are the quickest but cost eight times as much as regular calls. International calls can be dialed direct in some cases, or booked. Both systems are unpredictable. Sometimes, it is possible to get through immediately, at other times, it can take 24 hours. Book through your hotel operator, if possible, to avoid frayed nerves.

Telex services, both domestic and international, are good and reasonably priced.

Publications: With a large number of English dailies and hundreds in Indian languages, the press in India provides a wide and critical coverage of national and international events. Among the better known national English language dailies are *The Times of India, The Hindustan Times, The Hindu, The Statesman, The Telegraph* and the *Indian Express*. Major English news magazines include

India Today, Sunday and *Mainstream*. The leisure magazines include, *The Illustrated Weekly, The India Magazine*, and *Imprint*, which carry a variety of interesting features. There are also several women's magazines, city weeklies, general periodicals and special-interest journals.

Radio and Television:
Both radio and television are government-run and controlled, and are huge national networks. Programs in regional languages, Hindi and English, vary with the location of relay stations. With the recent addition of a second TV channel in Delhi and Bombay together with a renewed emphasis on commercial sponsoring, television programs are improving, both in coverage and in quality.

Photography:
Film is expensive and not always available, so make sure you bring your customs allowance of five rolls. Batteries can be bought from photography shops in the larger cities. However, what you particularly require may not always be available, so it is advisable to be well stocked. Additional equipment like lenses etc, are not available. Protect both your camera and film from excessive exposure to heat, humidity, and dust. Don't leave a camera lying directly in the sun or in a hot car when not in use, since heat affects film by giving it a green cast when processed and could also damage the mechanism of the camera.

Do not leave exposed film in luggage, as incoming and outgoing baggage is scanned and not all machines are photo-safe. For the same reason, don't mail unprocessed film. Make sure that scanning equipment at airports is photo-safe. Kodachrome cannot be processed in India.

Processing is reasonably fast with adequately good results. If you are not in a hurry, it's best to wait till you return home to get your films processed.

Most Indians are good-natured about being photographed, although some, in tourist centers, now demand a fee. If you are willing to pay, try and fix an amount before you shoot. However, photography is prohibited in some tribal areas, inside most temples and, for security reasons, at airports, seaports, bridges, railway stations and defence installations. Special permission from the Archaeological Survey of India is required for the use of a tripod and artificial light to photograph archaeological monuments and in museums.

Pharmacies:
Even the smallest town has at least one pharmacy. Larger towns and cities have one for each area, and some that operate round the clock. Contact your hotel desk or the tourist office for detailed listings of pharmacies.

Medical:
There are several privately run nursing homes and government hospitals in all large towns. Most hotels are also able to call in a house doctor and have 24-hour pharmacies.

Security & Crime:
Standard precautions are necessary. It is advisable to lock all valuables in hotel lockers, and to be particularly careful of handbags or hand luggage. Keep a record of passport details and of travelers checks, so that you are not stranded if you lose either. For police assistance or other emergencies, contact your hotel desk or the tourist office.

Tourist Information:
Government of India Tourist Offices in major cities both in India and abroad are valuable sources of information. Pick up a selection of their wide range of brochures on popular destinations. They are primarily information and advice centers and are not equipped to make reservations. They are however able to assist in itinerary planning and have a list of Government Approved Travel Agencies. Should you want to meet the local people, tourist offices also have lists of families who would be happy to have you visit. They can also help you get in touch with people in your line of business.

Guides proficient in English and other world languages can also be arranged. Charges range from Rs 50 to Rs 75 for a half day to Rs 75 to Rs 100 for a full day's sightseeing information on current cultural events is also available with Tourist Offices.

The governments of the various States of the Indian Union also run tourist offices in all big cities. Levels of efficiency vary, but most are useful stops for detailed information. The following is a list of Tourist Offices:

North Zone:

Delhi
88 Janpath. Tel: 320005-8, Palam Airport. Tel: 391196.

Jaipur
State Hotel. Tel: 72200.

Varanasi
15B The Mall. Tel: 43189.

Agra
191 The Mall. Tel: 72377.

East Zone:

Calcutta
'Embassy' 4 Shakespeare Sarani. Tel: 441475, 441402. Dum Dum Airport. Tel: 572611/444.

Patna
Tourist Bhawan, Bir Chand Patel Marg. Tel: 26721 (PP).

Bhubaneswar
B 21 Kalpana Area. Tel: 54203.

South Zone:

Madras
154 Anna Salai. Tel: 88685, 88686. Meenambakam Airport. Tel: 431686.

Bangalore
KFC Building, 48, Church Street. Tel: 579517.

Hyderabad
2nd Floor, 25 Sandozi Building, 26 Himayat Nagar. Tel: 66877.

Cochin
Willingdon Island. Tel: 6045.

Trivandrum
Trivandrum Airport.

West Zone:

Bombay
123 Karve Road. Tel: 291585, 293144. Santa Cruz Airport. Tel: 569031.

Aurangabad
Krishna Vilas, Station Road. Tel: 4817.

Khajuraho
Near Western Group Temples. Tel: 47.

Panaji
Communidade Building, Church Square. Tel: 3412.

TOURS

Package tours of varying durations and itineraries are offered for individuals as well as groups by the principal travel agencies in India and abroad. Costs naturally vary. For details, contact Government Tourist Offices and ask for their brochures covering tours operated by major agencies. Several short local tours from major destinations are also offered by the central and State Tourism Corporations, and also by private agencies of varying dependability.

All big agencies and many others offer a wide variety of special-interest tours (ranging from adventure to gourmet tours). These can be either the focus of a visit or a short interlude in your itinerary. Well-organized mountaineering and trekking tours, costing from $25 to $50 per day in the spectacular Himalaya, are carefully planned to cater to beginners as well as seasoned enthusiasts. Facilities for whitewater rafting are also well developed and expertly guided. The "Sail Trek" down the Ganga River is one of the most exciting ways of exploring India's ancient culture and heritage.

India's wealth of wildlife and its many sanctuaries, bring to photo-safaris a constant interest and excitement. Fishing holidays are also organized, both for the famous fighter, the mahseer, as well as for trout. There are also camel safaris in the Thar Desert, skiing holidays in the Himalaya, and beach holidays with the option of deep sea fishing. Other categories of tours cover architecture, golf, food, ayurvedic medicine and almost anything else you may want. Here again, Tourist Offices and Air India can give you further information.

TRANSPORT

Air: Indian Airlines (not to be confused with the international carrier, Air India), covers one of the world's largest domestic networks. It carries an average of 25,000 passengers every day to 73 destinations within the country and in Afghanistan, Bangladesh, the Maldives, Nepal, Pakistan and Sri Lanka.

The previously lengthy and time-consuming reservations system has now been dramatically improved by the recent introduction of computers. Instantaneous responses to reservation requests for multi-sector itineraries are now possibel through CRT units installed at the six major stations (Delhi, Bombay, Calcutta, Madras, Hyderabad and Bangalore) which are connected by automatic teleprintercircuits to other stations. The system is also linked to the international circuit and this has obviated delays in obtaining confirmations. For travel during the peak season (from September to March), try and make reservations well in advance as flights are usually heavily booked.

With time-consuming check-in and security procedures, you must be at the airport a good hour before departure time. Coach services from the city terminal are available and are reliable. In-flight service is adequate. Snacks and meals are served by pleasant English-speaking air hostesses. Alcohol is only available on inter-country flights. Incidentally, an airport tax of Rs 50 is levied on all flights to neighboring countries, as against the Rs 100 for travel to other countries.

Indian Airlines has a good safety record. Its fares are considerably lower than those charged for comparable distances elsewhere. The free baggage allowance per adult is 44 pounds (20 kg). International passengers with first class tickets are allowed an additional 22 pounds (10 kg).

Cancellation charges on tickets purchased locally are extremely high, but none are applicable for domestic sectors covered by international tickets.

The US$375 **Discover India** fare valid for 21 days of travel all over the country is particularly attractive. Travel must, however, be in a roughly circular direction. You are permitted to return to a city only to make a connection. Change of flights and even re-routing are allowed at no extra charge. This ticket must be purchased abroad, or paid for in India using foreign currency. Other concessional fares include a youth discount of 25 percent for students and travelers under 30. A recent innovation is the **India Wonderfare**, which for US$200 allows travel in any one of the four regions of the country for seven days. For details contact your travel agent or an Air India office abroad, or write to the Traffic Manager, Indian Airlines House, Parliament Street, New Delhi.

Vayudoot, a feeder airline, links 88 destinations. It also offers two popular schemes—"Rent a Plane" and "Own a Plane." For further details contact Vayudoot, Commercial Department, Safdarjang Airport, New Delhi 110 003.

Rail: Carrying about 30 million people every day to over 7,000 stations, the Indian Railways constitutes the largest system in Asia and the second largest in the world. Rail travel is safe and comfortable, but can be confusing. Of the many different categories of accommodation available, those recommended are air-conditioned First Class (the most expensive and comparable with the best anywhere); two-tier air-conditioned sleeper, and air-conditioned chair car (both second class). Travel by non-air-conditioned first and second class can become dusty and uncomfortable especially during the hot dry months. To avoid disappointment, make advance reservations.

Trains are slow compared to those in the West, so if you are in a hurry, stay with the expresses. Fares are generally low. The **Indrail Pass**, to be paid for in foreign currency, offers particularly good value for those on an extended tour of India. Prices range from US$160 for air-conditioned first class for seven days and US$600 for 90 days in the same class, to US$80 and US$300 for the air-conditioned chair car and first class non-air-conditioned for the same periods. The passes can be bought only in India through leading travel agents or Railway Central Reservations Offices in Delhi, Bombay, Calcutta, Madras, Secunderabad and Hyderabad.

Tourist Guide Offices at railway reservation centers are helpful in planning itineraries and obtaining reservations. Railway time-tables available at Indian Tourist Offices abroad, also contain much useful information. For the enthusiast, the more detailed *All India Railway Time-Table* or the concise but comprehensive *Trains at a Glance* can be bought at railway stations.

Remember to check which station your train departs from and do allow at least an hour to find your seat/berth. Lists of passengers with the compartment and seat/berth numbers allotted to them are displayed on platforms, and on each compartment an hour before departure. The Station Superintendent and the conductor detailed to the train are available for assistance.

Food can usually be ordered through the coach attendant and, on some trains, the fare covers food as well. Snacks, tea, coffee and soft drinks (colas etc.) are also usually available. Refreshment rooms are provided at big stations and stalls at others. Bed rolls are provided free in the air-conditioned first routes in the first and second class, provided this request is made at the time of reservation.

Retiring rooms (for short-term occupation only) are available at most railway stations, but these are usually heavily booked and should be reserved well in advance. All first class waiting rooms have couches for passengers using their own bedding.

Trains are usually overcrowded, so remember to reserve your seat well in advance.

Bus: Almost every part of the country is connected by bus services with the rest of it. These range from the noisy dilapidated off-line services to de luxe air-conditioned expresses that ply trunk routes. Frequent departures and low costs are major attractions for shorter journeys.

All cities have inter-state bus terminals. In some, reservations can be made in advance in city offices.

Bus travel within a city (except, perhaps, in Bombay) is arduous. Services tend to be unpunctual and buses are frequently overcrowded. However, if you have the time and the inclination, a full day's **Travel As You Like** ticket is inexpensive and can be a fun way of seeing the city and its people, but do avoid rush hours.

Car: Chauffeur-driven cars can be rented through major agencies and most hotels. No self-drive hire system is available, which, given traffic and road conditions, is just as well. Taxis are both air-conditioned and non-airconditioned. Charges vary, ranging from Rs 275 for eight hours and 100 km to Rs 400 for an air-conditioned car. For out of town travel, there is a per km charge, usually between Rs 2.30 and Rs 3 per km in the plains, with an overnight charge of Rs 85. Package tours, sold by travel agencies and hotels, include all assistance, guides, hotel accommodation and so on, in addition to the taxi charges. Hire charges vary considerably for private taxis.

The local yellow-topped black-bodied taxis are metered, but, with constant hikes in fuel prices, charges may often be higher than indicated. If so, this will be prominently stated in the taxi and the driver will have a card showing the excess over the meter reading that can be legitimately charged. The fare for three-wheelers that ply in almost every Indian city are roughly half those of taxis. They are also metered. Do not forget to ensure that the meter is zeroed before being flagged down to the minimum fare.

WHAT TO DO

Shopping: Leave plenty of space in your luggage for the shopping you are bound to do in India. The assortment of wares is staggering, and so are the comparatively low prices.

Places selling handicrafts (of all kinds) are an inevitable first stop for the shopper. Their incredible variety are themselves statements of the diversity that is India, and are at the same time products of its remarkably varied and attractive artistic traditions. Nowhere else could such colorful variety exist. Interesting as souvenirs, many are also valuable investments.

Carpets from Kashmir, at the upper end of the price range, crafted in the Persian tradition, are available in different sizes and counts. Unless you know a lot about carpets, shop at government emporia. Less expensive but lovely, rugs and druggets from all over the country are attractive accessories for your house. Then there is the huge assortment of precious and semi-precious gem-stones, jewelry set both in gold and silver, traditional as well as modern, chunky or dainty, all at prices that are irresistible.

Textiles for which India is justly famous, present a bewildering array of tex-tures, weaves, prints, de-signs and colors, which would make unusual and attractive dresses, cushion covers or bed spreads. Shawls, rich evening stoles and silk scarves make excel-lent gifts. Remember that many hotel tailors offer 24-hour tailoring.

Carved figurines of ivory or sandalwood and elabo-rately worked wooden pan-els from the south could be memorable souvenirs. Ob-jects in brass, copper and gun metal, inlaid, enamelled, worked or sim-ply beaten, offer a wide choice.

Exquisite marble inlay work and papier-maché items with intricate designs are painstakingly crafted in traditions that have existed for centuries. Reproductions of miniature paintings on ivory, paper or cloth must be chosen carefully. Look at several before you decide.

Leather wallets, shoes and bags, if less exotic, are also good buys. Hand-printed pottery, and cane goods ranging from table mats to furniture, are excellent value. The incredible array of ready-mades, both the cheap cotton casuals, and the more sophisticated boutique clothes could be interesting additions to your wardrobe. Antiques and semi-antiques of every kind are tempting, but bear in mind laws gov-erning the export of antiques and beware of fakes.

With the amazing variety of goods offered, shopping can be bewildering, so look around before you start buy-ing. For safe shopping, gov-ernment emporia and shops on the approved list of the Department of Tourism are recommended.

The Central Cottage In-dustries and the various state emporia have branches in major cities. They help make the diversity of Indian wares accessible at central points. If you prefer to wander in the bazaars and bargain, visit these first to get a feel of quality and prices. Be wary of shops to which guides or taxi drivers seem over-eager to take you. You'll pay more jn these shops to cover their commission. Exports of skins and furs is either banned or strictly regulated. Remember to get a certifi-cate of legitimate sale and permission for export.

Sports: Most large hotels offer facilities for tennis, squash, golf and swimming, and are able to help arrange equipment. Riding is also possible in some places and is particularly popular in bill

stations and Kashmir. At beach resorts boats can be hired, and water sports, sail-ing etc, organized. Gulmarg (Kashmir) offers skiing; the hills, climbing and trekking. Fishing and white-water rafting are other exciting possibilities.

International and national tournaments for most major sports are held throughout the year. Particular favorites include tennis and, of course, polo. Horse racing is also popular in some major cities.

Museums: India's nu-merous archaeological and artistic treasures are dis-played in museums located in all major towns and at several historial sites. Many have a specific focus, such as folk art, textiles, traditional objects of everyday use, cooking utensils, modern art and even trains. Check with your hotel or the Tourist Office for information on periodic exhibitions in multi-purpose galleries.

Delhi:

National Museum, Janpath.
National Art Gallery, Jaipur House.
Nehru Memorial Museum, Teen Murti House.
Red Fort Museum.
Hall of Nation Builders, Tees January Marg.
Crafts Museum, Pragati Maidan.
Shankar's Doll Museum, Bahadur Shah Zafar Marg.
Museum of Natural His-tory, FICCI Building, Bara-khamba Road.
Children's Museum, Kotla Road.

Rail Transport Museum, Chanakyapuri.

Calcutta:

The Academy of Fine Arts, Cathedral Rd.
Birla Academy of Art and Culture Museum, Southern Avenue.
Crafts Museum, Art Industry Museum, Old Court House St.
Indian Museum, Jawaharlal Nehru Rd.
Marble Palace Art Gallery and Zoo, Muktaram Babu St.
Nehru Children's Museum, Chowringhee Rd.
Rabindra Bharati Museum, Dwarkanath Tagore Lane.
The Asiatic Society, Park St.
Victoria Memorial Hall, Calcutta.

Bombay:

Prince of Wales Museum, Mahatma Gandhi Road, Fort.
Victoria and Albert Museum, Dr, Ambedkar Road, Byculla.
Jehangir Nicholson Museum of Modern Art, National Centre for Performing Arts, Nariman Point.
The Gandhi Memorial, Laburnum Road, Gamdevi.
Bombay Natural History Society, Hornbill House, near Prince of Wales Museum.

Madras:

Government Museum, Pantheon Rd.
Fort St. George Museum.

Andra Pradesh:

Salar Jang Museum, Hyderabad.
Archaeological Museum, Public Gardens, Hyderabad.
Ajanta Pavilion, Public Gardens, Hyderabad.
Khajana Buildings Museum, Golkonda Fort, Golkonda, Hyderabad.
Yelleshwaram Museum, Gunfoundry, Hyderabad.
Prince Azmatajah Museum in former Nizam's Palace, Hyderabad.

Bihar:

Archaeological Museum, Bodh Gaya.
Gaya Museum.
Archaeological Museum, Nalanda.
Patna Museum, Buddha Marg, Patna.

Goa:

Archaeological Museum and **Portrait Gallery,** Old Goa.
The Museum of Goa, Daman and Diu, St. Inez, Panjim.
Institute Menzes Braganza, Panjim.

Gujarat:

Sanskar Kendra Municipal Museum, Ahmedabad.
Calico Museum of Textiles, Calico Mills Premises, outside Jamalpur Gate, Ahmedabad.
Gandhi Memorial Museum at Sabramati Ashram.
Shreyas Folk Museum, ahmedabad.
Tribal Research and Training Institute, Gujarat Vidyapath, Ahmedabad.

Arts and Crafts Museum, Gandhi Smriti, Bhavnagar.

Jammu & Kashmir:

The Pratap Singh Museum, Lal Mandi, Srinagar.

Karnataka:

Museum of Art & Archaeology, University of Mysore, Mysore.
Folklore Museum, University of Mysore, Mysore.
Archeological Museum, Hampi, Bellary Dist.
The Government Museum, Cubbon Park, Bangalore.
Karnataka Govt. Museum and Ventatappa Art Gallery, Kasturba Rd., Bangalore.
Sri Chamlajendra Art Gallery, Jaganmohan Palace, Mysore.

Kerala:

Art Museum, Trivandrum.

Madhya Pradesh:

The Archaeological Museum in the Gujari Mahal, Gwalior Fort.
Archaeological Museum, Khajuraho.
State Museum, Banganga Marg, Bhopal.
Roopankar, Bharat Kala Bhavan, Bhopal.
Archaeological Museum, Archeological Survey of India, Sanchi.

Orissa:

Orissa State Museum, Bhubaneshwar.
Archaeological Museum, Konarak.

IN TRANSIT

Rajasthan:

The Government Central Museum, Ram Niwas Garden, Jaipur.
Maharaja Swawai Man Singh II Museum, City Palace, Jaipur.
Metrangah Fort Museum, Jodhpur.
The Museum in the City Palace, Udaipur.
The Government Museum, Udaipur.
The Archaeological Museum, Udaipur.
The Manuscript Library, Udaipur.
Archaeological Museum, Amber.

Tamil Nadu:

Gandhi Memorial Museum, Tammukam, Madurai.
Art Museum, Sri Meenakshi Sundareswara Temple, Madurail.
Art Gallery, Thanjavur.
Saraswati Mahal Library, Thanjavur.

Uttar Pradesh:

The Taj Mahal Museum (within the Taj Compound), Agra.
Archaeological Museum, Sarnath.
Bharat Kala Bhavan, Banaras Hindu University Varanasi.
Maharaja Banaras Vidya Mandir Museum, Fort Ramnagar, Varanasi.

West Bengal:

Himalayan Mountaineering Institute, Darjeeling.
Lloyds Botanic Garden, Darjeeling.

Art Galleries: India has a large number of talented contemporary painters and sculptors. Art galleries in all big cities are heavily booked and mount regular exhibitions, where paintings can be purchased.

Cultural Events: For those interested in classical music and dance, performances and festivals are regularly organized all over the country and are held throughout the year. Check locally for current shows and events. Some hotels, particularly those of the Ashok group, arrange cultural evenings for their guests.

India has a strong dramatic tradition, and theater is very popular. Most plays, however, are in local languages, though several talented amateur or semi-amateur groups present performances in English from time to time. These are usually well advertised in the local press. In Delhi, the Indian Council for Cultural Relations organizes a weekly program which is open to all.

Book Shops: Books in English published in the West and in India are freely available at bookshops in all cities. Those in hotels and major shopping centers also stock airmail editions of international news magazines and newspapers in English.

Libraries: Although most towns down to District headquarters level have public libraries, they are not always well maintained and stocked. Among the best libraries are those attached to educational centers and research institutions.

Movies: Every town in India has at least one movie hall. Most run Hindi or regional language films. Only a few English movies, usually those released months earlier in their country of origin, are shown.

WHERE TO STAY

India's immense range of hotels caters to every budget and preference. Star ratings range from five-star luxury or deluxe, comparable with the best anywhere in the world, to inexpensive one-star hotels for the budget traveler. Major private sector hotel chains with centralized reservations systems offer a variety of options. These include the eight hotels of the Oberoi group, 23 of the Welcome group, and 13 of the Taj group. Operating superb hotels in key destinations and resorts with every facility and excellent service, they are at the top end of the price scale. Those in converted maharajas' palaces offer a unique glimpse at life styles of a vanished era. In addition to group-run hotels, there are, of course, a number of well run, privately owned hotels, many offering modest, but comfortable and clean accommodation, at moderate rates.

The widest range is provided by the Indian Tourist Development Corporation (ITDC) hotels—the Ashok group. Its 24 hotels include every category from the most luxurious to the inexpensive, two beach resorts, nine moderately priced travelers' lodges, and four forest lodges.

State Governments also operate several moderately priced lodges or motels. There are also YMCA hostels, a huge variety of guest houses, and families offering paying guests accommodations, which can be arranged through the Tourist Offices. Kashmir offers the attraction of living in a houseboat. Here again costs range from super de luxe accommodation for Rs 325 per day to Rs 220 per day for the less lavish boats.

HOTELS

Ambassador (Govt. aprroved). 4-star.
Sujan Singh Park, New Delhi 110003. Tel: 690391. Cable: HOTEL AMBASSADOR. Telex: 031-3277.

Ashok (Govt. approved). 5-star deluxe.
50-B, Chanakyapuri, New Delhi 110021. Tel: 600121, Cable: ASHOKA HOTEL. Telex: 031-65207 600412.

Claridge's (Govt. approved). 5-star.
12, Aurangzeb Rd., New Delhi 110011. Tel: 3010211. Cable: CLARIDGES. Telex: 031-67526 CLAR IN.

Diplomat (Govt. approved). 4-star.
9, Sardat Patel Marg, New Delhi 110021. Tel: 3010204. Cable: DIPLOMATIC. Telex: DIP IN 2532.

Imperial (Govt. approved). 5-star.
Janpath, New Delhi 110001. Tel: 311511. Cable: COMFORT. Telex: 031-3162603 HIMP IN.

Janpath (Govt. approved). 4-star.
Janpath, New Delhi 110001. Tel: 350070. Cable: RESTWELL. Telex: 031-2468.

Maidens (Govt. approved). 4-star.
7, Sham Nath Marg, Delhi 110054. Tel: 2525464. Cable: OB-MAIDENS. Telex: 031-66303.

Maurya Sheraton (Govt. approved). 5-star deluxe.
Diplomatic Enclave, New Delhi 110021. Tel: 3010101. Cable: WELCOTEL. Telex: 031-61447 WELC-IN.

Oberoi Intercontinental (Govt. approved). 5-star deluxe.
Zakir Hussain Road, New Delhi 110003. Tel: 363030. Cable: INHOTELCOROBHOTEL. Telex: 63222 OBOL.

Qutab Ashok (Govt. approved). 5-star.
Off Sri Aurobindo Marg, New Delhi 110016. Tel: 660060. Cable: QUTABOTEL. Telex: 031-62537.

Taj Mahal (Govt. Approved). 5-star deluxe.
1 Man Singh Rd., New Delhi 110011. Tel: 3016162. Cable: TAJDEL. Telex: 031-4758 TAJD IN.

Y.M.C.A. International Guest House
Parliament Street, New Delhi 110001. Tel: 389821. Cable: MANHOOD.

Meridien (Govt. approved). 5-star.
Windsor Place, New Delhi 110001. Tel: 383960. Telex: 031-63076 HOME IN.

Centaur (Govt. approved).5-star.
Delhi Airport, New Delhi 110037. Tel: 391421. Telex: 031-62744.

Kanishka (Govt. approved). 5-star.
19, Ashoka Road, New Delhi 110001. Tel: 343400. Telex: 031-62788.

Hyatt Regency, (Govt. approved). 5-star.
Bhikaji Cama Place, Rk Poram, New Delhi 110066. Tel: 609911. Telex: 031-61512.

Sofitel Surya (Govt. approved). 5-star.
Friends Colony, New Delhi 110065. Tel: 6835070. Telex: 031-63092.

Taj Palace, (Govt. approved). 5-star.

Diplomatic Enclave, New Delhi 110021. Tel: 3010404. Telex: 031-62756 TAJS IN.

Calcutta:

Airport Ashok (Govt. approved). 5-star.
Calcutta Airport, Calcutta 700 052. Tel: 575111 574440. Cable: AIRPORTEL. Telex: 021-2271.

Hotel Hindustan International (Govt. approved). 5-star.
235/1, Jagadish Chandra Bose Road, Calcutta 700020. Tel: 442394. Cable: MODERN. Telex: 7464.

Oberoi Grand (Govt. approved). 5-star.
15, Jarwaharlal Nehru Rd., Calcutta 700013. Tel: 292323. Cable: OBHOTEL. Telex: 7248; 7854.

Park Hotel (Govt. approved). 5-star.
17, Park Street, Calcutta 700016. Tel: 248301. Cable: PARKHOTEL. Telex: 7159 PARK IN.

Bombay:

Ambassador (Govt. approved). 4-star.
Nariman Road, Churchgate, Bombay 400020. Tel: 2041131. Cable: EMBASSY. Telex: 011-2918.

Bombay International (Govt. approved). 3-star.
29, Marine Drive, Bombay 400020. Tel: 2026060. Cable: LUXURIOUS. Telex: 11-3428 BINTAN.

Centaur (Govt. approved). 5-star.

Bombay Airport, Bombay 400 099. Tel: 6126660. Cable: CENTAUR. Telex: 011-71171 CHTL.

Fariyas Hotel (Govt. approved). 4-star.
25, Off Arthur Bunder Road, Colaba, Bombay 400005. Tel: 2042911. Cable: FARIYAS. Telex: 3272.

Holiday Inn (Govt. approved). 5-star.
Juhu Beach, Bombay 400049. Tel: 571425, 571435. Cable: HOLIDAY INN. Telex: 11-71266; and 11-71432.

Nataraj (Govt. approved). 4-star.
135, Marine Drive, Bombay 400020. Tel: 2044161. Cable: HOTELRAJA. Telex: 2302.

Oberoi Towers (Govt. approved). 5-star deluxe.
Nariman Point, Bombay 400021. Tel: 2024343. Cable; OBHOTEL. Telex: 011-4153 OBBY IN; 011-4154 OBBY IN.

The Oberoi (Govt. approved). 5-star deluxe.
Nariman Point, Bombay 4000021. Tel: 2025757. Telex: 011-4153.

President (Govt. approved). 5-star deluxe.
90, Cuffe Parade, Colaba, Bombay 400005. Tel: 4950808. Cable: PIEM HOTEL. Telex: 11-4135 PRES IN.

Sun-n-Sand (Govt. approved). 5-star.

39, Juhu Beach, Bombay 400049., Tel: 571481. Cable: SUNAND SAND. Telex: 011-71282.

Taj Mahal Intercontinental (Govt. approved). 5-star deluxe.
Apollo Bunder, Bombay 400039. Tel: 2023366. Cable: INHOTELS. Telex: 11-2442 TAJB IN.

Welcomgroup Searock (Govt. approved). 5-star.
Lands End, Bandra, Bombay 400050. Tel: 6425454. Cable: SEAROCK. Telex: 011-71230 ROCKN; 011-71190 ROCKN.

Hotel Leela Penta (Govt. approved). 5-star.
Opposite Sahar International Apt., Bombay. Tel: 6363636. Telex: 011-72204.

Madras:

Chola Sheraton (Govt. approved). 5-star.
10, Cathedral Road, Madras 600086. Tel: 473347. Cable: HOTEL CHOLA. Telex: 041-7200 WELCN.

Connemara (Govt. approved). 4-star.
Binny Road, Madras 600002. Tel: 810051. Cable: CONNEMARA. Telex: 041-8197 CH IN.

Taj Coromondel (Govt. approved). 5-star deluze.
17, Nungambakkam High Road, Madras 600034. Tel: 474849. Cable: HOTELORIENT. Telex: 041-7194 TAJM IN.

Adyar Park (Govt. approved). 5-star.
132 T.T.K. rd., P.O. Box

1534, Madras 600019. Tel: 4525. Telex: 041-8881 WELCN.

Savera Hotel (Govt. approved). 4-star.
69 Dr. Radhakrishnam Rd., Madras 600004. Tel: 474700. Telex: 041-6896.

Andhra Pradesh:

Banjara (Govt. approved). 5-star.
Banjara Hills, Hyderabad 500 034. Tel: 222222. Cable; WELCOTEL. Telex: 0155 329.

Krishna Oberoi (Govt. approved). 5-star.
6-2, 249/10 Road, No. 1, Banjara Hills, Hyderabad. Telex: 425-6931.

Ritz (Govt. approved). 4-star.
Hill Fort Palace, Hyderabad 500483. Tel: 33571. Cable: RITZ. Telex: 10155-6215.

Hotel Sampurna International (Govt. approved). 4-star.
Mukramjahi Rd., Hyderabad 500001. Tel: 40165.

Maurya Patna (Govt. approved). 5-star.
South Gandhi Maidan, Patna 800001. Tel: 22061, 22065. Cable: MAURYA. Telex: 022-352 MAURN.

Satkar International (Govt. approved).
Frazer Road, Patna 800001. Tel: 25771/8. Cable: SATKAR.

Goa:

Cidade De Goa (Govt. approved). 5-star.

Vainguinim Beach, Dona Paula, Goa. Tel: 3301, 3308. Cable: WELCOTEL. Telex: 0194-257 DONA IN.

Fort Aguada Beach Resort (Govt. approved).
Beach Resort, Gandolim, Bardez, Goa 403515. Tel: 440112. Cable: FORT AGUADA. Telex: 0194-206 TAJ-IN.

Oberoi Bogmalo Beach (Govt. approved). 5-star.
Bogmalo Goa 403806. Tel: 2191. Cable: OBHOTEL. Telex: 0191-297.

Taj Holiday Village (Govt. approved).
Candolim, Bardez, Goa 403-515. Tel: 4414-7. Cable; FORT AGUADA. Telex: 0194-206 TAJ IN.

The Whitesands Hotel and Cottages, Colva Beaches.

Gujarat:

Cama (Govt. approved). 4-star.
Khanpur Road, Ahmedabad 380001. Tel: 25281. Cable: HOTELCAMA. Telex: 0121-373 CAMA IN.

Ambassador Hotel (Govt. approved). 4-star.
Khanpur Road, Ahmedabad 380 001. Tel: 392244.

Nilambagh Palace (Govt. approved).
Bhavnagar 364002. Tel: 24340, 24422, 29329.

Jammu & Kashmir:

Broadway (Govt. approved). 5-star.
Maulana Azad Road,

Srinagar 190001. Tel: 71211-14, 71284-85. Cable: BROADWAY. Telex: 0375-212.

Gurkha Houseboats (Govt. approved).
P. O. Box 57, Srinagar 19001. Tel: 75229. Telex: 0375-286 GRKAN.

Hotel Gulmarg, Boulevard Srinagar. Tel: 71331. Cable:HOTEL GUL. Telex: 0375-219.

Nedou's
Hotel Road, Srinagar.

Palace Hotel (Govt. approved). 5-star.
Gupkar Road, Srinagar 190001. Tel: 75617-18. Cable: OBHOTEL. Telex: 0375-201 LXSR IN.

Highlands Park (Govt. approved). 3-star.
Gulmarg. Tel: 30, 91. Cable: HIGHLANDS.

Hotel Pahalgam (Govt. approved). 4-star.
Pahalgam, Kashmir. Tel: 26.

Asia Jammu-Tawi (Govt. approved). 4-star.
Nehru Market, Jammu 180001. Tel: 43930, 43932. Cable: ASOAPTEL. Telex: 0377-224 ASIA IN.

Oberoi Shambhala
Ladakh Sarai, Leh.

Karnataka:

Taj Residency (Govt. Approved). 5-star.
14, M.G. Road, Bangalore 560001. Tel: 568888. Telex: 845-8367 TBLR IN.

Ashok (Govt. approved). 5-star.
Kumara Krupa, High Grounds, Bangalore 560001. Tel: 79411. Cable: 0845-433.

Shilton (Govt. approved). 2-star.
St. Mark's Road, Bangalore 560001. Tel: 568184-86, 578672. Cable: SHILTON HOTEL. Telex: 0845-251 SHIL IN.

West End (Govt. approved). 3-star.
Race Course Road, Bangalore 560001. Tel: 29281. Cable: WESTEND. Telex: 0845-337, 0845-8188 WEND IN.

Woodlands (Govt. approved). 2 -star.
5, Sampangi Tank Road, Bangalore 560025. Tel: 225590. Cable: WOODLANDS. Telex: 0845-311.

Windsor Manor (Govt. approved).
25, Sankey Road, Bangalore 560052. Tel: 28031, 79431. Cable: WELCOTEL BANGALORE. Telex: 0845-8209 WINDN.

Hotel Highway (Govt. approved).
New Bannimantap Extn., Mysore 570015. Tel: 21117. Cable: HIWAY.

Mayura Hoysala Hotel
2, Jhansi Lakshmi Bai Road, Mysore. Tel: 26677.

Lalitha Mahal Palace (Govt. approved). 5-star.
Mysore 570011. Tel: 27650. Cable: TOURISM.

Kerala:

Malabar (Govt. approved). 4-star.
Willingdon Island, Cochin 682003. Tel: 6811. Cable: COMFORT. Telex: 0885-661 MLBR IN.

Hotel Belair (Govt. approved).
Agricultural College Road, Vellayani Post Office, Trivandrum. Tel: 3402-3,. Cable: ACBEE. Telex: 0884-230 ACBI IN.

Mascot Hotel (Govt. approved). 3-star.
Trivandrum. Tel: 68990. Cable: MASCOT. Telex: 0884-229.

Kovalam Ashok Beach Resort (Govt. approved). 5-star.
Kovalam, Vizhinjam, Trivandrum 695522. Tel: 68010, 65323. Cable: TOURISM VIZHINJAM. Telex: 0884-216.

Madhya Pradesh:

Jehan Numa Palace Hotel
Shamla Hill, Bhopal 462 013. Tel: 76080, 76190. Cable: JEHANUMA.

Ramsons International
Hamidia Road, Bhopal. Tel: 72298, 72299, 73331. Cable: SETHIBROS.

Chandela, (Govt. approved). 5-star deluxe.
Khajuraho. Tel: 54. Cable: CHANDELA.

Jass Oberoi, (Govt. approved). 5-star.

By Pass Road, Khajuraho. Tel: 66. Cable: OBHOTEL.

Maharashtra:

Ajanta Ambasador (Govt. approved). 5-star.
Chikalthana, Aurangabad 431210. Tel: 8211-15. Cable: AMBASSADOR. Telex: 0745-211 AMBA IN.

Rama International (Govt. approved). 5-star.
R-3, Chikalthana, Aurangabad 431210. Tel: 82455, 82457. Cable: WELCOTEL. Telex: 0745-212.

Orissa:

Hotel Konark (Govt. approved). 4-star.
Bhovaneshwar 751014. Tel: 53330. Telex: 0675-343.

Hotel Safari International (Govt. approved).
Rasulgarh, Bhuvaneshwar 751010. Tel: 53443. Telex: 0675-345.

Kalinga Ashok (Govt. aprpoved). 2-star.
Gautam Nagar, Bhubaneshwar 751014. Tel: 53318. Cable: TOURISM. Telex: 0675-282.

Hotel Prachi (Govt. approved). 2-star.
6, Janpath, Unit III. Bhubaneshwar 751001. Tel: 52689, 52521. Cable: DESTINY,. Telex: 0675-278.

TDC Travelers Lodge.

Toshali Sands (Govt. approved).
Puri 752002. Tel: 2888, 2999. Telex: 0675-395.

S.E. Railway Hotel.
Panthaniwas, Tourist Bungalow.

Himachal Pradesh:

Kulu Valley Resort.

ITDC Travelers' Lodge.

H.P.T.D.C. Bungalow.

ITDC's Ashok Travelers' Lodge.

Sunshine Guest House.

Clarke's (Govt. approved). 3-star.
The Mall, Simla. Tel: 6091-5. Cable: OBHOTEL. Telex: 0391-206 OBCL IN.

Woodville Palace Hotel.

Hotel Lord's Grey.
The Mall, Simla.

Rajasthan:

Bharatpur Forest Lodge (Govt approved).
Bharatpur Bird Sanctuary, Bharatpur 321001. Tel: 2260, 2322, 2864. Cable: FORESTOUR.

Saras Tourist Bungalow (Govt. approved).
Bharatpur. Tel: 3700.

Shanti Kureler Guest House.
At the Ghana Bird Sanctuary.

Clarks Amer (Govt. approved). 5-star.
Jawaharlal Nehru Marg, Jaipur. Tel: 822616.Cable: CLARKSAMAR. Telex: 0365-276.

Jaipur Ashok (Govt. approved). 4-star.
Jaisingh Circle, Bani Park, Jaipur. Tel: 75121-26, 75171-73. Cable: ASHOKOTEL. Telex: 0365-262.

Mansingh (Govt. approved). 5-star.
Sansar Chandra Road, Jaipur 302001. Tel: 78771. Telex: 036-344.

Raj Mahal Palace (ex-Maharaja's Palace).

Rambagh Palace Hotel (Govt. approved). 5-star deluxe.
Bhawani Singh Road, Jaipur 302005. Tel: 75141. Cable: RAMBAGH. Telex: 0365254 RBAG IN.

Jai Mahal Palace (Govt. approved). 5-star.
Jacob Rd., Civil Lines Jaipur 302006. Tel: 73215, 73216. Telex: 365052 JMPH IN.

Umaid Bhawan Palace.
Jodhpur. Tel: Tel: 22316, 22366, 22516.

Lake Palace (Govt. approved). 5-star.
Pichola Lake, Udaipur 313001. Tel: 23241. Cable: LAKE PALACE. Telex: 033-203 LPAL IN.

Laxim Vilas Palace Hotel (Govt. approved). 4-star.
Udaipur 313 001. Tel:

24411. Cable: TOURISM.

Tamil Nadu:

Fisherman's Cove (Govt. approved).
Covelong, Chinglepur Distt. Tel: Via Mahabalipuram 947, 268. Cable: FISHCOVE. Telex: 041-7194.

Temple Bay Ashok Beach Resort (Govt. approved). 3-star.
Mamallapuram 603104. Tel: 251-58. Cable: TOURISM.

Uttar Pradesh:

Clarks Shiraz, (Govt. approved). 5-star.
54, Taj Road, Agra 282001. Tel: 72421. Cable: SHIRAZ. Telex: 0565-211.

Mughal Sheraton (Govt. approved). 5-star.
Taj Ganj, Agra 282001. Tel: 64701. Cable: WELCO-TEL. Telex: 0565-210 IT-CON.

Taj View Hotel (Govt. approved). 5-star.
Taj Ganj. Fatehabad Road, Agra 282 001.Tel: 64171. Telex: 0565-020 TAJV IN

Varanasi Ashok (Govt. approved). 4-star.
The Mall, Varanasi 221002. Tel: 42550-60. Cable: TOURISM. Telex: 0545-205.

NEPAL: ABODE OF THE GODS

Nestled in the cradle of the highest mountains on earth, Nepal has come to be known as the kingdom where deities mingle with mortals.

Here are the Himalayas, the "Abode of the Gods." Here, too, is the world's highest mountain, Mount Everest, or what the Nepalese call *Sagarmatha* ("The Brow of the Oceans"). Sherpa artists picture the peak as the god Chomolungma riding the snow lion through clouds of many hues. Ancient sages sought the highest climes for meditative seclusion among gods who bestowed love or sudden anger on a worshipful people. Such devotion remains among today's Nepalis: whether Hindu, Buddhist or animist, the people of Nepal live close to their gods.

Nepal is one of the world's most incredible countries—filled with geographical wonders and ethnological conundrum.

This is the home of 17 million Nepalis whose languages and customs are as diverse as the terrain. From mountain to mountain, valley to valley, plateau to plain, ethnic groups vary as much as the climate.

No fewer than 36 languages and dialects are spoken in Nepal. Similar diversity is observed in rites and religions with wide variations between one ethnic group and its immediate neighbor. The prevailing pattern is of Hinduism in the south and Buddhism in the north; but animist rites and shamanistic practices have survived in a highly integrated form. Both major religions co-exist in most of the country. And in the heart of the land, in the Kathmandu Valley, Hinduism and Buddhism merge, sharing the same festivals and the same places of worship.

Squeezed between the vastness of China to the north and India to the south, east and west, Nepal is the world's most precipitous staircase to the frozen heights of "the Roof of the World." Within a single day one can fly closely past Everest and its neighboring summits, pause in the capital city of Kathmandu, then descend to the plains to ride elephants through tropical jungles and to view wild tigers.

Nepal is the world's only Hindu kingdom, unified by King Prithvi Narayan Shah of Gorkha in the late-18th century. Nepal today is a rectangular 497 miles (800 km) long and from 56 miles (90 km) to 137 miles (220 km) wide. Except for the narrow strip of the Terai plains along its southern boundary, (once alive with rhino and tigers), and the temperate, terraced valleys spread across its middle (home of the famous Gurkha soldiers), the country is entirely mountainous. More than a quarter of Nepal's land area is over 9,843 feet (3,000 meters) in altitude and contains eight of the world's highest mountains.

Legends, more memorable than history, traditionally told the Nepalese all they needed to know about their origins, attributing unknown beginnings to great heroes and gods. But the sudden exposure of modern education, population pressure, communication and politics has altered age-old patterns and legends no longer carry the same meaning they once did. Still, the sense of belonging to one nation may not have spread to all the diverse people of this kingdom. To this day it is not uncommon to hear people refer to Kathmandu as Nepal—even though they all recognize King Birendra Bir Bikram Shah Dev with great reverence and affection. Kathmandu may be Nepal, but Nepal is not just Kathmandu.

Preceding pages: Sherpa painting of Namche Bazaar, with a yeti in the mountains above; roof of the world.   Left, Tantric priest dramatizing Buddha's life story.

Geography: The stupendous mountain pedestal of Nepal includes no fewer than eight of the world's giants: Everest, Kanchenjunga, Lhotse, Makalu, Cho Oyu, Dhaulagiri, Manaslu and Annapurna. Mountain relief is asymmetrical, with rock strata inclined to the north, leaving steep south faces. Deep river gorges incise across the range to fall rapidly to the lower valleys. The steep slopes prevent the formation of large glaciers; a snowline varying between 16,400 feet (5,000 meters) and19,700 feet (6,000 meters) also limit glaciation.

Below the Himalayas, running in a similar relief is less rugged, with wind-eroded landforms predominant.

Each of these mountain ranges is separated from the next by lowland or valley systems. On the south is the Terai extension of India's vast Gangetic plain. Between 15 miles (25 km) and 25 miles (40 km) broad within the Nepalese border, the Terai's gentle topography contrasts sharply with the rugged relief of the rest of the country.

At a slightly higher elevation, but with similar vegetation, lie the *dun* or Inner Terai Valleys between the Siwalik Hills and the Mahabharat Lekh. Until the mid-1950s, this region was im-

west northwest and east southeast direction, are two parallel ranges. Fifty-six miles (90 km) south of the great range, the Mahabharat Lekh rises to elevations of between 4,900 feet (1,500 meters) and 8,900 feet (2,700 meters). Broad tropical valleys are encased in the complicated folds, and three narrow river gorges slice through it.

Immediately south are the Siwalik Churia Hills, which rise abruptly from the Terai plains to a height of between 2,450 feet (750 meters) and 4,900 feet (1,500 meters). The hill's dry immature soils support only a sparse population.

In the northwest of the country, a fourth trans-Himalayan range defines the boundary between Nepal and Tibet. Peaks of 19,700 feet to 23,000 feet (6,000 meters to 7,000 meters) lie about 22 miles (35 km) north of the main Himalayas; their

penetrable, malaria-infested jungle. Today, with much of its rich indigenous wildlife endangered, it has become Nepal's most populous region. Almost all of the modern industries are in the Terai, whose flatlands are ideal for growing rice and other grains.

Summers are hot in the Terai and the *dun*, with temperatures often exceeding 100 F (38 C). Winters are considerably cooler with the temperature down to 50 F (10 C). Rainfall comes primarily in the June-to-September monsoon season, heaviest in the east. The strong straight *sal* tree, compared by some to the mahogany for its durability, and the *kapok* or silk cotton tree are frequently seen in Terai forests.

Between the Mahabharat Lekh and the main Himalayas lies the broad complex of hills and valleys. This *pahar* zone is heavily eroded by rivers and streams. It is the traditional heartland of the Nepalese people, the home of the Kathmandu Valley.

Nepal's capital is a city of about 500,000, at once medieval and modern. Despite its 4,368-foot (1,331-meter) elevation and the snowy summits looming at its northern horizon, Kathmandu has a mild climate. Summer maximums are about 86 F (30 C) and mean temperatures about 50 F (10 C). Winters are sometimes frosty, but are dry and snowless, while summer monsoons bring substantial rain. The moderate cli-

There is a distinctly alpine climate in the highlands above 13,000 feet (4,000 meters). Summers are short, winters severe and dry, with high snowfall, low temperatures and strong winds. In western Nepal and northern Himalayas, there are elevated valleys reminiscent of Tibet, with broad, open profiles and arid climates—particularly where the Himalayan rain shadow blocks out the monsoon rains.

A History Bathed in Legend: In the distant dawn of unrecorded time, so legend tells us, the Valley of Kathmandu was a turquoise lake. Upon this lake rested a wondrous lotus flower from

mate permits three harvests a year in the myriad terraces and small plantings in between. Oaks and alders are oft seen trees, and rhododendron and jacarandas are beautiful when in bloom.

Beyond Kathmandu, high in the mountains, thunderstorms are frequent and winter frosts limit agriculture. Nevertheless, rice is grown at 9,800 feet (3,000 meters), potatoes at 13,000 feet (4,000 meters) and barley even higher. The mountain population finds sanctuary in isolated valleys, where juniper and birch share the terrain of subalpine grasses.

Left, natives of Nepal. Above, a 1793 view of the Kathmandu Valley.

which emanated a blue light of awesome magnificence. This was the manifestation of Swayambhu or Adhi Buddha, the primordial Buddha. So beautiful was the lake, so sacred the flame, that the devout came from many lands to live in caves along the shore to worship and meditate. From a mountain retreat in China came the patriarch Manjushri. Wishing to worship the flame more closely, he sliced the restraining valley wall with his flaming sword of wisdom, draining the water and allowing the lotus to settle to the valley floor. There Manjushri built a shrine that was to grow into the great *stupa* of Swayambhunath.

Another version of this legend has the Hindu deity Krishna hurling a thunderbolt at the valley wall to release the waters of the lake. Flaming sword or thunderbolt, there is to this day a gorge at Chobar as narrow as a blade. Both legends are as acceptable to modern science as legends can be. Geologists have confirmed that the Kathmandu Valley was indeed under water at one time.

After the gods, the valley was settled by several successive waves of Tibeto-Burman migrants. These people may have come from today's north Bengal, after sweeping across the hills and valleys of northeast India from Burma and beyond, or perhaps they came down from Tibet, Mongolia and China.

The Kiratis who arrived in about the seventh or eighth century B.C. are nearer recorded history. These apparently fierce tribal people may have been the Kiriats of Old Testament Babylon. Invading from the east, they established a kingdom in the valley of Kathmandu and left a legacy of

architecture——the oldest inscription in stone (dated 467 A.D.) found at Changu Narayan, confirms Manadeva I to be a king of considerable talents, responsible for conquests in the east and west. Licchavi craftsmen left a legacy of stone masterpieces. And Licchavis left a tradition of a hierarchical society divided according to the Hindu caste structure.

In 602 A.D. the first of three Thakuri dynasties began with the ascent of Amsuvarman, who married his sister to an Indian prince and his daughter Bhrikuti to Tibet's powerful King Songtsengampo. Bhrikuti is believed to have taken as part of her dowry the begging bowl of the Buddha. Her role in converting Tibet to a Buddhist state made her a legendary figure—she is considered an incarnation of the Green Tara.

The Thakuris lived in considerable style. They

outstanding kings in the rich fabric of early Nepal. It was during the reign of the 28 Kirati kings that Gautama Buddha and his beloved disciple Ananda are believed to have visited the valley.

Two centuries later, the great Indian Emperor Asoka, who embraced Buddhism and set to converting everyone in his empire to the new religion, visited Lumbini, the birthplace of Buddha, and erected an engraved column. He is also said to have visited the Kathmandu Valley where he built *stupas* (which still exist) at the four cardinal points of Patan.

When the Kirati Dynasty succumbed to a Licchavi invasion from India in about 300 A.D., the Kiratis left the valley. The Licchavis brought with them the first golden age of Nepalese art and

inaugurated the three great festivals of Indian jatra, Krishna jayanti and the Machhendranath jatra. They erected monuments to the glory of various gods and it was during this time that the Kasthamandap or "House of Wood" was constructed from the trunk of a sacred tree, giving Kathmandu its name.

Little is known of this long, obscure period known as Nepal's "Dark Age" except that trade grew despite periods of domestic turmoil.

Peace and Plenty: The Malla kings came to power in 1200. Their early period is considered a stable age of peace and plenty, when art flourished and traders brought riches and recognition to the Kathmandu Valley. From South India, Taleju Bhawani was adopted as the royal goddess of Nepal. The Malla monarchs were considered incarnations of Vishnu, as are the present Shah rulers, and although Hindus follow strict Brahmin rituals, they were tolerant of Buddhism which was widespread among the people, especially in its Tantric form.

It was during the Malla rule that brick and tile were first used. Villagers clustered together in the familiar compact settlements seen today to preserve limited arable land and to protect themselves from invaders and bandits. The caste system ensured a tightly-knit social fabric.

This era of progress was interrupted by periods of earthquakes, instabiliy and a brief siege by the destructive Moslem armies from India. By the early 15th century however, the Mallas, their capital now in Bhaktapur, had unified the valley. Newari was introduced as a court language and in all the three cities of the valley, Kathmandu,

of today's dynasty. How alluring the lush valley of Kathmandu must have appeared to the mountain king. In 1768, after 10 years of preparation, seige and attack, the valley was conquered. The new Shah rulers, believed to have been descended from Udaipur's Rajput princes, transferred their seat of power to Kathmandu. Modern Nepal was born.

Prithvi Narayan Shah expanded and consolidated his new empire. Trade flourished with both Tibet and British India and by 1810 the kingdom of Nepal extended from Kashmir to Sikkim— double its present size. Frontier disputes with the British in the Terai led to a full scale war of almost two years.

The 1816 "Treaty of Friendship" curbed the Gurkha king's expansionist ambitions and also established a British resident in Kathmandu. The

Patan and Bhaktapur, a renaissance of art and culture flourished. Many of the great buildings, fine wood carvings and powerful sculpture seen today belonged to this period. Land was cultivated and trade encouraged.

The Founder of Modern Nepal: Political rivalries among the divided kingdoms led to the demise of the Mallas. The opportunity was seized by the king of Gurkha, then a principality situated about halfway between Kathmandu and Pokhara, which had been growing in strength under the leadership of King Prithvi Narayan Shah, founder

Opposite page: Left, King Prithvi Narayan Shah prepares to conquer the valley, and right, Jung Bahadur Rana. Above, Nepalese royalty and American diplomats.

first Europeans to arrive in the valley were the Italian Capuchins, who in 1730, had been permitted to establish a mission. The first British envoy had visited the valley in 1792.

The gallantry the Gurkha soldiers displayed in the 1816 conflict so impressed the British that they inducted Gurkha soldiers into the British Indian Army. Even today the Gurkhas are recognized as outstanding soldiers for the British and Indians.

The Fashionable Ranas: In 1846, after a period of palace intrigues, a young, shrewd and opportunistic Kathmandu army general named Jung Bahadur Rana had himself designated prime minister and later *Maharaja* with powers superior to those of the nominal sovereign. He made the office hereditary, thus establishing a unique line of succession that would pass first to his brothers than to his sons, and in so doing inaugurated the country-long Rana rule.

Early Rana rule was characterized by ruthless persecution with the Shah kings kept under strict vigil in their own palace, no longer permitted to exercise authority.

In 1850, Jung Bahadur took the highly unorthodox step of traveling to England and France, where he was much impressed by Queen Victoria and the fashions of the day. He launched an architectural vogue of neoclassical palaces and men adopted fanciful European attire and uniforms. Ladies of the court were forced into crinolines and bustles were converted from *saris*.

Succeeding Ranas who were more liberal eased the lot of the local people by abolishing slavery and reforming the forced labor system.

and the people fired by the ideal of freedom embodied by their two neighbors.

With the support of the Indian Congress Party, opponents of the Rana rule, which included some prominent Ranas, joined the Nepali Congress Party under the leadership of B.P. Koirala. The rightful sovereign of Nepal, King Tribhuvan, still powerless in his palace, was heralded as the embodiment of the democratic aspirations of his people.

In November 1950 King Tribhuvan, on the pretext of taking his family on a shooting picnic, escaped to the Indian embassy in Kathmandu and from there fled to India.

In Delhi he was welcomed by Nehru as Nepal's reigning monarch and on February 18, 1951, returned from his self-imposed exile to begin a new rule. The Rana rulers were forced to step

Newspapers were started in Kathmandu along with schools, colleges and dispensaries. The practice of *suttee*, immolation of widows on their husbands funeral pyres, was abolished and the application of capital punishment restricted.

Although there were some advances, the Ranas ruled Nepal as their own private feudal kingdom and are generally criticized for not doing enough for the country.

It was only during the years following World War II that major changes began to take place in Nepal, largely due to the newly found independence of India in 1947 and the establishment of the People's Republic of China.

Upheaval and Democracy: Within the kingdom, tensions were growing with the Rana prime ministers disagreeing on Nepal's position

down and more than a century of extravagant despotic Rana rule was ended.

The birth of modern Nepal was not without its problems. King Tribhuvan opened Nepal's doors to the world, initiating diplomatic relations with many countries, but his 1951 promise to establish a truly democratic government was not immediately realized. It was not until after the king's death in 1955 that his son, King Mahendra, finally established a constitution that provided for a parliamentary system of government.

The first general election in Nepal's history was held over several weeks in February and March 1959. The king took steps to ensure that he retained control after a 21-month experiment of democracy ended in 1960. The 1962 constitution established the *Panchayat* system, a legislative body with few real powers, as the prime minister and cabinet were appointed by the king. Reforms followed, giving more power to the common people of Nepal.

Nepal Today: When King Mahendra died in 1972 he was succeeded by his son, the youthful King Birendra. The new king affirmed that his government would turn its efforts towards improving the standard of living of his people, who were increasingly aware of their lack of progress on an international scale.

Despite attempted improvements, popular discontent, strikes and demonstrations in 1979 forced the king to again revise the national constitution, following a referendum in May 1980 confirming the people's support of the monarchy.

The constitution established the present party-

less *Panchayat* system with the national legislature directly chosen by the electorate and the prime minister chosen by that legislature. However, the king has the right to name one-fifth of the members of the legislature, thus retaining ultimate authority.

Today's government is faced with the herculean task of leading the country into the 21st century. The population is increasing at the rate of 2.6 percent per year and rural poverty remains Nepal's chief problem. Huge development efforts have gone into health services, education,

Section of Lal Durbar, largest of the Rana palaces. The new royal palace is now built on part of this site.

agriculture, banking, communication, water resources and population control. Foreign aid is an integral part of this and remains a mixed blessing. King Birendra himself has stressed the importance of self reliance though economic necessity may dictate otherwise. Dependence on India is considerable. As it has no access to the sea, Nepal relies on its southern neighbor for 80 percent of its trade. After aid, tourism is Nepal's major foreign exchange earner, attracting about 160,000 visitors and some US$60 million a year.

Nepal's precarious position between India and China may still be its best guarantee of survival as a Himalayan buffer state and indeed has been the basis of Nepal's foreign policy for centuries. Internationally endorsed as the "Zone of Peace," Nepal is the neutral headquarters of the South Asian Association For Regional Cooperation (SAARC).

If the rivalry between the two big neighbors has been put to good use, stability at home must be maintained in the face of an increasingly vocal opposition. In June 1985, bombs shattered the peace of the Himalayan kingdom, killing and injuring several, including a *Panchayat* member. Although an isolated expression by an extreme left-wing group, the incident was a startling reminder to the government that opposition exists and cannot be ignored.

A Cultural Mosaic: "Mutual tolerance and peaceful co-existence have been the basis of social harmony and cultural synthesis since the dawn of our country's history"—His Majesty King Birendra Bir Bikram Shah Dev, May 17, 1972.

Nepal is a veritable mosaic of dozens of ethnic groups with their own unique languages, cultures and religions. Nevertheless, it has a tradition of harmony rather than conflict and society here has always been accommodating to new ideas, new values, new peoples from afar. With ethnic elements as diverse as its landscape, the principles of integration and synthesis has been accepted in this land since ancient times.

Watch the faces of the Nepali people passing you at any busy crossroads in Kathmandu and you will soon discover what a fascinating melting pot of Himalayan cultures the city is. Wandering from the valley to Nepal's outlying regions, you will find many isolated pockets of distinct peoples and cultures.

Ethnic groups are too numerous to mention— Brahmins and Chettris have traditionally played an important role in Nepalese society, dominating the orthodox Hindu caste system. The Newars are the original people of the Kathmandu Valley. They are skilled artists and craftsmen, with their own language and unique occupational caste system.

Best known of the Tibetan-speaking mountain peoples are the Sherpas who inhabit central and eastern regions of northern Nepal. Although the name "Sherpa" has become synonymous with "mountain guide," it is only those in the Everest region who have achieved relative prosperity through mountaineering and trekking, their hardiness and reliability now famous throughout the world.

The middle hills are the home of many different types of people: Tamangs, Thakalis, Gurungs, Magars, Rai and Limbu, all have their individual characteristics. Many of the latter join the forces of the British and Indian Gurkha regiments, a confusing name as there is no Gurkha ethnic group as such. The name derives from the soldiers who came from the kingdom of Gurkha.

The original peoples of the lowland Terai were the colorful Tharu, and other non-caste ethnic groups including the Danuwar, Majhi and Darai.

puja, copper plates piled with grains of rice, red powder and tiny yellow flower petals, are the cornerstone of Nepal's Hindu religion. The Hindu pantheon of gods include many colorful characters and fanciful stories. Many of the gods and goddesses appear in different forms with different names, further confusing the casual visitor.

Most of Kathmandu's Newars are Buddhists—their family priests are tantric Buddhist priests rather than Hindu Brahmins. But Newari Buddhists recognize Hindu gods in different forms and likewise Hindus regard the Gautama Buddha as an incarnation of Vishnu. It has been said that if one asks a Newar whether he is Hindu or Buddhist the answer will be, "yes." The question is meaningless and implies an exclusive choice which is foreign to the religious experi-

These fragile animist cultures are now dominated by immigrant Indians and peoples of the middle hills in search of more land now habitable since malaria was eradicated in the 1950s.

A Unique Vision of the Divine: The two main spiritual currents underlying the religious practices of Nepal are Hinduism and Buddhism. It is often hard to distinguish the two, especially since they are interwoven with the exotica of Tantrism against a background of animistic cults retained from the distant past. The result is a proliferation of cult deities and festivals and celebrations in variations unknown elsewhere.

Ritual sacrifice, whether for a wedding, initiation, seasonal festival or as a blessing, is always a male animal and usually a chicken, goat or buffalo. This, along with the daily offerings or

ence of the Newar people.

Although political leaders of the Kathmandu Valley have always been Hindu, Buddhism since its emergence in the sixth century has always been tolerated and indeed the religion's founder, a Sakya prince named Siddharta Gautama, was born in Nepal at Lumbini in about 543 B.C. (The actual date is disputed). Gautama preached his doctrine for 45 years after his enlightenment. In the centuries following his life, many doctrinal disputes arose, leading to various schisms in the philosophy. Most important was the break between the Theravada school, which adhered more closely to the original teachings and today predominates in Southeast Asia and Sri Lanka, and the Mahayana school, which spread north and east from India.

Tibetan or Mahayana Buddhism, highly developed for centuries in remote Tibet with its adaptions from the original shamanistic *Bon* faith, now thrives in Nepal's atmosphere of religious tolerance. Today there are many new monasteries at Bodhnath and Swayambhunath, and Lumbini is being restored for visitors.

Tibetan Buddhism stresses the inter-relatedness of all things. Through the faithful practice of meditation under the guidance of a personal teacher, one strives towards understanding or *nirvana*. There are four main sects of Mahayana Buddhism and all believe in reincarnation, the rebirth from one life into the next, and all also acknowledge the Dalai Lama as their leading figure.

One cannot speak of religions in Nepal without mentioning the practice of Tantrism, a legacy of Nepal is of the essence. With religion a major part of daily life, one can well believe there are more gods than people in the valley of Kathmandu.

Artistic Heritage: The masterpieces of art produced by the great civilizations of the Kathmandu Valley are almost entirely religious in character; whether architecture, sculpture, woodcarving, metalwork, literature, music or dance, the marvelous legacy left by the people of the valley is all inspired by their gods. No visitor can fail but be impressed by the wealth of richness to be found literally lying around.

The basis of the Licchavi and Malla artistic genius in stone, wood, metal and paint was crystallized in its renaissance by the genius of the Newar people. Into the Kathmandu Valley crucible had been poured the cultural talent of people from India, Tibet and China, Mongolia, Central

the pre-Buddhist medieval cultures of India. *Tantra* is originally a Sanskrit word, referring to the basic warp of threads in weaving. Literally, Tantrism reiterates the Buddhist philosophy of the interwoveness of all things and actions. It expanded the realm of Hindu gods, cults and rites and created within Buddhism a major trend which reached great importance in Nepal. At its highest level Tantrism is a synthesis of spiritualism and materialism, but it often finds expression in esoteric practices.

With such diversity, religious tolerance in

Left, a 100-rupee note, featuring King Birendra. Above, Nepalese girls in their ceremonial finery.

Asia and perhaps even Burma. Fired with religious fervor, these peoples decorated temples, religious courtyards and palaces. Important temples were crowned with gold fused by a mercury process. The fine skills of the Nepali goldsmiths, silversmiths and workers in bronze, stone, wood and ivory carvers, terra-cotta and brick makers were celebrated throughout the region.

With the passing of the Malla Dynasty in the 18th century, art floundered and was even suppressed during the Rana period. Since the Shah Dynasty regained power in 1951, there has been a revival of the arts and crafts through such international agencies as UNESCO and the World Bank, though much of the work done today is aimed at the tourist industry.

EXPLORING THE VALLEY

The rich fabric of the cultural and artistic history of the Kathmandu Valley cannot fail to impress even the most casual visitor, despite some of the magic having been lost amidst the modern additions of dust, hooting vehicles and indiscriminate building.

Don't miss the three medieval city capitals of Kathmandu, Patan and Bhaktapur and include visits to the great shrines Swayambhunath, Pashupatinath and Bodhnath. Because of the valley's compact size and its relatively flat terrain, it is not difficult to get around.

For the more adventurous visitor who really wants to know the valley, there are many more villages and shrines, pilgrimage sites and settlements to explore. These are best discovered on foot or by bicycle. Within minutes of leaving the new tarmac roads, you return to the spiritual atmosphere of ancient Nepal, where villagers tend their terraced fields.

Kathmandu: A half-day visit to **Kathmandu** city center and Swayambhunath is a perfect introduction to the diverse culture of Nepal.

Start at the Durbar Square and you will find yourself in a medieval city. Although supposedly founded at the end of the Licchavi period, Kathmandu first became capital of the valley in the 14th century under King Jayasthiti Malla. Spreading from old trade routes which are still visible today, Kathmandu was said to have grown in the shape of a sword, though it is impossible to trace this today.

Architectural styles generally changed very little for centuries and only a trained eye can differentiate between earlier and later artistry in traditional Newari buildings. It was only in the mid-19th century during the Ranas rule, that dramatic changes in architecture occured, with the introduction of many western-influenced styles.

On your way to the Durbar Square you may pass the most dramatic Rana palace, **Singha Durbar,** a building of gigantic proportion and size, said to be the largest private dwelling in Asia and originally the home of the prime ministers. It now houses some government ministries.

As you wind your way around the one way system towards the old city, you pass the **Tundikhel,** a long, open expanse used as a parade ground, or as common grazing for the domestic stock which still roam the streets of Kathmandu.

From the Tundikhel you turn under the arch up **New Road,** so called because it was reconstructed after the major earthquake of 1934. It runs straight into Basantapur and the Durbar Square in front of the old palace to the heart of the old city. The new city is to be found farther northeast with **Durbar Marg** forming the central axis with its rows of airline and travel agencies, restaurants and banks. At the northern end of Durbar Marg is the western-style new **Royal Palace,** built by an Indian-American architectural collaboration.

New Road remains the paradise of the consumer society and here imported goods can be found in the shops and supermarkets between the jostling crowds and exhaust fumes. Half-way down, a big *peepul* tree shades a small square, a welcome respite from the whine of transistor radios. Farther still is forgotten **Freak Street** leading off to the left from an open area known as **Basantapur,** after the biggest tower looming on the right. Formerly the home of royal elephants, this area was also used as a vegetable market before being replaced by the present brick platform and curio sellers.

The Living Goddess: As you enter the Durbar Square on the left, note the carved

windows of the **Kumari Bahal**. This is the house of the Living Goddess, built in the mid-18th century. Two painted lion statues guard the entrance steps and inside the small courtyard, the wood carving on all four walls is truly remarkable. With a small payment per visitor, the *kumari* or living goddess appears at the window. No one is allowed to take photographs of the *kumari*.

The *kumari* is considered to be the incarnation of the "Virgin Goddess," a form of Parvati, Shiva's consort. Others consider her a manifestation of the goddess Taleju. She is called the royal *kumari* to distinguish her from other living goddesses in Nepal. She lives in her courtyard except for once a year when she is worshipped by the king and is paraded through the streets during *Indrajatra*, enthroned in her flower-bedecked chariot.

The living goddess is always chosen from a selection of young girls of the Sakya clan of goldsmiths and silversmiths. Her body must be flawless and must satisfy a number of distinctive signs, and astrologers ensure that her horoscope is in harmony with that of the king. Once selected, she is settled in the *bahal* or courtyard which becomes her home until she reaches puberty, or until she loses blood, as from a small wound. As soon

as this happens, her term as living goddess is ended and a new *kumari* is selected.

The girl then leaves the temple, richly endowed and free to marry. It is believed that a man who weds an ex-goddess brings bad luck to his household and an early death on himself. However, recent *kumaris'* husbands have so far survived this fate.

As you leave the Kumari Bahal, the **Temple of Narayan**, a three-roofed structure built about 1670 on a tiered plinth, is to the immediate left. You are now entering the **Durbar Square**. This wide area has less charm and less cohesion than its counterparts in Patan and Bhaktapur but it contains more than 50 important temples and monuments dominated by the impressive bulk of the **Taleju Temple**, which houses the tutelary divinity of the royal family.

The best view of the Durbar Square is from its western end. Walk on the left and you find the famed **Kasthamandap** or "House of Wood" built in the 12th century on the main trade route crossroads. The name 'Kathmandu' is said to be derived from Kasthamandap. Originally a community center where people gathered for ceremonies and other events, it was later turned into a temple dedicated to Gorakhnath. The god sits in the center of the platform on a

Drying grain in Kathmandu's Durbar Square.

small wooden enclosure. The Kasthamandap was seen all over the world, beautifully restored for the visit of the Queen of England in early 1986.

Hidden by the Kasthamandap is the small but very important **Ashok Binayak shrine** of the Kathmandu Ganesh. Returning to the square you come to a **Shiva temple** on the left with three roofs and a nine-step plinth. Just before entering this second square, notice the **Shiva Parvati Temple House** on the left. The deified couple, carved in wood and crudely painted, look benignly down on their worshippers from the center window of the upper balcony.

Opposite the entrance of the Hanuman Dhoka stands the **Krishna Mandir**, one of the few octagonal temples in Nepal. On the right hand corner, a large wooden lattice screen hides an enormous gilded face of the Seto Bhairav, a fascinating masterpiece of popular art.

Leaving the temples of the outer Durbar Square, you come to the entrance of the Royal Palace, the **Hanuman Dhoka**. On one side stands a 1672 statue of the monkey-god, Hanuman, under a small umbrella, wrapped in a red cloak and his face smeared with holy red dust.

The brightly-painted palace gates are guarded by royal guards whose uniforms date back to the Malla times. The gate opens upon the **Nasal Chowk**, the most important of the 14 courtyards which make up the palace. *Nasal* means "the dancing one" and this is the courtyard in which the actual royal coronation ceremonies take place. On the right is the entrance to the **museum** dedicated to King Tribhuvan.

Mostly built in Malla times, and adapted by King Prithvi Narayan Shah with later Rana additions, the Hanuman Dhoka was carefully restored by UNESCO for King Birendra's coronation in 1975.

The nine-storey Basantapur tower, the oddly-shaped Kirtipur tower, Lalitpur and Bhaktapur towers, which date from the late-18th century, are set in a square around and above the **Lohan Chowk**.

A Garland of Skulls: Leaving the Hanuman Dhoka, turn right out of the entrance and note the highly admired, fierce-looking **Black Bhairav** relief. The black-skinned god wears red and yellow ornaments, a tiara and a garland of skulls and is much respected by the people.

The northeastern end of the Durbar Square is dominated by the magnificent three-tiered **Taleju temple**, honoring the Goddess Taleju Bhawani, a south Indian

mari
ndidate
d
ends.

deity brought to Nepal in the 14th century. Everything here is gilded and particularly resplendent at sunset. The walled precinct is off limits to all but the king and certain priests except during special festivals, when Hindus are allowed access. Legend has it that the temple, restored in 1562 by the Malla kings, was a site for human sacrifices.

In the northwestern corner of the Durbar Square is the site of the original *Kot*, or amory, where the court massacre which secured Rana supremacy in 1846 took place.

From here, technically the end of the Durbar Square, you can stroll through the bazaar down **Makhan Tole** into **Indra Chowk** and **Asan Tole**.

Explore the tiny side streets and crumbling courtyards and appreciate what is left. So many are being replaced by ugly brick and concrete structures and the classical centers of commerce are being polluted by hooting rickshaws and roaring motorbikes.

If you wind your way far enough through the streets of the bazaar, you come to trendy **Thamel**, an area more easily reached from the new Royal Palace.

Recently replacing Freak Street as the home of world travelers and so-called hippies, Thamel is a welter of guest houses, restaurants and tourist shops. Spreading all the way to Chhettrapati, this is "where the action is," and certainly the center of evening activity.

Eyes of the Buddha: Atop a green hillock west of Kathmandu, at a point where the legendary patriarch Manjushri discovered the lotus of the ancient valley lake, stands the great *stupa* of **Swayambhunath**.

Although its origins are obscure, there must have been a monument here well before the advent of Buddhism. An inscription dated 460 A.D. confirms construction work on the sacred site and, certainly by 1234, Swayambhunath was an important center of Buddhist learning.

Three hundred flagstone steps lead to the terrace on which the *stupa* sits. Buddha's eyes are painted on all four sides of this ancient structure, gazing compassionately from beneath heavy eyebrows.

Swayambhunath is a model *stupa*, adhering to specific construction rules. Each segment has a symbolic meaning, from the dazzling white mound representing the four elements of earth, fire, air and water through the 13 gilded rings on the spire, representing the 13 degrees of knowledge and the climb to *nirvana*, which is symbolized by the umbrella on top.

Two views of the Swayambhunath.

Around the *stupa* runs a row of prayer wheels, each turned by the faithful during their clockwise circumambulation. Images of the goddesses Ganga and Jamuna, masterpieces of Newari bronze art, are in a temple behind the *stupa*. Continuing the circumambulation, you encounter a *gompa* (monastery). The *stupa* is especially exciting to visit at festival times when a sea of people overwhelms the hill, making offerings and enjoying picnics under the trees.

A delightful legend relates how Manjushri had his hair cut at Swayambhunath, each hair subsequently becoming a tree and the lice becoming monkeys who are today so profuse that Swayambhunath is sometimes irreverently referred to as the "monkey temple."

At the foot of the hill, many more *gompas* are being built in triumphant shades of red, white and black, testifying to the ever-expanding interest in Buddhism.

Patan of the Golden Roofs: The city of **Patan** is located on a high plateau above the course of the Bagmati River just south of Kathmandu. Sometimes called the "town with a thousand golden roofs," it was formerly known as Lalitpur, "the beautiful city."

Patan was built in concentric circles around its royal palace. Four main roads radiate from the palace to four directional *stupas*, earth and brick mounds which can still be found today. They were supposedly erected by Emperor Asoka and date back to at least the fifth century.

The city's great building period took place under the Mallas, particularly from the 16th century to the 18th century. With no fewer than 136 classified *bahals* (two-storey Buddhist monastery) and 55 major multi-roofed temples, Patan is really the cradle of arts and architecture of the valley, a great center both of the Newari Buddhist religion and of traditional arts and crafts.

The making of these can be seen in the **Patan Industrial Center** where local craftsmen are gathered. For those interested in carpet making, be sure to visit the **Tibetan Camp** in the north of the city where there are daily demonstrations of carpet weaving. Around the **Tibetan Center** are many private shops selling carpets.

The **Durbar Square** and **Royal Palace** complexes are an oblong space constituting perhaps the most spectacular example of Newari architecture at any urban context. Look north (right of the palace) to experience one of the greatest townscapes in Asia.

The palace consists of three main *chowks*

(courtyards). The central **Mol Chowk**, built in 1666, is the oldest. The smallest southern courtyard, the **Sundari Chowk** holds in its center a masterpiece of stone architecture, the sunken royal bath called **Tusha Hiti**. The walls of the bath, created around 1670, are decorated with a double row of statuettes, though sadly, many are missing. Two wriggling *nagas* (snakes) girdle the top of the basin into which water flows— through a conch-shaped stone spout covered with gilded metal. The surrounding three-storey buildings are decorated with wood carvings and windows of gilded metal and carved ivory.

Shiva and Parvati crown the much-admired "Golden Gate" gilded doorway leading to the third courtyard, the **Mani Keshab Narayan Chowk**. Completed in 1734 after 60 years of construction, it is currently undergoing restoration.

Temples and Traders: Facing the Sundari Chowk is a large octagonal **Krishna temple**, a stone *shikara*-style building. King Siddhi Narsingh is immediately to the north, praying on top of his pillar. The *shikara* behind him dates from 1590 and beside him, beyond the small **Narayan Temple**, is probably the oldest surviving temple in the square, built in 1565 for the god Char Narayan.

Facing the northern *chowk* of the palace is the **Krishna Mandir**, probably the rarest, most remarkable stone building ever raised in the valley. It is currently undergoing restoration by the Nepal Heritage Society. Completed in 1637, it portrays influence of Mughal architecture from India.

Ending the long row of temples is the **Bhimsen Mandir**, dedicated to the god of traders. This three-roofed brick building, with artificial marble facade from Rana times, was erected in the late-17th century.

At the corner of the northern *chowk* of the palace, the lotus-shaped, deeply recessed **Manga Hiti** has three beautifully carved water spouts in the shape of crocodile heads.

There are countless temples to explore in the back streets of Patan, off the main Durbar Square. Notable is **Mahapaudha** or the "Temple of the Thousand Buddhas," a tall structure entirely covered by terra-cotta plaques, now sadly dominated by surrounding buildings.

The temple, intended to be a copy of the Mahabodhi Temple at Bodh Gaya in India, was built at the end of the 16th century in *shikara* style. It was renovated after the 1934 earthquake.

Farther north is the marvelous "Golden

Activity centers of Patan's Durbar Square.

Temple," more properly known as **Kwa Bahal** or Hirana Varna Mahavir. This Buddhist monastery is a large, rectangular building with three roofs and a facade richly embossed with gilded copper. Guarded by a pair of temple lions, the main shrine is lavishly embellished with silver, gold and early bronze images, many with a strong Hindu influence. This is an ancient sanctuary. Legend connects its origin with a 12th-century queen and the earliest records date to 1409.

West is the **Rato Macchendranath Temple**, home of Macchendras, a popular tantric expression of the god Avalokiteshwara. He is also venerated as Shiva by Hindus. He is worshipped by all as a god of rain and plenty and inhabits the towering Macchendra chariot during the annual festival, Patan's biggest annual festival.

The Rato Macchendranath Temple structure dates from 1673 but a temple existed as early as the 15th century on the same site.

Big Bodhnath: The largest *stupa* in all of Nepal is **Bodhnath**. Sitting on flat land as a crown above pastel-painted facades of shops and houses, it is directly opposite Swayambhunath from the orientation of the old Royal Palace.

Bodhnath's great size and huge red, white and blue painted eyes are even more remarkable and striking than Swayambhunath's. The *stupa* combines planes and surfaces in a manner that can only be called simple, even austere, but with powerful effect. Built on concentric, gradually ascending terraces, with the overall pattern of a mandala, prayer wheels surround the base.

Worshipped by Tibetan Buddhists, this *stupa* has always been closely linked with Lhasa. It is thriving today, with new monasteries, private houses, shops, lodges and carpet factories all forming a recently established new township.

The Tibetan New Year festival, *Losar*, normally in February, attracts people from far and wide to watch *lamas* perform year-opening rites. The cold months in the high mountains are a good time to make a pilgrimage to Bodhnath when Buddhists from the northern regions of Nepal and India, Tibet, Ladakh, Sikkim, and Bhutan can be seen in their colorful traditional dress heavily adorned with coral and turquoise jewelry. The *stupa* is newly decorated with multi-colored prayer flags stamped with Tibetan *mantras*. Blessed with fragrant juniper incense, each breath of wind achieves a prayer. Magenta-robed *lamas*

blow great copper horns. At the climax of the prayers, all throw fistfuls of *tsampa* (ground barley) into the air.

The shops surrounding the *stupa* remain a good place for antique and curio shopping. Bodhnath is now the focus of Tibetans living in Nepal and has become a center of Buddhist learning.

Shiva Shrine: Pashupatinath is the great temple dedicated to Shiva, the Destroyer and Creator, and is one of the four most important pilgrimage sites in Asia for devotees. Shiva appears in many incarnations and, together with his popular and helpful son Ganesh, the elephant-headed god, he is one of the most awesome and revered gods in the Kathmandu Valley.

Of the many temples in the valley dedicated to Shiva in his various forms, none is more important than Pashupatinath. Throughout the year Pashupatinath is alive with the activities of the devout, bathing, making offerings or cremating their dead. Religious fervor reaches a crescendo in February and March, when thousands gather to celebrate *Mahashivaratri*, the birthday of Lord Shiva.

The sacred temple precinct is forbidden to non-Hindus, but from outside you can glimpse pigeons swarming on a huge sculp-

ture of Nandi the Bull—vehicle of Shiva and an ancient symbol of fecundity. This large, gilded, triple-roofed temple, built in 1696, can best be viewed from the wooded hill opposite, across one of the two stone bridges that span the sacred **Bagmati River.**

Before the bridge to your left are the *ghats* reserved for the cremation of the members of the royal family. The *ghats* to the right are for commoners, but only orthodox Hindus may be cremated at Pashupatinath.

Dharmasalas (rest houses) line the river, providing shelter for the many pilgrims who come to cleanse themselves in the holy water or to tend to their dying family members. The main square in front of the temple is shared—holy cows, street vendors and peddlars add to the busy atmosphere of the place.

Note the smaller temples in the complex with erotic carvings and colorful tantric paintings on the roof struts. Small shrines cluster the other side of the river, former sites of caves for meditating *sadhus* (holy men).

City of Devotees: **Bhaktapur**, also known as Bhadgaon, is said to have been designed in the shape of Vishnu's conch by its Malla founder in the ninth century. The capital of the Kathmandu Valley between

Perform religiou rites at Bodhna stupa.

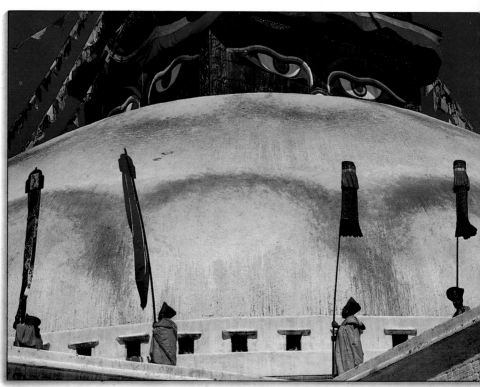

the 14th century and the 16th century, Bhaktapur has best preserved its character and identity, perhaps because of its position—a half-hour drive northeast from Kathmandu.

Bhaktapur is the most self-contained and self-sufficient of the valley's major settlements. Its farmers provide the city with food and the city's craftsmen build and decorate its houses, make its pottery and adorn its temples. The original traditions have been retained here and are typified in the red-edged black *sari*-like dresses (*patasi*), worn by the women of Bhaktapur.

Those who arrive by road, begin in the **Durbar Square**. Created by King Bhupatindra Malla at the beginning of the 17th century, Bhaktapur Durbar Square is more empty than its Patan and Kathmandu counterparts, due to considerable damage caused by the 1934 earthquake. Early prints and etchings show Bhaktapur Durbar Square over-crowded with highly decorated buildings.

One of the most precious masterpieces of art in the valley is preserved here, the **Sun Dhoka** or Golden Gate, leading to the **Taleju Chowk** and the **Kumari Chowk**. Erected in 1753, it is a monument to the skill of the craftsmen who produced it. The gilded copper gate is skilfully carved and masterfully decorated with many divinities.

From the Golden Gate, you can see what remains of the former Royal Palace. The restored earthquake-damaged palace to the left now houses the **National Art Gallery**.

Although the Taleju Chowk, Kumari Chowk and Sundari Chowk, the ritual bathing courtyard of the Bhaktapur king, are forbidden to non-Hindus, you can catch a glimpse of these superb courtyards through the doorways.

Returning to the Durbar Square, past the life-sized gilded statue of Bhupatindra Malla seated on a tall stone pillar, you can see a fine stone *shikara* dedicated to Durga. Note the big stone 18th-century bell used to call the faithful to prayer at the Taleju shrine and pause at the two-roofed shrine known as the **Pashupati Temple**. It is one of the oldest temples in the valley, dating from the end of the 15th century.

Take **Taumadi Tole**, Bhaktapur's famous small street lined with shops selling *thangkas*. This leads to the lower **Taumadi Square**, dominated by the famous **Nyatapola Temple**, Nepal's tallest, standing more than 98 feet (30 meters) high. Carved wooden columns support five roofs and form a balcony around the sanctum. The

shupati-
h, the
at Shiva
ple.

temple is balanced superbly upon five receding square plinths. A steep central stairway is flanked by huge guardians on each of the plinths, each pair believed to have 10 times the strength of the pair on the plinth immediately above them. Power culminates in the Nyatapola's main deity, Siddhi Lakshmi, a mysterious tantric goddess to whom the temple was dedicated in 1702. Exactly 108 colorfully painted wooden struts show the goddess in her manifold forms.

At right angles to the Nyatapola in the Tamaudi Square is the **Kasi Bishwanath Temple**, dedicated to Bhairav. This three-tiered structure was completely rebuilt after 1934, using many parts of the previous temple, but it is again in need of restoration. This massive building is a perfect architectural foil to the spire-like, vertical Nyatapola. Both temples show the Nepalese version of the balance of terror: the Tantric goddess in her sacred shrine is counterbalanced by the awesome powers of Bhairav, to whom this temple is dedicated.

Paradoxically, the image of Bhairav, which is taken out for chariot processions across town during the Bisket festival, is hardly a foot high. It usually rests in a niche about one meter from the ground. A hori-

zontal brass ledge cuts the central door in two; above it is a small hole through which offerings are thrust into the temple's mysterious inner space.

The real entrance to the Kasi Bishwanath is from behind, through the small Betal Temple. Betal, enshrined as a human figure in metal, accompanies Bhairav on all his journeys in Bhaktapur.

The pottery market of Bhaktapur, where thousands of pots dry in the open square surrounded by the whirling potters' wheels, is a fascinating place to visit. As the men make pottery, their women pound grain and children swarm around. The back streets of Bhaktapur provides endless diversions for the wandering visitor.

From the pottery bazaar, the nearest lane south goes straight to the **Hanumante River**. Here is **Ram Ghat**, one of the bathing and cremation places serving the western part of the city. The lane across the river leads to the **Surjaya Binayak Shrine**.

Make your way to the oldest square on the original site of Bhaktapur, the **Dattatraya Square**. The **Dattatraya Temple**, tall and square, faces the rectangular and squat **Bhimsen Temple**, built in 1605 from across the whole length of the square.

The Dattatraya Temple is probably the

A Hindu
mendica

136

earliest structure on this site, dating from 1727. It is the only temple in the valley dedicated to Dattatraya, a deity who is considered to be an incarnation of Vishnu. Devotees of Shiva venerate him as Shiva's teacher and local Buddhists, who consider Dattatraya to be a cousin of the Buddha, also offer gifts to the deity at the temple.

The Dattatraya Temple is reminiscent of the Kasthamandap in Kathmandu and, like it, must have served as a community hall for local citizens. Later, a front section was added, accounting for its rather unusual form. Guarding the entrance are the same Malla wrestlers found at the base of the Nyatapola Temple and erotic scenes are carved around the base of the temple.

Today, the West German Bhaktapur Development Project headquarters and museum is housed in the **Pujari Math**. Built in 1763, this priest's house was so renowned that until this century the government of Tibet annually sent a caravan laden with gifts. Note the excellent woodwork.

Behind the Dattatraya Temple, down a side alley, is the famed **peacock window.** Acclaimed as the Mona Lisa of Nepal's art, there are nevertheless many wood carvings of similar quality.

Many temples and courtyards wait to be discovered in the brick-paved lanes of ancient Bhaktapur. Relatively isolated from the rest of the valley and carefully restored, this is the pulse of old Nepal.

Valley Settlements and Shrines: Of the wealth of shrines and settlements to be visited in the valley, too numerous to be described here, the fourth city of **Kirtipur** must be mentioned. Perched on a ridge southwest of Kathmandu, Kirtipur was first established as an outpost to Patan in the 12th century. It later became an independent kingdom and the last stronghold of the Mallas, falling only after a prolonged seige, to King Prithvi Narayan Shah. The Malla soldiers held out with such persistence against the invaders that, when conquered, the vengeful Gurkha ruler had the noses and lips of all Kirtipur's male inhabitants cut off. A certain atmosphere of fortified isolation remains among the Kirtipur people to this day.

Although seldom visited, Kirtipur has a number of remarkable temples including the **Kyath** on top of the northern hill, which commands a wonderful view of the valley. Visit also the **Chilanchu Vihar**, a central *stupa* surrounded by eight small shrines and several Buddhist monasteries. Where the two hills of Kirtipur meet, north of the

central tank, stands the famous **Bagh Bhairav Temple**, a place of worship for Hindus and Buddhists alike. It contains an image of Bhairav in his tiger form.

Besides farming, traditional occupations of Kirtipur are spinning and weaving and the handloom cloth of the people of Kirtipur is supplied to Kathmandu.

The most spectacular, open religious worship performed in the valley takes place where the main road south ends, some 13 miles (20 km) south, past the narrow gorge of Chobar, now dominated and perpetually polluted by a cement factory. Beyond the village of **Pharping** is the **Dakshinkali Shrine**, set at the base of a wooded hill.

Sacrifices at the pit of Kali are performed here twice a week, and also during the annual festival of *Dasain*, when the image of Kali literally runs with blood. Pilgrims and tourists flock to witness the slicing of throats and severing of the male animals' heads to placate the fearsome goddess Kali. Legends say that Kali herself commanded a 14th-century Malla king to build her a shrine at this site.

On the way home, stop at the **Gorakhnath Cave**. Marked by prayer flags, the cave commands a fine view of Tibet. Here, an ancient sage is said to have meditated so long that he grew into the rock, forming a hollow in the roof of the cave.

Designated as one of the seven valley sites of world importance by the World Heritage Society, **Changu Narayan** is built on a hilltop some 7.5 miles (12 km) east of Kathmandu, accessible by a road from Bhaktapur or by a steep walk up from the Sankhu road.

Rebuilt after a fire destroyed it in 1702, the origins of Changu Narayan go back to the fourth century. There is also an inscribed stone pillar dated 467 A.D.

Dedicated to Vishnu in his form as Narayan, this temple complex is literally scattered with many of the priceless sculptures and treasures of the Licchavi age.

Apart from the various early Vishnu and Garuda images, note the graceful statues of Bhupatindra Malla and his queen in a gilded cage facing the highly decorated entrance to the shrine.

Valley Forests and Views: Other than temples, palaces and cities, there are a number of valley sites of natural beauty that have been developed for visitors.

Beyond Bodhnath and Jorpati on the Sankhu road, just across the newly constructed bridge, is the entrance to the **Royal Forest of Gokarna**. Pony and elephant rides are among the attractions of this forested park where the *chital* or spotted deer can easily be seen. A favorite weekend picnic spot, Gokarna boasts a small golf course and a restaurant.

For the cultural minded, don't miss the **Gokarna Mahadev Temple** on the banks of the Bagmati, a majestic ochre-colored three-roofed building dedicated to Shiva which has recently been restored with American funds.

As might be expected, the rim of the valley provides spectacular views and a number of places have been developed to enjoy these.

Most historic is **Kakani**, on the road north to **Trisuli**, where from the 19th century, the British envoy has been permitted to own a cottage.

Nagarkot at sunrise is a favorite spot for visitors who, with some luck and imagination, can see Mount Everest. Certainly the view in all directions is worth the drive.

For those prepared to go a little farther afield, continue past Bhaktapur on the road to Kodari, the Chinese/Tibet border. About an hour from Kathmandu is the mountain village of **Dhulikhel** and a little beyond, the **Dhulikhel Mountain Resort**, an ideal place to lunch, stay the night or pause en route to Tibet.

Cultivate foothills the Himalay

MOUNT EVEREST: THE HONOR LIST

Although all the world may not know Nepal, there are few who have not heard of Mount Everest, at 29,028 feet (8,848 meters) above sea level, the highest peak in the world. Everest dominates the Khumbu region of East Nepal and is the tallest of the eight of the world's 10 highest mountains that fall within Nepal. Marking the border with Tibet, the frontier actually runs across the summit of the mountain.

Named after a British Surveyor-General in late-19th century India, Sir George Everest, the Nepalese know the massive rocky peak as *Sagarmatha*.

The first attempt to climb the mountain was made in 1922 by Britons from the Tibet side. Seven Sherpas from India died in an avalanche, the first recorded fatalities on Everest. It was not until 1953 that Edmund Hillary, the New Zealander and Tenzing Norgay, a Sherpa from India, became the first mountaineers to reach the summit, climbing by the southeast ridge.

Perhaps the greatest achievement on Everest since it was first climbed was in 1978 when Italian mountaineer Reinhold Messner and his Austrian partner Peter Habeler proved that humans could survive at such a high altitude without artificial oxygen. Other men have since duplicated this feat and Messner himself repeated it in 1980 when he soloed Everest—with no oxygen, no companions, no fixed camps, no ropes or any other mountaineering aids.

The approach to climbing Everest followed the pattern of climbing in the European Alps a century earlier. Man first succeeded in scaling the mountain by its easier approaches and then went on to attempt increasingly difficult methods and in colder, windier seasons. In 1963 two Americans, Willi Unsoeld and Tom Hornbein, became the first climbers to ascend by one route (the west ridge and the north face) and descend by another (the southeast ridge). In 1975, Mrs. Junko Tabei of Japan became the first woman to reach the summit. In 1979 a West German expedition led by Gerhard Schmatz was the first to send all of its members to the summit.

Permission to climb Everest from Nepal is granted by His Majesty's Government of Nepal, with the most popular seasons being the spring and fall. In 1980, Leszek Cichy and Krzysztof Wielcki of Poland made the first winter ascent in February, braving the bitter winds and violent storms. In 1982 Yasuo Kato of Japan became the first person to reach the summit in three different seasons (spring, autumn and winter) though he died in a storm on his descent.

Despite advances in equipment, skills and technical knowledge, the chances of being killed attempting to climb Everest are still high. Most deaths are caused by avalanches, rocks or ice pinnacles falling on climbers, though some are killed in falls on the more difficult routes. Not surprisingly, Everest has claimed more lives than any other mountain in Nepal. As of June 1987, 57 lives had been lost on Nepal's side of the mountain alone. But Everest has also attracted by far the largest number of expeditions in the Himalayas— only 2.1 percent of all climbers perished on the mountain between spring 1971 and June 1987.

While mountaineering exploits are the stuff legends are built from, the best known, and still unexplainable myth, concerns a shaggy-haried wild beast of the snows. It is on the slopes of Mount Everest that the legendary *yeti*, or "abominable snowman," is believed to live. Whether fact of fiction, it is certain that the towering majesty of the highest mountain on earth will continue to work its magic on all who behold it.

BEYOND THE
VALLEY

Although 80 percent of visitors do not venture beyond the Kathmandu Valley, this is precisely where the true Nepal waits to be discovered. Whether trekking along ancient mountain trade routes through the Himalayan foothills, or enjoying river running on some of Nepal's great rivers, this is the ideal place for the person who enjoys camping and the outdoors.

There are a limited number of destinations with facilities accessible to visitors. The popular golden triangle of Kathmandu, Pokhara and Tiger Tops has now been extended to include a lodge in **Royal Bardia Reserve** in the far west and facilities at Lumbini, the birthplace of Buddha. Other than some modest lodges on the main trekking routes and on the road to the Tibet border, Nepal remains largely undeveloped.

Beyond the valley the monsoons from mid-June to mid-September close down many operations and make travel difficult, so the winter months are best to explore the great cross-section of climates, wildlife, peoples and cultures that the kingdom has to offer.

Shadow of the Fishtail: One hundred and twenty miles (200 km) west of Kathmandu, nestled in a valley beneath the Annapurna massif, the town of **Pokhara** has quietly won the hearts of travelers from around the world. Many visitors' most lasting impression of Nepal is not of the temples and palaces of the Kathmandu Valley but of the awesome "fishtail" peak of majestic **Macchapucchare** reflected in the still waters of Pokhara's **Phewa Lake**.

Second only to Kathmandu as a visitors' destination, Pokhara is virtually in the geographical center of Nepal. Until three decades ago, Pokhara was a small trading town of Newari and Gurung brick and tile shops catering to the mule caravans from Mustang and heavily laden porters from Butwal who congregated to exchange goods. The growth of tourism can be felt dramatically here where the unstructured town, strung out for several miles along the main road, gives a general impression of a recent, hasty and unplanned expansion. There is no other place in the world from which the great Himalayan peaks can be admired from so close. **Annapurna I** (26,700 feet/8,091 meters) and its panoply of peaks lie only 31 miles (50 km) away. Macchapucchare

142

(23,080 feet/6,994 meters) shoots straight up, without a single intervening ridge between it and Pokhara, 19 miles (30 km) distant.

The valley of Pokhara itself lies at about 3,000 feet (900 meters), significantly lower than Kathmandu, with a subtropical climate and heavy monsoon rainfall annually. The land is lush with vegetation, citrus trees, bananas, cacti, rice and mustard fields.

This is the contact point of two cultures, the Hindu groups from the Terai plains and the mountain people from the flanks of Annapurna. The ochre, thatch-roof houses of the former and the white slate-roof homes of the latter add variety to the landscape.

The sleepy life and the spectacular views have attracted many of the former denizens of Kathmandu's Freak Street to the series of unpretentious lodges and restaurants that border Phewa Lake. Above all, Pokhara is an ideal start point for treks and expeditions into the spectacular Annapurna region.

Birthplace of the Buddha: Once uninhabitable because of widespread malaria, the Terai is now the fastest growing area of Nepal with people from the hills mingling with the immigrating Indians from the south. Here, at the edge of the vast Ganges plain, the alluvial soil is rich and bountiful. This is the "bread basket" of Nepal where in some areas, farmers manage up to three crops a year.

Thirteen miles (20 km) west of **Bhairahawa**, a substantial Terai town, is **Lumbini**, where the Gautama Buddha was born over 2,500 years ago.

Located some 155 miles (250 km) west of Kathmandu, Lumbini lies on the plains of former Kapilvastu. In the sixth century B.C., when the Buddha lived, a confederacy of Sakya clan people was situated here. There are numerous buildings of religious significance in Lumbini, the most important of which is a massive stone pillar erected by the Mauryan emperor Asoka in 250 B.C. It was discovered only in 1895.

Nearby is the shrine of **Mayadevi**, which has been recently restored. Said to be located in the exact spot in a palace garden where the Buddha was born, it contains a stone relief depicting the story of the Buddha's birth. There is also a rectangular pond, said to be the remains of a sacred pool; the brick foundations of a ruined monastery; some small votive *stupas*; and several large plinths. In the area are modern Buddhist shrines and an older Tibetan *gompa*.

About 17 miles (27 km) west of Lumbini is **Tilaurakot**, which archaeologists have

e
napurna
ge as
en from
khara.

established as the actual capital of ancient Kapilvastu and the home of King Suddhodhan, father of the Buddha.

Tigers and Tharus: Today, the government of Nepal administers six national parks and five wildlife reserves, to protect the dwindling species threatened by increased population and cultivation. The national parks have been selected to represent the three principal zones of terrain, trans-Himalayan, Himalayan and tropical. It is interesting to note that although the country contains only a fraction of 1 percent of the earth's land mass, about 10 percent of the planet's birds (roughly 800 species) can be found in Nepal.

The preserves of the Terai constitute by far the richest wildlife zone of Nepal and indeed one of the best natural areas in Asia. Once the private hunting grounds of Nepal's ruling families and their guests, these areas were the sites of rhinoceros and tiger hunts, organized every few years, with hundreds of royal elephants bearing the royalty of Europe and India.

Nepal's best known and most accessible national park, **Royal Chitwan National Park**, was also its first. Established in 1962 by the late King Mahendra as a rhinoceros reserve, and officially gazetted in 1973 to enforce laws against poaching, it is in the **Rapti Valley** about 75 miles (120 km) southwest of Kathmandu. Covering an area of 360 square miles (932 square km), Chitwan is largely flood plain jungle and elephant grass at an elevation of about 500 feet (150 meters) above sea level with *sal* and mixed riverine forest on the higher ground.

In the heart of the Royal Chitwan National Park is the famous **Tiger Tops Jungle Lodge**, where elephants greet those who fly into Meghauly airstrip, carrying them to their treetop accommodation. Trained naturalists take visitors on safaris by foot, elephant, landrover or boat to search for rhinos, tigers, crocodiles and the colorful, rich birdlife.

The Royal Bengal tiger and the One-horned rhinoceros are both endangered species. It is estimated that the tiger population of the entire Indian subcontinent has, over the past 50 years, dwindled from 40,000 to a little over 2,000. About 200 tigers live in Nepal and of these, about 40 are within the precincts of Royal Chitwan National Park.

The tiger by nature is a solitary, shy animal which hunts by night. By day it hides in thick undergrowth to avoid disturbance.

A privileged sight: one horned rhino and calf.

Tiger Tops visitors, if fortunate, may spot one of these big cats in the dawn or twilight hours.

There are some 1,000 Great One-horned rhinoceros left in existence, most of them in India and Assam. An estimated 360 are resident in Royal Chitwan's tall grass swamplands.

Another endangered animal is the gharial, a rare fish-eating crocodile. A breeding center has been established near the park's headquarters at **Kasra** to ensure its survival. Other animals in the Royal Chitwan National Park that visitors are likely to see include leopards, gaur, sloth bear, wildboar, various species of deer and marsh mugger crocodiles. There are two species of monkeys, and river dwellers include the Gangetic dolphin. More than 450 species of birds have been identified, making Chitwan a paradise for birdwatchers.

Tiger Tops is a half-hour flight or five-hour drive from Kathmandu. Alternatively, it is a three-day trip by river through the Himalayan foothills. In addition to the Lodge, accommodation includes, for those more culturally inclined, a comfortable Tented Camp on an island in the **Narayani River** and the **Tharu Village**, an indigenous-style longhouse on the edge of the

national park.

At the western end of Royal Chitwan National Park, accessible by a five-hour drive from Kathmandu via the Terai town of Bharatpur, is another major entrance to the Royal Chitwan National Park, **Saurah**. The best known lodges and camps are **Gaida Wildlife Camp**, **Hotel Elephant Camp**, **Chitwan Jungle Lodge**, **Jungle Safari Camp** and **Machan Wildlife Resort**.

Wild West: In the remote far west, five hours drive from Nepalgunj, is **Karnali Tented Camp** and the **Karnali Lodge** in the undisturbed **Royal Bardia Reserve**.

Comprising 378 square miles (983 square km) of riverine terrain and short grassland areas, many species of mammals thrive here, including Nepal's second-largest tiger population and the rare swamp deer, black buck and wild elephant as well as a large variety of birds.

The reserve is at the foot of the *sal*-forested **Siwalik Hills** where the great **Karnali River** and its less turbulent tributary, the **Babai**, spill out from the mountain gorges onto the rich alluvial plain.

In addition to wildlife viewing and visiting the local Tharu villages, visitors can fish for mahseer, the great golden sporting fish of the subcontinent.

iger Tops
s home
ase for
hese
vildlife
eekers.

OUTDOORS

Taking the High Road: Astride the long frontier between Nepal and Tibet lies the greatest concentration of high mountains on earth. Considered the consummate climbing challenge, the peaks of such giants as Mount Everest, Annapurna, Dhaulagiri, Makalu and Cho Oyu have long stirred the imagination of travelers and adventurers.

Fascinating glimpses of these wild regions are accessible to those willing to exert a little extra physical energy. One of the great charms of Nepal, they are still largely without roads. Access to its interior, its villages and valleys, its mountains and hills, is by ancient foot trails and trade routes, interlaced across the country.

An increasing number of visitors to Nepal walk or trek. Trekking allows you to discover many new horizons, the haunting beauty of Himalayan reaches and the peculiar warmth of the mountain people.

Trekking in Nepal was established in 1965 when a British citizen named Jimmy Roberts, a veteran of numerous Himalayan expeditions, founded Nepal's first trekking agency, Mountain Travel. In doing so, he created an industry which has benefited the mountain people and has since grown to become one of Nepal's major foreign exchange earners. Today there are dozens of trekking agencies in Nepal. In many villages, lodges and tea houses provide accommodation for those wishing to explore on their own.

All treks require a permit, which is valid for one specific route. Permits can be obtained from the Central Immigration Department in Kathmandu or Pokhara, or from your trekking agent. Although 20,000 to 30,000 people trek every year, trekking should not be taken lightly, and advice and books on the subject should be studied. Treks can last from a few days to a few weeks and it is important to set out well-equipped.

There are three principal regions of interest to the trekker: The West, starting from Pokhara and the Annapurna massif, or venture farther to Jumla or Lake RaRa; the spectacular Langtang Valley and Helambu north of Kathmandu; and the best known of all, the Khumbu of east Nepal, homeland of the Sherpa people, in the shadow of Mount Everest.

Pokhara and the West: Starting at

Magar tribesmen lounge in front of Manaslu and Ganesh Himal.

Pokhara, a five-hour drive or a half-hour flight twice daily from Kathmandu, there are a wide choice of trails in the serene and beautiful Annapurnas.

Routes ranging from just a few days, take the trekker through rhododendron and oak forests above the lakes and ridges of the Pokhara Valley to **Siklis** in the **Madi Valley** or to **Ghandrung**, a beautiful Gurung village in the **Modi Valley**. For those with more time, trek up the spectacular **Kali Gandaki Valley**, pausing at **Pun Hill** above **Ghorepani** to see one of the great views of the Himalayas.

The best of all possible routes in this region is the **Around Annapurna** walk. Requiring at least 20 days, this is considered a classic trek. It offers some of the most breathtaking high Himalayan scenery and at the same time gives the traveler a cross-section of Nepali culture.

The Around Annapurna trip can begin or end in Pokhara, though most trekkers choose to start their walk from **Dumre**, a village midway between Kathmandu and Pokhara on the main road. From there proceed through the **Marsyangdi Valley**, across the high **Thorong La Pass** and back down the famous Kali Gandaki gorge (allegedly the deepest gorge in the world)

which runs between the Annapurna and Dhaulagiri massifs.

Lovely Langtang: Most accessible from Kathmandu is **Langtang**, north of the Kathmandu Valley where the area is dominated by **Langtang Lirung** (23,909 feet/7,245 meters) the highest peak in the area. Start walking at **Dhunche**. The Langtang Valley is located some 19 miles (30 km) directly north of Kathmandu close to the boundary with Tibet. Glaciers spawned by slopes of the Dorje Lhakpa, Lhakpa Lirung and other peaks feed the **Langtang Khola** (river) before emptying in a raging torrent into the **Bhote Kosi**.

In 1976, Langtang became Nepal's second largest national park. It is inhabited mainly by Tibetan-speaking people, thought to have originated across the border from Khirong, an ancient Tibetan fort. Tamangs and Sherpas live in the **Helambu** region, an area easily accessible to those with limited time and spectacular in spring when the rhododendrons are in bloom. The region does not have the enormous peaks of the Everest and Annapurna areas but the mountains between 16,500 feet and 20,000 feet (5,000 meters and 6,000 meters) are wild and beautiful.

Everest and Eastern Nepal: Perhaps

every Nepal visitor dreams of trekking to the foot of the world's highest peak, **Mount Everest** (29,028 feet/8,848 meters), in the **Khumbu** region of east Nepal. Much of the area is now contained within the boundary of **Sagarmatha National Park**, which was established in 1976. The Khumbu region is not only high and beautiful but the scene of much early exploration and mountaineering accomplishments. The exploits and writings of climbers like Eric Shipton, Sir Edmund Hillary, Chris Bonnington and Reinhold Messner have made the Khumbu famous.

As great an attraction as the mountains are the Sherpas. Now best known for their accomplishnents as high altitude porters and mountain guides, the Sherpa people have traditionally been traders, herders and subsistence farmers. They originally came to Nepal from east Tibet.

A deep adherence to the Tibetan Buddhist religion dominates their home lives and their biggest festival, the dance-drama *Mani Rimdu*, depicts the victory of Buddhism over the ancient *Bon* faith.

You can walk into the Khumbu area, starting from the road head at **Jiri**. Follow the old expedition route through the Solu Khumbu. Most visitors take their chances with the weather and take 40-minute flight from Kathmandu to **Lukla** (9,403 feet/ 28,209 meters), perched high above the **Dudh Kosi** river.

The Khumbu is too beautiful and too friendly a place to hurry through. Besides, its high elevation makes it dangerous to trek too high too fast. Attempting to walk from Lukla to the Sherpa capital of **Namche Bazaar** in less than two days is dangerous. Acclimatisation to altitude has nothing to do with physical fitness and trekkers should be aware of the early symptoms of mountain sickness—headache, nausea, sleeplessness, breathlessness, etc.—and heed them by stopping or descending until the symptons disappear.

The trekker can explore up the **Bhote Kosi** towards the monastery at **Thame** or continue up on the main trail to **Kala Pattar** (18,299 feet/5,545 meters) above Everest Base Camp. The Sherpa villages, with their stone-walled fields and flat-roofed houses, are rewarding and hospitable places to explore.

Rest for a day at the great **Thyangboche Monastery**, perched on a high ridge at 12,790 feet (3,876 meters). This is the leading Buddhist center in the Khumbu and its location is one of the most scenic, especially

Trekking in eastern Nepal.

148

in the spring. The *gompa* rests amid stunning views of Everest, **Lhotse** (27,923 feet/ 8,848 meters) and **Ama Dablam** (22,493 feet/6,856 meters).

One attractive side trip is to **Gokyo** in the shadow of **Cho Oyu** (26,748 feet/8,153 meters), with its sacred lake and wild mountain scenery. The more adventurous can explore the wild, rugged **Hongu Basin** or **Rolwaling Valley** and there are a number of "trekking peaks" in the area, the most popular being **Island Peak** above **Pheriche**.

Throughout the Sherpa villages, and especially on the main trail to Everest, there are plenty of Sherpa-run lodges in which to stay. There is a hospital at Kunde, funded by Sir Edmund Hillary's Himalayan Trust, and a Trekkers Aid Post at Pheriche run by the Himalayan Rescue Association.

Running the Rivers: Rising from the glaciers of the highest mountains of the world and from the mysterious plateau of Tibet, the rivers of Nepal plunge through the gorges of the Himalayas and traverse their rugged foothills. Before the melted snows reach the peaceful waters of the holy Ganges, the rivers course through the lush tropical jungles and meander through the plains of the Terai.

The rivers of Nepal take the traveler to the very heart of a magical land: one of the most exciting ways to explore Nepal's ancient cultures and unspoiled landscapes is by boat. In a country of few roads, it is the mighty rivers that penetrate the peoples and villages of the foothills.

On their river journey, travelers pass through a continually changing, rural landscape. And they don't have to invest the time and energy required of long treks. The serenity of cruising the rivers' gentle and tranquil stretches, with the excitement of shooting white water rapids, combines to provide a truly unique experience.

Some rafting trips require you to paddle your own way in inflatable rubber rafts. Others provide you with professional oarsmen. Either way, rafting can be a combination of introspective tranquility and tremendous excitement.

Most popular is the three-day trip on the Trisuli or Seti rivers to Tiger Tops and the Royal Chitwan National Park. For those with more time, the **Sun Kosi** in eastern Nepal offers remote trips in combination with trekking. In the west you can combine river running on the **Bheri River** with mahseer fishing on the Karnali River, ending your four-day trip at the Karnali Tented Camp near **Chisopani**.

Left, saddling up in the Khumbu region and right, in search of white water.

DESTINATION NEPAL

GETTING THERE

By Air: Kathmandu's Tribhuvan International Airport is served by flights from Hong Kong, Bangkok, Singapore, Rangoon, Dhaka, Calcutta, Patna, Colombo, Varanasi, Delhi, Karachi and Dubai, with some direct charters from Europe. Nepal is served by a number of airlines and Royal Nepal Airlines (RNAC) is the national carrier. Most visitors arrive either from Delhi or Bangkok by air, though there are 11 official land entry points along Nepal's border with India and one land entry point by road to Tibet.

Reporting time for international flights is two hours before departure and there is a Rs 150 international departure tax levied at check-in. Be sure to reconfirm your departure flight.

Visas: All passport holders require a visa for Nepal, except for Indian nationals who require an identity card only. A tourist visa can be issued by a Nepalese embassy, and is valid for 30 days. A seven-day visa can be issued on arrival at Kathmandu's airport or at official land entry points for US$10. This can be extended for a full 30-day period at no additional cost. Tourist visas can be extended for up to three months but longer stays require the recommendation of the Home Ministry.

Persons intending to trek must obtain a trekking permit valid for a specific region, from the Immigration Office in Kathmandu or Pokhara.

Health: Certificates of innoculation against cholera and yellow fever are necessary if originating from or transiting an affected area. Checks are random.

Although not compulsory, travelers are advised to get the whole range of injections against typhoid, hepatitis, cholera and tetanus.

Although there is no more danger to health in Nepal than in many other Asian countries, it is easy to get sick here and there are some basic guidelines to follow in order to avoid the many intestinal disorders, known locally as the "Kathmandu Quickstep."

Never drink unboiled and unfiltered water. Avoid eating raw vegetables and peel fruits before eating. Never walk barefoot. Do not trust ice or water anywhere, except in the best hotels. Mineral water is now widely available.

Medication, mostly manufactured in India, is cheap and readily available without prescription in Kathmandu pharmacies. But bring a basic medical kit, especially if trekking is on your itinerary.

Malaria is on the increase, but Kathmandu is too high for the kind of mosquito that carries it. However if you plan to visit lowland areas you should bring malaria pills. Bring mosquito repellant during the warm months. Medical care is not available outside the valley except for the occasional clinic. Within the valley, major hospitals are: Patan Hospital, Jawalakhel, tel: 522286, 522278, 521034, 521048; Tribhuvan University Teaching Hospital, Maharajguni, tel: 412303, 412404, 412505; Bir Hospital, Kantipath, tel: 221119.

Money: The official rate of exchange fluctuates against a basket of currencies. In 1987, the rate was between 21 and 22 Nepalese rupees to US$1. The official exchange rate for all major currencies is published daily in Nepal's newspaper, *The Rising Nepal.*

Import and export of Nepalese rupees is forbidden. Whenever foreign currency is exchanged during the stay, retain the official exchange receipt. You may convert excess rupees into hard currency at the end of your stay, as long as what remains does not exceed 10 percent of the total amount exchanged.

American Express and Visa charge cards are widely accepted in Kathmandu.

Customs: The duty free import of 200 cigarettes, 20 cigars, one bottle of spirits and a dozen cans of beer are permitted.

Also duty free are the following personal effects: a pair of binoculars, a still camera with a reasonable

INSIDE NEPAL

amount of film, an 8 mm movie camera, a video camera for personal use only, a record player with 10 records, a tape recorder with four tapes, a musical instrument, a transistor radio and a fishing rod with accessories.

Controls are quite strict at Tribhuvan airport and customs officials chalk up your luggage before you leave. Special permits are required for 16 mm movie cameras.

GETTING ACQUAINTED

Time: Nepal time is 15 minutes ahead of Indian Standard Time and 5 hours 45 minutes ahead of Greenwich Mean Time. Nepal shares a common border with China but is three hours 15 minutes behind Chinese Standard Time!

There are no less than five different calendars in simultaneous use in Nepal. The official calendar is the *Bikram Samvat* in which day 1 was February 23, 57 B.C. in the Western Gregorian calendar. Also observed is the Tibetan calendar, the *Sakya Era* calendar and the *Newari* calendar.

Climate: Although Nepal enjoys extreme varieties in climates, the Kathmandu Valley knows three distinct but pleasant seasons.

The cold season from October to March is the best time to visit the country. Although nightime temperatures may drop to nearly freezing, the sun warms the atmosphere by day with the temperature climbing from 50 F to 77 F (10 C to 25 C). The sky is generally clear and bright and there is frequently an early morning mist, the result of the rapid heating of the cold night air.

In April, May and early June, the weather becomes hot and stuffy with occasional thunderstorms. Temperatures in Kathmandu can vary between 52 F and 83 F (11 C and 28 C) with a maximum of 97 F (36 C).

By the end of June, the monsoon rains arrive, lasting until mid-September. During this time the Himalayas remain out of sight though the rains create spectacular lighting effects and some flooding. Trekking stops with the proliferation of leeches and the lowland Terai is cut off by swollen rivers and occasional landslides. It is still possible to visit the Kathmandu Valley and this is the best season to visit Tibet.

Pokhara is noticeably warmer than Kathmandu, being 1,000 feet (305 meters) lower, and the Terai warmer still, approximately 4,000 feet (1,200 meters) below Kathmandu Valley.

What to Wear: Your wardrobe will depend on when you are going to Nepal and what you intend to do there. Unless you are planning to meet embassy officials, there is no need to bring anything but the most casual clothes. For winter months, arrange your clothing in layers so you can easily adapt from the cold nights, when you will need a sweater and jacket, to the sunny days when a safari shirt is enough. Comfortable shoes and sneakers are ideal. From April to June, light clothes will suffice. Avoid synthetic fibers which irritate the skin. Do not bother to bring a raincoat as a local umbrella will be more useful against the rain and sun.

Special gear required foor trekking can be hired or bought in Kathmandu or Pokhara. Be sure you are properly equipped for the high, cold mountains.

Electricity: Major towns in Nepal have electricity. The voltage is 220. On festival occasions Kathmandu is ablaze with lights at night, especially during the *Diwali* Festival of Lights. The big hotels have their own generators as power failures are frequent. A small flashlight is useful.

Communications: Although Nepali is the official language in this country of many languages and dialects, English is widely spoken, especially in Kathmandu Valley and beyond, where visitors are familiar.

The Central Post Office is in Kathmandu but it is easier to ask your hotel to handle your mail.

International telex and cable is available though FAX has yet to reach the valley.

International telephone

connections, since the installation of the British earth satellite station in 1982, are excellent. Dial 186 for the international operator. However, telephone connections to other parts of the country remain intermittent and unreliable.

The Rising Nepal is the official English daily newspaper. A number of excellent bookshops throughout Kathmandu sell a wide variety of maps and books on Nepal.

TRANSPORT

Air: There are extensive domestic air connections operated by RNAC, the most popular being Pokhara (twice daily), Meghauly (for Tiger Tops), Nepalgunj (for Karnali Tented Camp), Bhairahawa (for Lumbini) and Lukla (for trekking in the Everest region). Early morning mountain flights to view Mount Everest are operated daily and occasion-

ally, small aircraft can be chartered for rescues or sightseeing. There is a departure tax on domestic flights of the equivalent of Rs 30. Foreigners are required to pay the tax with foreign currency.

Taxis & Hired Cars: From Tribhuvan airport to Kathmandu a taxi ride should not cost more than Rs 40 on the meter. Taxis are small Toyotas which can

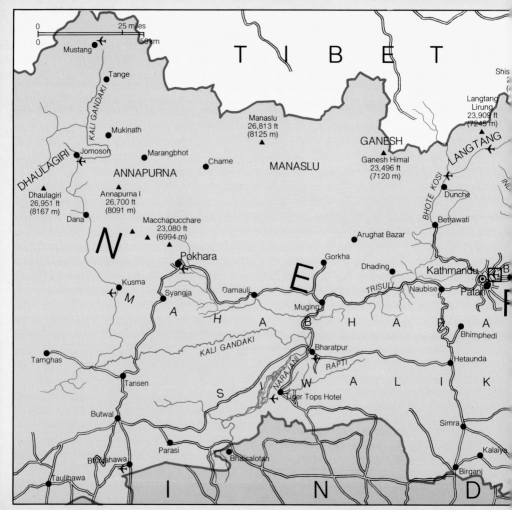

accommodate three passengers though often the driver is assisted by a co-driver occupying the front seat.

Taxis have black registration plates with white numbers while private cars have white numbers on red plates.

Cars can be hired from travel agents at approximately US$50 a day, depending on where you want to go. It is more expensive if you wish to travel to Pokhara, the Chinese border (for onward travel to Tibet), or to Royal Chitwan National Park. Roads are generally not good in Nepal and journeys can be slow but rewarding as the scenery is so spectacular. Beware of occasional landslides.

Buses: All roads are plyed by local bus services with express coaches on the main routes. Fares are extremely cheap. There are mini buses on some of the tourist routes which are less crowded.

Rickshaws & Scooters: Within Kathmandu you will see three-wheeled public scooters cluttering the roads. More fun are the gaudily-painted, honking rickshaws which are an integral part of Kathmandu's street scene. They are large tricycles with two seats in the back covered by a hood with a man pedaling up front. Settle the price before you start, as you may find they cost more than a taxi!

On Foot: Be prepared for a lot of walking as vehicles can only take you so far. Do not hesitate to venture off the beaten track. A leisurely stroll amid the rice and mustard fields of the valley is the best way to absorb its way of life.

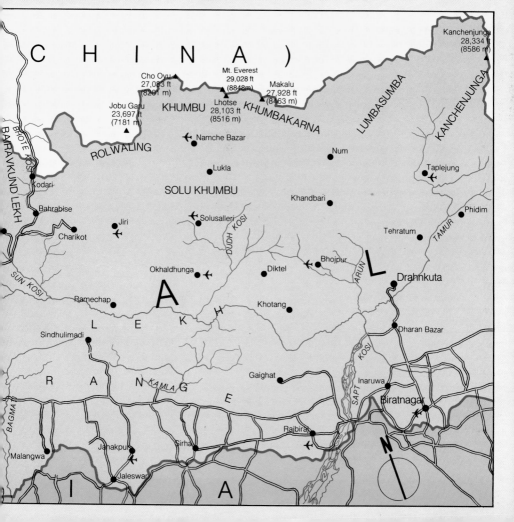

ACTIVITIES

WHAT TO DO

Although Kathmandu lacks a nightlife, there is a casino at the Hotel Soaltee Oberoi and a discotheque at the Everest Sheraton. Some hotels have evening folk dances and cultural shows in their restaurants.

The festivals of the people of the valley provide the best entertainment. Dates, which follow the lunar calendar, vary from year to year, but October and November remain the most colorful festival months. Check with the hotel or your agent when you arrive, as to where festivals might be taking place.

Trekking: See specialist books on this subject. Either you go with a trekking agent, who supplies tents and all camping equipment, or individuals may stay in the lodges and tea houses found on main trails.

Trekking prices vary from tea shops which can cost as little as Rs 50 to trekking with full service trekking agencies for about US$50 per day.

Shopping: Kathmandu is a treasure trove for the uinwary. Children sell *khukris,* belts, coins. Traders appear wherever tourists stray. Merchants wait on temple steps. Junk, guaranteed fake antiques, souvenirs are everywhere. Peer into the shops, take your pick or take your leave; try the next boutique or the next mat. There are good buys to be found here:

—Clothes are certainly good value, from lopsided *topis* (caps) to knitted mittens and woolen socks; from Tibetan dresses that button at the side to men's cotton shirts tied diagonally with ribbons across the chest. *Topis* come in two types: somber black ones and multicolor variations. They are like ties, a must for all Nepalis visiting the administration, but with a difference—their asymmetric shape is said to be a replica of Mount Kailash, the most sacred mountain for Buddhists and Hindus.

—Pieces of Nepalese cloth, red, black and orange, checkered with dots, that women wrap around their shoulders. Shawls are made with the same cotton cloth, but are covered on both sides with thin muslin that gives pastel overtones to the cloth.

—Wool blankets are a typical product of Nepal; made of the finest goat wool called *pashmina*, they are extremely soft, warm and strong.

—Tibetan-style multicolored wool jackets, shoulder bags and boots of geometric design. Most are made in India, and jackets sell for about Rs 100. The "real thing," sewn in the Jawalkhel Tibetan camp, is more expensive.

—Various Nepalese folk objects. Among them are the national knife, the *khukris,* worn at the belt and sometimes highly adorned, and the *saranghi*, a small four-stringed viola cut from a single piece of wood and played with a horse-hair bow by the *gaine* (Nepal's begging minstrels).

—All kinds of copper or brass pots, jugs and jars, sold by their weight (but rather heavy to take home).

—Tibetan tea bowls made of wood and lined with silver on the inside.

—Embossed prayer wheels of all sizes.

—Hand-made paper beautifully tie-dyed by the women of Bhaktapur, or woodblock printed in traditional designs.

—Papier-mache dance masks and terra-cotta elephants used as flower pots, made by the hundreds in Thimi, a village close to Bhaktapur.

—Copper or bronze statuettes of the Buddha and of various Hindu deities, none of them too old. All are produced semi-industrially, together with filigreed brass animals or ashtrays inlaid with small pieces of colored stones, and dreadful copies of erotic sculptures that seem to excite tourists so much.

—Numerous Tibetan trinkets, to be found primarily around Bodhnath but also in Patan and Kathmandu. They include everything from human skuls and leg bones to thankas (painted scrolls). There is silver-plated jewelry inlaid with coral and turquoise (earrings, necklaces, amulets, belt buckles,

IN TRANSIT

plaited silver belts and daggers), as well as bronze mandalas, charm boxes, pieces of furniture and musical instruments.

—Carpets, the production of which is flourishing, with substantial exports and sales to places like Hong Kong and New York. The new ones, made in private homes or refugee centers, are done in bright colors with chemical dyes, or with more subtle (and more expensive) vegetable dyes in traditional Tibetan designs. Older carpets, with intricate motifs and natural dye colors, are still available at higher prices.

—Bamboo flutes are also a good buy and cheap gifts. You will find them in the main streets of old Kathmandu. Hookahs (water pipes) are also tempting, but you might have trouble getting tem past suspicious customs officials.

—Beautiful marriage umbrellas in a variety of designs and colors can be bought in Bhaktapur, but these are for decoration and are not waterproof.

Shopping Tips: Before embarking on a buying spree, remember a few things:

• Genuine prayer wheels are supposed to hold a roll of parchment or paper bearing a *mantra* (prayer formula).

• An authentic *khukri* should have a small notch at the bottom of the blade to divert blod away from the handle. In the back of the scabbard, there should be two small knives for skinning and sharpening.

• Gold jewelry should show a slight tooth mark when bitten.

• A fine sculpture will have the fingers of its subject's hand separately sculpted, not merely outlined. This qualification leaves out about 99 percent of the modern works to be seen in Kathmandu.

• Unless otherwise certified by specialists, consider "antique" pieces to have been made the week before you see them in the shop, and pay the appropriate sum for them. Tibetans and Nepalis will not willingly part with their jewels and adornments; it is impolite to pressure them to sell their personal heirlooms.

Suggested Shops:
Jawalakhel, near Patan, for the best Tibetan carpets, old and new. They are displayed in the Tibetan refugee center and also in many shops in that area.

Cheez Beez Bhandar, "the Nepalese Handicraft Center" near Jawalakhel. This shop has handicrafts from all parts of Nepal.

Tibet Ritual Art Gallery, Durbar Marg, above the Sun Kosi restaurant. Excellent quality antiques and rare art objects are found here.

Patan Industrial Estate, to see woodcarving, metalwork and *thanka* painting. See also the **Bhaktapur Crafts Center** in Dattatraya

Square.

The main shops in Kathmandu for imported articles are in and around New Road. Handicraft shops are centered around Durbar Marg and the big hotels. Remember that old *thankas* and bronzes are forbidden for export if they are more than 100 years old. Certificates of proof are necessary to dispel any doubts.

WHERE TO STAY

Kathmandu

Kathmandu in the last decade has seen the mushrooming of international class hotels. Accommodations range all the way from first class to modest guest houses and lodges, mostly in Thamel district. Below is a list of some hotels and guest houses.

It is advisable to book well in advance as hotels of all types tend to get very full. It is necessary to pay for accommodation in foreign exchange. Prices listed below do not include the 12-to-15 percent government tax (depending on star rating) and 10 percent service charge.

First Class (above $35)

Soaltee Oberoi
Tel: 211211, 211106, telex: 2203, US$70 single US$90 double.

Yak & Yeti
Tel: 412351, 411436, telex:

2237, 110 rooms and two suites, $59 single, $81 double.

Everest Sheraton
Tel: `224960, 220389, telex: 2260, $80 single, $88 double.

Annapurna
Tel: 221711, 221522, telex: 2205, $59 single, $72 double.

Kathmandu Hotel
Tel: 412103, telex: 2256, 120 rooms, $58 single, $71 double.

Himalaya
Tel: 521887, 521888, 100 rooms, three suites, $55 single, $70 double.

Malla
Tel: 410320, 410966, 410968, telex: 2238, 75 rooms, $41 single, $58 double.

Shangrila
Tel: 412999, 410108, telex: 2276, 50 rooms, $44 single, $55 double.

Intermediate (under $35)

Summit
Tel: 521810, 521894, telex: 2342, 30 rooms, $23 single, $38.50 double.

Dwarika's Kathmandu Village
Tel: 414770, 412328, telex: 2239, 19 rooms, $30 single, $40 double.

Narayani
Tel: 521711, 521442, telex: 2262, 88 rooms, $32 single, $45 double.

Crystal
Tel: 223397, 223611, 223636, 55 rooms, $24

single, $33 double.

Vajra
Tel: 224545, 224719, telex: 2309, 40 rooms, $14 single, $17 double.

Budget (Under $15)

Ambassador
Tel: 214432, 410432, telex: 2321, 32 rooms, $15 single, $17 double.

Nook
Tel: 212627, 216247, 24 rooms, $10 single, $16 double.

Kathmandu Guest House
Tel: 216328, 80 rooms, $6 single, $8 double.

Tibet Guest House
Tel: 214383, 215893, 32 rooms, $11 single, $12 double.

Beyond The Valley

Dhulikhel

Dhulikhel Mountain Resort
Tel: (Kathmandu) 411031, 414206, 30 rooms in chalet-style cottages, $30 single, $32 double.

Himalayan Horizon Sun & Snow
Tel: (Kathmandu) 411696, 12 rooms, $20 single, $30 double.

Pokhara

Fish Tail Lodge
Tel: (Pokhara) 71-72, 35 rooms, $27 single, $39 double on full board basis. Situated beside the lake, superb location.

New Crystal Hotel
Tel: (Pokhara) 35-36, 46 rooms, $27 single, $39 double, close to Pokhara air-

port.

Hotel Mount Annapurna
Tel: (Pokhara) 27-37, 64 rooms, $14 single, $21 double.

Dragon
Tel: (Pokhara) 52, midway between the airport and the lake, 20 rooms, $19 single, $28 double.

Up-Country

Tiger Tops Jungle Lodge
Tel: (Kathmandu) 222706, 222958, telex: 2216 TIGTOP NP. Set in the heart of the Royal Chitwan National Park, 20 rooms, $165 per person per day inclusive of full board and wildlife excursions.

Tiger Tops Tented Camp has luxury tented accommodation for 16 people at $100 per person per day. **Tiger Tops Tharu Village** on the edge of the park, with accommodation in the style of traditional Tharu tribal long-houses, 12 rooms, $90 per person per day.

Adjacent to Royal Chitwan National Park at Saurah, accessible by road via Bharatpur from Kathmandu, are several lodges, camps and numerous tea houses. Best known are **Gaida Wildlife Camp, Hotel Elephant Camp, Chitwan Jungle Lodge, Jungle Safari Camp, Machan Wildlife Resort**.

•**Karnali Tented Camp**
A five-hour drive from Nepalgunj airport in the Royal Bardia Wildlife Reserve, accommodation is for 16 people at $110 per person

FOOD DIGEST

per day fully inclusive of meals and excursions.

Lumbini

About one hour's drive from Bhairahawa or three hours from Tiger Tops Tharu Village, the modest **Lumbini Hotel** provides limited accommodation

WHAT TO EAT

Despite centuries of isolation and a variety of vegetables and fruits, Nepal has failed to develop a distinctive style of cooking. An exception is Newari cooking, which can be very elaborate and spicy; but this is found only in private homes. Nepalese dishes are at best variations on Indian regional cuisines.

In most parts of Nepal, including the Kathmandu Valley, rice is the staple food. It is usually eaten boiled, supplemented with *dhal* (lentil soup), vegetables cooked with a few spices (notably ginger, garlic and chillies), and—in times of festivity—plenty of meat. There is a predilection for enormous radishes. Hill people eat *tsampa*—raw grain, ground and mixed with milk, tea or water or eaten dry—as a complement to, or substitute for, rice. *Chapatis* diversify the diet. Some castes eat pork. Goat, chicken and buffalo meat— or in the mountains, yak meat—is available to all, but beef is forbidden in this Hindu kingdom.

The Nepalis enjoy eating sweets and spicy snacks such as *jelebis* and *laddus*. These come in a variety of shapes, and wrappings, not to mention ingredients and tastes. Fruit from the lowlands can also be found in Kathmandu. Transportation costs have pushed prices up, so that fruit is often sold by the unit or even by the quarter-unit for a few rupees.

Buffalo milk is turned into clarified butter (*ghee*) or delicious curd sold in round earthernware pots. Curd is a good buy, but be sure to scrape off the top layer. Dairy products are rare elsewhere in Asia, but fresh milk, butter and cheese are plentiful in Kathmandu. The main dairy is at Balaju. Excellent cheese is available at the Nepal Dairy at Mahabouda, located behind Bir Hospital.

Fresh bread can be found in food shops, and doughnuts are sold in the streets. The Annapurna and Nanglo cake shops (both in Durbar Marg) are good but best of all is The Bakery in Kanti Path.

Certain areas of Nepal have developed regional dishes. The introduction of a potato crop in Sherpa country has revolutionized eating habits there. Sherpas now survive on potatoes, eating them baked or boiled, dipped in salt or chilies. More elaborately, they enjoy *gurr*—raw potatoes peeled, pounded with spices, grilled like large pancakes on a hot flat stone, then eaten with fresh cheese. Tibetan cooking, including *thukpa* (thick soup) and *momos* (fried or boiled stuffed raviolis)—is widespread in the mountains and is also available in many parts of Kathmandu.

Drinks: The national drink, *chiya* (tea brewed together with milk, sugar and sometimes spices), is served in glasses, scalding hot. Up in the mountains, it is salted with yak butter and churned, Tibetan-style. Another popular mountain drink is *chang,* powerful sort of beer made from fermented barley, maize, rye or millet. *Arak* (potato alcohol) and *rakshi* (wheat or rice alcohol) are other popular drinks.

Coca-cola is bottled in the Kathmandu Valley and *Lemu* (a lemon drink), Fanta orange and soda are also available. Restaurants serve good Nepalese beer, Star, Golden Eagle and Iceber, as well as imported brews, while the classiest establishnments in Kathmandu suggest bottles of imported wine at prohibitive prices. Good quality rum, vodka and gin are produced locally. If you are a whisky drinker, though, be warned against the local variety. Imported Scotch whisky is widely available, though expensive.

Where to Eat: Kathmandu restaurants have vastly improved in the last few years. Prices are low by Western standards. Indian, Chinese, Tibetan and even Japanese cuisine is found, as well as a variety of Western menus. The large international hotels have three or four restaurants each, some of them excellent. New restaurants keep opening while others disappear from one season to the next. Hygiene is not always a priority in the smaller establishments, so keep our health tips in mind.

Outside of Kathmandu, it is often difficult to find appealing food in the Valley, even for a snack. Travelers on day outings should carry their own food; snacks from the Annapurna or Nanglo bakeries and some fresh fruit will do for a midday picnic before repairing to the more substantial menus of Kathmandu. Hotels will provide packed lunches upon request if ordered the night before.

The following listing covers some of Kathmandu's better restaurants:

Chimney Restaurant, Yak & Yeti Hotel. The original Boris' restaurant, this is one of the best in town for good Western cuisine. A meal of pate maison, shrimp cocktail, chicken a la Kiev and vegetable au gratin costs Rs 400 for two people, excluding drinks. The atmosphere of this former Rana palace is cozy and congenial, with a central fireplace blazing in winter.

Ghar e Kebab, Durbar Marg, serves wonderful *tandoori* and Indian cuisine in comfortable surroundings, accompanied by Indian classical music. It is excellent value at around Rs 80 a head. It is advisable to book in advance as this is one of the most popular restaurants in town (Tel: 221711, 221552).

Al Fresco, at Hotel Soaltee Oberoi, offers Italian cooking in elegant surroundings at elegant prices.

Far Pavilion, Hotel Everest Sheraton, an elegant Indian dining experience on the top floor next to Ropes for barbecues and the Bugles and Tigers bar for a drink before. Unrivaled views.

La Marmite, Durbar Marg. French cooking of an ambitious nature. Popular with local residents. Closed Mondays.

Kowloon, Lazimpat, offers delicious spicy Chinese cuisine in unpretentious surroundings for about Rs 50 per person.

Old Vienna Inn, Thamel, has reasonable, hearty Austrian and German specialties. Try the Apple Strudel.

Zen, Thamel, good Mexican-style food in simplest surroundings.

Arirang Restaurant, Durbar Marg. The only Korean food in town.

Sun Kosi, Durbar Marg, next to Tiger Tops office. An excellent selection of traditional Nepalese and Tibetan food is offered in pleasant surroundings. This is the only real Nepalese cooking outside private homes. Service can be slow and prices run about Rs 80 per person.

Mountain City Chinese Restaurant, Malla Hotel. Szechuan cuisine is prepared by Chinese cooks from Chengdu. A meal will cost about Rs 150 per person.

Golden Gate, Durbar Marg. This Chinese restaurant, also run by the Malla Hotel, offers Peking and Canton specialities.

Tso-Ngon and **New Om**, both in Chetrapati. Tibetan

and Chinese cuisine runs about Rs. 50 for two.

Fuji Restaurant, Kantipath, newly opened, Japanese food in an imaginatively converted Rana bungalow with a picturesque moat.

Nanglo Chinese, Durbar Marg. The Chinese food here is good, though the decor is rather dark. It is good value at Rs. 50 per person.

Nanglo Pub and **Snack Bar**, Durbar Marg. The same management offers good Western food and sandwiches for lunch, served in the courtyard or on the roof. Excellent value.

Rumdoodle, Thamel. Named after a climbing spot, this fun restaurant caters to mountaineers and trekkers with hearty appetites. Select steaks and hamburgers from an amusing menu for about Rs. 45 per dish. Atmospheric bar.

K C's Restaurant, Thamel, is a favorite hangout for aging hippies and world travelers. This is "where the action is" and K C is an amiable host. Good Western food. Get a table in the recently opened section upstairs.

Kushi Fuji, Durbar Mar. This Japanese restaurant can be found above the Tiger Tops office. There is an open counter with good food for about Rs 50 per person.

Sakura-Ya Restaurant, Lazimpat. Newly opened spectacular Japanese restaurant with beautiful garden, authentic cuisine. Menu from Rs 65 to Rs 350.

BHUTAN: LAND OF THE THUNDER DRAGON

Bhutan, or *Druk Yul* ("Land of the Thunder Dragon"), as the locals call it, is today still a mysterious and unknown destination which has only recently begun to appear in the catalogues of specialized tour operators.

What may sound like a cliche is certainly true about Bhutan. Hidden in the southern folds of the Himalayas and for centuries forbidden to foreigners, Bhutan has succeeded in preserving its independence and its ancestral way of life.

The 18,000-square-mile (47,000-square-km) area of Bhutan is protected by natural obstacles: in the north, the great Himalayan range forms the border with Tibet (China) and is pierced with few passes—most of them snowbound in winter. In the south, a thick tropical forest infested with wild animals and small but feared leeches, constitutes a very efficient buffer between the central valleys of Bhutan and the Indian plains of Bengal and Assam. Till the completion of the first road in 1962, it was a strenous five-day journey from India to the center of the country. Like Nepal, Bhutan is a gigantic staircase: from the 1,000-foot (300-meter) altitude of the southern fringe, the landscape soars up to 25,000 feet (7,600 meters) along the border peaks, just 93 miles (150 km) away.

Changes in ecological patterns over a short distance are commonplace in Bhutan. These sharp contrasts are one of its main attractions. A one-day trek is sometimes sufficient to go from subtropical valleys where rice and banana trees grow, to wide yak pastures.

But for all its variety, Bhutan remains a uniformly traditional country—so uniform, in fact, that the people, by law, go to work in national dress. The 1.2 million Bhutanese are mainly Buddhist, and hold traditional Buddhist values. They believe in hierarchy and deferring to authority.

The strong religious influence of the country is evident from the white prayer flags fluttering on hillsides, and from the numerous examples of religious architecture. So strong is the Buddhist faith that climbing expeditions which fail are attributed to the displeasure of deities. The 24,700-foot (7,500-meter) Gangkar Punsum, one of the world's highest unclimbed peaks, was closed after numerous failed expeditions and complaints by local people that the expeditions disturbed the deity living on top.

Bhutan is quite happy with its way of life and is careful to preserve its tradition and culture. It does this by setting a quota on the number of tourists going into the country—only 2,405 were admitted in 1986, and the government's target for 1992 is just 3,000. Also, tourists can only enter the country if they are part of a tour group of at least six persons.

While strict entry regulations only add to its relative inaccessibility, Bhutan is also assured of remaining blissfully unspoilt, with just the right amount of mystical appeal.

Preceding pages: Wall painting of Buddha in wrathful form, to scare away evil spirits; the impressive Tashichodzong, or "Fortress of the Glorious Religion." Left, angelic youth takes a break from his scriptures.

Bhutanese society was historically hierarchical in nature, consisting of three basic groups: the nobility, peasantry and slaves. In a special relationship to them was still another hierarchy based on theological training and religious function, the Buddhist clergy, whose members enjoyed high standing in the society, regardless of their birthright.

The nobility's lifestyle was not much different from that of the rest of society—except that they had access to the country's limited resources and political power.

The peasants, the majority of the population, were tenant farmers living on semi-feudal estates of the nobility. They worked the fields and tended the herds, and sometimes, when fighting broke out between provincial chiefs, served as warriors. There were also slaves of Indian descent, whose forefathers were captives of the Bhotes.

Bhotes make up the majority of Bhutan's population of one million. There are also a large number of Nepalese, a few Indians of various castes and at least two tribal groups, the Lepcha, an indigenous people, and the Santal, whose forebears migrated from the northern part of India's Bihar state.

The population is distributed mainly along the country's southern border and in the high valleys to the north, particularly those near the western end of the east-west lateral route.

Geographic Differences: Bhutan is divided into three main zones: the foothills, which have a tropical climate and luxuriant vegetation, the inner Himalayas, which enjoy temperate climates, and the high Himalayas. Foothills are mainly inhabited by Nepalis, inner Himalayas by Drukpas and the high Himalayas by semi-nomads who live on yak-related products.

All the mountain chains except the border Himalayan range run from north to south, forming real barriers between the different parts of the central area. This area can be divided longitudinally into three zones, western, central and eastern Bhutan.

Western Bhutan, consisting of the valleys of Ha (9,240 feet/2,800 meters), Paro (7,425 feet/2,250 meters), Thimphu (7,590 feet/2,300 meters), Punakha and Wangdiphodrang (4,290 feet/1,300 meters), is the rice basket of Bhutan. Situated along gentle slopes are orchards producing apples, plums and peaches. Coniferous forests cover the higher part of the mountains. Blessed by fertile lands, the western Bhutanese, called "nagalong," are probably the most prosperous of all the Bhutanese and their relative wealth is evident from the size and the decoration of their

houses, from the food they eat, and from the way they serve their meals.

Central Bhutan has a very different outlook. As rice cannot grow in high altitudes, the main crops are wheat, barley and buckwheat. Big herds of sheep and yaks share the highland pastures. The main valley of Bumthang is inhabited by people who are very attached to their language and proud of their customs and religious traditions.

Eastern Bhutan, which includes the districts of Mongar, Tashigang, Samdrupjongkhar and the lower part of Lhuntshe, is the land of the Sharchops, the "people of the East." A warmer

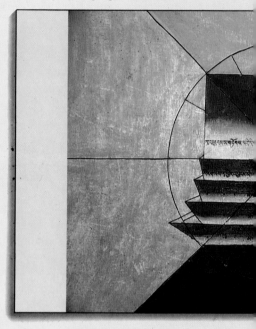

climate, steep slopes which are bare in many places, villages perched high in the mountains and fields of maize are the distinctive features of this area.

Common Bond: A common feature shared by all parts of Bhutan is religion—about 75 percent of the population is Buddhist, and Buddhism is the state religion. There are about eight major monasteries and some 200 minor shrines scattered throughout the country.

Bhutan's religious history begins in the seventh century. At that time, Bhutan was known as "the Southern Country of the Mons" and a Tibetan, King Songtsengampo built two monasteries, one in Paro Valley and one in Bumthang Valley. These were the first Buddhist establishments in the country but Buddhism was not really introduced on a large scale until the eighth century, when the Indian tantrist Padmasambhava (or Guru Rinpoche) founded the Nyingmapa religious school in Bhutan.

After two centuries of obscurity, Buddhism revived in the 11th century, spreading throughout the nation. In the 12th century, the religion expanded in Tibet, leading to missionary activities in Bhutan. The Lhapas, a branch of the Kagyupa school, arrived first in western Bhutan followed by the Drukpas, another branch of the Kagyupas. These two schools fought for religious and economic predominance over western Bhutan till the

17th century when the Drukpas emerged victors. However, from the 13th century, other schools settled in western Bhutan. Besides the Nyingmapas, the Lhapas and the Drukpas, there were the Sakyapas, the Nenyingpas and another subsect of the Drukpas.

Political Beginnings: Everything changed with the arrival in 1616 of the *Shabdrung* Nagawang Namgyel (1594-1651). Nagawang Namgyel, who belonged to the ruling family of the Drukpas, fled his monastery in Tibet and took refuge in Bhutan.

Above, cosmic mandala symbolizes the Buddhist universe.

He took the title of *Shabdrung* ('to whose feet one submits') and started bringing Western Bhutan under the Drukpa hegemony. At the same time, he faced, and repelled many Tibetan attacks. The *Shabdrung* devised a judicial and political system for the country. Each valley was dominated by a fortress, or *dzong*, which was an administrative and religious center, and each *dzong* was headed by a *dzongpon*, a "chief of the fort." Three larger regions were commanded by *penlops*, (governors).

With much political sense, and help from local allies, the *Shabdrung* gradually had the central and eastern parts of the country unified under the Drukpa rule. When he died in 1651, the *Shabdrung* left an original dual system of government which lasted until Bhutan became a monarchy in 1927.

Under the *Shabdrung's* rule, there were two high monks: one was the temporal ruler or *Desi*, the other was the head of the monk-body, the *Je Khenpo*. In the 18th and 19th centuries, this system of government led to political inertia and inter-factional struggles, allowing the governors to increase their powers. At the end of the 19th century, two powerful governors of Tongsa and Paro emerged. In the ensuing struggle, the Tongsa *penlop*, Ugyen Wangchuk, defeated his opponent.

Advised by Kazi Ugyen Dorje, he maintained excellent relations with the British. In the 19th century, the relations turned sour due to a dispute over the question of the Duar foothills. In 1865, the treaty of Sinchula obliged Bhutan to give up its rights to the fertile Duars but in exchange, it received an annual allowance from the British. The British knighted Ugyen Wangchuck in 1905 for his role in the Younghusband expedition to Tibet, and for stabilizing the country. He was proclaimed king in 1907.

The monarchy signaled an end to years of internal feuds, and brought a guarantee of stability. Ugyen Wangchuck died in 1926 and was succeeded by his son Jigme Wangchuck, who reigned peacefully until 1952. His son Jigme Dorje Wangchuck is considered the Father of Modern Bhutan. His reign marked the gradual opening of the country to the world, beginning with entry into the United Nations in 1971.

In 1961, economic and social development in the form of the first Five-Year Plan was launched. Since his father's death in 1972, the present king, His Majesty Jigme Singye Wangchuck, has continued to promote this progressive program of development, while maintaining the ancestral and cultural values of the country.

LOWLANDS

Phuntsholing is the gateway to Bhutan. Situated at an altitude of 1,155 feet (350 meters), between the plains of Bengal and the first Bhutanese hills, Phuntsholing is a bustling border town. It is close to the **Torsa River**, and houses a number of small commercial enterprises. The town stops where the jungle, teeming with wild animals, starts. On the top of a hill, near the **Kharbandi Hotel**, a small **Buddhist monastery** surrounded by eight *chortens* (reliquaries) has been built by the Senior Royal Grandmother. It overlooks the town and the vast plains of Bengal.

Paro Valley is so beautiful that there is something unreal about it. The clusters of white farmhouses with shingle roofs, the patchworks of the paddy fields surrounded by slopes covered with blue pines, the small irrigation channels shadowed by willows, the white mass of the **Paro Dzong**, dominating the valley and the small airstrip where the tiny plane bearing Bhutanese colors lands—all these contribute to an atmosphere of peace, beauty and enchantment.

Paro Valley is endowed with beautiful temples and monasteries, testimonies to its rich religious past. Among the most famous is **Kyichu Lhakhang**, which was built by the Tibetan King Songtsengampo in the seventh century, to suppress a demon. Kyichu Lhakhang appears amidst a forest of prayer flags.

Taksang, "the tiger's lair," takes its name from the tiger that Guru Rinpoche supposedly rode when he arrived there. From the valley, Taksang looks almost impossible to reach, small buildings clinging to the face of a vertical rock, 2,640 feet (800 meters) above the valley. In fact, it takes three hours of strenuous walking through a forest of oaks decorated with lichens to cross the threshold of the monastery. The curious *chorten*-shaped temple called *Dungtse* contains beautiful paintings of the 19th century, depicting the Drukpa hierarchy as well as the Tantric Buddhist pantheon.

A fascinating ruin, **Drukyel Dzong**, stands at the end of the Paro Valley, barring access to the north. It was built to commemorate the Bhutanese victory over the Tibetan armies in the 17th century but it was accidentally burnt down in the mid-1950s, and was never rebuilt. In clear skies, the snow-clad peak of the Jomolhari (24,136

feet/7,315 meters) can be seen on the horizon, like a sentinel on the road to Tibet.

A visit to the museum, or **Tadzong**, located above the *dzong* in an old watchtower, is a must. The traditional architecture enhances the beauty of the items, which range from statues and paintings to stamps and artifacts of daily life. As there are frequent power failures, it is advisable to bring a torch.

The **Paro Bazaar** is very small, as towns did not exist in Bhutan until a few years ago. The traditional pattern was a *dzong* and clusters of houses scattered throughout the valley. The only hotel is situated about two miles (three km) from the bazaar and all the other places of interest are quite far from each other. It is difficult to visit the valley without a car.

The Big City: Thimphu (7,920 feet/2,400 meters) is situated in the fertile valley of the Wangchu, which is still largely devoted to agriculture. Formerly the summer capital and since 1955 the permanent capital of Bhutan, Thimphu has grown rapidly in the last decade. It is now a town of 15,000 inhabitants which, by Bhutanese standards, is a lot. However, there is nothing congested about Thimphu and except for the main bazaar street, most of the houses and build-

Left, nimble footwork in Thimphu. Right, memorial chorten to King Jigme Dorje Wangchuck.

ings have gardens where chillis, maize and potatoes grow.

On the banks of the Wangchu, among roses, weeping willows and terraces of rice fields, stands the **Tashichodzong**, the fortress which is Bhutan's central secretariat and the Drukpa monk-body's headquarters. Built in 1641 by the *Shabdrung* Nagawang Namgyel, "the fort of the auspicious religion" was rebuilt by the third king in the 1960s to house the nation's secretariat. The architectural features of the old building were faithfully respected and its restoration was completed in 1969.

A characteristic feature of Thimphu is the tall white *chorten* crowned by golden canopies which was built in 1974 in memory of the third king, Jigme Dorje Wangchuk. Inside, the three storeys filled with paintings and statues are dedicated to the most important teachings of the Nyingmapa religious school and the representations are highly symbolic.

A visit to the old **Simtokha Dzong** which guards the entrance to the **Thimphu Valley** is enlightening. Built in 1629, it contains, behind a row of prayer wheels, exquisitely carved slates which represent different gods and religious masters. They are a unique testimony to an art which was not practiced anywhere else in the Himalayas. Simtokha Dzong now houses the school for traditional studies, where teachers of *Dzongkja*, the national language, are trained.

The main streets of Thimphu are lined with houses gaily decorated with auspicious motifs. The shops, which seem to sell the same things, smell of butter, betel, tea and dried fish. Anybody can enter, look around and leave without buying anything. The shopkeeper will smile placidly, or give an indifferent look to the *pchilimp* (foreigner) before returning to his occupation.

Two little-known places, the **hospital** and the **National Library**, can be visited on special request. The hospital is the center for traditional medicine, which is based on Indian and Chinese medicines. Treatment is mostly herbal. Bhutan was for centuries called "the country of medicinal herbs." The National Library, not far away, houses thousands of Bhutanese and Tibetan manuscripts as well as xylographs which are representative of traditional literature. It also has an English section where books of general interest on the Himalayas and Bhutan can be consulted.

One of the main attractions of Thimphu is the **Sunday Market**, where for a few hours each week, most of the local population

Taksang, the precariously perched "Tiger's Lair."

congregates. It is a wonderful occasion to mingle with the people as they buy their foodstuffs for the week. Vegetables, cheese, fruit, dried fish, rice, artifacts, chinaware and traditional books are displayed for customers. In a corner, religious men chant prayers in front of a portable chapel, a *tashigomang*, which is a religious tradition peculiar to Bhutan.

Excursions: Around Thimphu, some wonderfully rewarding excursions can be organized. The **Cheri Monastery**, perched on a hill at the top of Thimphu Valley, is easily reached after a 45-minute walk, following a drive among the paddy fields. Built in 1619 by Nagawang Namgyel, it became his first permanent residence in Bhutan. It features interesting statues and paintings.

Phajoding Monastery is a full-day excursion, requiring three hours of steep climbing. Situated at 11,220 feet (3,400 meters), Phajoding overlooks the Thimphu Valley. Two 18th-century temples contain gilded copper work and statues and paintings of great artistic value. A school for religious studies has been set up but is not open to visitors. This is to maintain calm and concentration among the pupils. A small, simple guest house provides shelter for the night but a sleeping bag and candles have to be brought along.

Dochula Pass is a 45-minute drive from Thimphu. Dochula (10,900 feet/3,300 meters) has a beautiful view of the Himalayan summits on winter mornings. In other seasons, the mountain is usually not visible.

A two-to-three-hour drive through a dense forest takes one to the low valley of **Punakha** (4,290 feet/1,300 meters). The valley, dotted with paddy fields and banana and orange trees, enjoys a warm climate. This attracts the central monk-body into spending the winter months in the valley's gigantic *dzong*, the one-time capital of Bhutan. Built in 1637, the fort symbolizes the Drukpa power which unified the country in the middle of the 17th century. The *dzong* is deserted in the hot summer, but bustling with activity in winter. A small town has sprouted on the bank of the river, and will probably become a trade market when the road to northern Bhutan is completed.

Wangdiphodrang (4,290 feet/1,300 meters) is the last *dzong* along the road to **Pelela Pass** (10,890 feet/3,300 meters), the traditional boundary separating western and eastern Bhutan. Built in 1638, it stands proudly and almost defiantly on a spur barring the road to the eastern region. The *dzong* is unique in that its administrative and

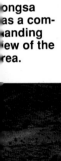

religious departments are separated by a small bridge. The *dzong*, which is covered with shingles, has a lot of charm, despite being beseiged by howling winds for most of the year.

Tongsa (7,425 feet/2,250 meters) is probably the most impressive *dzong* in Bhutan. It has a striking strategic position and an aura of grandeur, created by intricate courtyards and temples. The Tongsa *penlop* (governor) was the most powerful man in Bhutan. Ugyen Wangchuck, who in 1907 became the first king of Bhutan, was a Tongsa *penlop*. Above the dzong is a watchtower. The *dzong* commands the view of the road to the east, west and south, making it difficult for anyone to enter or leave the area without being seen.

Bumthang (8,745 feet/2,650 meters) is composed of four valleys: Chume, Choekhor, Tang and Ura. Bumthang is known for its broad and high valleys, dense forests of coniferous, austere stone-houses, *chortens* and small monasteries. The best way to discover Bumthang is on foot, although the road network is good enough for vehicles to traverse this bewitching area.

Interesting temples and monasteries of Bumthang are:

In **Chume Valley:** Pra (or Prakhar);

Domkhar Tashichoeling; Zugney. Nyimalung, Buli, Tharpaling and Choedrak are accessible only to trekkers and hikers.

In **Choekhor Valley:** Jakar Dzong, Lamey Gompa (now a forestry school), Jakar Lhakhang, Jampey Lhakhang, Kuje, Tamshing, Koncho Sum and Wangduchoeling Palace. Petsheling, Thangbi and Ngang Lhakhang are accessible only to trekkers and hikers. In **Lamey Gompa** is an old craftsman who prepares Bhutanese paper the traditional way. The sheets can be used as wrapping paper. Next to **Chamkhar**, the center of Choekhor, is an apple juice production unit which makes excellent apple juice, cider and apple brandy. There are also cheese and butter production units, but production is irregular.

In **Tang Valley:** Mebartsho, a holy site, although there is no temple. Kunzandra, Ugyenchoeling and Thowadra are accessible only to trekkers and hikers.

In **Ura Valley:** Ura Village, Sombrang, Shinkar and Thangsibi.

There is no handicraft shop in Bumthang, but villagers come here to sell their weavings to tourists.

Perched on a slope and offering some beautiful scenery, **Mongar** (5,610 feet/1,700 meters) is a great way to spend a night from Bumthang, en route to Tashigang or Lhuntshe.

Lhuntshe Dzong (5,610 feet/1,700 meters) is situated on a spur at the end of a gorge. Lhuntshe is still very much like it was in the old days, with only a few houses grouped below the *dzong*. Numerous villages with famous temples and a strong community of renowned weavers are scattered high on the steep slopes of the mountains. Like Bumthang, Lhuntshe has a rich past closely related to the Pemalingpa's lineage. Again like Bumthang, the Lhuntshe region has to be explored on foot to be fully appreciated, although walking here is more difficult because the slopes are steeper.

Tashigang (3,960 feet/1,200 meters), in the heart of 'Sharchop' country, is, by Bhutanese standards, a fast-developing town. With its small piazza, colorful bougainvillea and people strolling around at dusk, or drinking in the cafes, it has a unique charm. Two hours drive from Tashigang is the small *dzong* of **Tashiyangtse**, with its beautiful old cane bridge and the impressive white *chorten* of **Chorten Kora**. On the way back, stop at the temple of **Gom Kora** to learn another story about Guru Rinpoche. The temple is situated next to a huge black rock and surrounded by banana trees.

eft, hardy llager ith boots at were ade for alking. ight, rayer ags are ver-resent.

TREKKING

Trekking in Bhutan is refreshingly different from trekking in other parts of the Himalayas. Much of the country is covered by a dense carpet of vegetation ranging from semi-tropical jungle to alpine shrubs, and provides a unique approach to Himalayan flora. Bhutan has a small population, and human settlements are concentrated in certain areas, leaving large sections of the country empty. In the north, it is sometimes more than a day's walk from one settlement to the next. Unlike Nepal, it is impossible to trek alone in Bhutan. The lack of maps, difficulty in obtaining food and shelter on the trail, and the absence of porters makes trekking a different proposition. Expeditions, which have to be planned well in advance, are undertaken by the Bhutan Tourism Corporation. The BTC only accepts groups of six or more trekkers. A guide, a cook and a helper are assigned to each group. Food, tents and the personal belongings of members are carried on horses or yaks, depending on the altitude of the trek.

Trekking routes range from the easy mid-altitude short trek, to the long and challenging high altitude route. All routes are impressively devoid of any of the unwanted trappings of trekking, presenting an unspoiled character and clean paths often difficult to find in other parts of the Himalayas. As a bonus, fishing is also possible and along some routes, trout is plentiful, providing some pleasant diversions from the rigors of the trek.

Trekking Variety: One of the shortest treks is the **Druk Path**, which in three days takes the trekker from Thimphu, the capital, to the enchanting valley of Paro, through a 12,870-foot (3,900-meter) pass. The trail climbs steeply through the forest to the monastery of Phajoding, a charming cluster dating to the 18th century. On the way to Paro, the **Jimilangtsho Lakes** provide a wonderful opportunity for fishermen.

Botanists find paradise during the four-day **Gantey Gompa Trek**. Starting from the rich and impressive **Gantey Monastery** which belongs to the Nyingmapa school, the trek crosses two passes at 11,220 feet (3,400 meters) in a setting of coniferous, giant junipers, small bushes of daphne and a symphony of rhododendron. Mid-April to the end of May is the best time to see and

Trekkers are rewarded with breathtaking views of Jichudrak mountain.

admire the different species in full bloom. The last day is a fantastic three-hour climb down—an ecological adventure which starts in the rhododendron and magnolia forest at 10,000 feet (3,000 meters), continuing through a semi-tropical forest with trees bearing broad shiny leaves, realm of orchids and unknown creepers, and finishing at 4,620 feet (1,400 meters) among the neatly maintained paddy fields, the pretty farmhouses and the banana trees of the **Shar Valley**.

The **Bumthang Trek** (five or six days) is an introduction to the fascinating region of Central Bhutan and has a more cultural tone, featuring an interesting selection of monasteries. Never exceeding an altitude of 11,220 feet (3,400 meters), it leads to the discovery of traditional villages, nestled between forest and fields, retaining their centuries-old way of life, and to the artistic treasures hidden in the temples scattered all over the different valleys of Bumthang. This region boasts a rich past, with the Nyingmapa religious masters making a significant contribution to its fame.

From the exquisite early-16th-century paintings of **Tamshing**, to the cloister of **Tharpaling**, from the holy shrine of **Kuje** to the regal atmosphere of **Ugyencholing**

Palace, this trek is a walk in a lively open-air museum. A visit to a farmhouse can often be arranged, and if the villagers have buck-wheat, the staple food of the area, they can show how the renowned *buta* (buckwheat noodles) is made. A few miles from Jakar Dzong, in Lamey Gompa, an old craftsman demonstrates the Bhutanese way of manufacturing paper from the bark of a daphne bush. Everywhere, women are weaving the famous woollen checked pattern called *matra*, used to make the day-to-day men's and women's clothes, and the woollen strip, the *yatra*, which makes splendid baskets, cushion covers or jackets.

One of the most popular high altitude treks is the seven-day **Jomolhari Trek**, which goes from Paro to Thimphu via the northwestern region. It provides beautiful views of the high Himalayan range and especially of **Mount Jomolhari** (24,186 feet/7,329 meters) and **Jichudrake** (22,417 feet/6,793 meters). It is a trip which takes to the remote and wild world of the yak herders, nomads who live in black tents and who tend their yaks in pastures shared with blue sheep. The fortress of **Lingshi**, which used to guard the frontier against invaders, stands in a lonely and majestic landscape. Primulas, poppies and gentianas add color to the

stoic beauty of the mountain. After the steep pass of **Yalila** (15,510 feet/4,900 meters), the trail to Thimphu follows the **Wang River** in a spectacular gorge and a dense forest. Before reaching the upper part of the Thimphu Valley, it passes near the ruins of the once-famous **Barshong** fortress.

The **Laya Trek** is a challenging 16-day trek in high altitude. It starts from Paro and up to **Lingshi Dzong**, following the same route as the Jomolhari Trek. But instead of going south after reaching Lingshi Dzong (13,530 feet/4,100 meters), it heads to the northeast. For four days, it goes through the northern rugged terrain, ascending three passes of more than 14,520 feet (4,400 meters). It is the realm of one of the rarest animals on earth, the takin (*budorcas taxicolor*), an ungainly looking animal that is related to the goat but bears more of a resemblance to the antelope. In fact, the takin is actually rather agile.

The villages of **Laya**, dominated by the **Masagang** (23,760 feet/7,200 meters), are situated just above the tree line. Their stone houses are clustered together, surrounded by small fields of buckwheat, barley and turnips. Just after the harvest, yaks are brought to graze in the fields. Black tents, pitched next to the houses, serve as accommodation for younger people, while the elders stay inside the houses.

Like all yak herders, the Laya people make the best use of this hardy animal: the milk of the female is used to make cheese and butter, the meat is eaten or exchanged at lower altitudes for rice, the hair is woven into clothing, tents and ropes and their excrement serves as a combustible. Contrary to other Bhutanese women, Laya belles have long, loose hair and wear a most peculiar headdress: a pointy conical hat made of bamboo which gives them a unique look.

The way down to Punakha (four days) is a walk among the different levels of vegetation: the pinetree forest starts just below Laya and thins on arrival at **Gasa Dzong**. Gasa has one of the most outstanding positions in Bhutan, and from its semi-circular walls, the eye embraces, at one glance, the narrow gorge of tropical forest, 3,000 feet (1,000 meters) below which lies Punakha (two days away), as well as the huge rocky mass of the **Gangphu** (21,450 feet/6,500 meters).

The most difficult route is the **Lunana Trek**. This trek requires not only fitness and endurance but preferably previous experience in trekking. Lunana is a northern and extremely remote region of Bhutan. It is the

The Laya Trek makes it way past scenic Punakha Dzong.

home of one of the highest Bhutanese mountains, the **Gangkar Punsum** (24,885 feet/7,541 meters) and offers beautiful rugged landscapes, turquoise lakes, glaciers and snowcapped peaks. The population is scarce and like in Lingshi and Laya, lives mostly on yak products. The routes which lead to this fascinating area are a challenge for any serious trekker because there are three passes above 16,830 feet (5,100 meters) to cross. The trek to Lunana starts from Punakha. It takes four days to reach Laya, via Gasa, and another three to reach Lunana at the village of **Woche** (12,705 feet/3,850 meters). During this leg, the route crosses the famous **Ganglakarchung Pass** at 16,830 feet (5,100 meters) which offers a breathtaking view of the eastern Himalayas. From Woche, the trail crosses the **Kechala Pass** (15,015 feet/4,050 meters) and in two days, reaches the most inhabited part of Lunana, the villages of **Thega**, **Chozo Dzong** and **Thanza**, the capital of Lunana (13,365 feet/4,050 meters). A cluster of low stone-houses around the temple in a marshy green landscape contrast sharply with the snow-covered mountains in the background.

From there, five more days of unrelenting landscape are necessary to arrive at **Nikarchu Bridge**, the end of the trek. This route is used by the people of Lunana who bring yak meat, butter and cheese to the lower altitudes.

The Lunana Trek, combined with the Jomolhari Trek, offers one of the most exhilarating experiences for a seasoned trekker—it covers a walking distance of 226 miles (362 km) in 18 days and crosses 11 passes of northern Bhutan, providing unique views of the eastern Himalayan range. This formidable trekking combination is known as the **Snowman Trek** because Bhutanese believe that the wild north is the home of the mysterious and legendary Abominable Snowman, and that an encounter is always possible(!).

Advice to Trekkers: When walking in forest or dense vegetation areas, be sure to make some noise, to lessen the risk of stumbling on a wild animal. Bhutan has a lot of bears, which can be dangerous when surprised. Leeches exist below 6,600 feet (2,000 meters) during the rainy season. A leech bite does not hurt but can become septic.

Gum boots are also useful as paths are often muddy. They are especially good for walking during the monsoon season, or on the Jomolhari Trek.

snow-
vered
ya
age.

HANDICRAFTS

Bhutanese women take great pride in the traditional handicraft of weaving. Handwoven textiles are still worn daily by the majority of the population and weaving, like other Bhutanese traditions, is thriving.

Yarns include raw silk (*bura*), refined silk (*seyshy*), cotton, sheep wool and in the nomad regions, yak hair.

These yarns are woven on three kinds of loom: the very traditional backstrap body-tensioned loom, the 'tablet' or 'card' loom, used only to weave belts and the third loom, introduced recently, is the loom with pedals on which woollen fabrics are woven.

Each cloth, depending on the color and pattern combinations, has a special name. Some of the fabrics take many months to be completed because they involve the

made from them: bags, quivers, liquor containers, bows and arrows, strainers, the famous airtight containers known as *banchung* and modern conveniences such as table mats and lamp shades.

Many centuries-old traditions are still in everyday use in Bhutan. Men wear the *go* or *baku*—a long robe hitched up to the knees and held in place with a small belt. Women wear the *onju* or *gyenja,* a buttonless blouse and the *kira,* a large piece of cloth wrapped round the body and held by the *komas* (silver clips) at the shoulders, and by the *kara* (a tight belt). A small jacket, the *togo,* is usually worn over the *kira.*

A ceremonial scarf, the *kabney,* is worn to religious or official functions. The men's scarf is a long piece of cloth loosely wrapped around the body. The common man wears white scarves, the high officials, red and the ministers, deep orange. The king wears yellow. The women wear red floral scarfs. The only jewelry Bhutanese men wear are gold rings—either

technique of brocade in which a supplementary weave is introduced into the background weave to produce intricate and exquisite designs.

Bhutanese silversmiths and goldsmiths make delicately carved betel and lime boxes, the clips (*komas*) used in dresses, bracelets, ceremonial teapots, bowls and liquor containers.

Because of its large rainforests, Bhutan has a wide range of cane, bamboo and rattan and produces many daily artifacts

plain or adorned with turquoise or coral.

Women wear, in addition to the silver *komas*, decorative silver chains or *japtha*.

Other accessories include gold and silver bracelets with dragons or flower patterns. Necklaces, which are worn mostly on festive occasions, usually feature huge corals, strings of pearls and gold lockets. Bhutanese handicrafts have an authentic flavor which may disappoint people in search of a "cute souvenir," but real connoisseurs of beautiful objects will rejoice.

t,
rdant
s and
e fields
Punakha
lley.
ght,
ditional
utanese
velry.

DESTINATION BHUTAN

GETTING THERE

By Air: From Calcutta, a 90-minute flight by the national airline Druk-Air takes you to Paro airport, a 90-minute drive from the capital, Thimphu. Druk-Air operates on different schedules according to the season but it is usually three times a week. The plane is an 18-seater and the last leg of the journey is a marvelous mountain flight. However, during monsoon seasons, poor weather conditions may delay a flight. The cost is about US$280 return.

Druk-Air flight information can also be obtained from their office at 48 Tivoli Court, 1A Ballygunj Circular Road, Calcutta 700019, India.

Overland: Entering Bhutan by road requires more procedures because a permit is required to go into the crossing between Darjeeling, Bagdogra (the nearest airport), Ailiguri or the railway station of New Jaipalguri, all situated in West Bengal, and Phuntsholing, the border town. This permit is obtained strictly six weeks in advance by applying to the Bhutanese Embassy in New Delhi or to the Bhutan Tourism Corporation in Thimphu.

It takes four hours from Bagdora to Phuntsholing, and six hours from Phuntsholing to Thimphu/Paro.

Visas: The Bhutan Tourism Corporation needs 15 days to process the tourist visa, which must be paid for on arrival at Phuntsholing or Paro. The visa fee of US$20 is not included in the cost of a package tour.

It is only possible to enter Bhutan as a tourist, or to work officially for United Nations agencies and at government request.

Useful Addresses

Bhutan Tourism Corporation
Box 159
Thimphu
Bhutan Ph 2647, 2570
Telex: 3162377 SARC IN

Bhutan Travel Service
120 East 56th Street, New York,
New York 10022
Telex: 220-396 BST UR

Bhutan Travel Service
c/o Royal Bhutanese Embassy
Chamobragopra Marg, Chamarkyapore,
New Delhi 11021, India

Bhutan Travel Service
48 Tivoli Court, 1A Ballygunj Circular Road,
Calcutta 700019, India

Health: No special vaccinations are required. Major towns have hospitals and there are good drugstores in Thimphu.

Tap water must be purified before drinking.

Money: The Bhutanese unit is the *ngultrum*, which is equivalent to the Indian *rupee*. Hard currencies in travelers checks or cash can be changed at certain hotel counters and at the Bank of Bhutan in Phuntsholing and Thimphu. Moneychangers prefer traveler's checks to notes. Change all unused *ngultrum* before leaving the country as Bhutanese currency is virtually impossible to change outside Bhutan.

INSIDE BHUTAN

GETTING ACQUAINTED

Government: Bhutan is a monarchy. The king is helped by a cabinet which is the main executive body, and by the Royal Advisory Council, which has a consultative role.

The national assembly is the main legislative body. Created in 1953, it consists of 153 members who meet twice a year in Tashichodzong in Thimphu.

Bhutan is the only independent country which practises Mahayana Buddhism in its tantric form as state religion. The monks are headed by the *Je Khenpo*.

The judicial power is held by the king. A high court has its seat in Thimphu and all the districts have a local court.

Bhutan is divided into 17 districts headed by an administrator, the *Dzongda*, appointed by the King. At a lower level are the village headmen, *gaps*, and the people representatives, the *chimis*.

Economy: Bhutan is an agrarian country. It is favored by natural resources and fertile soil. It has limited land for cultivation, and its rugged terrain and lack of transportation facilities make it inaccessible.

Climate: The climatic conditions in Bhutan are extremely diverse, and can vary tremendously within a day.

The southern fringe bordering India has a tropical climate with a heavy monsoon and mild and clear winters.

In the central valleys, the summer rains are not as heavy as in the south and occur mostly in late afternoon and at night. From mid-May to the end of September, the weather is warm at night (63 F to 64 F/17 C to 18 C) and in the day (72 F to 78 F/22 C to 26 C).

In winter, the sky is bright and it is sunny but cold, especially when the sun hides behind the mountains in the mornings and evenings. At night, the temperature falls below zero.

Spring and autumn are very pleasant with warm days and cool nights but there are occasional showers in April and May.

Above 10,500 feet (3,200 meters), it snows a lot in winter, and many passes are closed.

What to Bring: From October to May, heavy clothes and coats or down jackets are required. From June to September, cotton clothes are sufficient for day wear but light wool is required in the evening, and a raincoat is useful for occasional showers. Comfortable shoes are a must. Except in summer, warm pajamas are recommended. Because of the different altitudes and weather conditions, clothing should be layered. One should refrain from wearing mini-skirts, shorts or low-cut T-shirts.

Flashlights are essential items, especially during power failures.

As this book goes to press, Bhutanese King Jigme Singye Wangchuck has decreed that starting from 1988, temples and other religious sites will no longer be open to tourists unless special permission is granted.

Photography: Photographers must bring all their equipment, rolls of film and extra batteries. Tourists are allowed to film with a super-8 camera but not with a 16mm camera. Film crews are welcome in Bhutan for commercial purposes based on certain rules and payments of royalties. All enquiries should be addressed to the General Manager, P.O. Box 159, Thimphu, Bhutan.

Survival Bhutanese: The *Dzongkha* spoken in western Bhutan is the national language. The *Bumthangkha* is spoken in central Bhutan and the *Sharchopka* in the east. However, English is spoken by all educated people as it is the medium of instruction.

Good morning
Kousousangpo
Thank you
Kadrinche

fortress-monastery	
dzong	
stupa, reliquary	
chorten	
monastery	
gompa	
temple	
lakhang	
temple for protective	
deities	
gonkhang	
pass	
la	
god	
lha	
okay, alright	
thub	
lake	
tsho	
water, river	
cho	
high mountain	
gang	
respectful word indicating	

a person is taking his leave
lass

Communications: Bhutan boasts beautiful stamps which are highly-prized by collectors. A wide assortment of stamps is available at the Philatelic Bureau in Phuntsholing and at the General Post Office in Thimphu. The mail service is very reliable. Letters to Europe and Australia take between 10 and 15 days; to Japan, between seven and 10 days; and to the United States, between 15 and 30 days. Only important letters need to be registered.

It is possible to telephone almost anywhere in the world. Complete phone codes should be given to the

operator to shorten delays.

Festivals: Festivals are one of the highlights of Bhutanese life and take place all year round, but most often in spring or autumn, after the harvest.

Festivals are a unique occasion to watch the religious dances, the *cham,* which depicts the victory of Buddhism over evil forces. The dances are performed by monks or laymen who wear colorful costumes and impressive masks. They turn, jump and stamp the ground according to a precise choreography, following the sound of the drums and cymbals. Among the most famous of these dances, which originated in Tibet, is

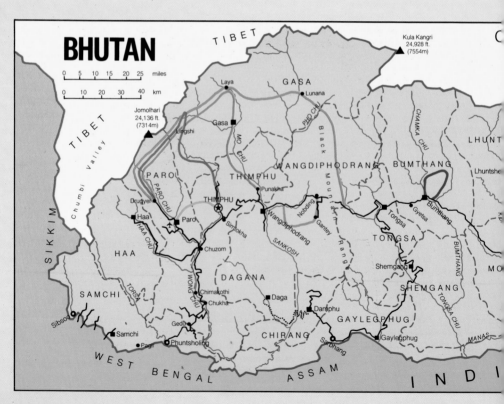

the dance of the drum-beaters from Dramitse, which depicts the celestial vision of a religious man, and the spectacular dance of the Black Hats, which relates how the *Shabdrung* Ngawang Namgyel took over the soil of Bhutan from the earth-deities.

A lot of these festivals are called *Tschechu*, which means "the 10th day." They commemorate, on the 10th day of different months, the great deeds of the revered saint, Padmasambhava (Guru Rinpoche).

During some of the festivals, a *thondrol* is displayed on the last day. It is a huge applique and embroidered banner, a *thangka*, whose very appearance brings liberation to those who see it which is the exact meaning of *thondrol*. It usually represents Guru Rinpoche, his two main consorts and his eight other manifestations.

The atmosphere differs greatly from place to place. The *Paro Tschechu*, a *dzong* festival, is a grand, but rather stiff, pageant. The village festivals are simpler, more jovial and family-like. But whatever the place, a festival is a wonderful occasion for the people to show their deep faith and to gather for merry-making and the latest news. Whole families dress in their best clothes. Ladies adorn themselves with jewels, pearls and corals. Everybody brings a hearty picnic in *banchung*, small bamboo baskets, and local liquor helps to foster the festive mood.

The dates of the festivals, which follow the lunar calendar, are available from the government-run Bhutan Tourism Corporation.

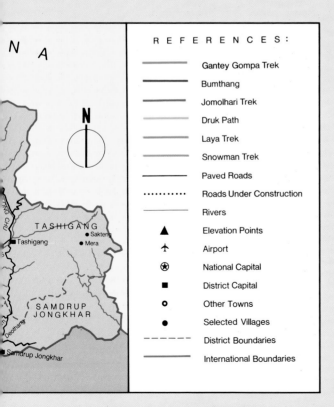

N A

N

REFERENCES:

——— Gantey Gompa Trek

——— Bumthang

——— Jomolhari Trek

——— Druk Path

——— Laya Trek

——— Snowman Trek

——— Paved Roads

·········· Roads Under Construction

——— Rivers

▲ Elevation Points

✈ Airport

⊛ National Capital

■ District Capital

o Other Towns

● Selected Villages

- - - - District Boundaries

——— International Boundaries

TASHIGANG
■ Tashigang ● Sakteng ● Mera

SAMDRUP JONGKHAR
■ Samdrup Jongkhar

TOURS

It is impossible to visit Bhutan as an individual. The government, in its efforts to protect the natural and social environment, has set a policy of a minimum of six persons per package tour.

The Bhutan Tourism Corporation proposes a certain number of package tours. Hotels, food, guides and transport are included in the overall price.

Two package tours depart from Calcutta. **Journey to the Dragon Kingdom** is a six-day tour with departures every Friday from Calcutta airport. The tour goes to Paro, Thimphu and Punakha, the three main valleys of western Bhutan. **Journey to Druk Yul** is an eight-day tour which departs every Wednesday. It is basically the same tour as Dragon Kingdom, but the sojourn is longer in each place, allowing tourists to better appreciate Bhutanese life.

Every Monday, there is a departure from Bagdogra Airport or Sinclairs Hotel at Siliguri. This tour goes through the border town of Phuntsholing and then to Paro, Thimphu and Punakha.

Getting Around: The main towns are linked by regular bus services. It is always possible to hire a car, or a four-wheel drive landcruiser with a driver. The hiring charges are fixed.

Tourists' transport usually comes in the form of Japanese mini-buses and cars.

WHAT TO DO

Mountaineering: Mountaineering in Bhutan started in 1983. The Bhutanese Himalayas are known to contain some 18 peaks over 23,000 feet (7,000 meters).

Alpinists who have visited Bhutan say that Bhutanese peaks present serious difficulties, even to the toughest climbers. An added challenge is the climatic conditions, which are more unpredictable than the rest of the Himalayas.

The first peak to be scaled was the **Jomolhari** (24,136 feet/7,315 meters) in 1937 by Spencer Chapman and Pasang Dawa Lama. The Jomolhari was climbed a second time in 1970 by a joint Royal Bhutan Army and Indian Army expedition under Colonel N. Kumar.

The government opened the **Jichudrake** (22,417 feet/6,793 meters) in 1983 on a commercial basis. That same year, two expeditions, an Austrian and a Japanese all-woman team led by the famous Junko Tabei, tried to reach the summit, but were ultimately unsuccessful.

The next year, the **Gangphu** (21,450 feet/ 6,500 meters) in the Jomolhari group and the **Namshila** (21,747 feet/6,590 meters) in the Lunana group were opened, and were scaled successfully by two Japa-

nese teams. In 1985, two more peaks, the **Gangkar Punsum** (24,700 feet/7,500 meters) and the **Masagang** (23,760 feet/7,200 meters) in the Laya region, were opened.

So far, only the Masagang has been scaled. This achievement was accomplished in 1985 by a Kyoto University expedition.

Like tours and trekking, mountaineering is handled by the Bhutan Tourism Corporation, which has published a booklet explaining the mountaineering rules and regulations in Bhutan. It can be obtained from: The Trekking Manager, BTC, P.O. Box 159, Thimphu, Bhutan.

Trekking Equipment: Cooking gear, foodstuffs, tents and mattresses are provided by Bhutan Tourism Corporation. Trekkers must bring their own sleeping-bags, clothes, shoes and photographic equipment.

Nights tend to be cold, so good sleepingbags and downjackets are a must. A nylon poncho is most useful for the occasional rainshowers. Leather shoes will do for easy treks such as the Druk Path and the Gantey Gompa, but mountaineering shoes are needed for the other treks, which are rocky, rough and sometimes snow-bound. It would also be advisable to bring along a pair of slippers.

Shopping: Thimphu is the only place which has shop-

IN TRANSIT / FOOD DIGEST

ping. In Thimphu bazaar, a lot of shops which sell foodstuffs also sell handicrafts, and one should not hesitate to enter the shop to look around. A Few shops specialize in handicrafts. The biggest is the government-run **Handicrafts Emporium** which has a good selection of cloth, paintings, ceremonial masks and other souvenirs. At the back, there is a workshop where it is possible to see the craftsmen at work.

Three private boutiques share the rest of the market: **Pel Jorkhang** has mainly traditional fabrics and is situated at the main crossroads of the town. **Tshering Dolkar** and **Ethometho** are both located on the ground floor of the Tourism building next to the cinema hall. Both have a good assortment of Bhutanese fabrics and jewelry, besides bamboo handicrafts and woodworks. Tshering Dolkar has a wider choice of clothes while Ethometho sells postcards, stamps and books on Bhutan. The prices are the same in all the shops.

Compared to neighboring countries' handicrafts, Bhutanese handicrafts are expensive, but this does not mean that foreigners are subject to higher prices—so don't bargain—bargaining is not usually practised.

Because of the government policy to keep its cultural heritage in the country, the export of antiques is forbidden. It is advisable to ask for a receipt for purchases.

WHERE TO STAY

There are very good hotels, decorated in Bhutanese style but with all the modern facilities, in Phuntsholing, Paro and Thimphu. In the rest of the country, the accommodation is usually very simple and consists of government guest-houses. In Tongsa and Bumthang, the two guest-houses are managed by the Bhutan Tourism Corporation.

Phuntsholing: The best and more expensive hotels are the **Druk Motel** in town and the **Kharbandi** situated on a hill three miles (five km) from the center of the town. They both have Western standard rooms and services.

Paro: The only hotel in Paro is the **Olathang Hotel** run by the Bhutan Tourism Corporation.

Thimphu: Motithang Hotel, situated in a beautiful park outside the town, is considered the best hotel. Not surprisingly, it is operated by the Bhutan Tourism Corporation.

In town, **Bhutan Hotel**, also run by the BTC, has attractive rooms with terraces and a nice view of the mountains. The privately-run **Jomolhari Hotel** and **Druk Hotel** are in the heart of town. They have efficient service. These three hotels are similarly priced.

WHAT TO EAT

Bhutanese food is very spicy due to the large quantities of chilli, *hema*, which go into the preparation of a dish. The national dish is the *hemadatsi*, a dish made from fresh chillis cooked in a cheese sauce.

The staple food is red rice, but in some high valleys, rice is replaced by buckwheat pancakes or barley and wheat flour. Rice is consumed in huge quantities and is accompanied by vegetables cooked in a gravy or in a cheese sauce, and always with chillis added. The favorite meat of the Bhutanese is pork, especially the fat part, which is a delicacy, and yak which is consumed or cooked after having been dried in long strips. Beef and more recently, chicken, is also eaten, but not mutton.

Drinks: Tea is the most popular drink. Bhutanese offer visitors either butter tea or sweet tea.

Bhutan produces its own alcoholic beverages. The traditional drinks are homemade; they are produced by fermenting different cereals: barley, wheat, millet and maize. The most popular are *chang* and *temka*, which are low in alcoholic content. *Arak*, a product of the distilling of *chang*, has a higher alcohol content. A very special drink, called *chang keu*, made from *chang*, butter and eggs, is consumed on festive occasions.

Bhutan also produces very good quality whiskies such

as the famous Bhutan Mist and Special Courier, as well as an assortment of rum and gin. Very tasty tinned fruit juices are also produced for export.

Where to Eat: Restaurants are found only in Thimphu, Phuntsholing and Paro. The restaurants serve continental, Indian and local food. Chinese restaurants are found only in Thimphu. As regular supplies are a problem, restaurants could run out of items listed on the menu.

Phutsholing: Kharbaaron, outside the center, serves very good food.

Paro: The only restaurant is located in the **Olathang Hotel.** Food usually has to be ordered in advance.

Thimphu: Thimphu offers a greater variety of restaurants. The best and most expensive are located at **Bhutan Hotel** (continental and Bhutanese), **Jomolhari Hotel** (Indian and Chinese) and **Druk Hotel** (continental, Chinese and Indian). There is also a continental and local food restaurant at **Motithang Hotel**, but it requires advance orders.

Local liquors are available everywhere in small bars, but the restaurants only serve imported drinks and beer.

There is no nightlife in Bhutan. Entertainment is provided only at private dinners or official parties.

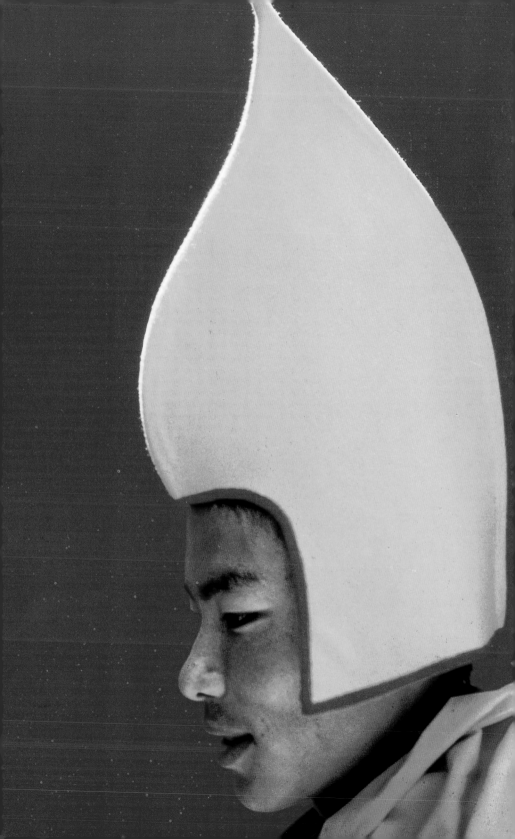

TIBET: THE FORBIDDEN LAND

Sandwiched between China and the Indian subcontinent, yet wholly distinct from both, Tibet was, until recently, one of the last great unexplored regions of the earth. We are now just beginning to learn about its extraordinary variety and unparalleled culture and history.

Tibet covers an area larger than France, Spain, Germany, Italy and Great Britain put together and has an average altitude of over three miles (five km) above sea level. A large part of it is so inhospitable that it has been described as "making the Gobi Desert look fertile;" yet parts of Tibet, rich with citrus fruits and tropical vegetation, are little higher than the plains of Bengal.

It is a country protected from the outside world both by its own geography and by its fear of foreigners. No other has captured man's imagination in the same way. Tibet has always been a magnet for explorers. For 500 years after the first reports of Lhasa from Portuguese Jesuits, missionaries, cranks, scholars and adventurers risked body and soul to try to get there.

Few other cultures hold such contrasts—a lifestyle of medieval simplicity coexists with sophisticated philosophy, debate and architecture. The ancient science of Tibetan medicine is still astounding Western medical researchers with its methods of diagnosis and cure in areas that perplex the technological West. Yet until this century, the only "wheels" in Tibet were prayer wheels; the first vehicle to be seen was the 13th Dalai Lama's car, which had to be carried over the mountains from India.

Geographically, Tibet is a land of spectacular extremes. The bleak northern plain, more than 745 miles (1,200 km) from east to west, is dotted with some of the highest lakes in the world. To the south are the vast mountains of the Trans-Himalayas and the Himalayas themselves. Although much of Tibet is a high altitude desert, it is also the prime water source for Asia with the Indus, Sutlej, Ganges and Brahmaputra rivers all beginning in the west and the Salween, Mekong, Yangtse and Yellow rivers having their sources in north Tibet.

Vegetation varies from little more than lichen on parts of the northern plateau to a botanist's paradise in the southeast, where the richness and variety of plant life is unmatched. Undisturbed by hunters, wildlife also flourishes—there is a wide range of animals and birds.

But perhaps the most fascinating thing of all is the authenticity and intensity of Tibet's religion. Buddhism in Tibet is not a matter of occasional ritual, it is an integral part of daily life. Paths are littered with small shrines, thousands of prayer flags flutter in the wind and ordinary people walk the streets spinning their prayer wheels. The long lines of pilgrims at every major religious site are proof that the recent history of religious oppression has had little effect on the people, who have been called the most religious in the world. After the ravages of the Cultural Revolution, only a fraction of Tibetan religious and architectural heritage remains and visits to the ruined sites leave travelers wondering at what might have been. But restoration is beginning everywhere and this rooftop world is far from becoming a museum piece. Visitors leave with an impression of a people seeking man's real place in the natural world and showing a level of tolerance and a depth of understanding that much of the rest of the world can learn from.

Preceding pages: Mural from Shalu Monastery depicts a typically religious theme; Potala dominates the Lhasa landscape. Left, Tibetan Buddhism is personified by this Gelugpa monk, or Yellow Hat.

The earliest records of Tibet are those of the seventh century and the advent of Buddhism. Of earlier history we can only piece together myth, legend and oral tradition. Legend has it that the land originally lay below a shallow sea—this has since been geologically supported—which later receded, leaving a vast area inhabited only by a monkey and the Ogress of the Rocks. The monkey, Chenrezi, was said to be peaceful and contemplative and an emanation of the *Bodhisattva* of Mercy. By contrast the Ogress was lustful, stubborn and full of rage; when she howled in loneliness for a mate the monkey took pity and

under the Franks, Lombards and Visigoths. According to the 13th-century Tibetan historian Sonam Gyamtsen there was some agriculture as early as 100 B.C. and oxen were being used to draw ploughs; the yak and *dzo* (cross-bred cow/yak) were domesticated at a very early stage.

A ninth-century chronicle traces the rulers of Tibet back through 36 generations to the semi-divine and divine, but credible Tibetan history begins late in the sixth century.

It was in the reign of the celebrated Songtsengampo (620-649) that Tibet began to develop as a recognizable power. Some trade

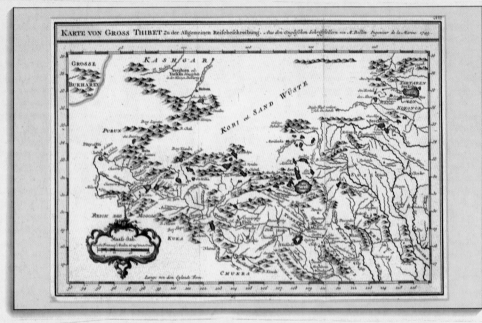

went to her. The six children of this unlikely union had no tails and few simian characteristics and are said to be the first Tibetans—some inherited the gentle wisdom of their father and others were cruel, lustful and insatiable—thus did the Tibetans explain their varied characteristics.

What the History Books Say: Historical accounts bring us a less fanciful picture of a nomadic population of sheep and cattle herders who seem to be descended from the non-Chinese Chiang tribes who were wandering around Central Asia many centuries before Christianity. They were clear clan-type groups, some of whom gradually became more sedentary, and the earliest records give us accounts of rival chiefs in fortified valleys living off a feudal system similar to that of Anglo-Saxon England and West Europe

links—first with China, then with what is now west Tibet, north India and Nepal—were created and gradually Tibet began to expand its borders until it became a force to be reckoned with. The Chinese of the Tang Dynasty looked on nervously and quickly arranged an alliance through the marriage of a Chinese princess, Wencheng to Songtsengampo—his other wife was a Nepali. What had begun as a small kingdom in the Yarlung Valley developed into an empire.

Tibetan historians make much of the introduction of Buddhism at this time, but it seems that initially it was little more than a pastime at court brought by the Chinese princess. It was not until the subsequent founding of the monasteries that it spread among the rest of the population.

The original faith of Tibet was referred to as

"Sacred Conventions" (*Llachos*) or "the pattern of heaven and earth." It developed into Bon, the indigenous Tibetan religion which was a kind of animism where trees, rocks, rivers and mountains were thought to be the homes of spirits to be placated at every opportunity. In some areas Bon is still practised but in many cases Bon customs have simply been absorbed into Tibetan Buddhism over the centuries. At the time of the introduction of Buddhism into Tibet, India was still predominantly Buddhist, but gradually Islam and Hinduism took precedence, causing Indian Buddhism to all but disappear. Eventually the

Tibetans inherited much of the Indian tradition.

After the reign of King Songtsengampo, what Buddhism there was declined and it was actually banned for some time before being reinstated by the second famed religious king, Trisongdetsen (755-797). Tibet's expansionist period continued throughout the eighth century and Central Asian territories were acquired. These were partially recovered by the Chinese but then won back again by the Tibetans. It was at this time that Buddhism was declared to be the state religion and Samye, the first monastery of Tibet, founded. It was

Left, 17th-century map of the Forbidden Land. Above, Buddhism in Tibet is steady as a rock.

modelled after a well-known temple in Bihar, north India, and two famous Indian Buddhists, Padmasambhava and Santarakshita helped the king set it up as a training place for Tibetan monks. Monks were placed above the Royal Law and some of the landowning families of Yarlung were made subject to the monastery rather than to the king, and had to support the monks with food, income and supplies. This caused considerable resentment among the nobles who tended to adhere to the Bon faith.

At this time rivalry between the older indigenous Tibetans and the 'newer' border Tibetans caused severe disruption. The former tended to be supporters of the king in his capacity as the "sacred ruler of divine origin." They were in general hostile to China and saw Buddhism as essentially foreign. In contrast the 'newer' Tibetans were more open in their acceptance of Chinese Buddhism. These disagreements culminated in "The Great Debate."

The Growth of Buddhism: "The Great Debate" was held at Samye in about 792 in order to decide whether to follow Indian or Chinese Buddhist doctrine. The basis of the Indian teaching was the assumption that it was necessary to accumulate vast quantities of knowledge and merit throughout innumerable ages, if one wished to progress towards the goal of Buddhahood. This favored the side of conventional intellectual and moral training which had given Buddhist monasticism stability since its foundation. The Chinese doctrine concentrated on the absolute nature of Buddhahood, which could be reached by anyone who attained a state of complete repose. This made conventional morality and intellect appear irrelevant, and even harmful or obstructive to the contemplative state. The Indian case, skillfully presented by the Indian scholar Kamalasila, won the day over the chief Chinese debator but political considerations may also have been important as Tibet was once again at war with China.

After the great Samye debate, the political potential of the new mainstream religion was quickly appreciated and before long monk-ministers from noble families were wielding great power. The rivalry between the lay nobles and the religious leaders grew steadily. During the reign of Ralpachen (815-838), much work was done on the translation of Buddhist texts. The devout king left the administration to a monk-minister, but the reign came to a dramatic end when Ralpachen was murdered by anti-Buddhist opponents and his successor Langdarma began to persecute Buddhism. Langdarma ruled for six years but was himself murdered by a monk. This marked the beginning of 200 years of infighting and the destruction of the Tibetan empire.

Contemporary histories disagree about what happened after Langdarma's murder. Some say he had a son, others claim that there was no heir. What is clear is that from 842, disorder reigned and cultural, religious and literary activities were all but non-existent. Tibetan unity and strength was destroyed by rivalry between generals commanding the frontier armies. Sometime early in the ninth century, a descendant of the old royal family migrated to the west and founded small kingdoms there, but by 899 Tibet was no more than a collection of separate principalities. A few Buddhist monks escaped to Kham (east Tibet) where they developed "the second diffusion of the doctrine" under Gongpa Rabsal around the turn of the ninth century, and in some parts of west

However, as the Tibetan kingdom was no longer united, the decentralized conditions led to the development of some 20 different sects. The Nyingmapa sect, the "Ancient Ones," claims to most purely preserve the teachings of the eighth century, and may therfore contain stronger elements of the more ancient Bon religion than the other sects. This sect follows the teachings of Padmasambhava (Guru Rinpoche), one of the founders of the Samye Monastery. The Nyingmapa became known as the "Red Hats."

The other important sects can be traced back to the 11th century when Atisha came to Tibet. Sakya Monastery, center of the Sakyapa sect, and Reting Monastery, center of the Kadampa sect, were founded, and the teacher Marpa, founder of the Kagyudpa school, was teaching.

Another famous person at this time was

TIBETAN GIRLS   J.SINGH
                      DARJEELING

TIBETAN BRIGHT-PRIESTS   J.SINGH
                            DARJEELING

Tibet, Buddhism still flourished. Throughout most of Tibet, however, Bon was once more predominant and Buddhist teachings were adapted, misinterpreted and undermined.

There were signs of a Buddhist Renaissance in west Tibet at the end of the 10th century when Yeshe O, king of Guge, sent the scholar Rinchen Sangpo to India to expand his knowledge of Buddhist teachings and to bring back Indian teachers and artists. This led to the foundation of the first monasteries in west Tibet.

Growth of the Sects: In 1042 Atisha, a celebrated Mahayana teacher from India, went to west Tibet at the invitation of the king. Later, Atisha expanded his missionary activities into central Tibet until he died in Nyethang, near Lhasa, in 1054.

Marpa's pupil, Milarepa, the poet, singer and ascetic who, it is reputed, lived only on nettles until his hair turned green. One of his caves, six miles (10 km) north of Nyalam, can still be visited.

Milarepa shunned the material life but the established sects became increasingly prosperous through the support of local lords. Although many lamas of different sects studied together there was considerable worldly competition.

The period of feuds and struggles between princely and monastic states continued until 1207 when centralized rule was once more achieved under the control of the Mongol Empire. The Tibetans had established relations with and—to avoid invasion—paid tribute to, the great Mongol chief, Ghengis Khan, after his armies had attacked Reting Monastery.

In 1247 Sakya Pandit's, a scholar from Sakya Monastery, was summoned to Mongolia and appointed the Mongol's viceroy for Tibet by Ghengis Khan's successor Godan Khan. The year after Sakya Pandita's death in 1251, the Mongols invaded once again. Three years later Kublai Khan, who was to become emperor of China, granted control of the many small Tibetan estates, which had been reorganized into 13 main districts, to Sakya's nephew, Phagpa Lodro Gyaltsan and later made him "Imperial Preceptor" over Tibet. This was the beginning of the priest-patron relationship that was later to develop into the patron-lama link between the Manchu Emperors and the Dalai Lamas.

The recognition of the Sakyapa sect was resented by the Drigungpa sect and in 1290 the support of local rulers and Mongol chiefs. The great monasteries founded in the first half of the 15th century—Ganden, Drepung, Sera, Tashilhunpo and Chamdo—were all founded by Tsongkhapa's disciples.

By the end of the 14th century, Buddhism had permeated the whole of Tibetan society. The monasteries developed on feudal lines, each having noble supporters, farmers and peasants providing tithes and military manpower in times of strife. Not only did the cultural life of the monasteries flourish but popular crafts, in the form of jewelry making, carving and carpet weaving developed. Literature was mainly in the hands of the monks, but traveling minstrels continued the oral tradition of singing of the glories of ancient kings and monasteries, and sometimes supplemented their repertoires with popular reli-

Sakya generals destroyed the Drigung monasteries. The main monasteries of the different sects were important political and military bases as well as theological centers. The Sakyapa sect remained in control until 1354 when they were overpowered by the Pagmotru sect and from this time on various new schools flourished.

The most powerful of the new sects was the Gelugpa or "Yellow Hat" sect. This had been founded in the 14th century by Tsongkhapa, the "great reformer" and is considered to have grown out of the Kadampa sect. It gradually gained the

Left: Attractive postcards of early Tibetans. Above, 19th-century Gurkhas at the Nepal-Tibet border.

gious tales.

The Dalai Lamas: Despite the inter-sect battles of the 15th century, the Gelugpa sect increased its power and influence. This was mainly through the appeal of their order which held to monastic simplicity, religious devotion and austerity—a considerable contrast to the other more worldly sects. Sonam Gyamtso, high priest of the Gelugpas, born and recognized as the reincarnation of the Abbot of Drepung in 1543, was the first to introduce an important political aspect to the sect. This he did by turning outside Tibet for help, when his Yellow Hats were lacking support. He found it in the form of Altan Khan, chief of the Turmed Mongols, who recognized his authority and conferred upon him the title of Dalai Lama. The title was then granted posthumously to his two predecessors. This meeting may have echoed the link between Sakya Pandit and Kublai Khan but in 16th century the Mongols were no longer in a position to offer more than rich gifts to the Tibetans. In exchange, Sonam Gyamtso, the third Dalai Lama, traveled through Mongolia, establishing a new "religious empire."

Conveniently, the reincarnation of Sonam Gyamtso was "found" in the family of Altan Khan himself (the only non-Tibetan Dalai Lama). This diplomatic move benefitted the Yellow Hats considerably as a large retinue of Mongolians followed the child back to Tibet. Although there was no physical opposition, the Red Hats of the Karmapa sect sent patronizing messages to the new Dalai Lama, which the Yellow Hats found insulting. This resulted in a new round of petty

to the Gelugpas. New monasteries were also built—some on hilltops in impressive and dominating positions. This new spirit in architecture reflected the grandeur and triumph of the Gelugpas and culminated in the building of the Dalai Lama's palace, the Potala. The great fifth Dalai Lama (1617-1682), was the first Tibetan ruler to effectively unite both spiritual and temporal power. He was a mighty scholar, architect and politician and he was served by worldly and able monk-politicians. His death appears to have been concealed by the regent, the provisional ruler of Tibet during a Dalai Lama's minority, while the new incarnation was being brought up, and the building of the Potala finished. This fact was not finally made public until 1697.

At this time the Manchu tribes, having won over the Mongols, ousted the Ming Dynasty from

violence and insults. The Gelugpas had now really descended to the worldly level of the other orders.

In the early-17th century, the U (Lhasa area) province collapsed in the face of Tsang (Shigatse area) opposition, resulting in the growth of Red Hat power. There were attempts to mediate but in 1664 Gusri Khan of the Qosot Mongols came to the Dalai Lama's aid and overthrew the king of Tsang, giving his territory to the Dalai Lama.

The pacification of the whole of Tibet took some time but by 1656 the fifth Dalai Lama's regime stretched from Mount Kailash in west Tibet to Kham. The abbot of Tashilhunpo was given the title Panchen Lama by the Dalai Lama. Tibetan theocracy was greatly consolidated with many of the Karmapa monasteries handing over

Peking where they remained until 1911. Relations between the Tibetan Gelugpas and the Manchu court developed in the form of diplomatic contacts. In 1652 the Dalai Lama himself visited China.

Invasions: In 1705 Lhajang Khan, king of the Qosot Mongols and the fourth successor of Gushri, invaded Tibet. Lhasa was conquered, and the sixth Dalai Lama deposed and sent to China. The 25-year-old Dalai Lama died en route. It was then declared that he had been a false reincarnation and the Khan enthroned a monk of his own choice. It was made clear that the original sixth Dalai Lama was deemed unsuitable to govern. He was considered to be more fond of wine, women and song than religion or politics. However, the strong Tibetan belief in reincarnation made his overthrow very unpopular and his replacement was more or less ignored.

The first Capuchin monks arrived in 1707, followed in 1716 by the Jesuit, Father Ippolito Desideri who became the first Western scholar of Tibetan. The Christians' descriptions of Lhajang Khan showed him to be extremely unpopular as the destroyer of the Dalai Lama and the murderer of Sangye Gyamtso, the regent. He was also seen as a puppet of the Chinese emperor. He remained in power until 1717 when he was killed by the Dzungar Mongols.

The Dzungars were welcomed as deliverers but instead behaved savagely and even ransacked the tomb of the fifth Dalai Lama. Religious foundations were persecuted and an elderly nobleman was made regent but he could do little to prevent the reign of terror. With the approach of the

Chinese army the Dzungars pulled out, leaving the Manchu Chinese to take on the role of friends and saviors. They installed the seventh Dalai Lama, the reincarnation of the deposed sixth Dalai Lama.

The Manchu overlordship established a system of Chinese resident governors (ambans) and they wisely conferred the title of Wang on Pholhanas, the noble governor of Tsang who had fought against the Dzungars. "Power man Pholha" became the effective ruler of Tibet. He governed peacefully for 30 years, maintaining virtual inde-

Prayer stones, left, and Buddhist scriptures, above, are an integral part of daily life.

pendence from the Chinese by giving them due respect for their suzerainty. In 1750, three years after his death, Pholhanas' son was put to death by the amban for plotting against the Chinese residency. Later, the seventh Dalai Lama himself plotted against the Chinese and was deprived of all effective power, which was transferred to a council controlled by the ambans. Chinese influence strengthened when the Tibetans appealed to them for help in the face of an invading Gurkha army from Nepal at the end of the 18th century. On that occasion a Chinese force was sent to defeat the Gurkha troops but in 1836, when Manchu power in Tibet was waning and another Gurkha army invaded, the Chinese did nothing to help. The Tibetans were forced to placate the invaders by paying an annual tribute to Nepal. By this time, the other neighboring states of Sikkim, Bhutan and Ladakh had all become independent political units.

The eighth Dalai Lama (1758-1804) was an unworldly figure taking no major part in the political scene, and his successors, the ninth, 10th, 11th and 12th Dalai Lamas all died under the age of 21, leaving power in the hands of a variety of regents. Rumors abounded about the reasons for their deaths. Generally, the country stayed peaceful and remarkably free of Chinese control. The ambans remained, but men chosen for the post usually regarded it as little more than punishing exile.

The great 13th Dalai Lama was born in 1876 and took full power in 1895. Thupten Gyamtso was the first Dalai Lama since the fifth Dalai Lama to have real influence over the destiny of his country. With the coming of the 20th century, the solitude and isolation of Tibet gave way to the encroaching modern world.

Pawn of the Superpowers: Tibetans had always been deeply suspicious of foreigners and at the beginning of the 20th century, they played upon their supposed imperial connection with China to avoid contact with Britain, claiming that it would displease their rulers. The British however, wary of rumored links between Russia and Tibet, and finding their own trading overtures with Tibet rebuffed, sent a diplomatic expedition led by Francis Younghusband to Tibet in 1904.

When the Tibetans refused to meet this mission, Younghusband was authorized to take his troops as far as Gyantse to force trade upon the lamas. Despite Christmas supplies of turkey and plum pudding, the British troops suffered miserably from the altitude and the extreme cold. When they finally met the pathetically-armed Tibetan troops, Younghusband's attempt to avoid combat failed. Shooting began by mistake and in four minutes 700 Tibetans were dead or dying. The Tibetans' bewilderment only increased when the British field hospital went in to treat the survivors. The British then took Gyantse and in August, when Younghusband marched into Lhasa, he found that the Dalai Lama had fled to Mongolia. A treaty was signed with the regent and, having obtained a trade agreement, the British withdrew and a flourishing trade relationship developed.

In 1910, the Chinese attempted to establish supremacy once again in Tibet. This time the Dalai Lama fled to India and the protection of the British. The Chinese Revolution in 1911 enabled the Tibetans to shake off unwanted Manchu rule and on his return to Tibet in 1912, the Dalai Lama resolved to rule without Chinese influence. British and Tibetan relations continued to improve—the trade route of wool out of Tibet in exchange for cotton cloth, kerosene, hardware, sugar, soap, matches and the greatly prized British Trilby hat became well established. In 1913-14, the British

However, society was still essentially feudal and many lay people were little more than serfs. The monasteries continued to flourish; it is estimated that a fifth of Tibet's male population was made up of celibate monks—every family was expected to give one son to the monkhood and even in the 20th century there was no other chance of becoming literate. The 13th Dalai Lama hoped to develop Tibet into an equal with its powerful neighbors but the religious establishment began to distrust his plans for modernization. He was forced to close the English school he had opened in Gyantse only two years earlier and the army fell into disarray again. He then sought to maintain a balance between Tibet's powerful neighbors.

The 14th Dalai Lama, Tenzin Gyamtso, was enthroned in 1940. Power was first held by the

arranged the Simla Conference where Tibet tried to gain recognition for its independence, while China continued to assert its claim over Tibet. A British compromise developed in which Tibet had autonomy within Chinese suzerainty. It was hoped thus that the Chinese would stay out of Tibet without "losing face," but the Chinese refused to sign the agreement.

The next 20 years were peaceful, with Tibet remaining neutral in both World Wars. European scholars, notably Sir Charles Bell, began recording Tibetan culture and the 13th Dalai Lama experimented with modernization. Tibetan officers were trained by the British Army, students went to study in England, a hydro-electric plant was established and the first car was carried over the mountains.

regent, Reting Rinpoche, a pious man, later replaced by Taktra Rinpoche, whose period of power was marked by corruption.

The Chinese Move in: In 1947, the British left India, effectively removing any deterrent to a Chinese invasion of Tibet. Chinese Nationalists had already established an office in Lhasa and in 1949 the new Communist government asserted its claims. In 1950 the Chinese captured Chamdo, the capital of east Tibet, while another Chinese force moved into west Tibet. The Dalai Lama sent a force to meet them but they were poorly equipped and the Tibetans had little choice but to negotiate. The Dalai Lama himself fled to the Sikkim border to return four years later, and the captured governor of Chamdo signed the "17-point agreement for the peaceful liberation of

Tibet," but later claimed he had been put under pressure to do so.

The Chinese appeared to come bearing gifts—talking of religious freedom and modernization. They spoke of "welcoming the Tibetans back to the Motherland." The promised break from the feudal past turned into a nightmare of confiscation, collectivization and shortages as the invaders lived off the land. Reactions from Tibet's first major resistance group resulted in the Chinese insistence that the Tibetan army be immediately integrated into the People's Liberation Army (PLA). The lay prime minister defied this request but the Dalai Lama then accepted both his and the religious prime minister's resignations and determined to deal directly with the Chinese himself. The Dalai Lama met Mao Tse Tung in Peking in 1954 and was led to believe that he would still

have some control of Tibet, but the longer he and his entourage stayed in Peking, the more they learned of the real intent of the Chinese. For the Chinese, Tibet, known as *Xizang* (The Western Treasure House), possessed mineral and forestry reserves and underpopulated tracts of land and they felt that by annexing it they could both obtain these and close their own back door. It also became clear that the Chinese Communist Party's ultimate aim was to shape all minoritiy groups of the region into the Han Chinese mould.

In 1954 rebellion broke out, started by the

Left, People's Liberation Army officials strike a benevolent pose in a Lhasa park. Above, the exiled Dalai Lama is on the minds of many Tibetans.

PLA's attempt to disarm the Khampa tribesmen. This led to the strafing and destruction of the Litang Monastery in east Tibet. The rebellion spread and although the details are little known it seems that in eastern Tibet there was full-scale war. Fifteen thousand Khampa families fled to Lhasa and many people joined the Khampa resistance. The rebellion reached its peak in 1959. There were mass demonstrations against the Chinese—the numbers swollen by the Khampa refugees—and the Dalai Lama, unable to control them and fearing reprisals, fled to India. A few days after his departure, the Norbulinka (Summer Palace), the Sera Monastery and the Jokhang (Lhasa Cathedral) were shelled. By the end of 1959 some 20,000 refugees had fled their homeland, many dying en route. Eventually there were over 100,000 Tibetan refugees. In Tibet, religious persecution was rife and thousands of people were killed.

As Tibet began to recover from the turmoil of the rebellion, it faced the Cultural Revolution. Information on this period (1966-1976) is again far from clear. After the flight of the Dalai Lama the remnants of the Tibetan government had been dissolved and in 1965 the Tibetan Autonomous Region was set up. This meant that China had complete administrative, political and economic control. While many thousands starved, Tibetans were forced to grow wheat for shipment to China. Historic buildings were dismantled and then destroyed and Tibetan religion and culture were banned.

Government-in-Exile: Meanwhile, the Dalai Lama established a government-in-exile in Dharamsala in India. In 1979, dialogue between the Chinese and the exiles began again and delegations from Dharamsala were allowed into Tibet. However, China has made it clear that if the Dalai Lama is to return anywhere it will be to a desk job in Peking. Within Tibet, there have been considerable changes since 1980. Tibetans are now allowed to grow the crop of their choice, their taxes have been reduced and collective farms dismantled. Most importantly for Tibetans, religious freedom has been restored and a limited number of young men and women are being allowed to become monks and nuns. Most of the destroyed monasteries are being repaired. Despite recent disturbances in October 1987, when Tibetan demonstrations calling for independence were quelled by Chinese troops, the Chinese appear to realize that Tibet's greatest asset is as a source of foreign currency through tourism. Dharamsala has become the center of Tibet in exile and the Dalai Lama's government now has offices in New York, London, New Delhi, Switzerland, Tokyo and Kathmandu. Their main task is to keep Tibetan culture and customs alive and maintaining links with their homeland in the Himalayas.

LHASA

The inspiration of generations of explorers and the heart of the Forbidden Land, the name of **Lhasa** still rings with mystery. The recent growth of a utilitarian Chinese town around the old Tibetan quarter, though, may disappoint modern travelers who arrive with romantic visions of the fabled city.

Still, the Potala Palace, towering above the city on a craggy red hill, cannot fail to impress. The old town, full of pilgrims, nomads or rugged traders with daggers in their belts, maroon-robed monks and jewelry-adorned women spinning their prayer wheels, is quite unlike anywhere else in the world.

Lhasa now has a population of 150,000, many of whom are Han Chinese. It is divided into two sections—the modern Chinese section and the Tibetan one that dates back to the seventh century when King Songtsengampo moved his court from the Yarlung Valley. Despite the Cultural Revolution, the main religious sites remain imposing and there are all kinds of gems to be discovered in the not-so-obvious corners.

Rooms to Spare: Begun in the seventh century, the awe-inspiring Potala now consists of 1,000 rooms and 13 storeys. Most of the building was constructed in the reign of the fifth Dalai Lama between 1645 and 1693. The main structure, the **White Palace** (Podrang Karpo), was completed in three years. The fifth Dalai Lama then moved his government and residence there and it became the power center of Tibet. The **Red Palace** (Podrang Marpo) was still only a plan when the fifth Dalai Lama died, and the regent, Sangya Gyamtso, went ahead with its construction, concealing news of the death until the building was finished. It was completed in four years by 7,000 Tibetan and Chinese workers. The original seventh-century structures were incorporated into the design. Minor alterations were made in the 18th century and the 13th Dalai Lama had a new set of apartments built in the White Palace during this time.

The construction was a huge undertaking. So much earth was dug up for mortar that the pit behind the Red Hill became a lake. The enormous walls are over 16 feet thick at the base and copper was poured into the foundations to help withstand earthquakes.

The White Palace is approached through the Shol village under the Potala. The

yellow **East Plaza** (Deyang Shar) is reached by a broad corridor with very thick walls. This large courtyard is surrounded by two-storey former offices.

To the west of the courtyard is the main seven-storey building of the White Palace. After going up some steps you reach the entrance foyer, the north and east walls of which have frescoes of Princess Wenchang's (the famous Chinese wife of Songtsengampo) journey to Tibet. The south wall shows the fifth Dalai Lama's edict proclaiming Sangya Gyamtso as regent and a frescoe of the building of the Jokhang.

On the top floor are the Dalai Lama's apartments, including bedrooms, chapels and meditation rooms. The suite of rooms on the east side, Nyiwod Shar, were built by the 13th Dalai Lama; those on the west are the original suite—Nyiwod Lho. The terrace outside the bedroom has magnificent views. A chapel on the west side of the roof level has a big statue of Maitreya and leads into the sixth Dalai Lama's quarters. From here a corridor connects the Red Palace to the White.

The Red Palace consists of a main hall, the biggest in the Potala, and numerous chapels. The Main Hall West, Tshomchen Nub, so called because it is west of the White Palace main hall, contains nearly 3,300 square feet (300 square meters) of wall paintings, many of which describe the life of the fifth Dalai Lama. The Dalai Lama's throne is in the center of the west wall. For important ceremonies, a huge pair of fabulous gold embroidered curtains are hung. They were given by the Qing Kangsi emperor to commemorate the palace's completion. The pillars are wrapped in Bhutanese fabric.

Four chapels open off this main hall: The **North Chapel** contains statues of the Dalai Lamas. A gold Sakyamuni and a silver fifth Dalai Lama are in the center. On the far left is the gold *chorten* (shrine) of the 11th Dalai Lama flanked by two rows of Medicine Buddhas. On the right is Chenrezi in all his historical incarnations. The **East Chapel** is dedicated to Tsongkhapa and contains images of him and other Gelugpa lineage holders.

The South Chapel is dedicated to Padmasambhava, whose silver image is in the center flanked by his two wives. East of this are eight sculptures of his lineage holders; to the west, eight of his manifestations. Fine *thankas* (religious paintings) hang above the **West Chapel**. The famous gold and sandalwood *chorten* of the fifth Dalai Lama is found here. It is said to have taken 814 pounds (370 kg) of gold and contains the mummified remains of the Lama. Flanking this are the burial *chortens* of the 10th and 12th Dalai Lamas.

The second floor windows of the Tshomchen Nub open on to the chapels and halls below. There is a gallery of excellent murals showing historical scenes from Tibet including the spirited celebrations after the completion of the Red Palace. On the third floor, you can have a cup of tea and browse in the souvenir shop.

On the fourth floor, the south side contains the seventh Dalai Lama's assembly hall and apartment while going east leads to the oldest section of the Potala—the original palace built by Songtsengampo. The ancient **chapel of Phagpa Lhakhang**, reached by a flight of wooden stairs, is the holiest part of the edifice and contains the most important statue of the Potala, a small jewel-encrusted **statue of Chenrezi**. It came from Nepal and has been kept here since Songtsengampo's time despite having been lost in Amdo during the 17th century. The small seventh-century meditation cave below the Phagpa Lhakhang contains sculptures of Songtsengampo and his wives.

Other chapels contain intricate mandalas,

scriptures and fine sculptures, but it can be difficult to visit them. The **Ornament of the World Chapel** that houses the 13th Dalai Lama's tomb must be visited in the company of a Potala official. Built in 1933, the three-storey *chorten* contains priceless jewels and uses 1,300 pounds (590 kg) of gold. The famous pearl mandala in the form of a pagoda is here. Its roof is made of pure gold, turquoise and coral and the whole structure is made with 200,000 pearls. Frescoes in the chapel depict the fifth Dalai Lama's life. There are also chapels for the *chortens* of the seventh, eighth and ninth Dalai Lamas. The maverick sixth was deposed and exiled, and has no tomb.

Soul of Tibet: The **Jokhang**, the so-called Grand Cathedral, is the soul and essence of Tibet—its best expression of religious and cultural achievement. When Tibetan pilgrims travel thousands of miles from remote corners of the country, prostrating all the way to Lhasa, it is to the Jokhang that they come. It is the center of Tibetan Lhasa and everything else revolves around it.

The **Barkhor**, a street that surrounds this most sacred of monasteries is at once a fascinating and bustling market and a holy circuit. The quickest way to gain an insight into Tibetan life is to spend an afternoon here. It is a fascinating market-cum-pilgrimage circuit where Nepalese, Chinese and Muslims mix with Tibetan traders to sell a wonderful array of goods, ranging from Stetson hats to daggers. Bargaining is essential.

Most pilgrims spend a great deal of time continuously circumambulating the Jokhang along the Barkhor, gaining additional merit with each new circuit.

The Jokhang, the first Buddhist temple in Tibet, was built, on the suggestion of his Nepalese wife Tritsun, by Songtsengampo around 645 A.D. Since then, three major renovations have brought the building to its present condition. Recently, repairs were undertaken in 1971 (under the personal orders of Chou-En-Lai), 1973 and 1985-86.

There are two main structures: the first is the Jokhang itself, the second is the surrounding complex of the **Tsuglhakhang**. Three sides of this complex are enclosed by big buildings; the fourth, on the west, is the main entrance. All of this is in turn surrounded by the Barkhor.

Follow the trail of pilgrims into the Jokhang and remember to keep going clockwise. Entering the ground floor of the Tsuglhakhang, you pass the **Gyalchen Zhi** **chapel** containing big statues of the Four

The Barkhor attracts traders from all over Tibet.

Guardian Kings. The frescoes on the left of the entrance foyer depict the Qosot Mongol prince, Gushri Khan, offering tribute to the 17th- century Regent Sangya Gyamtso. The large assembly hall, the Khyamra Chenmo or **Dukhang**, is covered with frescoes painted in 1648.

The first chapel (destroyed) on the left is the **Chapel of The Three Doors to Enlightenment**. After this is the **throne** of the Dalai Lama. Passing the **Drolma Lhakhang** (destroyed), you join the pilgrims' circumambulation along the **Nangkhor** (inner circuit) which surrounds the Jokhang, passing ruined chapels and numerous prayer wheels. Off a small courtyard at the eastern section is one of two main kitchens, remarkable for its 10-foot diameter metal cauldrons. The frescoes on the walls of the Nangkhor depict the 108 stories of Buddha's previous lives according to the Kashmiri poet Ksemendra Avadanakalpalata. They were commissioned by the 13th Dalai Lama.

At the entrance of the Jokhang proper, two small chapels (**Lukhang** and **Disakhang**) house the water and earth divinities. Next to the water dragon's shrine is a slab of flagstone which is the mythical opening onto the lake over which Lhasa was built. Every year in the second month it is opened to make offerings to the water dragon to prevent the lake from rising.

The entrance leads into an inner courtyard (**Kyilhor Thil**) which contains large sculptures of religious and historical figures. There are 100 very early sphinx-like lion figures around the top of the hall (one of these has a human face).

The chapels around this courtyard contain many recently restored sculptures. Pilgrims follow the prescribed circuit and visit every chapel. Along the north wing, the **Thuje Chenpo Lhakhang** contains the 11-headed image of Chenrezi. This is the most important statue in the Jokhang after the Jowo Sakyamuni. The original was destroyed in the Cultural Revolution.

After the **Wopagme Lhakhang** (Chapel of Amitabha, the God of Infinite Light), is the Holy of Holies: The **Jowo Sakyamuni Lhakhang**. This contains the statue of Jowo Rinpoche, representing the Buddha at the age of 12.

The second floor of the Jokhang includes many more chapels, all destroyed and locked up. There is a spot on the southeast corner wall where pilgrims often rub their backs to relieve the sins of the body and to cure backache. **Songtsengampo's Chapel**

roads ad to the tala.

is another chapel with a gilded roof. The statues of the king and his wives were commissioned by the Nepalese wife and created by Nepali craftsmen.

The third floor of the Tsuglhakhang consists of the Dalai Lamas's quarters. The third floor of the Jokhang itself is dedicated to the Goddess Palden Lhamo, and in the stairwell at the southeast corner of this floor are her two statues. The famous wrathful form, covered by a veil, is shown eating brains from a human skull and is clothed in the skins of dead men. The roof gives a fabulous view of the mountains surrounding Lhasa and the Potala, and consists mainly of four gilded pagoda-style roofs crowning the lower chapels.

A Summer Palace: The palaces, pavilions, zoo, gardens and woods of what is now called the **People's Park** cover 99 acres (40 hectares). It is pleasantly wooded and is a favorite picnic spot for Tibetans. With its vast open spaces, it is a refreshing place to visit after the challenge of the great religious sites. The park was actually built by the seventh Dalai Lama who began to use it as the Summer Palace. The eighth Dalai Lama expanded the Summer Palace and built the Debating Pavilion, the Palace on the Lake, the West Water Dragon Palace, the Retreat

Building and some of the park walls. The 13th Dalai Lama, influenced by Chinese architecture, then built more buildings and completed the gardens. The most recent construction was that of the present 14th Dalai Lama who built a palace in the mid-1950s.

The area really divides into two parts: The eastern part—the **Norbulinka** proper and the western part, or **Chensiklingka**.

The Norbulingka includes a section of the palace, the opera grounds and the Government offices. The **Chensiklingka** contains the rest of the palace section, the forest section and fields. Southwest of the palaces is the **Usilkhang**, the Pavilion for Hairwashing. The **Kalzang** palace is the building to the southeast where the Dalai Lamas used to administer affairs of state and religion. There is a big main hall and offices of the Dalai Lama. North of this is a small 18th-century meditation building, the **Woser Podrang** where the 13th Dalai Lama came often to meditate. This is the oldest building in the park. The big three-storey building of the **Chensel Podrang** with a tree-filled courtyard was used exclusively by the 13th Dalai Lama. Here he held audiences, watched dances, studied and relaxed.

The two-storey building to the west is the

Jokhang, the "soul of Tibet."

Kalzang Dhesi Podrang, and contained the 13th Dalai Lama's personal treasures. It was in the main chapel here that he received important visitors. The **Jigme Chutsi Podrang** was the favorite of the 13th Dalai Lama.

The so-called New Palace, the **Dhonden Migyur Podrang,** was built by the present Dalai Lama and was both his living quarters and office. It remains as it was when he left in 1959 and is an unusual mix of traditional religious style and the contemporary. The Dalai Lama's collection of 78 rpm records and gramophone can still be seen in his living room on the second floor.

The **Dhingcha Khang** or Debating Pavilion is near the **Khamsum Zikkyam** where the Dalai Lamas watched opera troupes from all over Tibet. The most important festival held here was the annual *Shotun* or Yoghurt Festival, when traditionally the nomads gave yoghurt to monasteries. This festival was revived again in 1986. For five days in July, there is a great celebration and many of Lhasa's inhabitants come to picnic and watch the operas.

The Horse Pavilions, or Dalai Lamas's stables, are designed so that horses can be viewed comfortably from the second floor. Soothing frescoes are painted inside the horses' stalls. In the center of the artificial lake is a small pagoda-style building, furnished with Chinese furniture from the Ching Dynasty emperor. This was used for the birthday ceremonies of the Dalai Lamas. The square Chinese-style pavilion nearby is known as the **West Water Dragon Place.**

Near Lhasa: About six miles (nine km) west of Lhasa along the main airport road and then up the hill slopes on the right is **Drepung,** the largest monastery in Tibet. It is an extensive monastic town with a surprisingly European feel to its orderly jumble of white-washed buildings. Drepung is one of six major Gelugpa centers of Tibet. Drepung once had a population of 8,000 monks (now there are 300), and was the political center of the Gelugpas before the Potala was built. A disciple of Tsongkhapa founded it in 1416 after the pattern of an Indian Tantric monastery. It suffered badly in the internecine wars, was destroyed twice by the Mongols and suffered more recently under the Chinese but, phoenix like, it always seems to revive.

Drepung is divided into four specialist colleges grouped around the central hall. Each college had its own administration and domestic arrangements and the entire community came together only for important

occasions.

The main hall is on the west side of the complex. A massive flight of steps leads up to the eight red pillars of the entrance. Behind the hall is a small unpretentious chapel, the Jampayang Lhakhang, flanked by white chortens. This was the original foundation of Drepung and parts of its walls are formed of a carved rockface. The **Losaling** is the college to the south of the hall and its inmates specialized in logic. It has a spacious courtyard and its chapels contain numerous sculptures and scriptures. The back wall of the assembly hall opens onto the small chapels of Neding, Champakhang and Dongsar Lhakhang. Debates are held in the garden under fine old trees. The **Trashi Gomang** is to the northeast. The most notable of the images in the main hall is a 1,000-armed version of Chenrezi. The **Deyang Chapel** (south of Trashi Gomang), dedicated to the Gods of Medicine, has images of Tsongkhapa and the fifth Dalai Lama. The **Ganden Podrang** to the southwest was the administration base of the Dalai Lamas before it was moved to the Potala. It is here that the celebrations of the Yoghurt Festival are held.

Between the Drepung complex and the airport road is Nechung Monas**tery**, the seat of the state oracle of Tibet. The activities of the oracle are fascinating and accounts of this can be found in John F. Alvedon's *In Exile from the Land of Snows*. The main door of Nechung is of very fine metalwork with thin silver inlay. The main assembly hall is small and has three chapels at the rear.

Sera and Ganden: North of Lhasa is the Gelugpa monastic town of **Sera** or Sera Choding. It is in remarkably good condition but looks deserted as there are few monks here. It was founded by a disciple of Tsongkhapa in 1419. The **Sera Me Tratsang** was the college reserved for teaching novices. It has an imposing statue of the Sakyamuni flanked by Champa and Jampayang and many chapels dedicated to different deities.

The Ngagpa Tratsang college is for the teaching of esoteric mysticism. The third college, Sera Je Tratsang, was reserved for the wandering monks of Kham. It contains a statue of the 13th Dalai Lama and the relics of important Sera Lamas. One of the chapels is dedicated to a Tantric divinity, Tamdrin, which has the head of a horse. There is a debating garden behind the building.

The most sacred object in Sera is a magic dagger (phurbu). Legend has it that this dagger belonged to a 13th-century Indian

Religious and physical heights a scaled at Drepung Monaste

ascetic and it flew to Tibet from India, landing on a small hill near Sera.

An hour's walk up the hill behind and to the east of Sera is the restored chapel of the oracle. It is often closed and the walk is steep but the prize is a panoramic view of Lhasa.

To get to Ganden **Monastery**, the most famous and most important of all Gelugpa monasteries, take the main East road, from Lhasa, heading towards Medugonggar. Turn off after 24 miles (39 km) at the 1529 road marker. Follow the winding road up the Ganden Valley for a further 11 miles (18 km) to the monastery.

The relentless and total devastation of Tsongkhapa's great monastic town reduces many returning Tibetans to tears. The whole town was destroyed by dynamite during the Cultural Revolution. Today it is being slowly rebuilt, largely by volunteer efforts.

The monastery was founded in 1409 as a training place for monks of the new discipline that was to become the Gelugpa sect. It was gradually expanded to become a huge institution. The first temple you come to after the bus and truck stop is a small *Lhakhang* (chapel) on the right. This is a vital and charming place, the congregation point of pilgrims and monks. A small assembly hall is on the ground floor. The second floor contains a private room for the Dalai Lama.

The big red fortress-like restored building further up the road, the **Serdhung Lhakhang**, once contained Tsongkhapa's tomb, the most sacred object of Ganden. This destroyed relic has been replaced by a new golden *chorten* on the second floor. The restored building of the Ganden Abbot is located to the right of the Serdhung. The office of Abbot (*Tripa*) in Ganden is neither transmitted by incarnation nor by inheritance, but is a seven-year appointment. The *Tripa* is usually chosen from among the most learned monks of the main monasteries in the Lhasa area.

Near the topmost building of the complex, the **Lubum**, which is consecrated to subterranean spirits, the sacred *Lingkhor* circuit starts. Most pilgrims visiting Ganden perform this highly important ritual. The route encircles the entire Ganden ridge, first passing rocky shrines and then coming to a flat black rock known as the **Vision Rock** where visions may supposedly be seen. To the left is a good view of the **Lhasa River Valley**. You then come to the sky burial site where pilgrims roll on the ground to rub off bad karma. Then a short descent to the **Sin Gauge**—a rock with a narrow cleft. It is

difficult to squeeze through—if you get stuck you have too much sin and have to turn back. Towards the end of the circuit is Tsongkhapa's cave and hermitage. Within are brightly painted images. Tradition has it that the knob of rock at the back was used by the saint to pull the cave wall closer to him. On the right of the path you pass a black conical rock about five feet high. Pilgrims put their stomachs on the top and then spit, or if possible vomit, to exorcise sickness and evil spirits.

Also known as the Little Jokhang, **Ramoche** is, after the Jokhang, the most important monastery in Lhasa. The entrance, on the west side of a big courtyard, is a 10 minute walk due north from the **Tromsikhang market** (the north section of the Barkhor, where all the Khampas congregate all day).

This badly sacked monastery has been restored since the Panchen Lamas's visit in 1986. Now nearly everything is new, and the place is full of life. Ramoche was founded by Songtsengampo's Chinese wife Wenchang in the seventh century, about the same time as the Jokhang. The famous Jowo statue of the Jokhang was first kept here. Ramoche's most important statue, the **Jowo Mikyod Dorje**, represents the Buddha at the age of eight. It is also called the Little Jowo or the Jowo Chungba. During the Cultural Revolution this important statue was 'lost' but was 'found' again in 1986 and returned to the inner sanctum. Eight *bodhisattvas* guard it.

Some of Ramoche's best features are on the roof where the original Chinese-style pagoda roof with its original ceramic tiles is still intact. It is a wonderful foreground for a magnificent view of the Potala. According to legend, Ramoche has a direct link with hell and there is a crystal palace of subterranean spirits deep beneath the monastery.

Other Holy Places: About a two-hour walk west from the **Lhasa Military Hospital** (north Lhasa, west of Sera) is the renovated **Paronka Monastery**, one of the most hallowed sites in all Tibet. At the hospital compound entrance, take the path to the left along the perimeter wall, continue around a bluff and into a side valley. From here you will be able to see the monastery perched on a huge granite rock. The main structure is unusual and comprises of the base of a large round tower built by King Songtsengampo but destroyed in the Cultural Revolution. There are few old objects here but Paronka is wonderfully photogenic and there are good views of the valley.

Also starting from the Military Hospital

Horse races are regular festival feature.

206

area, go north through Sera Monastery and take the zigzag footpath, which follows a cypress-lined ravine. On the left are some white buildings where the monks of Sera live. On the right is an impressive gilded roof chapel, with painted rock carvings nearby. Continue along the trail, following the small ravine to reach the hermitage of **Sera Utse** (about 90 minutes walk). The retreat, built before Sera Monastery, consists of an attractive group of buildings with a delightful courtyard and a sensational view. Only a handful of monks live there now.

Most of the lesser-known religious sites of Lhasa are within the Lin*gkhor* (the pilgrims' circuit around the center of Lhasa) and generally close to the Jokhang. Many were destroyed during the Cultural Revolution but others were converted into Government buildings or offices and are easy to miss because of the recent extensions and renovations.

The **Four Royal Monasteries** have all been badly damaged but you can still find some gems among the rubble. They were decreed by the fifth Dalai Lama and the regents of Tibet are often chosen from their abbots. All four were built after the 17th century. **Tangyeling**, originally the most important of the four, was no longer considered a royal monastery after it sided with the Chinese in 1921. It was badly damaged at that time by the Tibetan Government. It is located in a big complex directly in front of the **Snowland Hotel** but well hidden by other buildings. Inside the entrance portal, there is a maze of Tibetan houses ranged around the former courtyard. Ask for directions to the small chapel which has been rebuilt on the roof of the main hall. **Tsomoling**, south of Ramoche, apparently has been taken over by a crew of Chinese carpenters but there are still some original wall paintings left and the roof is worth a visit. The entrance is just north of the junction between the **Banak Shol Hotel** street and the Snowland Hotel street. The third royal monastery, **Kundeling**, is south of **Bhamari Hill**. From the **Post Office**, walk west towards **Lhasa Hotel**, pass **Chokpori Hill** and its cave monastery of **Dragla Lugug**. Below the small hill on the left is a new gas station, then a disused one. After this hill, a dirt road turns left, leading to a village and to the small rebuilt chapel of Kundeling.

Nearby, also on the sacred Bhamari Hill, are some ancient Chinese-style buildings—they are small Chinese/Tibetan temples known as the **Gesar Lhakhang**. Dedicated

to the Chinese God of war and linked with the Tibetan folk hero Gesar of Ling, these were built to celebrate the Chinese victory over the Gurkhas in 1792. They are one of the few reminders of the Chinese presence in Tibet in the 18th century. The architecture is quite unique in Tibet.

The fourth royal monastery, **Tsecholing**, is south of the Lhasa River in the village of **Trib**, at the entrance to the **Tungo La Valley**.

Three monastic teaching colleges (*tratsang*) can still be found near the Jokhang, while others are attached to the major monasteries. **Shide Tratsang** is quite difficult to find but the almost roofless main chapel still contains wonderful original wall paintings and the ruins still house interesting but damaged sculptures.

Across the street from the **Kirey Hotel** is the big stone building of the Tibet Theatre group. This is the monastery of **Muru Tratsang**, founded originally in the seventh century and where work on the Tibetan alphabet by Thonmi Sambhota, a famous minister of King Songtsengampo's, was completed. The monks here converted to the Gelugpas at the time of the third Dalai Lama and were connected with an important Tantric school known as the **Gyurme**

Tratsang whose building is next door to the west. **Gyurme Tratsang** is an extensive complex now used as a printing press to print Buddhist texts from old woodblocks. It is not officially open but it may be possible to persuade the guard to let you in.

Southwest of the main Lhasa **mosque** is the mellow oasis of **Tsangung Nunnery**. It is the only nunnery in old Lhasa and has over 80 nuns. Tsangung is a small, low yellow building with a courtyard in front of the main entrance. In the northeast corner, a small entrance leads to the oldest part, the **tsangkhang** (possibly seventh century), where there is an unusual hidden chamber and the meditation well (**tshamkhung**) of Songtsengampo, presided over by a sculpture of the king.

The small **Muru Nyingpa Monastery** attached to the southeast corner of the Jokhang is a pleasant find. Usually overlooked by tourists, the monks are surprised and delighted to have visitors. Take the small lane south from the north section of the Barkhor where the free market is. This lane passes a stone archway and leads to a flight of stairs (on the right) going up to some small rooms and a chapel on the second floor. The balcony is festooned with prayer flags. The chapel contains good

Youngsters shoulder their share of religious responsibility.

paintings and sculptures and is an important pilgrim stop. The main and larger chapel with a courtyard next to the entrance is around the corner. It is recently restored and is usually alive with religious activity. This monastery is the residence of the Nechung Oracle when he visits Lhasa.

The raised yellow stone dais on the south side of the Jokhang is known as the throne or *shugtri* and is used for important events. The small courtyard in front of it is the **Sung Choera**. This area was blocked from view by ugly shops but the Panchen Lama recently ordered that these be cleared to restore the pleasant plaza to its original splendor. The Sung Choera is where the geshes are examined in debate during the Monlam Festival of the New Year. Geshes are the Gelugpa equivalent of Doctorates of Theology.

The **Dragla Lugug Cave Monastery** is a very special hermitage and one of the most interesting monasteries in Lhasa. It is located on the southeast side of Chokpori Hill, about five minutes walk from the main Lhasa Hotel-to-Jokhang road. The inner sanctum cave chapel is off the second floor of the monastery. The dark rock walls of the cave glisten with smeared yak butter and 71 ancient (some restored) images are carved

directly onto the rock wall.

A popular picnic place immediately north of the Potala is **Liberation Park**. An island on a small lake holds the charming **Dzongyap Lukhang**—a small Naga chapel. In the park there are also two *dorings* (pillars with inscriptions) housed in small yellow buildings: one commemorates the defeat of the Dzungar Mongols in 1727; the other proclaims the defeat of the Gorkhas in 1791. In the southwest corner of the park is the **Langkhang**, the shed for the 13th Dalai Lama's elephant, a gift from the Maharajah of Bhutan.

There are five mosques in Lhasa used by the estimated 2,000 Muslim residents. Muslims first came to Tibet from Ladakh and Kashmir as traders at the time of the fifth Dalai Lama. They also came to Lhasa to work as butchers. Recently, many more have come from the Sala area of Qinghai. Notice the *halal* restaurants with blue banners outside the entrances. The original Muslim area is the **Khache Linka**, two miles west of the Potala. There are two mosques and a cemetery. The main mosque, **Gyal Lhakhang**, is near the southeast corner of the Barkhor. It was first built in the 18th century but was destroyed by fire. The present complex was built in 1959.

etan
dical
ctices
highly
arded.

THE FRIENDSHIP HIGHWAY

Parts of the Sino-Nepalese highway, the northern route between Lhasa and Shigatse, were built in 1955-56, but the **Friendship Highway**, constructed by the Chinese, was not opened until 1966. The purpose was to encourage trade links between the two countries, although there were initial fears that it was simply opening up Nepal to an imperialist threat. Now that the road has been open for some time it has become the main artery for trade as well as a major tourist route into Tibet. Linking Lhasa, Gyantse and Shigatse, it includes some of Tibet's most important religious sites as well as bridging two very different countries and cultures.

From Lhasa to Shigatse there are two routes. Try both if you have the opportunity. The northern road goes over two high passes and the 203 miles (328 km) cover some varied countryside. However, the southern route includes the important town of Gyantse and should not be missed.

The Northern Route: This is the oldest stretch of the Friendship Highway. From Lhasa, follow the first section of the Tibet-Qinghai highway to **Yangpajen**. Then turn southwest down the Uyug Valley to the Bon monastery of Yumdroling across from Tachuka. From there a ferry crosses the Tsangpo and the road continues west to Shigatse. The road markers are numbered from the road junction immediately after Yangpajen.

From the geothermal station of Yangpajen (about nine miles/15 km out of town), it is just over a mile further to the **Yangtse Monastery.** This is a Karmapa monastery built beside the **Lhorong Chu River** in 1490. It was rebuilt in 1986 and there are now about 20 monks. The road goes past areas of nomad camps and at the 25-mile (40-km) mark there is a good view of **Mount Chomo Ganggar** (20,260 feet/6,139 meters). The next few miles zigzag up to the **Shogar La**, a pass of 17,490 feet (5,300 meters) from where you have a fine view of a striking snow dome, part of the Chomo Ganggar range. The next pass is the 15,972-foot (4,840-meter) **Donggu La** at marker 104. Continue to the small town of **Uyug Qu** (134 miles/216 km from Lhasa) and enter an area of Himalayan-type terrace cultivation which is quite unusual for Tibet.

About 19 miles (30 km) from Uyug Qu, at

Preceding pages: Traders take a te break in Lhasa. Below, crossing the Tsangpo

marker 168, is the ferry over the Tsangpo. This crossing only takes five minutes by an iron barge.

The Bon monastery of **Yumdroling,** probably the most important Bon center in Tibet, is a short distance to the east on the north side of the river. To get there you have to wade the wide Uyug estuary and walk for about 45 minutes. From the monastery there are excellent views of the area. Yumdroling is nearly 900 years old and despite almost total destruction during the Cultural Revolution, it has been rebuilt.

The Southern Route: The first section covers the road from Lhasa to the airport. Shigatse is 51 miles (82 km) further west. From Lhasa, the road follows the west bank of the Kyi Chu. After passing Nyethang Monastery, cross the Tsangpo River at the big Chusul Bridge, turn right and climb up to 16,170 feet (4,794 meters) at the **Khamba La Pass.** From here there is a spectacular view of the **Yamdrok Tso** or Turquoise Lake, which is a freshwater lake about 150 miles (240 km) in circumference. It supports a small population of fishermen. The road then rises again to cross the **Karo La** (17,160 feet/5,010 meters), the site of the highest battle in history. It was here that Younghusband's British expedition fought

3,000 Tibetans in 1904. The road then descends to Gyantse. It takes about six hours from Lhasa to Gyantse in a four-wheel drive vehicle (12 hours by bus).

Lying at 12,540 feet (3950 meters), **Gyantse** is 130 miles (210 km) from Khasa or Zhangmu (Nepal border), 59 miles (95 km) from Shigatse. Originally a fort, Gyantse was once Tibet's third largest city and a trading link with the outside world. It is divided into two parts by a high rocky ridge topped by an imposing fortress. The west side contains the main monastery complex while the east is the principal approach to the fortress.

In the monastery complex, the **Kumbum,** known as the Chorten of 100,000 Images, is, at 100 feet (30 meters), the highest and most important surviving *chorten* in all Tibet. The 15th-century frescoes in the chapels are untouched and superb. Designed as the Holy Chorten of Many Doors (Trashi Gomang), one of eight *chorten* designs, it is a prime example of the best of Tibetan architecture. The *chorten* is constructed of successively smaller levels, each having chapels that contain statues and frescoes by artists of various schools. There are eight floors and a basement, the top being a one- room chapel reached by a rickety ladder. The design follows strict Tantric laws laid down by Buton, the well-known scholar, and was planned as a gigantic three-dimensional mandala. To circumambulate the various levels and visit all the chapels is the equivalent of going through all the esoteric liturgy of Mahayana Buddhism.

There are 73 chapels in total. Each contains a central sculptured figure and accompanying thematic murals. Many of the chapels have rare examples of 15th-century Newari art. The **Palkhor Chode Monastery** was founded under Sakyapa influence by Rabten Kunsang Phagpa, second prince of Gyantse, in 1418. Nine years later he built the Kumbum. At this time the Gelugpas were very influential and precepts of their sect were also included in the monastic curriculum. Eventually, many sects co-existed here and by the 19th century, seven different sects were represented. Much of Palkhor Chode has been destroyed but the original art that remains is an unique and unequalled example of a distinct Tibetan genre. Palkhor Chode and the Kumbum are perhaps the most important monuments in Central Tibet in terms of their artistic and cultural heritage.

The **Gyantse Fort** is one of the few forts in Tibet to have survived the Red Guards,

The Kumbum reflects Tibetan architecture at its best.

apparently because the British had already damaged it extensively in 1904. However, it remains very impressive and commands a great view of the area. There are no monks here. The fortress served as the Royal Palace of the Gyantse king and the monastery within was built in 1390.

The important Nyingmapa monastery of **Nenying** is seven miles (11 km) from Gyantse on the Chumbi Valley road. Half a mile west of Gyantse, take the left hand branch at the main road junction until you reach the 265 km road marker. A dirt road leads through Nenying village to the monastery's massive walls.

The monastery was founded by a Samye monk and became one of the most important Nyingma centers in Central Tibet. It was later taken over by the Gelugpas but both traditions continued to be followed.

Shigatse, the historical rival of Lhasa, is the second city of Tibet. It stands near the confluence of the Yarlung Tsangpo and the Nyangchu rivers on the north west end of the wide and fertile Nyang Valley. It is the administrative center for the huge region of West-Central Tibet and one of Tibet's most important agricultural centers. In the summer, the valley is richly colored with barley fields, all kinds of vegetables and the brilliant yellow of rape seed in flower. However, apart from the very vital Tashilhunpo Monastery, probably the only true monastic town in Central Tibet, and the old Tibetan market, the town itself is modern and unprepossesing.

It was not until the 17th century that the fifth Dalai Lama succeeded in uniting the Shigatse region, the province of Tsang, with the Lhasa region, the province of U. For centuries there were power struggles between the princely families and the diverse sects. Tsang was the center of the Nyingmapas at the time of the founding of Tashilhunpo—the Gelugpa monastery of Shigatse. The fifth Dalai Lama united the country and gave the Abbot of Tashilhunpo the title of Panchen Lama. From then on, Shigatse's religious importance was centered around the Panchen Lamas.

Tashilhunpo Monastery : This great Gelugpa monastery with perhaps the best religious atmosphere of all the principal Gelugpa monasteries, was founded in 1447 by Tsongkhapa's nephew and disciple Gedundrub. It was later enlarged by the fifth Dalai Lama. In 1642, he conferred the title of Panchen Rinpoche (Precious Teacher) upon his former tutor, the Abbot of Tashilhunpo, Lobsang Chokyi Gyaltsen.

View of Gyantse from the fortress.

The Panchen Lama was recognized as an incarnation of the Present Buddha, Amitabha, and of the two *Bodhisattvas* of Manjusri and Vajrapana. From this time on, the abbots of the monastery, whether appointed or elected, became the highest incarnates in Tibet along with the Dalai Lamas.

At one time, the monastery had over 4,000 monks, now reduced to about 600. The south facing rose-colored monastery is a spectacular sight and an important religious center. The tall building on the west side is the **Champa Chenmo** and houses a huge statue of the Future Buddha—the Maitreya or Champa. This 86-foot (26-meter) statue was built in 1914 and is said to have used nearly 660 pounds (300 kg) of gold and 330,000 pounds (150,000 kg) of copper and brass. The left hand holds a *bumpa* (vase), symbolising hidden treasure, and the right the *khorlo*, (wheel), emblems of the Sakyamuni.

The **Kesang Lakhang** is the big complex off the main courtyard of the monastery. The courtyard walls are painted with many small figures of Sakyamuni. In the main hall to the west, there is a throne for the Panchen Lama along with statues representing the different forms of Chenrezi.

vo
habitants
Tashil-
npo.

Left of the hall are chapels dedicated to Sakyamuni and Dorjechen, and a printing room. On the second floor many small chapels are arranged around a courtyard from where the hall can be seen. The chapel called **Chukhang Shar** contains the *chorten* of the first Panchen Lama. A long gallery, also on the second floor, contains hundreds of fine small bronzes. The kitchen of the complex, with its huge copper cauldrons, is worth seeing.

The tantric college **Ngapa Tratsang** is west of the main path. It is the only one of four colleges that survived the Cultural Revolution and it is now used by the monks for tantric ceremonies accompanied by memorable ritual music.

The free-standing *thanka* wall in the northeast corner of the complex is visible for several miles. This is used for an ancient ceremony when for three days in July, a huge *thanka* is hung from it. This festival drew tens of thousands of pilgrims when it was performed in 1985, for the first time since the Cultural Revolution.

A two-mile *khora* surrounds the monastery, hugging the perimeter wall of the complex and then ascending the hill from the west, passing small shrines and prayer wheels. The circuit offers a fine view of Shigatse and an opportunity to see the many fascinating rituals performed by pilgrims along the route. Some of them prostrate themselves the whole way.

After following the north wall the path splits: one path continues along the circuit, the other goes east to the ruined fort and the Tibetan market, where an assortment of jewelry, cloth, leather and copperware is on sale. To the west of Tashilhunpo is a sky burial site where the dead are disembodied and then fed to the many vultures which arrive on cue every morning from unknown mountain refuges.

The important **Shalu Monastery** is 12 miles (20 km) from Shigatse. Take the road to Gyantse and travel southeast from Shigatse center. A black rock (next to a village) covered with prayer flags marks the entrance to the Shalu Valley. Shalu is a marvellous combination of unique architecture, unusual historical background and fabled artwork. Its artistic heritage ranks with the great monasteries of Sakya and the Palkhor Chode and the Kumbum at Gyantse. It combines Chinese style with Tibetan tradition both in architecture and paintings.

Shalu was founded in the 11th century by a descendant of the Shangshung (west Tibet) royal family and a member of the Sakyapa sect. The site was consecrated by

Atisha himself during his trip from India to Central Tibet . It was destroyed by an earthquake in 1329 and subsequently rebuilt on the orders of the Mongol emperor of China. Apart from the main temple, rebuilt by Tragpe Gyaltsen at the beginning of the 14th century, the design and renovation was credited to the great Buton (1290-1364) who also built the Kumbum at Gyantse. He imported craftsmen and artists from China and Nepal and conceived the entire iconographic program for the monastery. Buton founded the Shalupa school here and wrote prolifically on many aspects of Tibetan Buddhism. He completed three great treatises on Tantra and his greatest accomplishment was probably the re-organization of the *Tanjur* and the *Kanjur* , the compendia of all sacred Tibetan texts.

What we see today at Shalu was mostly built around 1320. Originally there were four primary and six secondary sections. Only parts of the main chapel have survived. The rest has been absorbed by the Shalu village.

Shalu represents not only the coming together of diverse artistic currents which co-existed but did not mingle, but also the the beginning of an authentic Tibetan style of art.

At Shalu there are **Four Sacred Objects** held in great esteem by the monks. The most important is a sandalwood woodblock, carved jigsaw-like from 108 individual pieces. The monks maintain that it is 700 years old and say that once taken apart it will never be reassembled. In the main hall is a sealed bronze receptacle containing sacred water which is distributed to lucky pilgrims once every 12 years and which is said to have the power to remove sin. The water level supposedly remains constant throughout this period. Outside the main entrance is a bowl-shaped rock that collects rainwater. Shalu's founder used to wash his face here. The fourth object of veneration is the stone plaque in the courtyard inscribed with Tibetan script and carved with four *chortens*. This has survived from Shalu's founding.

The famous cave hermitage of **Shalu Ripug** is in the mountains to the northeast. This underground retreat was where hermits were supposedly sealed up for 12 years. Here, disciples of the Shalupa sect acquired skills such as levitation, running (in a meditative trance) for very long distances, and regulating body temperature.

Nine miles (14 km) from Shigatse on the north side of the westbound Friendship Highway (towards Lhartse) is **Narthang**

Tashilhunpo's giant thanka is displayed for three days each July.

Monastery. Narthang was an important 12th-century monastery famed for its wood-block library and printing press. It was completely destroyed in the Cultural Revolution. You can see little from the road but a walk through the adjacent village gives some idea of the extent of the ruins.

From Narthang go south across the main road towards the eastern base of a well-defined and isolated hill. Skirt the southeast side to **Harm** and then continue due south up the left hand valley to **Biron** village. Leave your vehicle here and walk half an hour further up the valley to **Ngor Monastery.** The monastery was founded in 1429 by Kunga Zangpo, the Sakyapa master. A Ngorpa subsect then developed here. At one time there were 18 different colleges under five masters. Ngor was famous for its Sanskrit manuscripts and its fabled art collection. The Nepalese wall paintings were outstanding and there were magnificent Indian and Pala sculptures.

Sakya Monastery: The most important sacred site between Shigatse and the Nepal border is the well-known **Sakya Monastery**. The road from Shigatse goes over the 14,850-foot (4,500-meter) **Po La Pass** just before the Sakya turnoff. Turn left immediately after crossing the Sakya River

Bridge at the road marker 377. A rough road takes you the 16 miles (25 km) to Sakya village.

As you approach, the huge fortress-like walls of Sakya can be seen rising from the valley floor in the red, blue and white colors of the Sakyapa sect. At each corner there are watchtowers showing a Mongolian tradition in the architecture that echoes the monastery's political history.

Originally, there were two monasteries on the north and south banks of the Trum River. The northern site, now ruined, was the earlier of the two and founded in 1073. The southern part, dating back to the 13th century, was built on the order of the famous Sakya patriarch Phagpa. Phagpa (1235-1280) was the fifth of the Five Sakya Patriarchs. He was a child prodigy and nephew of the great Sakya Pandita. At the age of nine he was already giving teachings to the *sangha*. Later, he accompanied his uncle to Mongolia. Phagpa was much favored by Kublai Khan and became the emperor's spiritual advisor. At the same time he was able to accumulate much wealth for the construction of the new monastery. It is claimed that 100,000 people were present at Phagpa's feast to celebrate the completion of the monastery. With the support of the

estora-
on work
n the
urals at
halu.

Mongols the Sakya sect became very powerful and Phagpa was effectively the ruler of Tibet.

The principal building of the monastery is the **Tsogchen Dukhang**, the 64,000-square-foot (5,760-square-meter) assembly hall.The surrounding walls are 53 feet (16 meters) high and 12 feet (3.5 meters) thick. The roof of the very impressive assembly hall is supported by 40 pillars, four of which, each a massive single tree trunk, are especially famous and sacred. One was carried all the way from China as a gift of the Kublai Khan, another is said to have been carried from India on the back of a tiger, the third was delivered on the horns of a black yak. The yak wept en route, creating a sacred spring at the Yak's Tears Pass, south of the Yalung district. The last, also from India, was said to have bled the black blood of its protector spirit when it was cut down.

The best time to see the magnificient main hall is when the morning sun lights up the murals and sculptures to show them in all their natural majesty. The main images are the big statues of Sakyamuni, Jampayang and Jetsun Champa Gonpo. Sakya patriarchs are also represented. Between the statues are shelves of ancient Buddhist texts.

In front of the great hall is a paved courtyard. Stone steps lead from here to the second floor of the East Wing, to the chapels of **Phuntsok Potrang** and **Drolma Potrang.** Notice the fine original paintings in the stairwell between the ground and second floor.

In the **Nguldhung Chapel** to the north side of the courtyard, there are 20th-century paintings with scenes depicting the construction of the monastery. The 11 *chortens* in the hall contain the relics of the Sakya rulers.

The monastery suffered during the internecine strife of the 16th century and was subsequently renovated. Another major renovation was carried out in 1948. Unfortunately, many of the old wall paintings were repainted over at this time.

At the back of the main hall are the libraries known as **Kunga Rawa**, where over 20,000 texts are kept. This is a very rare and important collection. Sakya also has over 300 *thangkas*, over 20,000 sculptures and numerous pieces of rare porcelain dating back to the Yuan, Ming and Sung eras. The whole monastery is a treasure trove and more mundane items such as safety pins offered by pilgrims, or modern Dalai Lama pictures, are mixed with rarities of great

The distinctive red, blue and white walls of Sakya.

value.

Lhartse: This small town is little more than a trucker's resting place but it is worth breaking your journey to visit the few sites in the area. **Lhartse Chode**, 7.5 miles (12 km) north of Lhartse, is a large three-storey restored monastery in the center of the village, next to a small hill with fortress ruins on top. **Gayadara Lhakhang** is a cave temple inside the hill next to the monastery, and was named after the 11th-century Kashmiri pandit who died in Tibet. You can see the door to the temple, marked with prayer flags, from below the hill.

The 14th-century **chorten of Gyang Bumoche** is a 90-minute walk from Lhartse Chode. To reach it, take the path through the cultivated fields from the left of the wide valley (where Lhartse Chode is), to the right. The big earth *chorten* can be seen just a little outside the village. It stands on a small hill and is badly ruined. The wall paintings have now been eroded by rain. These were quite unique as they were done by local Tibetans but had absorbed foreign influences in a primitive and interesting way. Nearby are the ruins of a small Nyingmapa monastery called **Gyang Yonpolung** and Padmasambhava's **meditation cave** is also in the neighborhood.

From Lhartse the route on to Shegar crosses the **Lhakpa La Pass** (17,225 feet/ 5,220 meters) and takes three hours. **Shegar** itself is the base for trekking and climbing expeditions to the Everest region. The town is four miles (seven km) north of the main road. The old Tibetan town has an impressively situated rebuilt monastery on the slopes of an imposing ridge. Shegar, the "Shining Crystal Monastery," once housed 400 monks.

From the Shegar turnoff to the village of **Tingri** is 37 miles (60 km). Here, there are marvellous views of the Himalayas to the south including the peaks of Everest and Cho Oyo. The panorama continues as you drive towards Nyalam beyond the spectacular **Lalung Leh Pass** (16,665 feet/ 5,050 meters). Just north of Nyalam, between the main road and the river is the small village of **Zhonggang**. A path leads from the road through the village to the recently rebuilt cave monastery of **Phenkyeling**. This is one of the many cave retreats of the famous 11th-century hermit, Milarepa.

The small town of **Nyalam** is perched on the mountainside at the head of a dramatic gorge. The lush Nepalese scenery here is in sharp contrast to the dry and arid plateau.

akya's
rayer
wheels
rovide
ilgrims
with
piritual
uidance.

The hour's drive along a precipitous gorge on to the border town of Zhangmu/Khasa begins the spectacular descent to the Kathmandu Valley. The road goes through luxuriant greenery and cascading waterfalls. **Zhangmu** itself, a busy trading depot full of Nepalese, Chinese and Tibetan merchants, is built along a series of hairpin bends—the road that snakes through the town is 2.5 miles (four km) long.

The Chinese border post for passport control and customs is next to the **Zhangmu Hotel**. There is a **Bank of China** where you can change your Chinese money for foreign currencies.

The actual border is the Friendship Bridge over the Sun Kosi River and is several miles below Zhangmu. The Nepalese immigration checkpost is at **Kodari** (five miles/eight km) after Zhangmu, while the customs office is a bit further down at **Tatopani**. Kodari to Kathmandu takes about four hours by car.

The Everest Region: Known to the Tibetans as *Chomolungma*, the "Goddess Mother of the World," **Mount Everest** has fascinated mankind for centuries. At 29,028 feet (8,848 meters), it is nearly 5.5 miles (nine km) above sea level and was conquered for the first time in 1951, after 30 years of attempts.

Reaching the base camp on the Tibetan side of the mountain is surprisingly easy. Although the road is rough it is possible to drive all the way. The best time to visit the area is in May/June when the roads are usually clear and the sun not too hot. Be well prepared for cold, dehydration, sunburn and the high altitude.

There are two routes to the base camp, both starting from the Friendship Highway, and you can combine driving with some hiking.

Everest can be reached from Tingri, which is 434 miles (700 km) from Lhasa. After the Shegar checkpost, the first approach turns off at road marker 494 to Everest. The second is just before crossing the bridge at Tingri. Turn left onto a rough track which heads southeast towards Everest. After 20 minutes **Rizong** (Razam) village and monastery is reached. Turn right in the main square and continue across a plain, taking the right fork where the road splits. The road, although quite level, can be difficult to follow and you have to cross several streams. About one hour from Tingri is the friendly village of **Lungjang**, where you can camp by the river at the Nelung yak pasture. Hire yaks here or arrange a guide

Highland pasture: grazing at 14,000 feet

for trekking.

From here you can drive to **Lamdu**, another good campsite, or on to **Zambu** village. There are foot trails between these places and it is possible to combine an energetic outing with a less strenuous vehicle journey, as the trail rejoins the road at various points. Nelung to Lamdu is a four-hour walk. Lamdu to Zambu takes seven hours and goes over a 16,150-foot (4,895-meter) pass. Everest can be seen from Zambu. From Zambu to Rongbuk Valley is a wonderful six-hour walk along a ridge with panoramic views of Everest, Cho Oyu and Gyachung Kang. However there is no trail, so do not go this way if visibility is poor. The road remains lower down, and it rejoins the trail at the Rongbuk River.

Destroyed in the Cultural Revolution, **Rongbuk Monastery** once housed over 100 monks. It is situated at the head of the valley and is quite spectacular. Founded in 1904, it was formerly a sacred pilgrimage site. Now a handful of monks and nuns have returned to help with restoration.

It is another 40 minutes drive to the **Everest Base Camp** (17,150 feet/5,200 meters). On the way is a ruined nunnery and a meditation cave. From the Base Camp, those who are well enough acclimatized can walk a little further to get a good view of the Everest **North Face**. A flatter walk two hours along the Advance Base Camp trail gives a distant view of the blue/green seracs of the **Rongbuk Glacier** with the west ridge of Everest in the background. It is another two hours on to the **Advance Base Camp**. You can camp here or do the round trip in one long day but do not consider it unless you are well acclimatized and fit.

The drive down from the base camp to the main road is a four-and-a-half-hour journey. As the road descends to Rongbuk it passes an imposing ruin on the east side, then curves northeast to a small village. The road heads in a more northerly direction, fording the **Rongbuk River** before reaching another village. The river can be impassable in August.

Continuing north through an area of cultivation it reaches **Peru**, a village at the base of the **Pang La Pass**. From the Pang La, there is a spectacular panorama of some of the highest peaks of the Himalayas—Everest, Makalu, Lhotse, and Cho Oyu. The descent to the main road includes some dramatic hairpin bends and passes a picturesque village on the right. From there it is a 40-minute drive to Shegar and 390 miles (630 km) to Lhasa.

WEST TIBET, EAST TIBET

West Tibet: The main areas of west Tibet or Ngari that are of interest are the ancient kingdom of Guge and the sacred mountain of Kailash—the holiest pilrimage site for both Buddhists and Hindus.

From Lhasa, it is a long but unforgettable journey along the North Route. Although the South Route along the Tsangpo River is shorter, it is closed for many months of the year. The only reliable way is the 1,061-mile (1,712-km) northern road across the Changtang Plateau to Shiquanhe, the capital of west Tibet. The high plateau has some small villages but few other inhabitants apart from nomads. However, there is abundant wildlife and the scenery is stunning.

The North Route: Although hitching is possible, the only way of making a scheduled visit is to hire a vehicle in Lhasa or take one of the tours offered by the CITS. From Lhasa, take the Friendship Highway west through Shigatse and Sakya to Lhartse. Then, cross the Tsangpo by ferry to Raka. From there the road turns sharply north past amazing geysers and hotsprings (make an

effort to stop here) and on to Coqen. Continuing, skirt the western shores of the Zhari Namtso lake and then the road joins the Amdo-Shiquanhe route at Gerze.

Shiquanhe is a thriving modern town built recently at the confluence of the Indus and Gar rivers. There is nothing of historical interest to see but the market area is fascinating, various ethnic groups come here to sell their goods.

To reach Toling Monastery and the kingdom of Guge at Zanda and Tsaparang, take the main road south towards Purang (the main town near Mount Kailash). At Gar, turn west to Zanda (174 miles/280 km from Shiquanhe).

Two hours before reaching **Zanda** the road enters an awe-inspiring canyon system. Lama Govinda's book *The Way of the White Clouds* has marvellous descriptions of this area.

Toling Monastery, on the outskirts of Zanda, is still impressive. The roofs are gone and the larger than life-size statues were systematically broken up, leaving only their outlines on the temple walls.

Toling was built around 1020 by Rinchen Zangpo and it became the most influential Buddhist center in west Tibet. Zangpo came to the region on the invitation of King Yeshe

Preceding pages: Harsh Tibetan landscape Below, pretty countryside on the road west

O and while Buddhism declined in India, many important texts were translated into Tibetan here.

To reach Guge, drive west along the Sutlej gorge for nine miles (14 km) to **Tsaparang**. Here you will need to find the custodian of Guge who has the keys to unlock the monasteries.

Two-and-a-half miles from the village, the astounding ruins of **Guge** are spread over an entire mountain.What is left of this ancient monument is a vast array of semi-ruined temples, *chortens*, cave villages, forts and houses interlinked with paths and secret passages. At the top are the remains of the royal castle. A secret tunnel leads down into the innards of the mountain to the empty chambers of the Winter Palace. The **Demchog Chapel** is also at the top. Inside is a half-destroyed three-dimensional clay mandala. The frescoes are original and in good shape. The floor is littered with bits and pieces of ancient armor.

Sacred Mount Kailash: To visit Mount Kailash, return to the main Shiquanhe-Purang road. **Mensi**, near a coal mine, is 44 miles (71 km) northwest of **Barga**, a village near Kailash. Eight miles (13 km) from Mensi is the sacred hotspring and chapel of **Tirthapuri**.

The approach to Kailash is spectacular. Kailash is to the north and the massive Gurla Mandhata (25,500 feet/7,728 meters) with Lake Rakastal below it, to the south. In the distance are the Nepalese Himalayas. Six miles (10 km) before Barga, take the dirt track on the left to the small pilgrim village of **Darchen**. This is the starting point of the *khora* of the mountain.

Kailash is a stunning mountain. Standing alone and symmetrical, it is the most holy mountain for Hindus, Buddhists and the followers of Bon. In Hinduism it is Shiva's throne, the central peak of the world and a means to enlightenment. For Tibetan Buddhists, Kailash is the center of the universe and home to the god Demchog—the mountain is the soul and protector of Tibet.

Its sides have horizontal and vertical striations that give it the name of Swastika Mountain. Pilgrims from India, Nepal and Tibet come to walk, or even prostrate, around the mountain—a circuit of 32 miles (52 km). One circuit is said to remove a lifetime of sin, and 108 circuits achieves *nirvana*. The two lakes in the area, **Manasarower** (Mapam Tso) and **Rakastal** (Langak Tso) representing the forces of light and darkness respectively, lie to the south of Kailash. The 60-mile (100-km) circuit of

the sacred Manasarower is also an important pilgrimage. Pilgrims perform ritual bathing and visit the monasteries of Seralung,Yerngo, Thuguhul and Chiu on the lakeshore.

Some 64 miles (104 km) south of Barga is **Purang**, the second town of west Tibet. A very interesting and colorful Nepalese market operates near the town in the summer. The important and beautifully-sited monastery of **Khorja**, founded by one of the early kings of Guge, is nine miles (14 km) southeast of Purang.

East Tibet: East Tibet (Kham) is geographically, culturally and ethnographically different from central and west Tibet and well worth a visit should the opportunity arise. The 1,495-mile (2,412-km) Sichuan-Tibet highway goes from Chengdu, the main city of Sichuan, to Lhasa through Chamdo, the capital of Kham.

Kham contains the mighty rivers of the Mekong, the Salween and the Yangtse, which cut deep valleys across the eastern extremity of the Himalayas. There are the snowcapped mountains and desolate and arid high plateaus familiar to central Tibet, but Kham also has vast tracts of lush alpine country and some spectacularly luxuriant rain forests, situated as low as 5,600 feet

(1,700 meters). The remarkable flora of eastern and southeastern Tibet is well known to botanists throughout the world.

The Khampas, the tall people of the Kham region, are renowned as fierce fighters. In the past they were often involved in clan rivalries and were quick to go to battle. There were many Chinese-Khampa confrontations in the first three decades of this century and, despite the Chinese invasion of Chamdo in 1950, it was the Khampas who set up the guerrilla force that has been a thorn in the side of the Chinese army since the 1950s. Khampa men are easily recognizable by the tassles of red yarn plaited into their long hair.

Chamdo (10,500 feet/3,200 meters) is the capital of east Tibet and Tibet's third largest city. At the end of the 19th century, it had a population of 12,000, one quarter of whom were monks. Today, it is a mixed Tibetan-Chinese city, very much involved in trucking and trading between China proper and Tibet.

Mount Namche Barwa: The highest unclimbed peak in the world—**Namche Barwa** (25,595 feet/7,756 meters), is near the big town of **Ningchi**, about halfway between Chamdo and Lhasa. The Chinese have not allowed foreign climbers to make an attempt on it. However, the incredibly scenic base camp area is open to trekkers and is fascinating for its geographic and botanical variety. It is about 335 miles (540 km) from Lhasa to Namche Barwa.

Beyond Namche Barwa is one of the most sacred regions of Tibet, known as Pemako or **Meito** (flower country).This centers on the great knee-bend of the Tsangpo and has a fantastic variety of vegetation—the richest flora of all Tibet—and many sacred sites.Within a 28-mile (45-km) radius, there is an altitude difference of 23,000 feet (7,000 meters), a more dramatic gorge than the Kali Gandaki in Nepal or the Grand Canyon. Plants vary from those of the alpine snow belt to that of the sub-tropical. The rhododendrons are especially rich and resplendent. Between 7,590 feet (2,300 meters and 12,200 feet (3,700 meters), in more humid regions, there is a magnificient girdle of forests—silver firs in the higher reaches and broadleaf trees, including maples and cherries lower down. Below 5,940 feet (1,800 meters), there are wild bananas and betel nut palms and in the lowest areas centering around Baibung and Meito villages there are tangerine and lemon groves. Here the lowest temperature is always well above zero. The Monpas, as the local Tibetan tribes are called, have no word for ice.

Tassle-haired couple from Kham.

TIBETAN ICONS

Tibetan religious art is rich with characters and symbols from the Buddhist pantheon. The brilliantly colored and ornate wall paintings, *thankas* and sculptures can be overwhelming to the uninitiated. The following are some iconographic conventions that make the identification of these religious and historic figures easier. The names are in romanized Tibetan unless otherwise indicated.

Sakyathupa: The historical Buddha is often seated under the tree of wisdom. He is shown as a beautiful youth, often with a golden complexion with long ears, in the simple robes of a religious mendicant.

Chenrezi: This mythical Father of Tibet, the *Bodhisattva* of Compassion (Sanskrit: *Avalokitesvara*), is seldom portrayed as a mere man. He often has several hands and arms and in his wrathful form has 11 heads. He can be encircled by as many as 1,000 pairs of arms and have 1,000 eyes.

Dorje Jigje: This is the tutelary divinity in the form of the destroyer of the king of the dead. He usually has several heads (the lowest one being in the form of a bull) and numerous legs and arms holding weapons. He may wear a necklace of human heads, and is often seen in sexual embrace with Prajna (Wisdom).

Jampayang: The *Bodhisattva* of Wisdom (Sanskrit: *Manjusri*) in the benign form. Usually seated in the lotus position and holding the book of wisdom and the flaming sword of knowledge.

Drolma: The most popular female deity (Sanskrit: *Tara*). Usually represented as the Green Tara—a beautiful bejewelled lady seated on a lotus with her left leg pendant and holding a long-stemmed lotus flower, associated with Tritsun, Songtsengampo's Nepalese wife. The White Tara, seated in the 'Buddha pose', is connected with Wencheng, Songtsengampo's Chinese wife. Drolma symbolises fertility.

Guardian Kings: Often seen as statues or depicted on murals at monastery entrances. The north is yellow and often carries an umbrella; the south is green/blue and carries a sword; the west is red and usually holds a *chorten* or a *dorje* (thunderbolt); he is also the God of riches. The most popular, from the east, is white and carries a musical instrument. These celestial kings guard the heavens from attacks of outer demons.

King Songtsengampo: He is consid-ered to have introduced Buddhism into Tibet in the seventh century. He is easily recognized by the tall gold turban he wears. Chenrezi's head often peers out of the top. He is frequently shown with his wives. The Chinese Wencheng sits on his left; the Nepalese Tritsun is on his right.

Guru Rinpoche: The 'lotus born' (Sanskrit: *Padmasambhava*), the Indian teacher famed for his exorcising powers. Often shown seated, he carries a staff topped with human heads and sometimes holds a skull and a *dorje*. He has several forms, two of which are wrathful. He commonly wears a crownlike red hat.

Tsongkhapa: As the founder of the Yellow Hat (Gelugpa) sect he is easily recognized by his pointed yellow cap. He is always seated and usually smiling.

Milarepa: This 11th-century religious master and hermit is usually shown with his hand cuppéd to his ear as he sings. He is depicted smiling and has the long hair of a hermit.

Fifth Dalai Lama: The great Dalai Lama who unified Tibet in the 17th century is frequently depicted in murals. He wears the Gelugpa yellow hat and is distinguishable from Tsongkhapa by his moustache and his slightly protruding eyes.

The musically-inclined Guardian King of the east.

DESTINATION TIBET

Travel in Tibet usually begins in Lhasa. It is the administrative center where permission for visiting other areas is granted, transport arranged and supplies bought. At slightly below 13,200 feet (4,000 meters), it is a good place to acclimatize and it is the center of Tibet's greatest cultural monuments. Traveling there by land gives you an opportunity to see large areas of Tibet en route but permission to use land routes may change so be sure to check up in advance.

By Air: The airport for Lhasa is Gonggar, 60 miles (96 km) from Lhasa itself. The Civil Aviation Administration of China (CAAC) provides free transport into Lhasa taking about 90 minutes. Luggage follows separately so try to take an overnight bag with you on the plane. The rest of the luggage should arrive at the CAAC office in Lhasa on the same day. The return journey with CAAC involves an overnight stay at Gonggar but Lhasa Hotel provides a 20-*Yuan* shuttle service which leaves early in the morning, thus avoiding the night at the airport hotel. Plane schedules are often subject to delay.

Chengdu-to-Lhasa: The main flight route for Lhasa. Planes leave Chengdu daily at around 7 a.m. and 11 a.m. and the flight takes about two-and-a-half hours. It costs Y421, payable in FECS (see Money), approximately US$110. In clear weather it is a superb flight over the ranges of eastern Tibet passing near the peaks of Minya Konka (24,783 feet/7,556 meters) and Namche Barwa (24,783 feet/7,756 meters). The best view is from the left side of the plane.

Golmud-to-Lhasa: CAAC operates a twice-weekly flight from Golmud, Qinghai Province, taking two hours and 10 minutes at around US$85 one way. Golmud is reached by plane from Xian or by train in 21 hours from Xining.

Kathmandu-to-Lhasa: The possibility of Kathmandu—Gonggar flights is under discussion. A once-a-week charter operated by CITS(US$400 round trip) started in September 1987.

Overland: Kathmandu-to-Lhasa: The land route from Nepal is usually open to individuals and groups. Summer landslide damage to the road may mean that part of the journey has to be on foot. For the individual traveler, transport from the border to Lhasa can be uncertain. It is difficult to tag onto an organized group for the journey. The best bet is to get a seat on a Landcruiser (Y150 - Y400) or a bus (Y80).

All travelers can exit from Tibet to Nepal by land. The route takes at least three days with overnight stops in Zhangmu (border) and Shigatse and is about 500 miles (900 km) long. The journey to Lhasa can be very exhausting as the roads are mostly unpaved and the passes are over 16,000 feet (5,000 meters). Travelers going the other way are usually well acclimatized and so find it much easier. Many of the important religious sites of Tibet are on the Kathmandu—Lhasa road (at Gyantse, Shigatse and Sakya).

This road near both sides of the border is sometimes closed to vehicles for extended periods in the summer because of landslides. In the winter, it can be blocked by avalanches.

Golmud-to-Lhasa: A journey of 691 miles (1,115 km) along the Tibet—Qinghai highway taking between 30 and 50 hours by bus. This costs about 60Y payable in *Renminbi* (see Money). Buses and trucks leave Golmud regularly. Short stops are made at Nagchu and Damxung. Take your own food and warm clothing: the road goes over the high Tangula Pass and vehicles often travel all night irrespective of seasons. Portions of this route can be bitterly cold. Try to travel in a warmer and more reliable Japanese vehicle.

Golmud is a major town of the Qinghai Province and is at the end of the railway line.

Chengdu-to-Lhasa: 1,495

miles (2,412 km)—not officially open but many do come through this way. Bus or truck journeys take anywhere from one week to three weeks. Bridges often break in the summer rains and snow may block the passes in winter. This is a risky route to take but undeniably beautiful and at times, rewarding.

Visas: You cannot enter Tibet without a Chinese visa. These may be obtained by contacting by telex the Foreign Independent Travel Division (FIT) at the China International Travel Service (CITS) in Beijing. (FIT Division, CITS Head Office, 6 Changan Avenue, Beijing. Telex 22004 CIFITCN) Give your name, age, sex, nationality, itinerary, length of stay, planned point of entry and passport number, and request a visa. At the same time you have to send a sum of money (handling fee for CITS) to the Bank of China, check the amount with the nearest Chinese consulate or embassy—it is about US $20 (Group visas are cheaper). The CITS should then send a telex of confirmation to your nearest consulate and when you have filled in an application form, paid your visa fee, and provided two passport photos you should receive your visa. This may take two to three days or two to three weeks.

The visa application form includes questions on your religion, political party, occupation and previous occupation. To save complications it is easiest to put 'none' for religion and political party and to avoid 'awkward' occupations such as journalist, priest or government worker. 'Student' will cover most things. The form also includes requests for names and addresses of friends in China. It is simpler to put 'none.'

Visas are generally issued for one month. If you are planning a longer trip, try to get three months right away (more or less standard in Hong Kong). Visas are extendable at major Public Security Bureaus (PCB) in China and Tibet at a cost of five *Yuan*, but this can be difficult. If you are going to leave China by a land border it is helpful, but not necessary, to have an exit permit, which is also obtained from the PSB. Lhasa PSB issues them on the spot for exit to Kathmandu.

Visa in Hong Kong: Visas are issued by many agencies in Hong Kong. Usually there is a choice of visas: by itself or a package deal including transport to China. Recommended agents are: **Wah Nam Travel** (Rm 1003 E. Commercial Centre, 397 Hennesy Rd. Warchai. Tel 5-8911161) **Trinity Express** (Rm 614, 6th floor, New World Centre, Salisbury Road. Tsimshatsui, Kowloon), **China Travel Service** (China Travel Building, 77 Queen's Road, Central, Hong Kong Island (Tel. 5-259121), **Mera Travel** (Rm 1307 Argyle Center 688 Nathan Road, Kowloon Tel.3-916892). The process should take two to three days. Express visas

(24hrs) can be obtained for a surcharge.

Visa in Kathmandu: If you are going on a group tour from Kathmandu the agent will arrange your visa for you. Individuals still have to go through the telex process. As of now, it is not possible to get a visa direct from the embassy.

It is important to realise that regulations change all the time and you will need to check up for the most up to date news.

Visa for Nepal: Available in Lhasa for 45Y FEC at the Nepalese Embassy and Consulate (near the Lhasa Hotel and Norbulinka). Opening hours: 10 a.m. to 12 noon and 4 p.m. to 6 p.m. Visas are ready the next day. Seven-day visas are also readily available at the Nepalese border (Kodari) for US$10. They are extendable to one month at Central Immigration in Kathmandu.

Money: There are two different money systems in China: *Renminbi* (RMB, people's money) for locals, and Foreign Exchange Certificates (FEC or Waihuizhan) for foreign travelers. There is a double pricing system. As a foreigner you are usually charged double for buses, lodgings, etc. You can use RMBs on the streets and it is not illegal to hold them. If you are out of the main centers you will need RMBs. There is a black market of 40 percent to 50 percent more for FECs as they are used locally to buy imported

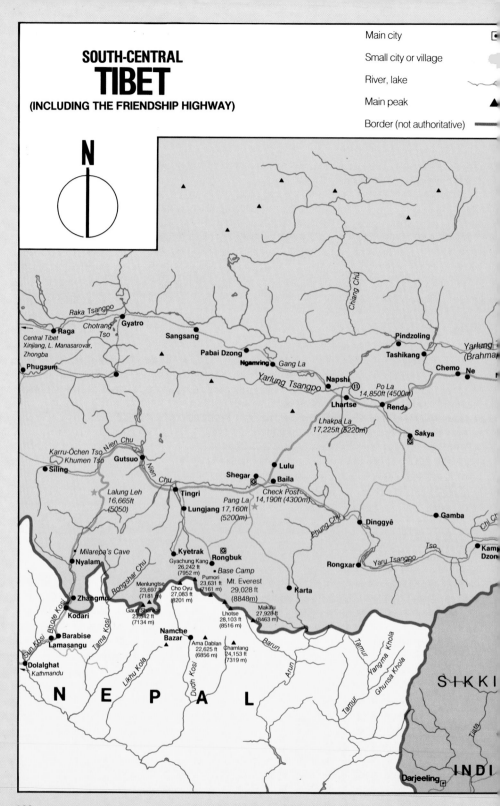

SOUTH-CENTRAL
TIBET
(INCLUDING THE FRIENDSHIP HIGHWAY)

Main city

Small city or village

River, lake

Main peak

Border (not authoritative)

N

Raka Tsangpo

Raga *Chotrang* **Gyatro**
Tso
Central Tibet
Xinjiang, L. Manasarovar,
Zhongba
Phugsum

Sangsang

Pabai Dzong

Ngamring *Gang La*

Yarlung Tsangpo

Chiang Chu

Pindzoling

Tashikang

Yarlung
(Brahma

Chemo **Ne**

Napshi ⑪ *Po La*
14,850ft (4500m)

Lhartse **Renda**

Lhakpa La
17,225ft (5220m)

Sakya

Karru-Öchen Tso Nien Chu
Khumen Tso
Siling

Gutsuo

Nien Chu

Lulu

Shegar **Baila**

Check Post
14,190ft (4300m)

☆ *Lalung Leh*
16,665ft
(5050)

Tingri

Lungjang *17,160ft*
(5200m)

Pang La
17,160ft
(5200m) ☆

Phung Chu

Dinggyê

Gamba

Chi Ch

Tso

Kam
Dzon

Rongxar

Yaru Tsangpo

• *Milarepa's Cave*
Nyalam

Kyetrak

Rongbuk

Gyachung Kang
26,242 ft
(7952 m)

• *Base Camp*
Pumori
23,631 ft
(7161 m)

Mt. Everest
29,028 ft
(8848m)

Karta

Makalu
27,928 ft
(8463 m)

Menlungtse
23,697 ft
(7181 m)

Cho Oyu
27,083 ft
(8201 m)

Rongshar Chu

Zhangmu

Kodari

Gauri Shankar
23,542 ft
(7134 m)

Lhotse
28,103 ft
(8516 m)

Barabise
Lamasangu

Namche
Bazar

Ama Dablan
22,625 ft
(6856 m)

Chamlang
24,153 ft
(7319 m)

Barun

Tamur

Yangma Khola

Ghunsa Khola

S I K K I

Dolalghat
Kathmandu

Sun Kosi

Bhote Kosi

Tama Kosi

Likhu Kola

Dudh Kosi

Arun

Tamur

N E P A L

Tista

I N D I

Darjeeling

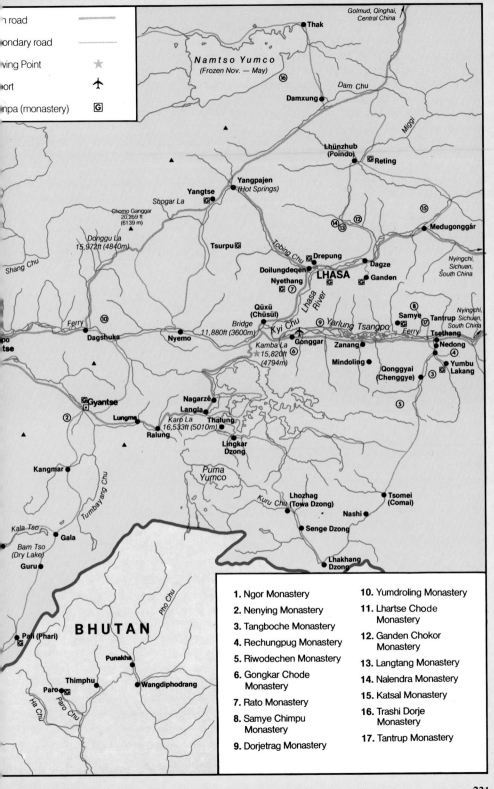

Legend (partial):
- road
- ondary road
- ving Point ⭐
- ort ✈
- npa (monastery) Ⓖ

Thak

Golmud, Qinghai, Central China

N a m t s o   Y u m c o
(Frozen Nov. — May)

⑯

Dam Chu

Damxung

Miggi

Lhünzhub (Poindo)

Ⓖ Reting

Yangpajen (Hot Springs)

Yangtse
Shogar La Ⓖ

Chomo Ganggar 20,259 ft (6139 m) ▲

Dönggu La 15,972ft (4840m)

Tsurpu Ⓖ

Tobing Chu

⑭ ⑬ ⑫

⑮

Medugonggár

Shang Chu

Drepung

Doilungdeqen
Nyethang Ⓖ ⑦

LHASA Ⓖ

Dagze
Ganden Ⓖ

Nyingchi, Sichuan, South China

Qüxü (Chüsül) Ⓖ

Lhasa River

⑧
Samye

Tantrup ⑰

Nyingchi, Sichuan, South China

Bridge 11,880ft (3600m)

Kyi Chu ✈

⑨ Yarlung Tsangpo

Ferry

Tsethang

Ferry ⑩

Dagshuka

Nyemo

Kamba La ⭐ 15,820ft (4794m) ⑥

Gonggar

Zanang

Mindoling ●

Nedong ④
Yumbu ③ Ⓖ Lakang

Qonggyai (Chenggye)

⑤

po tse

Gyantse Ⓖ
②

Lungma

Ralung

Karo La 16,533ft (5010m)

Thalung

Lingkar Dzong

Nagarzê
Langla

Kangmar ●

Tumbayang Chu

**P u m a
Y u m c o**

Kala Tso

Bam Tso (Dry Lake)

Gala

Guru ●

Kuru Chu

Lhozhag (Towa Dzong)

Nashi ●

Senge Dzong

Tsomei (Comai)

Lhakhang Dzong

Pho Chu

B H U T A N

Pari (Phari) Ⓖ

Punakha

Thimphu ●

Paro ● Ⓖ

Wangdiphodrang

Ha Chu

Paro Chu

1. Ngor Monastery
2. Nenying Monastery
3. Tangboche Monastery
4. Rechungpug Monastery
5. Riwodechen Monastery
6. Gongkar Chode Monastery
7. Rato Monastery
8. Samye Chimpu Monastery
9. Dorjetrag Monastery
10. Yumdroling Monastery
11. Lhartse Chode Monastery
12. Ganden Chokor Monastery
13. Langtang Monastery
14. Nalendra Monastery
15. Katsal Monastery
16. Trashi Dorje Monastery
17. Tantrup Monastery

goods like TV sets etc. If you are coming through China, change your FEC for RMB in Canton, Beijing or Guilin for a better rate. Otherwise,in the Barkhor area of Lhasa, and the Tibetan market area in Shigatse. This is a fairly accepted procedure but use your discretion. The unit of money is the *Yuan* which is divided into 100 *Fen* or 10 *miao*.

The only places that change traveler's checks or foreign money in Tibet are the Lhasa hotel; the Bank of China in Lhasa, Shigatse, Zhangmu (border), Shiquanhe (west Tibet; traveler's checks only). If you are traveling around Tibet make sure you get enough cash in Lhasa and have notes of small denominations and some coins.

At the Nepal border you can change Nepalese *rupees* to RMB informally but the rate is not good. It is better to change money in Kathmandu with tourists returning from Tibet.

Bank hours are officially 8:30 a.m. to 12:00 noon and 3:30 p.m. to 6:30 p.m.

Customs: You have to register watches, radios, cameras, calculators, etc. on entering China and account for them when you leave. Do not lose your declaration form. It is not advisable to take in anything that could be constituted as detrimental to China's way of life, particularly in the form of printed matter or cassettes. Flaunting Tibetan flags, etc. is frowned upon.

You can take in four bottles of liquor, two cartons of cigarettes, up to 72 rolls of still film and 3,000 ft of 8mm. There are no obvious restrictions on video equipment. Artifacts made before 1959 are officially antique and cannot be exported. Rugs and the small religious objects available in the open market can be taken out but tourists considered to be carrying "too much" may have goods confiscated. Body searches are unlikely.

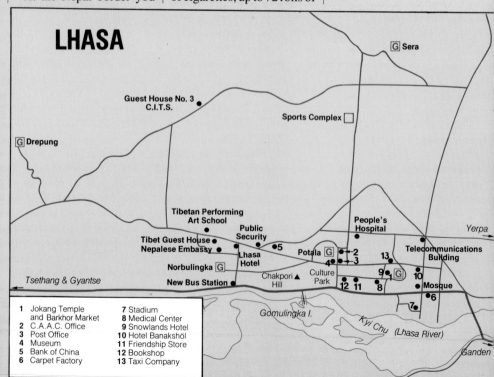

LHASA

G Sera

Guest House No. 3
C.I.T.S.

Sports Complex

G Drepung

Tibetan Performing
Art School

People's
Hospital

Yerpa

Public
Security

Tibet Guest House
Nepalese Embassy

Lhasa
Hotel

Potala G

Telecommunications
Building

Norbulingka G

Chakpori ▲
Hill

Culture
Park

Mosque

Tsethang & Gyantse

New Bus Station

Gomulingka I.

Kyi Chu (Lhasa River)

Ganden

1	Jokang Temple and Barkhor Market	7	Stadium
2	C.A.A.C. Office	8	Medical Center
3	Post Office	9	Snowlands Hotel
4	Museum	10	Hotel Banakshöl
5	Bank of China	11	Friendship Store
6	Carpet Factory	12	Bookshop
		13	Taxi Company

INSIDE TIBET

GETTING ACQUAINTED

Cost: How much will it cost? Apart from the airfare and travel expenses which vary greatly, you can survive in Tibet on about US$5 a day or less, although Lhasa is slightly more expensive. If you trek it is hard for you to spend any money. Lodging and local food are very often *gratis*. Economy hotels and truckstops are cheap and local internal travel is not expensive. However, organized tours are expensive.

The more limited your time the more expensive on a daily basis your trip will be. A two-week trip to Lhasa can really only be done on an organized tour basis and will cost between US$500 to US$1,500 from Kathmandu.

When planning your itinerary bear in mind that if you fly in you should allow at least a couple of days in Lhasa for acclimatization. If you intend to go off the main routes you will probably be walking so give yourself time to adapt to the altitude.

Climate: The best time is early spring to late autumn. It can be very pleasant in Lhasa as late as the end of December. On the land routes, some passes may be blocked, however. During the winter months many nomads converge on Lhasa and there are few tourists—a very interesting time to visit. As Tibet is in the Himalayan rainshadow, the summer months are fairly dry while countries further south are in mid-monsoon. From July onwards there is rain and a danger of flooding as the rivers get swollen by the melted snow and once again roads jam as the transport systemfalterss. Light rain is frequent in July, August and early September.

There are wide extremes of temperature in Tibet. The summer midday temperature can reach 101 F (38 C) but the same evening, it can fall to below zero. Generally, Tibet is cold in winter and mostly very pleasant in the summer (although the afternoons can be very hot, and a forced siesta necessary). The Himalayan rainshadow keeps the rainfall down to between 0.8 feet and 1.6 feet (25 cm and 50 cm) per year. In the summer, dust is a big problem, so bring a face mask.

What to Wear: Because of the changes in temperature it is advisable to have many layers of clothing. Silk protective clothing of the kind used by skiers is very useful against the cold and takes up little space; polypropylene underwear is especially good in the cooler seasons. Make sure you have good gloves, scarves, socks, etc. European and American outdoors and ski shops can usually provide suitable gear. You need only casual clothes but do not wear skimpy shorts and T-shirts. Protection against the dust is a good idea. A silk scarf over the mouth and nose helps and you can get gauze masks in Lhasa. If you wear contact lenses you are probably better off leaving them at home.

What to Bring: You must take good dark glasses—preferably with side protectors to help against the dust and the glare. A hat is useful, though they can be bought in Lhasa. Take a good sunblock cream and lipguard.

Also recommended are strong, comfortable shoes, a good windproof jacket—a down jacket is good against cold, and as padding on uncomfortable journeys. Pile jackets take up more space but they dry quickly. Other essentials: a water bottle, a flashlight for visiting monasteries, batteries, (local ones are not good), film (see Photography) a can opener, water purifying tablets such as Micropur, or iodine, toilet paper and soap. Take some food goodies for when times are hard. Kit for a long off-road trip would need careful planning.

What to Buy: In many ways, Tibetan artifacts are more easily available in Kathmandu, where there is more choice and fewer customs restrictions. However, you can still find interesting things in the markets and Tibetans will approach you with personal items of jewelry, etc. to sell. You can buy Tibetan boots ready-made or have them made to measure next to the main mosque. Tibetan carpets are readily available and you can get the traditional type tents and canopies from the Lhasa Tent and Banner Factory.

For more mundane things, try the general stores. The Nong Ken Ting Department store has cotton clothing, mugs, tinned food. soap, toothpaste, towels, writing paper, etc. On the third floor is the Friendship Store which sells imported cigarettes, alcohol, Coca Cola and some better quality tinned food. The main bookshop, Xinhua Shudian on Renmin Lu has maps, posters and Chinese and Tibetan books. Near the new cinema, across from the Tibetan hospital, a shop sells a beautiful book on *thangkas*, and picture guidebooks to major monuments. The Lhasa Hotel has an adequate tourist shop.

Officialdom: Chinese officialdom is a mass of red tape illustrated most graphically by the China International Travel Service (CITS) and the Public Security Bureau (PSB). One small problem can cause havoc with your plans.

There appears to be no logic to the replies the CITS gives to queries. Sometimes they are helpful. Sometimes they will claim that things are closed just because it is the answer that requires the least energy. The main problem is that they do not have a systematic program for staff training. They are, however, the body responsible for looking after foreign tourists

throughout China and they can do anything from organizing full tours and hiring out vehicles to booking specific tickets. Remember that most things they do will be charged at tourist prices which is often 75 percent over the local going rate. Efficiency and helpfulness of CITS varies from city to city in China. Chang Chen, a senior official of the Lhasa office, is an anomaly. He is pleasant and efficient.

The CITS' most useful service is the hiring out of vehicles—anything from a 4-WD Toyota to a full-size bus. A driver is always provided. (Rates for a Landcruiser are around 2-to-3 FEC per km.) CITS also have guides of varying standards who speak English, French, German and Japanese, after a fashion. Try to get a Tibetan speaker.

CITS mainly works with groups. They have a section for individual travelers in an office at the CAAC building, but few people have found it useful.

CITS will arrange special tours for botanists, art historians, etc. if given advance warning.

Public Security Bureau: The Public Security Bureau is China's police force—both uniformed and plainclothes. It covers anything from traffic problems to political dissidence. The branch responsible for foreigners is the Foreign Affairs Branch which is also responsibile for issuing Alien Travel Permits (ATP). The PSB have a reputation of friendliness to foreigners

and there are a few English speakers among them.

There are two offices in Lhasa: one is north of the Potala, across from the Bank of China; the other is a couple of blocks south of the Banak Shol Hotel.

Alien Travel Permits (ATP): Travel in China is restricted to certain areas and sites. Until recently, Alien Travel Permits (ATP) were required for travel to some areas. These are now nearly obsolete but they can still be very useful for west Tibet.

Useful Bits of Paper: The Chinese are fond of bits of paper—you may find it useful to carry business cards, and as many kinds of identity cards as you can lay your hands on. ID cards can sometimes be used as deposits so you can avoid relinquishing your passport. Carry several spare passport photographs.

Communications: Airmail is quite reliable. Telegrams are commonly used but unpredictable. The telephone is unreliable even within Lhasa. There is one telex which is available to guests at the Lhasa Hotel, and another at the telecommunications office.

Electricity: There is a supply in the main centers and nearly all towns and major villages, but it can be unpredictable. The supply is 220 volts 50 cycles AC. Make sure that all your equipment is battery operated rather than mains reliant.

Photography: Photography is controlled in monasteries. In some cases you may have to pay for every photograph you take; in others you may be refused permission to film at all. Respect these rules but you may quite often get around them by being nice to the monks. Do not take photographs of Chinese military installations, bridges or airports.

Technical Problems: Take plenty of film with you—sometimes print film can be completely out of stock even in Lhasa. Kodachrome/Fujichome is not available. Be prepared for the very strong light and the appalling dust. A lenshood and a good polarizer can help the exposure problem. It is best to photograph in the early mornings and late afternoons to avoid the harsh light and worth underexposing by half a stop to one stop at other times. Kodachrome 25 film is very useful. Nothing will completely keep out the dust but plastic bags help. A strong flash is needed for many of the temple interiors. Take flash photographs of wall murals at an angle to avoid reflection problems.

Social Attitudes to Photography: Try to get to know people a little before you intrude and take photographs. Don't take photos if people don't want you to and do send a copy of the photo to your subject if you promised that you would. Don't give money in exchange for

taking photos—it is a quick way of creating beggars. On the whole, people are happy to let you photograph them.

Medical Tips: Travel in Tibet is strenuous—do not consider it if you have serious health problems.

Altitude Sickness: Tolerance for altitude is not related to age, sex or personal fitness. Altitude sickness or Acute Mountain Sickness (AMS) can affect anyone above 8,250 feet (2,500 meters). Most travelers adapt quickly to the altitude after a few days and find that unpleasant symptons such as headaches recede with increased liquid intake and aspirin. The body needs time to adapt to the diminished oxygen so take it easy especially for the first few days. If, however, symptoms are severe you must act immediately. The best thing to do is to get to a lower altitude as quickly as possible—i.e. flying out, even if this means sacrificing your trip. Pulmonary or cerebral edema brought on by high altitude can be fatal in two days.

Mild Symptoms: Nausea, loss of appetite, mild shortness of breath with exertion, disturbed sleep, irregular breathing especially during sleep, dizziness, mild weakness or lethargy, slight swelling of the hands and face. Rest, aspirin, and increased liquid intake should cure these.

Serious Symptoms: Serious shortness of breath, rapid breathing after resting

(25 breaths per minute), "bubbly" breathing, severe coughing spasms, coughing up watery or pink-tinged sputum, persistent vomiting, vomiting blood, severe persistent headache, loss of coordination, severe lassitude, delirium, confusion and rapid heart rate after resting. Anyone developing any of these symptoms should descend immediately and they must be accompanied. There is no substitute for going to a lower altitude but if this is not immediately possible go to the Regional Military Hospital on the west side of Sera Monastery. This is the best hospital in Lhasa which, however, isn't saying much. There is a decompression chamber here. A nasty machine but it may save your life.

Sensible precautions for everyone are: to avoid overexertion and take time to acclimatize; to drink plenty of fluid (make sure you are urinating normally); avoid smoking if possible; avoid sedatives and tranquilizers and avoid excessive salt.

The drug Diamox has been proven to help against symptoms of mild altitude sickness and it may benefit those flying in. However it only prevents some symptoms and not the serious life-threatening ones and it can create a false sense of security. Take plenty of water with Diamox.

Lhasa is not well supplied with pharmacies so take your own medical supplies. Include medicines for coughs, colds, sore throats and more serious bronchial problems. These are common afflictions and hard to shake off. Take broad spectrum antibiotics as well as ones for stomach problems such as amoebic dysentery.

Stick to boiled water both for drinking and for cleaning your teeth and if you cannot make sure it has been boiled for a good length of time, use purifying tablets or iodine.

There are no official obligations for vaccination for Tibet but take medical advice on the need for injections against hepatitis, meningitis, rabies and tetanus before you go and remember to take into consideration the areas you may be going through en route to Tibet. Dog bites are frequently reported. Vaccines for rabies are hard to come by even in Lhasa.

TOURS

Group travel is certainly the easiest, if the most expensive, option. The organizing agency will deal directly with the Chinese authorities, thus reducing your own problems with the bureaucracy considerably. Tours can be organized by the CITS (see below) or through Nepal trekking agents and their counterparts throughout the world. Traveling as an individual can be much cheaper and leads to a far wider range of adventurous possibilities but it is also more unpredictable and time consuming.

The Chinese Mountaineering Association (CMA)

organizes trekking and climbing in the mountain regions. They have strict rules for expeditions and are usually expensive.

Travel Agents organizing Tibet trips:
Mountain Travel
Kathmandu, Nepal. (They have the best Sherpa support.)
Mountain Travel
Albany, California, USA.
Wilderness Travel
Albany, California, USA.
Exodus
London, UK.
Himalayan Rover Trek
Kathmandu, Nepal (Specializes in good value budget tours).
Himalayan Journey
Kathmandu, Nepal
Mera Travel
Hong Kong (Specializes in adventure travel).

If you have no prior arrangements in Lhasa, the Sports Association of Lhasa may be able to put together trekking or jeep-touring to more exotic places. Make enquiries through their office in the Lhasa Hotel.

TRANSPORT

The transport system in Tibet is poor. Before 1950, wheels were believed to scar the sacred surface of the earth. Even now, the main forms of transport are still donkeys, ponies, yaks (and feet).

CITS, Lhasa Hotel, Taxi Company (next to the Yak Hotel) and Lhasa City Tourist Company (Sunlight Ho-

tel, formerly known as Lhasa No.2 Guesthouse), Xuelin (Snow Lotus) Hotel, inside the Military Compound adjacent to the Lhasa River, all rent out 4-WD vehicles with drivers. Toyota Landcruisers taking four-to-five persons cost 2-to-3Y FEC per mile. Beijing jeeps are about half the price, but should be avoided if possible as they are very dusty and often break down. Lhasa City Tourist Company also hires out Japanese minibuses for about 3Y FEC per km. This can work out cheaper as they can seat between seven and eight people. Lhasa Hotel usually give priority to their guests, but they have cars for rent for short day excursions.

Bus: Buses are unpredictable and decrepit (unless you luck in on a Japanese model). Try to avoid a back seat if you want to keep your skull intact. Check that your luggage is securely tied on and well-protected against the elements. Keep a day pack with you and carry food. Always try to get a Japanese vehicle. Bus stations in Lhasa: Central Bus station next to the Norbulinka; another is one block east of the Post Office; a third is across from the University of Tibet. These service different routes. Buses cost double for tourists in FECs but try bargaining. Buy your ticket one to two days in advance. There are buses to the Nepal border and to Golmud but Chengdu is very difficult.

IN TRANSIT

Truck: Almost everything enters Tibet by truck. Roads usually are unpaved, dusty and bumpy. The condition of the vehicles is usually uneven. The very recent (1986 and later) Chinese models, and, of course, the Japanese ones are very good. The dark green pre-1950 Chinese models should be avoided like the plague. You can sometimes negotiate a ride on the back of a truck or, if you are lucky, in the cab. This, however is getting more and more difficult due to clampdowns by the police. Truck travel is greatly improved by trying to speak a bit of Tibetan or Chinese (depending on the driver's origin), providing cigarettes and sharing food. If you're going to be on the top of a truck, make sure you have plenty of warm clothes, a hat and sun protection cream.

You might be able to arrange a ride at truck depots, petrol stations and friendly checkpoints. Otherwise, just try waving down vehicles in the road. However, hitching rides is also getting increasingly difficult.

Bicycle: Bikes can be hired in Lhasa at nearly every hotel at 10 *yuan* per day. They are a good way of getting round the immediate area but remember the altitude—don't overdo it.

Trekking: In small villages you can often hire a guide and pack animals—but remember that farmers are likely to need their animals during harvest. A yak can take 110 pounds-to-175 pounds (50 kg-to-80 kg) in weight and will travel up to 16 miles (25 km) in a day. Horses and donkeys are also possible depending on the type of terrain involved. Bargain for the price—it is likely to be around Y10-to-Y20 per day per beast (this includes handler).

WHERE TO STAY

In Lhasa, hotels range from the top-ranked **Lhasa Hotel** (managed by Holiday Inn as of 1986), a western-style complex with the potential to house 1,000 guests, to simple Tibetan inns. Elsewhere, the choice is limited. Guesthouses *(Zhao Daisuo)* in bigger towns may provide showers and a restaurant of a minimum standard, but otherwise guesthouses usually offer a cheap bed, a rough dining room and outside toilet pits. You can also stay at truckstops for around 1Y-to-3Y (shared accommodation) for a four-bed room. In remote areas army camps may provide accommodation. Some towns have solar-heated bathhouses.

You may be able to find accommodation with Tibetan families but there are stories of this causing problems with the PSB. Tibetan homes can be very smoky and there is usually no privacy, but they are certainly an experience.

It is sometimes possible to stay in monasteries along with other pilgrims.

Rating system:
(1): Quite good facilities, most expensive.
(2): Reasonable, some plumbing. Reasonable price.

Lhasa:

Lhasa Hotel—atrocious location. Your movement's greatly dependent on the once-an-hour shuttle. Holiday Inn management has upgraded previously non-existent service considerably. Western style rooms with private bathrooms, good food (Western and Chinese) by Lhasa standards. Telex. (1).

Tibet Guesthouse—Western Suburbs next to the Lhasa Hotel, swimming pool! private bathrooms, good set meals. Owned by CITS but clobbered by Lhasa Hotel—usually very few guests. (1).

No.1 Municipal Guesthouse—near Friendship Store and bookshop, Chinese compound, good location (10-minute walk to the Jokhang) showers in the evening, good laundry service, plain Chinese food. (1)

No. 3 Guesthouse (CITS guesthouse)—six miles (10 km) west of Lhasa, very pleasant setting, bungalows with shared bathrooms, good food. Operatons being phased out. (1).

Sport Association Hotel—near university, new (open 1988). (1).

FOOD DIGEST

No. 2 Municipal Guesthouse—east side of Potala, inside bus station. Shared bathrooms. Expanding. (2).

No. 2 Lhasa City Guesthouse (Sunlight Hotel)—across from the university, Tibetan-style architecture, fairly central location, restaurant being built. Tibetan management. (2).).

Shigatse:

Shigatse Hotel—new hotel with Western trappings, few of which work; caters mainly to tours. (2).

No.2 Guesthouse—across from the cinema. Used to cater to tour groups. Very nice suites to dormitory-style rooms. (2).

Tsethang:

Tsethang Hotel—double rooms with Western bathrooms and haphazard solar showers. Caters mainly to groups. Adequate Cantonese food (very good in 1986 when genuine Cantonese cooks were stationed here). (2).

Shiquanhe:

Shiquanhe Hotel—newly completed (1986) near the center of town. Y15 per person. (2).

WHAT TO EAT

In Lhasa and Shigatse, hot, spicy and rather ordinary Sichuan food is *de rigueur*. There are some Muslim restaurants in the old part of Lhasa and Shigatse where the food is simple and reliable: noodle and mutton dishes are recommended. Elsewhere, restaurants and menus are limited. The staple of Tibet food is *tsampa* (roasted barley flour) which is mixed with yak butter tea into doughy mouthfuls. The tea is brewed and then salt and yak butter added.

Tibet is not a place for gourmets. In fact, the situation in Lhasa has improved over the last couple of years and fish and locally grown vegetables are readily found. A well-known Tibetan dish is *momos*—dumplings filled with meat or vegetables, and *thukpa*—soup noodles with meat or vegetables. These dishes are also popular in Nepal and Bhutan. You can get dried yak meat and yak cheese in most places but if you are going off the beaten track, be sure to take supplementary foods.

As in Nepal and Bhutan, the favorite drink, apart from buttered-tea, is the flat, sour, barley beer called *chang*. You can also get Chinese beers in most places.

Eating Out:

Lhasa Hotel: The only Western restaurant in town (so far)—yakburgers, spaghetti, chicken in a basket, etc. Good breakfast, surprisingly good coffee. Dynamite Viennese cakes— one of the best in Asia. The Chinese restaurant is one of the best in Lhasa and reasonable in price; small portions.

Hotels Banak Shol, Snowlands and Kirey have restaurants where you can choose your own vegetables and meat and have it cooked while you wait—a feature pioneered by the Banak Shol in 1984.

Tibet Guesthouse: Good Chinese set meal with five or six dishes, good value.

Muslim Restaurants: Recognized by their blue banners outside—good plain food, noodles, mutton, etc. Note how the noodles are shaped from the dough entirely by hand.

Chinese Restaurants: Tend to be indistinguishable from each other and mediocre, some good dumpling restaurants across from the Kirey Hotel. Most have menus written in English, a vast improvement; too bad the quality still lags.

Tibetan Restaurants: Very basic, serving noodles and *momos*.

PAKISTAN:CROSSROADS OF ASIA

Stretching from the Himalaya and Karakoram mountains to the Arabian Sea, Pakistan is the land of the Indus River, which flows for 1,500 miles (2,400 km) through the country. Born in 1947, 'The Land of the Pure' is a new Islamic nation created as a homeland for the Muslims of the Indian subcontinent. It is a land of variety and extremes: of the highest mountains and the hottest deserts; of terraced valleys and irrigated plains. Pakistan stands at the crossroads of Asia, where travelers from China and the Mediterranean meet those from India and Central Asia. Its four provinces, Sind, Punjab, Baluchistan and the Northwest Frontier Province, all have a distinct character and culture.

For thousands of years the fertile Indus River basin has tempted warriors and traders to cross barren mountains and empty deserts in search of fortune. Today's visitor to Pakistan follows a long line of distinguished adventurers: Alexander the Great, St. Thomas the Apostle, Marco Polo, Genghis Khan, Tamerlane and the great Mughal emperors, all rode along the banks of the Indus.

The history of the area is well chronicled and richly illustrated with ruined cities and Buddhist monasteries from the pre-Muslim era, and marble tombs, Mughal forts and decorated mosques that are the pride of the Islamic world.

A journey through Pakistan is full of contrasts, from the well-watered fields of the Punjab and central Sind, where lush fields of rice and wheat, cotton and sugar-cane, oranges and bananas flourish along the rivers and canals, to the sparse deserts either side of the irrigated belt, that stretch across the borders with India, Iran and Afghanistan.

But it is in the north that Pakistan is unsurpassed. Here, close to the heart of Central Asia, is the hub of the world's greatest mountain chains: the Himalayas, Karakorams, Pamirs and Hindu Kush radiate out like spokes on a wheel. Eight out of the world's 20 highest peaks and the longest glaciers outside the polar regions, are in northern Pakistan. And hidden amidst this mountain network are some of the remotest valleys on this planet.

The new Karakoram Highway connecting Pakistan to China winds for 800 miles (1,280 km) through some of the world's most spectacular mountain scenery. Opened to tourists in 1986, this road is now the most exciting route to China for modern-day Marco Polos.

The four major cities of Pakistan also have much to offer, reflecting the many historical influences that have created modern Pakistan. Islamabad, the federal capital, is a modern garden city with wide, tree-lined boulevards. Peshawar, on the northwest frontier with Afghanistan, is a city straight out of the *Arabian Nights*, where turbanned tribesmen stroll proudly through the colorful bazaars. Lahore, once the Mughal capital, is the cultural and intellectual center of the country, full of graceful mosques and tombs. And Karachi, with a population of seven million, is a huge bustling port and the industrial hub of the country.

Whether your particular interest is driving through mountain scenery, exploring Mughal forts and tombs, rummaging through the bazaars for antique brass, hiking up remote valleys, or just lazing on the beach, Pakistan awaits you.

Preceding pages: Truck art: painted lorry panel; the Karakoram Range. Left, The enormous courtyard of Lahore's Badshahi Mosque.

CRADLE OF CIVILIZATION

The Indus was the most eastern of the three great rivers that made up the Ancient World. The Nile, the Tigris-Euphrates and the Indus were the cradles of mankind and of early civilization. About two mllion years ago, *Homo*, our genus, evolved in this area and made stone tools which he left scattered along the river banks. *Homo Sapiens*, our particular species of man, was living in Pakistan at least 50,000 years ago, and about 9,000 years ago, discovered how to tame animals and plant crops.

Indus Valley Civilization: Three great civilizations rose at about the same time, around 3,000 B.C.: the Egyptian, the Mesopotamian and the Indus. The Indus Valley Civilization grew out of the indigenous farming communities. It was a well-organized society, living in large cities, and uniting the Indus Valley under a strong central government. Its pictographic writing has still not been deciphered.

From then on the history of Pakistan is one of invasion. Migrants and armies followed each other across the mountains to the rich Indus Plains. First came the Aryans in about 1700 B.C. These warlike nomadic herders overthrew the Indus Civilization, settled along the Indus River, and founded the Hindu religion (Hindu and Indus have the same derivation).

Next came the Persians who absorbed northwest Pakistan, then known as Gandhara, into their expanding empire in the sixth century B.C. Gandhara grew in importance and developed into a great cultural center. By the fourth century B.C. Taxila, one of its capitals, was one of the most famous universities of the ancient world.

After the Persians came the Greeks. Alexander the Great conquered Gandhara between 327 B.C. and 325 B.C. Alexander's army revolted and refused to go further, so he marched down the Indus and turned westward along the coast, heading for home. Alexander had been wounded in Pakistan, and died before he reached Greece.

Buddhism spread westwards to the Indus River basin in the third century B.C. under the great Mauryan emperor, Ashoka.

From the first century to the fifth century A.D., the kingdom of Gandhara was at its most powerful under the Kushan kings. The Kushans were Buddhists, and Gandhara became the center of the Buddhist world, from where Buddhism spread to Afghanistan, China, Tibet and Japan.

Islam arrived in Pakistan in the eighth century A.D., about 80 years after the religion was founded in Saudi Arabia by the Prophet Muhammad. It came from two directions: first by sea, in 711 A.D., to the coast of Sind and up the Indus

River to lower Punjab. Later, in the 11th century, it arrived by land from Afghanistan, and spread south.

Wave after wave of Muslim rulers invaded the Indian subcontinent from Central Asia in search of plunder. The most famous were Genghis Khan in the 13th century, Tamerlane in the 14th and Babur, the first Mughal emperor, in the 16th century, who established his capital in Delhi.

Conquering Hordes: At its height the Mughal Empire stretched from Kabul to Calcutta and halfway down the Indian subcontinent. For nearly 200 years from 1526, the Mughals held

power. The great Mughal emperors, Babur, Humayun, Akbar, Jehangir, Shah Jahan and Aurangzeb, followed each other on the throne. Aurangzeb died in 1707 and the empire began to disintegrate. In 1739, Nadir Shah of Persia marched across the Indus, sacked Delhi and carried off the famous peacock throne.

In the early-19th century, the Sikhs rose to power. They were a religious group founded by Guru Nanak, who was born near Lahore in 1469. The religion evolved over three centuries and became a strong militant brotherhood centered in the Punjab. By the 1830s the Sikhs had pushed the Afghans back across the Khyber Pass. Ranjit Singh, their greatest leader, ruled from Lahore from 1799 to 1839.

As the Mughal Empire declined, the British

gradually extended their power. By 1843, Sind (the lower Indus region) was in British hands, taken from its local Talpur rulers because it was a useful corridor to Afghanistan. The Sikhs were still in control of the Punjab, but not for long: after two Anglo-Sikh wars, in 1845 and 1849, the British overthrew the Sikhs, and annexed the Punjab and the Northwest Frontier area.

In 1857 the Indians staged their First War of Independence (known by the British as the Indian Mutiny). In retaliation, the British government took direct control of India. This was the beginning of the British Raj (British rule). In the name

border, and five million on the Afghan side. The British left the Pathan tribal areas to govern themselves under the supervision of British Political Agents, a system which has been continued by the Pakistani government.

Modern Pakistan is strongly influenced by the old British colonial system of administration. The British divided the country into Divisions and Sub-divisions in the charge of Commissioners and Deputy Commissioners, and while some of the borders have changed, the system is largely intact today. They mapped the entire country and built an impressive network of roads, railways

of Queen Victoria, the British continued to expand their empire, taking Kashmir and the other small northern kingdoms. Hunza, on the Chinese border, was the last area to fall into British hands in 1891.

Fearful of the Russian advance southwards, the British decided to make a clear northern boundary to their empire. In 1893, they drew the Durand Line, separating British India from Afghanistan. This line cut straight through the homeland of the Pathans, a fierce mountain tribe. There are now about 10 million Pathans on the Indian side of the

Left, early inhabitant of Lahore. Above, ancient map of Pakistan, showing its numerous mountain ranges.

and canals. The most noticeable sign of British rule is the architecture in the old British sections of the main towns. The British built separate 'cantonment' areas for themselves, with wide, tree-lined avenues and imposing public buildings that are a curious mixture of Victorian gothic and classic Mughal.

The Emergence of Pakistan: The idea of splitting India into two separate states for the Hindus and the Muslims was first voiced in 1930 by the poet-philosopher, Muhammad Iqbal. In 1933 the name 'Pakistan' was coined by Choudhury Rahmat Ali, an undergraduate at Cambridge University who founded the Pakistan National Movement. 'Pakistan' means 'Land of the Pure' and includes the initials of Punjab, Afghan Province (officially called the Northwest Frontier Province) and Kashmir, combined with the ending of Baluchistan. The Muslim League adopted the political goal of a separate Muslim state called Pakistan at a meeting in Lahore in 1940. Under the dynamic and determined leadership of Q*uaid-i-Azam* (Great Leader) Muhammad Ali Jinnah, the idea was espoused by almost all the Muslims in India (about a quarter of India's population was Muslim in 1940).

Mahatma Gandhi, who led the campaign for India's independence, strongly opposed the partition of the country, but was overruled. On August 14 and 15, 1947, Britain gave independence to an India divided into three parts. Pakistan was created out of the east and west wings of the country—where there was a Muslim majority—while India retained the predominantly Hindu center and south. Both countries remained in the

cerned Kashmir, where the people were mostly Muslim, but the Maharaja was Hindu. The Maharaja opted to join India at Independence. About a third of Kashmir started a liberation movement and joined Pakistan. The Northern Areas and Azad (free) Kashmir are now districts of Pakistan, but do not have full provincial or voting rights. Both sides now claim Kashmir, and a UN-supervised 'line of control' separates the two halves.

Pakistan Since Independence: The greatest difficulty facing the new Pakistan was that nearly 1,240 miles (2,000 km) of hostile India separated West Pakistan from East Pakistan. The people of the two halves of the country had nothing in common except religion. East Pakistan had the larger population, but West Pakistan was dominant both politically and economically. The

British Commonwealth with Jinnah as the first governor-general of Pakistan, and Liaquat Ali Khan as prime minister.

Deciding on the boundary between the two countries proved a difficult task, especially in the fertile Punjab, where Hindus, Muslims and Sikhs were inextricably mixed. When the borders were announced, an estimated six million Muslims, mostly from the Punjab, streamed into Pakistan, and about 4.5 million Hindus and Sikhs went the other way. Refugees arrived penniless on either side of the border. About half a million never arrived at all: they were murdered en route in some of the worst communal rioting the world has ever seen. Gandhi fasted to try to stop the bloodshed, but was assassinated in January 1948.

There were other serious problems. One con-

nation soon lost its most able leaders. Jinnah died of tuberculosis in September 1948 and Liaquat Ali Khan was assassinated in Rawalpindi in 1951.

Widespread discontent followed with sectarian riots, a slump in trade, a shortage of consumer goods, famine and political disagreement. A series of leaders jostled for power, and in 1956 a new constitution was proclaimed, turning the dominion into the Islamic Republic of Pakistan with a president replacing the governor-general: but political affairs showed no improvement. In 1958 General Ayub Khan took control, declared martial law and ruled by decree until 1962. Elections in 1964-65 kept Ayub in power, but his handling of a short war with India in 1965 lost him many supporters. In 1969, Ayub handed over to

General Yahya Khan, who, once again, imposed martial law.

In the meantime, East Pakistan was becoming increasingly unhappy with its position in the power structure. Things came to a head in 1970, when there was a disastrous cyclone in the eastern half. In December of that year elections were held, resulting in wins for the Pakistan People's Party in the western half and for the Awami League in the eastern half. The dispute over which party had the right to form a government led first to strikes, and then to outright revolt in East Pakistan. India supported the creation of an independent Bangladesh.

Zulfikar Ali Bhutto, the leader of the Pakistan People's Party, became President of Pakistan, and ruled until 1977, pursuing a policy popular with the urban masses and rural poor, especially

in his native Sind. He nationalized basic industries, banks and insurance, began to democratize the civil service and started reforming the health and education systems. When Britain recognized Bangladesh, Bhutto pulled Pakistan out of the British Commonwealth. He strengthened ties with China in an attempt to balance the threat of India. Bhutto's downfall came after the general elections in 1977, which opposition parties alleged were rigged.

General Zia-ul-Haq took over the administration of Pakistan, and again imposed martial law.

Left, the rich farmlands of the Indus Valley. Above, Islamic-inspired mosaic tiles are a common feature.

Bhutto was charged with murder, tried twice, found guilty and hanged. Under President Zia, Pakistan enjoyed steady economic growth favoring the private sector. There were also some efforts to Islamize the political, legal and economic structures. In 1985 'non party' elections were held and a civilian government installed. Martial law was lifted in 1986, but President Zia remains in power.

Economy, Religion and Culture: Agriculture is the backbone of the Pakistani economy. A drive up the Indus from Karachi to Lahore takes you through the rich irrigated farmland of the plains, past fields of rice and wheat, orchards of oranges, bananas and dates, rows of sugar-cane and cotton and patches of chillies and tobacco.

Pakistan produces five percent of the world's cotton. Cotton possibly originated here. In Mesopotamia, cotton was called *sindu*, and in ancient Greece cloth was known as *sindonian* —names derived from the Indus and Sind. Textile manufacture has been the most important industry along the Indus for 4,000 years. Pakistan's other industries include light engineering, food processing, pharmaceuticals, cement, tobacco and steel. Pakistan also has good deposits of oil, natural gas and coal.

Pakistan is filled with many different racial types, from tall, pale-skinned mountain people with blue eyes, to small, dark-skinned fishermen on the coast: From round-faced traders in the Punjab, to wiry farmers in Sind. Waves of invaders from the north, refugees from the south, holy men from the west and pilgrims from the east have all left their cultural and ethnic marks. The one uniting force is Islam.

Islam pervades every facet of society, and is evident everywhere, from the call of the *muezzin* reverberating from the minarets of the mosques, to the men bowed in prayer in the fields and shops: from the veiled women in the streets, to the crowds thronging the holy shrines. About 96 percent of the population is Muslim, with Hindus, Christians and Zoroastrians (Parsees) making up the rest.

Islam is the inspiration behind Pakistan's art and architecture, its music and poetry, its festivals and celebrations. Islamic architecture is at its finest in the tombs, mosques and forts of the 12th to 17th centuries, especially in Lahore, Multan and Thatta. The most beautiful examples of Pakistan's art is the decoration of these buildings—delicate floral mosaics, intricate wood carving and stylized writing from the *Koran* (Islam forbids the representation of human or animal life). The most haunting poetry is sung in the shrines of famous saints throughout Pakistan.

The most lively festivals are *Id-ul-Fitr*, celebrating the end of *Ramadan*, the month of fasting, and the various saints days at the most popular Sufi shrines.

KARACHI

A hundred years ago, **Karachi** was a tiny fishing village clustered on three islands just to the west of the Indus estuary. It is now a sprawling city with seven million inhabitants, Pakistan's major port and biggest industrial center. The first impression is one of glass-fronted hotels, multi-storey banks, spacious British colonial buildings with domes and spires and wide lawns, and the normal hazard of any big city—fast flowing traffic.

Karachi is not old enough to be graced with elegant Mughal mosques or tombs. Its main attractions are the sea, the seafood, the busy bazaars, the museum, the shrine of Abdullah Shah Ghazi, and the tomb of Muhammad Ali Jinnah, Pakistan's illustrious founder.

As the sun sets, the fishing boats in Karachi harbor unfurl their sails and float silently out into the quiet water. This is *bundar* boat time when family parties and tourists sail around the harbor, fish for crabs to be cooked and eaten on board, and stop off on the Sandspit to watch the giant turtles lum-

ber up out of the sea to lay their eggs in the sand (laying season July to November). To hire a boat (a modest Rs 50 to Rs 100 an hour for a boat seating 10), go to **Keamari Harbor**, 15 minutes from downtown Karachi. As darkness falls, local fishermen paddle by in rowing boats, and overhead, long lines of cormorants and flamingoes fly home to roost. For a bigger choice of seafood: crayfish, giant prawns and fish, try Karachi's famous restaurants. Chances are you won't be disappointed.

By day, you can laze on the miles of smooth sand, swim in **Hawkes Bay**, or visit the aquarium and take camel rides along **Clifton Beach**. At the fish harbor on **West Wharf**, hundreds of small fishing boats with colored sails line up to unload. Nearby, boat-builders using old-fashioned tools still make wooden fishing boats in the traditional style.

A Bazaar Time: Karachi's bazaars are good sources of antique silver and copper, tribal embroidery, oriental carpets and a multitude of modern onyx, brass and wooden ornaments. The most colorful bazaars are in the **old city**, to the north of **M A Jinnah Road** (also known as Bundar Road), behind **Boulton Market**. Here nomad women in full red skirts over baggy trousers and tribal men wearing enormous turbans, stride through the narrow alleys. In the wider streets, camel carts jostle with laden donkeys and hooting taxis. Each lane is a separate market selling a different commodity. The **Sarafa Bazaar** is lined with jewelry shops offering both modern and antique pieces. Deeper into the bazaar is **Bartan Gali**, selling copper and aluminium pots and pans. Next comes the wholesale **cloth bazaar**, and beyond that the **Khajoor** (date) **Bazaar** full of carefully arranged pyramids of fruit, and hawkers selling everything from twigs to clean your teeth, to pyjama cords to hold up your trousers.

Karachi's newer markets are in the **Saddar Bazaar** area between **Abdullah Haroon** (Victoria) **Road**, and **Zaibun Nisa** (Elphinstone) **Street** (both the old British, and the new Pakistani street names are used). These have less local color, but offer a good selection of new copper and brass, onyx, inlaid woodwork and hand-printed cloth and applique bedspreads.

A wander round **Empress Market** shows the modern Karachi housewife doing her morning shopping. The market, opened in 1889, is a huge Victorian Gothic building with a square clock tower, housing hundreds of stalls selling fruit, vegetables, meat, fish and groceries. Behind the market are the *hookah* shops with pipes of all shapes and sizes.

Karachi's **National Museum** has well-organized displays from the Indus Civilization of 4,000 years ago, and an impressive selection of 1,500-year-old Gandharan Buddhist sculptures. Its ethnological gallery, illustrated manuscripts and coins room, all illustrate and document the history of Pakistan.

The **tomb of Muhammad Ali Jinnah** stands on a hill at the end of Jinnah Road, from where its tall marble dome with pointed arches gaze down over the city. The colorful changing of the guard ceremony takes place every two hours.

The **shrine of Abdullah Shah Ghazi** is the center of Karachi's spiritual life. Abdullah Shah Ghazi was a ninth-century Sufi saint: patron of Karachi, he has one of the largest followings in Pakistan. His square, green-domed shrine dominates the top of the hill near **Clifton Viewpoint**. Visitors interested in discovering the real Pakistan should go to the shrine on a Thursday evening to watch the pilgrims and listen to the devotional singing.

Trips From Karachi: From the 14th to 18th centuries, when Karachi was just a fishing village, **Thatta**, 60 miles (100 km) to the east, near the Indus River, was the capital of Sind. Its Mughal mosque and fine tombs illustrate 500 years of Sind's history, evoking the grandeur and wealth of a former age.

A day tour to Thatta takes in the **Chaukundi tombs**, graves dating from the 15th century to the 19th century, decorated with carved stone. Also included in the trip is **Banbhore**, an archaeological site with the excavated remains of the earliest mosque in Pakistan, dated 727 A.D.; and **Makli Hill**, the largest necropolis in the world, where a million tombs and graves cover the top of a ridge, five miles (eight km) long. Bird-watchers can also stop off at **Haleji Lake**, a wildlife preserve, where hundreds of species of birds migrate in winter. Thatta's **mosque**, built by the Mughal Emperor Shah Jahan in 1647, is the climax of the tour—its long arcades of red brick tempered with the cool blues and greens of glazed tiles.

Other day trips take you west along the coast to visit the beaches and **Paradise Point**, or north to the **shrine of Pir Mangho**, another Sufi saint whose shrine stands beside hot sulphur springs and a pool of crocodiles. Twenty miles (33 km) north of the shrine is **Hub Dam**, and another wildlife preserve around **Hub Lake**. A

The ornately-carved Chaukundi tombs.

weekend trip to **Kirthar National Park** involves a rugged drive into the **Kirthar Hills** on the border between Sind and Baluchistan, where Chinkara gazelle graze in the eroded gullies stalked by jungle cats, leopards and desert wolves. Huge monitor lizards, pangolins and porcupines lurk among the rocks.

Four days are needed for a little safari, east of the Indus, into the **Thar Desert** along the border with India. Here the desert tribes live in round thatched huts, grow sparse crops near occasional wells, and breed herds of camels and goats.

Moenjodaro—City of the Dead: One of the greatest mysteries of Pakistan is the Indus Valley Civilization that flourished 4,000 years ago along the banks of the Indus and its tributaries. Over 400 cities have been identified, but only half a dozen are excavated. The most famous of these is **Moenjodaro**, in upper Sind, a short flight north from Karachi.

The Indus Civilization was contemporary with those in Ancient Egypt and Mesopotamia. Less is known about it since the writing is undeciphered, and the cities were built of fired bricks that have partially disintegrated over time. But from the excavations and museum at Moenjodaro you can still get a good impression of what life was like on the banks of the Indus in 2000 B.C.

The civilization's empire covered most of present-day Pakistan and stretched north to Kabul and as far east as Delhi. It was well organized with a central administration probably ruled by a priestly class. It had strong trading links with Mesopotamia. People lived comfortably in large houses set around courtyards with surprisingly modern bathrooms, and a city sewage system that worked remarkably well.

The stone seals used by the merchants are the most exquisite exhibits in the museum. Most are about an inch (2.5 cm) square, with delicate and naturalistic carvings of animals and deities on the front, and an inscription, presumably the trader's name, written across the top.

The ancient city was about three miles (five km) in circumference with a raised citadel on its western edge. Dominating this acropolis is the ruins of a Buddhist *stupa* that was built in Gandharan times, 2,000 years later than the Indus city. The original public buildings on the citadel were a great bath (for ritual cleansing) surrounded by a cloister; a state granary where the wheat, barley and sesame collected as taxes were stored; a palace and an assembly hall.

The main city east of the citadel is laid out in a neat chessboard pattern with wide main streets intersecting at right angles, and narrow alleys giving access to the houses. The rich residential area on the northern edge of the town is the most exciting part of Moenjodaro. Here you can stroll down the lanes between high brick walls. The walls are blank and forbidding. Like many Pakistani houses today, the windows all looked inwards to a central courtyard. Most of the houses had two floors with a wooden balcony round the second floor giving access to the upstairs rooms.

The city wells stand up like factory chimneys. As the centuries passed, the ground level in the city rose, and the well shafts were extended upwards. The excavators have cleared away the later levels of rubber leaving the walls of the wells sticking up in the air. The brickwork nearer the top is inferior to that lower down, showing a decline in workmanship as the civilization came to an end.

Moenjodaro lay safely buried for thousands of years until discovered by a British archaeologist in 1921. Now that it is exposed its bricks are crumbling. The water table is rising as a result of irrigation, and the lower levels of Moenjodaro are probably lost forever.

Seal from Moenjodaro.

LAHORE

Lahore is the heart of the cultural and intellectual life of Pakistan. For a thousand years it has been the capital of the Punjab, and for a short time at the end of the 16th century, was the center of the Mughal empire. Some of the richest treasures of the Mughal world are preserved here—graceful palaces and mosques, marble tombs, cool gardens and an impressive fort. The British embellished the city with elegant public buildings and tree-lined avenues. Here, they collected the best of the Gandharan Buddhist scuptures and the finest examples of Mughal art. Since the creation of Pakistan, Lahore has retained its reputation for the tastiest Mughal cuisine. It is Pakistan's second largest city with a population of about three million, and is an important industrial center.

City Sites: The soul of Lahore is the old walled city, dominated by **Lahore Fort** and the enormous Badshahi Mosque. The fort, built by Emperor Akbar in 1566, is a huge rectangle enclosed by massive walls. Inside are spacious lawns and a series of court-yards, each built by different Mughal emperors. The oldest is Akbar's court and hall of private audience, decorated with elaborate sandstone brackets, carved marble and with a few traces of the original gilded stucco work.

Jehangir's quadrangle is more austere. The emperor's private sleeping quarters are now a small museum containing, among other things, the *Akbar Nama*, the daily chronicle of Akbar's reign.

Emperor Shan Jahan, the greatest Mughul architect, added the most beautiful parts of the fort in the 1630s and '40s (at the same time as he was building the Taj Mahal in Agra). Loveliest of all are the private apartments for his empress, the **Shish Mahal** (palace of mirrors), the inside of which is covered in mirror mosaics, carved and gilded plaster work, and marble inlaid with semi-precious stones. Beside the Shish Mahal, with a bird's-eye view down over the Badshahi Mosque and the tomb of Ranjit Singh, stands a little marble pavilion, the **Naulakka**, where the emperor sat and dallied with his ladies. The inside is decorated with exquisite floral patterns of semi-precious stones inset into the marble.

The **Badshahi Mosque**, opposite the fort, was the Emperor Aurangzeb's gift to

The artist of Mughal architecture, Lahore.

Lahore in 1674. Its three onion domes seem to float over the city, and the four soaring minarets cast long shadows across the giant courtyard where 100,000 can gather to pray.

A short *tonga* ride from the Badshahi Mosque takes you through the maze of streets in the old walled city to the **mosque of Wazir Khan**, decorated in glazed mosaics, and one of the most beautiful in Pakistan. Continue on foot deeper into the bazaars of the old city. A hunt through the nearby **brass bazaar** turns up some fine antique pots and bowls.

The **Shalimar Garden**, about three miles (five km) from the center of town, was laid out by Shah Jahan in 1642, following the Mughal conception of the perfect walled garden, with three terraces of straight shaded walks, geometrically arranged ponds, bubbling fountains, rippling waterfalls and cool marble pavilions where the emperor and his ladies slept.

The **tomb of the Emperor Jehangir** stands in a walled garden, five miles (eight km) west of town. Built in the 1630s by Shah Jahan, its red sandstone walls and four minarets are intricately decorated with geometric patterns of inlaid white marble. The 30 rooms inside the tomb have polished floors of variegated marble: the walls and ceilings are covered in fresco paintings. In the center stands the marble cenotaph inlaid with semi-precious stones.

In adjoining walled gardens are the **Akbari Serai**, designed by Shah Jahan as a Moghul hotel, and the **tomb of Asaf Khan**, Shah Jahan's father in law. Nearby, the **tomb of Nur Jahan** (Shah Jahan's mother) has been recently restored.

Lahore Museum, opened by the British in 1894, with John Lockwood Kipling, Rudyard's father, as curator, is the biggest museum in Pakistan. This typical Victorian building with fluted columns, arches and cupolas, houses a superb collection of Buddhist stone sculpture from the Gandharan period; a world famous set of Mughal miniature paintings, illustrated manuscripts and engraved copper; plus a good ethnographic display and a prehistory section.

Outside the museum stands Zam-zama, the 18th-century cannon on which Kim played in Kipling's novel. It is said that whoever holds Zam-zama holds the Punjab.

North of the museum is **Anarkali Bazaar**, where a maze of lanes and alleys stock everything from handicrafts to refrigerators. The bazaar is named after Anarkali, a legendary favorite in the harem of the Emperor Akbar, and who was condemned to death when Akbar saw her return the smile of Jehangir. When Jehangir become emperor he built a marble tomb for his loved one, near the bazaar. On the cenotaph, Jehangir wrote the heartrending words:

'Ah, if I could again see the face of my beloved,
To the day of judgement I would give thanks to my Creator.'

More shaded gardens and a cool lake surround Jehangir's **hunting pavilion** about 20 miles (32 km) outside Lahore, near Sheikhupura. Beside the lake is the **Hiran Minar**, a tower built in memory of the emperor's pet deer.

Between Lahore and Islamabad is **Rohtas Fort**, built in 1540s, the most imposing of Pakistan's castles, with three miles of walls, turrets and battlement.

Twice a year Lahore is the focus of lively festivals. The feast of Data Ganj Baksh, one of Pakistan's most popular saints, is on the 18th and 19th of the month of Saffar in the Muslim calendar, when thousands of devotees throng to his shrine near the old city. The other great event is the National Horse and Cattle Show every spring, the biggest jamboree in the Pakistan calendar with a multitude of equestrian attractions—polo, tent pegging, dancing camels—besides the more serious busines of livestock judging.

nperor
‹hangir's
mb.

ISLAMABAD

The new garden city of **Islamabad** is tucked against the foothills of the Himalayas, and marches down in perfect order to the banks of Rawal Lake. The site of the new federal capital is well chosen, near the center of the country, close to the cool Murree hills, and on the main axis of Pakistan, the Grand Trunk Road. Started in 1961, the city grew rapidly and the government moved up from Karachi in 1962. Now 26 years old and still growing, Islamabad will soon join up with its neighbor, the old military city of Rawalpindi.

Urban Planning: Islamabad's Greek architects, Doxiadis Associates, planned the city in blocks one kilometer square, and laid it out in eight distinct zones: residential, commercial, government, diplomatic, educational, etc. Each sector was designed with its own shopping area and open space. Over six million flowering trees were planted, and the result gives a feeling of cool spaciousness, with long wide avenues of jacaranda and flame trees leading through the comfortable residential area to the well proportioned government buildings.

A drive halfway up the **Margalla Hills**, that rise steeply on the northern edge of town, gives a panoramic view over Islamabad. The **Shah Faisal Mosque**, designed to represent a desert tent surrounded by four 300-foot- (90-meter-) high minarets, is close against the hills, and Rawal Lake, Rawalpindi, and the Potwar Plains stretch off into the distance. From **East and West Viewpoints**, two low hills in **Shakarparian Park**, there is a photogenic view of Islamabad with the hills in the background. Also in the park is **Lok Virsa**, the Institute of Folk and Traditional Heritage, with a well-organized **Ethnological Museum.**

Though Islamabad is new, it, too, has its old and venerated Sufi shrine, in **Nurpur**, near the **Quaid-i-Azam University**. Pilgrims gather here from all over Pakistan, particularly on Thursday evenings and during the shrine's annual festival. From the shrine you can walk up into the hills to the **Holy Man's Cave**, where the 17th-century saint, Syed Abdul Latif Shah, lived in meditation for 12 years.

Murree, one hour's drive up into the Himalayan foothills, is an old hill station founded by the British in 1851. Surrounded by forests of enormous Himalayan pines,

Damaged Buddhist relics at Taxila.

Murree, at 7,414 feet (2,247 meters), is refreshingly cool in summer, and piled high with snow in winter. The town is a popular summer resort with fine views into Indian Kashmir, good shopping for furs and nuts, and pleasant walks in the forest.

Beyond Murree the road follows the ridge through the forest to other, smaller hill stations known collectively as the **Galis**.

Taxila, 20 miles (32 km) west of Islamabad, is one of Pakistan's most important archaeological treasures. Its three ruined cities and numerous Buddhist monasteries and *stupas* date from 600 B.C. to 500 A.D. Set in a broad valley behind the Margalla Hills, Taxila was once the university town of the kingdom of Gandhara. Alexander the Great stopped there in 326 B.C. and discussed philosophy with the univeristy intellectuals, who were naked ascetics. Students took courses in astronomy, mathematics, medicine, social sciences, law, history, the arts and military tactics.

When Gandhara was at its height, under the Kushan kings from the first to fifth centuries A.D., thousands of Buddhist monasteries were built throughout the empire. On almost every hilltop around Taxila, are the remains of such monasteries and *stupas*, more than 50 of them within a

six-mile (10 km) radius. **Taxila Museum** displays some of the best Gandhara Buddist sculptures, and an excellent collection of artifacts detailing the daily life of the inhabitants of ancient Taxila: utensils, weights, jewelry and toys.

Start your tour of Taxila at **Dharmarajika stupa and monastery**, one of the largest in Pakistan, about a mile east of the museum. First built in the third century B.C., the *stupa* and monastery were enlarged over the next seven centuries. All has been carefully excavated showing the main *stupa*, about 50 feet (15 meters) high, and dozens of smaller votive *stupas*, chapels that once contained giant plaster statues of Buddha, and the monastery courtyards surrounded by monks' cells.

Sirkap, the second city of Taxila, was built in 185 B.C. by the Bactrian Greeks who came from Greece with Alexander the Great in 328 B.C., and settled in Bactria in Afghanistan for 140 years, before moving south into Pakistan. The Greek city was rectangular, surrounded by a wall three miles (five km) long. Only the foundations remain, showing a wide main street with narrow side streets leading off at right angles. Large houses with courtyards, temples, *stupas* and a palace made up the old city.

The best preserved of all the ruins at Taxila is Jaulian Monastery, built in the second century A.D. on a hill with a sweeping view down the valley. The monastery was burned by the invading White Huns in the fifth century and lay buried until the 1920s. The main *stupa* and many of the votive *stupas* are still covered in their original plaster with rows of plaster Buddhas round all sides, and the high walls of the monastery with 28 monk's cells, dining room, assembly hall and kitchens, give a clear picture of the living conditions of the monks.

Tarbela Dam on the Indus River between Islamabad and Peshawar, is the largest earth-filled dam in the world, 1.7 miles (2.7 km) across the top. In July, August and September, when the giant spillways are open, it is a thundering, spectacular sight.

Attock, where the Grand Trunk Road to Peshawar crosses the Indus, about 20 miles (32 km) south of the dam, is where Akbar built an enormous fort in 1581. Its crenellated walls are still in perfect condition. The 16th-century caravanserai (hotel), beside Attock bridge, with its 200 rooms set around a huge courtyard, is an excellent place from which to view the fort and the confluence of the Indus and Kabul rivers.

king
re that
e spice is
ht.

PESHAWAR

The Wild, Wild West: Founded 2,000 years ago as one of the capitals of the ancient kingdom of Gandhara, **Peshawar** exudes an atmosphere that would do justice to a Western movie. Now capital of Pakistan's Northwest Frontier Province, on the border with Afghanistan, it is the chief town of the Pathan tribesmen. Patans stroll through the bazaars of the old walled city, hands hidden inside their shawls, and faces half covered by the loose end of their turbans. With their proud expressions and finely chiselled noses, they must be the handsomest men on earth. Afghan refugees, many of them in Peshawar for rest and recreation between bouts of fighting in their homeland, stride purposefully past in their huge black and white turbans. Smuggling, drug trading and arms dealing are normal business for the day, as they have been for centuries. Kidnapping and carnapping are other lucrative sources of income.

Bazaar follows bazaar in the warren of lanes—the romantically named Bazaar of the Story Tellers, **Qissa Khawani,** where tea is served from giant samovars, leads to the bazaars for brass and copper, baskets and bells. In the **bird bazaar**, fierce Pathans whistle gently to songbirds in cages. **Chowk Yadgar**, the central square of the old city, is lined with money changers and letter writers, and stalls piled high with carefully arranged fruit and vegetables. Leather bandoleers and holsters, lambskin Astrakhan hats, tribal silver jewelry, leather sandals and hand block printed fabric each has its own alley near the square.

To the east of Chowk Yadgar, **Cunningham's Clock Tower** marks the bottom of **Sethi Street**, whose tall houses with ornately carved wooden doors and balconies belong to an old merchant family. To the west, peeping above the rooftops in the silver bazaar, are the elegant minarets of the **Mahabat Khan Mosque**, built in the 1670s. Brooding over this exciting maze, stands the massive **Bala Hizar Fort**.

In striking contrast, the **cantonment area**, and the **University of Peshawar**, are graced with wide avenues, spreading chinar trees, English churches, colonial-style bungalows, gardens and an excellent **museum**.

Barren and forbidding hills rise up to the west of town. The road through them crosses the infamous **Khyber Pass**, a nar-

Preceding pages: A spectacular valley near Gilg Beaded and bejewelle Kafir Kalash girls.

row, easily-defended passageway to Afghanistan, in which many British soldiers lost their lives in the 19th century. The Khyber Pass is in tribal territory, and is currently closed to tourists.

North and east of Peshawar lie the rich, well-watered plains that were the center of the Gandharan kingdoms. Scattered along the banks of the Kabul and Swat rivers are many ancient villages and ruined Buddhist monasteries. At **Charsadda** is the excavated site of **Pushkalavati**, the first capital of Gandhara, captured by Darius the Great of Persia in the sixth century B.C., and by Alexander the Great of Greece in the fourth century B.C.

Perched on a hilltop near Mardan, stands **Takht-i-Bahi**, the most complete Buddhist monastery in Pakistan. Monks lived and prayed here from the first century to the sixth century A.D., with bird's-eye views down over the Peshawar Plains in one direction, and up to the Malakhand Pass and the mountains around Swat Valley, on the other.

Valley Deep, Mountain High: Swat, Chitral and Kaghan, three steep mountain valleys, run down parallel to the main Indus Valley in the north of the Northwest Frontier Province.

zaar opping Pesha-ar.

Swat, three hour's drive from Peshawar, is the most fertile, and was coveted by every invader. Alexander the Great marched through in 327 B.C. In the first centuries A.D., Swat became an important center of Buddhism, supporting 1,400 monasteries. First Hinduism, and then Islam, drove the Buddhists out, and the monastery tradition moved east to Tibet.

Saidu Sharif and **Mingora**, the twin capitals of Swat, are spread on the wide floor of the valley surrounded by terraced hills with a clear view south to the sacred **Mount Ilam**. A trading center for 2,000 years, this is the site of one of the oldest monasteries in Pakistan, **Butkara**, founded in the second century B.C. Butkara *stupa* originally contained some of the ashes of Lord Buddha. It was the most important shrine in Swat, visited by pilgrims from all over the Buddhist world. Over the centuries the *stupa* was enlarged five times by building new shells around the old core.

Throughout Swat, Buddhas carved on rocks gaze down protectively over the valley. The biggest, and best preserved is near the village of **Jahanabad**, just north of Saidu Sharif.

Other impressive ruins are the massive Hindu forts from the eighth to 11th centuries, that crown many of the hilltops. **Raja Gira's castle** is a steep climb above the village of **Udegram**. Raja Gira was overthrown by Mahmud of Ghazni, who brought Islam to northern Pakistan in the 11th century. Mahmud built a **mosque** on the mountainside below Gira's castle.

At the top end of Swat Valley, where the valley walls are too steep to terrace, and giant pines stand green against the white mountain peaks, the village mosques are decorated with intricately carved wooden pillars and beams. Carved chairs, chests and doors, richly embroidered shirts and hand woven shawls, complete the heritage of the mountain people.

A well-surfaced road leads from Swat across the Shangla Pass to the Karakoram Highway.

Chitral Valley is best known for **Tirich Mir**, the highest mountain in the Hindu Kush, and for the Kafir Kalash, a tribe of non-Muslims whose women wear headdresses decorated with cowrie shells similar to those in Tibet. The **Shandur Pass** with a summer jeep road connects Chitral to Gilgit.

The narrow, scenic **Kaghan Valley** with excellent fishing and walking, winds up the **Babusar Pass**, the old route to Gilgit before the Karakoram Highway was opened.

GANDHARA ART

Serene statues of Buddha, and detailed scenes illustrating the story of his life: the sculpture of Gandhara is famous for its vibrant portrayal of Buddhism and for the deep devotion of its artists. This tradition was developed about the time of Christ in the kingdom of Gandhara, to decorate Buddhist monasteries and *stupas*.

Gandhara, founded in the sixth century B.C., was at its height under the Kushan kings from the first to fifth centuries A.D. The Kushans controlled a vast area including most of modern Afghanistan, Pakistan and northern India. Their winter capital and main center was Peshawar in Pakistan. Power brought peace, and peace brought prosperity: the Kushans grew rich as middlemen in the trade between China and the Roman Empire.

The Kushans were Buddhist, and central Gandhara became a Buddhist holy land, full of monks and monasteries. The monasteries and *stupas* were piously decorated with statues of Buddha and scenes from his life, in a combination of styles drawn from all over the known world. Ideas from West and East are fused in Gandhara art: Greek, Roman, Persian and Indian influences are all present—small pillars with Corinthian and Persepolitan capitals, centaurs, garlands, vine motifs, and Atlas figures from the West are frequently seen decorating the Buddhist shrines.

The Gandharans were the first to represent Buddha in human form. Before that he was indicated by a symbol—a lotus, a tree, a wheel or a *stupa*. The earliest Gandhara Buddha figures have recognizably Greek faces and wear Roman-style clothes with deeply carved folds. As the school developed, the Buddha figure lost its Western look and assumed a more mask-like expression showing the ecstatic inner serenity of a man withdrawn into deep meditation.

The earlier statues were in stone, but later ones are made of beige colored limeplaster. Both were originally covered in gold leaf and colored paint.

Gandharan sculptures are full of little details of life in Gandhara. For though Buddha lived from about 563 B.C. to 483 B.C. in the Ganges River basin, the Gandharan sculptures show him surrounded by people in Kushan dress, using local tools, pens, pots, musical instruments and toys.

The purpose of the carvings was to tell the story of Buddha and spread the Buddhist message. The most important scenes from Buddha's life, and from many of his 1,000 previous lives are depicted.

Gandhara art has been prized in both the West and Japan since its recognition by scholars in the 19th century. There are fine collections in London and Rome. In Pakistan the most magnificent displays are in the Lahore, Peshawar, Taxila, Swat and Karachi museums.

Temptation scene from the life of Buddha, Taxila.

THE KARAKORAM HIGHWAY

The drive up the **Karakoram Highway** (KKH) is one of the most spectacular trips in the world. Connecting Pakistan to China, the KKH twists through three great mountain ranges—the Himalayas, Karakorams and Pamirs—following one of the ancient silk routes between West and East. For 800 miles (1,280 km), the road forces its way along narrow gorges, across high desert plateaux, round some of the highest mountains on earth. At times it is terrifying—no more than a dizzy ledge, blasted across cliff faces, hundreds of feet above the river. Built jointly by the Pakistanis and Chinese, the road took 20 years to complete, and was finally opened to tourists in 1986.

The Northern Areas of Pakistan, through which the KKH passes, used to be one of the most rugged and isolated places on earth, only explored and mapped this century. Until it became an integral part of Pakistan in the 1970s, each valley was a separate little kingdom, often speaking its own distinct language. Communication between the valleys was precarious, involving danger-ous journeys across frozen passes, or down rivers with sheer rock walls on either side.

The Karakorams and Himalayas are still growing. They quake and settle continu-ously, an average of one tremor every three minutes. India drifted north and collided with Asia about 55 million years ago, and ploughs relentlessly on, nosing under the Asian geological plate and forcing the mountains up by about three-tenths of an inch (seven mm) a year.

Northern Pakistan is outside the mon-soon belt, and receives very little rain. In this high altitude desert, every village is a man-made oasis where life depends on water channelled down from the glaciers and snowfields to irrigate the tiny terraced fields below.

The journey from Islamabad to Kashgar (in Xinjiang, China) up the Karakoram Highway takes four days, provided there are no rockfalls. An exciting alternative is to fly halfway, to Gilgit, and take two or three days for the remaining 436 miles (697 km) across the Khunjerab Pass and down to Kashgar.

The flight to Gilgit, at Rs 234 (about $14), must be one of the best value trips in the world. The PIA pilot of the small Fokker Friendship plane navigates by sight up the

rmland
ar the
rakoram
ghway.

Kaghan Valley, over the Babusar Pass, and then skirts round the shoulder of **Nanga Parbat**, 26,660 feet (8,080 meters), the westernmost peak in the Himalaya Range, and the ninth highest mountain in the world. Lying on her back across the top of the mountain is the fancifully named 'Sleeping Beauty', her outline formed by the various summits. On a clear day you can see 87 peaks over 23,000 feet (7,000 meters), with the sharp triangle of K-2, the second highest in the world, easily visible on the horizon.

Those traveling by road all the way, can reach the Indus River by three routes: via Taxila, via Murree or via Swat. The Taxila and Murree roads join at **Abbottabad** (two-and-a-half hours from Islamabad via Taxila, or four hours via Murree), a military cantonment town built by the British. Soldiers in uniforms are everywhere, marching, exercising, parading, playing polo and even practising the bagpipes.

Mansehra, 15 miles (24 km) further north, was an important junction on the ancient trade routes. The old Mughal road to Srinagar in India (now closed because of the border dispute), branches east at this point. At this busy junction, the Emperor Ashoka inscribed another set of his edicts in the third century B.C., outlining his policy of govern-ment and instructing his subjects how to lead virtuous lives.

The KKH joins the Indus River at **Thakot Bridge**, 77 miles (123 km) from Abbotta-bad and follows it for the next 200 miles (320 km), through **Kohistan** and round the base of Nanga Parbat.

At **Besham**, halfway to Gilgit, the road from Swat via the Shangla Pass, joins the KKH—this is the most unstable section of the highway, where the Indian geological plate ends.

Rocky Road: **Chilas**, 10 hours from Islamabad, was another important junction on the ancient trade route. Here the jeep track from the Kaghan Valley, over the Babusar Pass, joins the KKH. And nearby, the track from Srinagar (now closed) comes in via Astor. Hundreds of rocks along this stretch of the Indus are engraved with pictures and inscriptions dating from the first century B.C. to the present day. Most carvings are Buddhist— pictures of the seated Buddha, *stupas* and pagodas, drawn by Chinese pilgrims on their way to Swat. The inscriptions, in various languages, reflect the anxiety of the pious travelers on their difficult journey along the Indus, and often give the date, destination and purpose of the journey.

River crossing can be a tricky affair.

Nanga Parbat, in all her shimmering majesty, is at last in sight six miles past **Rakhiot Bridge**. Only then is the road out from under her shadow, and you are far enough away to see that whole mountain. Nanga Parbat behind, Rakaposhi ahead, and Haramosh to the east, are all visible from the same stretch of road. The Indus makes a sharp turn at this point: one trade route follows it southeast through Skardu and on up to its source in Tibet, while the Karakoram Highway continues north along the Gilgit and Hunza rivers.

Gilgit, a green, irrigated oasis, sits in a wide bowl 4,700 feet (1,400 meters) above sea level, surrounded on three sides·by barren mountains, and guarded on the east by the snow-clad pinnacle of Domani, one of the peaks of Rakaposhi. As the only market town for hundreds of miles in every direction, it is here that traders from Central Asia meet those from the south.

Capital of Pakistan's Northern Areas, Gilgit has expanded rapidly since the Karakoram Highway connected it with the rest of Pakistan in 1975. Always an important staging post on the Silk Route, it has been well known for nearly 2,000 years. Ruled in turn by China, Tibet and Kashmir, it finally threw off the yoke of foreign domination in the 11th century, and became the powerful independent kingdom of Dardistan.

Sometime after the 11th century, Gilgit was converted from Buddhism to Islam, which arrived from three different directions. Today, the Muslim tribes of the Northern Areas are divided fairly equally into three sects: Sunni, like the majority in the rest of Pakistan; Shia Ithanasheri, like the majority in Iran; and *Shia Ismaili*, the followers of the Aga Khan.

When Dardistan declined, each valley became a small kingdom, each with its own customs and language. There were seven kingdoms along the Gilgit and Hunza rivers alone, speaking five different languages. Marco Polo, when he passed through this area in about 1273, called it "noisy with kingdoms."

Strategically placed, close to the borders of Russia and China, Gilgit interested the British. Worried by the steadily advancing might of Russia, they set up an agency there in 1877. It was the most isolated outpost in the British Empire and only lasted four years. The second agency, established in 1889, survived, thanks to an improved footpath across the mountains to Srinagar. By 1913 most of the area had been surveyed, showing that there was no pass to the north

over which the Russians could bring an army to invade India.

At the Partition of India and Pakistan in 1947, the Northern Areas were designated as part of Hindu-ruled Kashmir. The people of Gilgit objected, staged a successful coup against the Kashmiri governor, and became part of Pakistan.

The bazaars of Gilgit are always bustling. Men of different ethnic types, each wearing their own distinctive hat or turban, parade up and down the streets, or sit bargaining and gossiping in the open-fronted shops. Fragile porcelain and lustrous silks from China are sold next to paraffin lamps, ice axes and iodized salt. There is not a woman in sight. Up the hill is the old British cantonment area with spacious bungalows.

Polo tournaments take place in June, August and November. Polo originated in this area: the British learned it here and carried a tamer version to the rest of the world. Polo, Gilgit-style, is rough and exciting. It has replaced the tribal wars, and the spectators become wildly involved, shouting and jeering in a solid mass. Drowning out all else is the band. Originally the kings directed their men in battle with the band, signalling to them with different tunes. The wailing clarinets are excruciatingly loud,

and the players cannot fail to hear the musical messages blasted at them by their coach.

A huge Buddha, carved on a cliff face in the seventh century A.D. at **Kargah**, just outside Gilgit, gazes down serenely on the valley. It marks the beginning of the old pilgrim path across the mountains to the Indus and thence to Swat, the once famous center of Buddhism. The irrigation channel below the Buddha leads back to the Serena Lodge hotel, an easy two-hour walk, through villages and farmland, with panoramic views down over the whole valley.

The jeep track from Gilgit to Chitral across the Shandur Pass follows the Gilgit River west. The side valleys of **Punial**, **Ishkoman** and **Yasin** are steeply terraced, and filled with fruit and nut trees. Once isolated kingdoms, they are now accessible by jeep in a few hours. **Naltar Valley**, two hours' jeep ride north of Gilgit, is the loveliest of all, with high alpine meadows and pine forests surrounded by snowcapped mountains.

Hunza, on the Karakoram Highway between Gilgit and China, was the model for Shangri-La in James Hilton's novel *Lost Horizon*.. Reached through a series of dramatic gorges with sheer sides, the Hunza River rushing below, the mountains tower-

View of Mount Rakaposh from Baltit Fort.

ing above, nothing prepares you for the miracle of central Hunza. In a wide bowl surrounded by jagged peaks, 25,000 feet (7,600 meters) high, the rippling terraces, supported on high, dry stone walls, cascade from the snow line to the river. Slender poplar trees, green in spring, golden yellow and orange in autumn, cut strong vertical lines across the horizontal terraces. And standing guard over the whole valley, is **Baltit Fort**, the old palace of the *Mir* (king), perched on a ridge below Ultar glacier. **Rakaposhi**, 25,550 feet (7,740 meters), the 27th highest mountain in the world, protects the valley to the south.

At 8,000 feet, (2,400 meters), the fresh climate of Hunza makes it the perfect place to break the journey, explore the villages, take gentle walks along the irrigation channels, and visit the forts of Baltit and Altit.

Ruled by the same family for nearly 1,000 years, the Hunza people are peaceful and friendly. Almost all are Ismailis, followers of the Aga Khan. The conspicuous green-roofed house in every village is the Ismaili community center. Until the Karakoram Highway opened the area to the outside world, Hunza was almost self sufficient, each family growing enough wheat, maize, apricots and walnuts for its own use.

Herds of yaks, cows, goats and sheep feed on the summer pastures at the top end of the side valleys. The people still spin their own wool, and do their own weaving.

Hunza women, dressed in bright clothes and little embroidered pillbox hats draped with a scarf, are much less retiring than other women in northern Pakistan.

The KKH makes a spectacular climb from central Hunza up through long barren gorges, and past the fertile oases of **Gulmit** and **Passu**, whose magnificent glaciers come down to the edge of the road. **Sost**, the border post, is the last village, 55 miles (88 km) before the **Khunjerab Pass**. Open and windswept, the pass, at 15,528 feet (4,700 meters), is the continental watershed dividing the Indian Ocean from the China Sea, and is the highest border crossing with a surfaced road in the world.

Skardu, on the Indus, east of the Karakoram Highway, is the capital of **Baltistan**, also known as Little Tibet. Accessible by air, and by a good, surfaced road, it is the starting point for some of the world's best trekking and mountaineering. Nowhere else is there such a large number of high mountains in such a confined space—60 of them over 23,000 feet (7,000 meters), culminating in **K-2**, the second highest in the world.

ountain-
ers
eparing
r an
cent.

DESTINATION PAKISTAN

By Air: International airlines from 35 countries call at Karachi, Islamabad-Rawalpindi and Lahore. Pakistan International Airlines flies to 35 countries in Europe, Asia, Africa and the Americas. On arrival you can change money at the airports to pay for transportation to the city centers. You should bargain with the taxi driver and agree on a fare before setting off. From Karachi airport to the downtown hotels should cost about Rs 90 by taxi, Rs 10 by airport coach and Rs 2 by bus. From Islamabad-Rawalpindi airport to Islamabad is about Rs 70 by taxi, Rs 5 by wagon and Rs 3 by bus. A taxi to Rawalpindi costs about Rs 50, a bus costs about Rs 2.

By Sea: Boats sail twice a week from Bombay to Karachi en route for the Gulf States. They are operated by the British Indian Navigation Company and McKinnon and McKenzie Company. There are also boats from the Gulf States to Karachi and from Mombasa and Dar es Salaam in East Africa.

Overland from China: The Kunjerab Pass is open from May 1 to October 31 for tours, and from May 1 to November 30 for individual travelers. The border post for customs, immigration and health formalities are open every day for outgoing travelers until 11 a.m. and for incoming travelers until 4 p.m. It takes five hours to travel from Taxkurgan (the last town in China) to Sost (the first village in Pakistan), not including the time taken with border formalities.

Overland from India: The border at Wagah, near Lahore, is currently closed (1987), due to unrest in Indian Punjab. India and Pakistan have agreed to open the railway line from Jodhpur in Rajasthan to Hyderabad in Sind, but it is not yet running.

Overland from Iran: The border is open only at Taftan, from where it is a 15-to-24-hour bus ride to Quetta in Baluchistan.

Overland from Afghanistan: Afghanistan is closed to foreigners because of the Russian occupation. The two possible entry points to Pakistan from Afghanistan (from Kabul via Torkham and the Khyber Pass, and from Kandahar via Chaman and the Khojak Pass) are both off limits to all but local traffic and authorized refugees.

Visas: A valid passport is required for all visitors. All nationalities need visas for Pakistan, except nationals of Hong Kong, Ireland, Malaysia, Singapore, Tanzania, Tonga, Trinidad and Tobago, and Uganda. Nationals from the following countries can enter Pakistan without a visa from between one and three months, depending on the country: Fiji, Japan, Republic of Korea, Maldives, Mauritius, Nepal, Philippines, Romania and Western Samoa. Israelis and South Africans are not admitted to Pakistan. A maximum of three months stay is allowed on a tourist visa. Short visa extensions can (in theory) be obtained from the passport offices in Islamabad, Karachi, Lahore, Peshawar and Quetta. The length of the extension is at the discretion of the officer in charge. Contact the Pakistan consulate or Pakistan International Airlines for further information.

Departure: Antiques may not be exported from Pakistan. Only jewelry and precious stones worth less than Rs 10,000, and carpets worth less than Rs 25,000 are allowed out, and you must produce foreign exchange certificates up to the value you claim for the articles. Unaccompanied baggage needs an export permit.

Airport Tax: Rs 100 for international flights and Rs 10 for domestic flights must be paid at the airport by all travelers.

Health: Visitors need cholera and yellow fever vaccination certificates if coming from an infected area. Malaria exists all year round in the whole of Pakistan below 6,600 feet (2,000

INSIDE PAKISTAN

meters) so malarial prophylactics are essential. Anti-malaria pills should be taken for one week before arriving and for six weeks after departure. Ask your doctor for the latest information on the recommended malaria prophylactics for Pakistan.

Tourists are advised to have up-to-date vaccinations against typhoid, tetanus and polio. Cholera vaccine is only 50 percent effective and may have quite severe side effects, so is not recommended. Some doctors suggest you have an injection of gamma globulin a few days before departure. It gives 80 percent protection for five months against hepatitis, which is prevalent in Pakistan.

Customs: Alcohol is not admitted to Pakistan (bags are often searched and the alcohol impounded if found). Non-Muslims can buy liquor in Pakistan if they have a liquor licence obtainable (for a small fee) in some large hotels authorized to sell alcohol to hotel residents, and from government liquor shops in the main cities if the non-Muslim has a permit from the Excise and Taxation Department of that area.

Officially, 200 cigarettes, half a pint of perfume and only one camera, tape recorder and typewriter are allowed in. Officials are less strict about these for tourists, though visiting Pakistanis and Indians are thoroughly

searched.

Money: Rupees and paise are the currency of Pakistan, 100 paise = one rupee. Approximate rates (1987) are: US$1 = Rs 17.50, English £1 = Rs 27.00, DM 1 = Rs 10.00

There is no restriction on the amount of foreign currency or traveler's checks brought into Pakistan. Only Rs 100 in cash may be taken in or out of Pakistan. Only Rs 500 can be changed back from rupees to foreign currency. Save your encashment slips; you may need them when leaving. It is is an offence to sell foreign currency in Pakistan except to authorized dealers. Black market rates are little better than official ones, and it is strongly recommended that tourists use the authorized dealers.

US dollars and traveler's checks are the most useful to carry (English pounds and Deutschemarks are also widely accepted). American Express has offices at Karachi, Lahore, Islamabad and Rawalpindi, but the Islamabad and Rawalpindi branches have a reputation for inefficiency and delays. Traveler's checks can be changed at the major cities and at some Divisional Headquarters (there are 14 Divisions in Pakistan). Only foreign banks, the National Bank of Pakistan and Habib Bank are permitted to deal in foreign exchange. The rates differ slightly depending on

the town and bank. Big hotels and tourist shops will change traveler's checks, but usually give a lower rate than banks. Big hotels also accept credit cards.

If you need to have money sent to you in Pakistan, it is better to get it by bank draft, sent registered air mail to a specific address. This is quicker than having it sent bank to bank.

GETTING ACQUAINTED

Time: Pakistan is five hours ahead of GMT. It gets dark at about 5 p.m. in winter and 7.30 p.m. in summer.

Climate: The climate in Pakistan is so varied that no matter what time of year you go there, somewhere will be pleasant at that time. Winter (November to February) is the best time to visit southern Pakistan (Sind and southern Punjab). The rest of the country is at its most beautiful in spring (March to May depending on the altitude) and autumn (mid-September to mid-November) when the spring flowers and autumn colors are at their best. For trekking and mountaineering, June to September are the recommended months.

During *Ramadan*, the fasting month, no food or drink is sold during the day except in the dining rooms of large hotels (poolside service is usually suspended), and in some restaurants.

Travel during this month is difficult; tourists should be careful not to eat, drink or smoke in public. The dates of *Ramadan* vary from year to year.

Medical Facilities: Pakistan has a good supply of doctors, many English-speaking, in the major towns. Chemists stock a wide range of medicines which can often be obtained without prescription and at low cost. There are hospitals in many towns; the best is the Aga Khan University Hospital in Karachi.

What to Wear: Loose cotton clothes are recommended for hot weather. In winter and in the mountains you will need sweaters and an anorak. Pakistanis wear a large woolen shawl day and night, a useful idea to copy.

Women should dress modestly in loose trousers and a long, loose skirt. Legs and shoulders should be covered at all times, so dresses should not be worn. The light-weight scarf *(dupatta),* usually 6.5 feet (two meters) long by 20 inches (0.5 meters) wide, that Pakistani women wear, is useful to carry to drape round your shoulders and head in remoter areas and when visiting mosques and shrines. The women's national dress of Pakistan, the *shalwar-kameez,* is very comfortable and can be bought cheaply, ready-made in Karachi, Lahore and Islamabad. Elsewhere it can be made quickly and inexpensively by a dressmaker.

Men should wear shorts

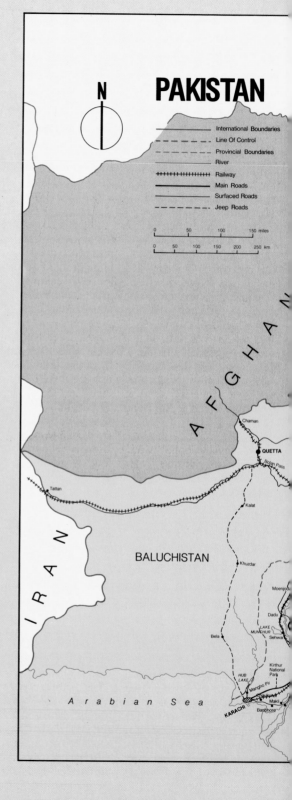

PAKISTAN

International Boundaries
Line Of Control
Provincial Boundaries
River
Railway
Main Roads
Surfaced Roads
Jeep Roads

0   50   100   150 miles
0   50   100   150   200   250 km

AFGHAN

Chaman
QUETTA
Bolan Pass
Tattan
Kalat

IRAN

BALUCHISTAN
Khuzdar
Moenjo
Dadu
LAKE MANCHUR
Bela
Sehwan
Kirthur National Park
HUB LAKE
Mangho Pir
Makli
KARACHI
Banbhore

Arabian Sea

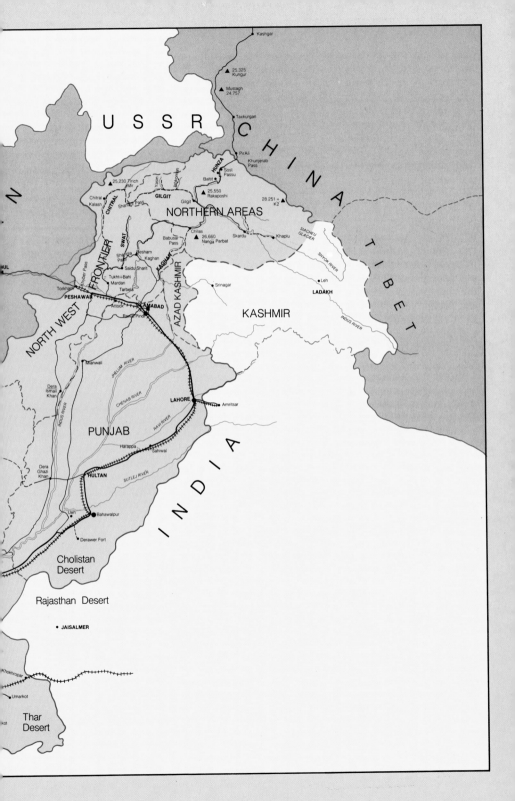

only for playing sports, and should wear a track suit to and from the sports ground.

What to Bring: Here is a checklist of useful items to carry with you in Pakistan: sunglasses, some sort of head covering to keep off the sun and dust and for women to wear in mosques and shrines, toilet paper, water purifying tablets and pills for upset stomachs, insect repellent, suntan lotion, a zippered bag for cameras and other possessions to keep out the dust, plastic water bottle and pocket knife. If you are using the cheaper hotels take a plug for washbasins, soap, towel, DDT powder and a sheet or sleeping bag.

Women should be sure to take all the moisturizing cream and sanitary napkins they need as they are difficult to find in Pakistan.

Religion: Tourists are welcome in mosques and shrines provided they remove their shoes, show respect and are suitably dressed. Women should cover their heads and shoulders. A pair of socks, or the little bootees that airlines sometimes give you are very useful, especially in summer, as the stones can get extremely hot. In some shrines women are not allowed into the inner sanctum, but may look in through a side window. Many mosques close their doors to tourists half an hour before prayers.

Etiquette: Pakistani women never travel alone: many never even leave their houses unless accompanied by a family member, friend or servant. Foreign women tourists are advised not to travel alone in Pakistan, not because there is any danger, but because it offends a good Muslim male to see a woman being so immodest as to travel unaccompanied.

Men are often seen holding hands and embracing; this means nothing more than that they are friends. Men and women never caress each other in public, and seldom even touch. Tourists should be sensitive about not offending the Muslim ethic with their Western habits.

Tipping: Service charges are not included and wages are low. It is normal to tip all hotel and restaurant staff, taxi drivers and porters.

What to Buy: Pakistan has some very beautiful handicrafts. Specialities are: rugs and carpets, leather goods, furs, embroidered and appliqued bedspreads and table linen, pottery, copper and brassware, onyx ornaments, woodwork and gold and silver jewelry. You can buy these in government-sponsored handicraft shops where the prices are controlled, or in the bazaars. It is necessary to bargain to get a good price.

Business Hours: Friday is the weekly holiday in Pakistan when all shops and offices are closed. Most offices also close on Saturday. Government office hours are 8.30 a.m. to 2 p.m. in summer and 9 a.m. to 2.30 p.m. in winter. Normal business hours are 7.30 a.m. to 2.30 p.m. in summer and 9 a.m. to 4 p.m. in winter.

Electricity: 220-240 volts, with fluctuations in voltage. In the north the electrical supply is erratic. Paraffin lamps or candles are usually supplied in hotels. Electric hairdryers and razors are useable only in large cities.

National Holidays:
March 23—Pakistan Day
May 1—Labor Day
August 14—Independence Day
September 6—Defence of Pakistan Day
September 11—Anniversary of the death of M A Jinnah, the Quaid-i-Azam
December 25—Birthday of the Quaid-i-Azam

Religious Holidays: The dates of these vary each year, as the Muslim calendar is about 11 days shorter each year than that of the west.

Publications: Three English language daily newspapers—*Dawn, The Pakistan Times* and *The Muslim* are available in most towns, with others just in Karachi. Foreign newspapers and periodicals are available at large bookstalls and the big hotels, as are English-language books.

Photography: Pakistan and its people are superbly photogenic. Very few travelers have time to wait for the perfect light, but beware the noon-day sun, when the strong light tends to flatten the subject and colors lose their brilliance. The best re-

ON THE MOVE

sults are with photos taken before 10 a.m. and after 3 p.m. or 4 p.m. (depending on the season). Deliberately underexposing midday shots by half a stop or even more can help, as will the use of a daylight or haze filter, but the results may be slightly disappointing and 'washed out.'

Film for color prints is available in many towns in Pakistan, but it is often old and overheated. Film for color slides and black and white prints is available only in Karachi, Lahore and Islamabad where it is expensive. Enthusiasts are advised to bring all the film they need with them and to store it in as cool a place as possible.

You are not allowed to photograph military installations, airports or bridges. People like to be asked permission before being photographed, then they usually assume manly poses and stare straight into the camera. A very discreet telephoto lens may be useful for spontaneous shots. Men should not attempt to photograph women, though female photographers usually have no problem at all, especially if there are no men around to disapprove, and if a little time is spent first making friends and asking permission.

TRANSPORT

Air: PIA operates flights to Karachi, Islamabad, Lahore, Peshawar, Quetta, Multan, Faisalabad, Mianwali, Sargodha, Hyderabad, Nawabshah, Badin, Moenjodaro, Sukkur, Jacobabad, Sibi, Sui, Jiwani, Gwadar, Turbat, Pasni, Panjgur, Saidu Sharif, Chitral, Gilgit, Skardu, Kohat, Bannu, Dera Ismail Khan and Shob.

Flights to Gilgit, Skardu and Chitral are extremely good value at about twice the bus fare. These tickets are cheaper if bought in Pakistan. The Gilgit and Chitral flights go only when visibility is good, so can be delayed for some days.

Journalists and groups can get discounts. Apply to the Public Relations Officer at the PIA offices at Karachi, Lahore, Rawalpindi, Peshawar, Multan or Quetta.

Rail: This is the best way of traveling if you are not in a hurry. The main lines run from Karachi via Multan, Lahore and Rawalpindi to Peshawar, and from Karachi via Sukkur and Quetta to the Iranian border. There is an extensive network of branch lines. There are frequent trains, but they are slow, unpunctual and crowded. There are two classes of train, express and ordinary, and three classes of compartment, air-conditioned, first and second. Air-conditioned and first class have sleeper compartments, and there are special ladies' compartments recommended for women traveling alone. Air-conditioned class is almost as expensive as flying. You usually need to book several days in advance, especially for sleepers. Most passengers bring their own bedding, but it can sometimes be hired at major stations. Buying a ticket can be time-consuming and frustrating. An agency or hotel employee willing to handle it is a great asset. If all else fails, you can pay a station porter (distinguishable by their red turbans and armbands) to buy you a ticket and find a seat.

Parties can hire a luxurious Tourist Car complete with dining and sitting room, which can be attached to certain trains and detached at any railway station for as many hours as the occupants wish. It can be hired from the Divisional Superintendent's office, Pakistan Railways, Karachi. The cost is reasonable if divided among a fairly large party.

Foreign tourists can get a 25 percent discount, and foreign students a 50 percent discount, on most rail fares. Apply to ·the Divisional Superintendent with passport and student card at Karachi, Lahore, Rawalpindi, Peshawar, Quetta, Sukkur or Multan railway stations for the necessary concession order before you buy your ticket. Indians and visiting Pakistanis are not given discounts.

Bus: Buses are the cheapest but most uncomfortable and dangerous way of traveling in Pakistan. Buses go anywhere from everywhere. Seats cannot be reserved in advance. Bus stations are usually near the railway stations in larger towns, and near the bazaar in smaller places. On longer journeys the buses make scheduled stops for food, but it is wise to take food (especially fruit) and drink with you.

Minibuses are faster, more comfortable and only slightly more expensive. Seats can be booked in advance. They often use a different station from the buses. There are several private luxury bus services between Rawalpindi and Lahore.

Jeep-taxi: Jeep-taxis are used for public transport in the northern valleys where the roads are too narrow for buses. The drivers are excellent, but the jeeps are neither cheap nor comfortable and they do not run to a timetable. As many passengers as possible perch on top of the cargo (usually sacks of grain or fertilizers), and crouch on the front and back bumper. In the more remote valleys, jeeps are very rare.

The Northern Area Transport Company (NATCO) runs buses and jeeps up the Karakoram Highway and into some of the side valleys off the main road. They offer a discount to a limited number of Pakistani and foreign students on each vehicle.

Car: The main roads in Pakistan are surfaced and generally in reasonable condition. Drivers are not conscientious about traffic rules, so those unused to driving in Asia may find it

dangerous. The main road, Karachi-Lahore-Rawalpindi-Peshawar, is always very crowded with particularly reckless drivers. The minor roads are often impassable for ordinary cars; 4-WD vehicles with high clearance are recommended. In the mountains it is essential to have a small 4-WD vehicle as the roads have been built for small jeeps and the bridges are very narrow.

Signposts are few and are often written in Urdu. There are frustratingly few in the big cities so finding your way round can be difficult. Driving at night is especially hazardous as trucks, bicycles and bullock carts rarely have lights. It is dangerous to drive in some parts of Sind at night because of the bandits.

Car Rental: Cars with drivers can be hired at the airport and big hotels. Hotel cars are fairly expensive (more so if air-conditioned), but are often worth it as the drivers can speak some English. Make sure with the hotel rental agency that the driver knows where you want to go before you set off. You can hire a small local taxi (black with yellow tops) in the street for about Rs 300 for the day, which is often the most satisfactory solution if you have several places to visit. Local taxi drivers usually know only the main locations in town. If looking for offices or private houses, they will expect you to direct them.

Jeeps with drivers can easily be hired in the mountains. The government-ap-

proved rate in 1987 in Punjab, on the Karakoram Highway and in Gilgit District is Rs 6 a mile and Rs 75 overnight charge. In Chitral it is Rs 8 a mile and Rs 30 overnight charge, and in Skardu the rate is Rs 10 a mile and Rs 200 halt charge.

Self-drive cars are not usually available.

Maps: Maps are difficult to find in Pakistan, and good maps do not exist. The best overall map is Bartholomew's road map covering the entire subcontinent. The best general road map of Pakistan is the 1:2 million 1976 road map. The most useful maps are the 1:1 million (10 km to 1 cm) contour maps issued by the Survey of Pakistan. Occasionally you can buy some of these in a bookshop or hotel lobby, but usually the only place to get them is in the Survey of Pakistan Office on Murree Road in Faizabad between Islamabad and Rawalpindi. (The office is 200 yards from the Airport Road—Murree Road intersection, on the right going towards Rawalpindi.) They may also be available in the Survey of Pakistan office in Karachi near the Metropole Hotel. These maps are reprints of old maps and are sometimes blurred, and the road grading is often 50 years out of date. New roads and lakes and even the present border with India are not shown.

The Pakistan Tourism Development Corporation publishes pamphlets with sketch maps which contain much useful information.

ACTIVITIES / IN TRANSIT

WHAT TO DO

Fishing: There is excellent deep-sea fishing off Karachi and equally good freshwater fishing in the northern valleys. Fishing permits usually cost Rs 10 a day and are available from the local fishing authorities.

Wildlife: Over 740 species of birds have been identified in Pakistan. The Indus is one of the major migration paths of the world so the lakes and reservoirs of Punjab and Sind are alive with migrant birds during the winter months. The coastline and the deserts are also good places to see unusual birds. Pakistan has seven national parks, 72 wildlife sanctuaries and 76 game reserves.

Sports: The Pakistanis are sports mad, and play all sorts of ball games. They excel at cricket, hockey, badminton and squash. They are also famous for their polo playing, and in the Northern Areas play a local variety of the game which is faster and visually more exciting than the staider international game. In many areas you can hire horses. There are golf courses in Islamabad, Murree, Quetta, Abbottabad and Swat.

Desert Safaris: Through a travel agent, you can arrange camel safaris in the Cholistan Desert.

Trekking: The Himalayas, Karakorams and Hindu Kush offer some of the best trekking in the world.

Mountaineering: Pakistan has five peaks over 26,400 feet (8,000 meters) and 101 over 23,000 feet (7,000 meters), some of which are still unclimbed. In 1985, 54 expeditions attempted 62 peaks. Applications for permission to climb K-2 must be made two years in advance and applications for other peaks, one year in advance. For rules, regulations and application forms write to the Tourism Division, College Road, F-7/4, Islamabad, Pakistan, or to any Pakistani Embassy or Pakistan International Airlines office abroad.

Rafting and Kayaking: This is allowed on the Indus, Hunza, Gilgit, Swat and Kunhar (Kaghan) rivers, but the sport is in its infancy in Pakistan and the rivers have not yet been graded for difficulty. Apply to a good travel agency for details.

Hunting: Officially, boar-hunting is the only hunting now allowed in Pakistan.

WHERE TO STAY

Hotels in Pakistan must be seen in perspective and not be compared with Western standards.

There are good international class hotels in Karachi, Islamabad, Rawalpindi, Lahore and Peshawar, but outside these major cities there is a shortage of good accommodation. This situation is improving with the Serena chain building and taking over hotels at Quetta, Faisalabad, Swat and Gilgit, and the Shangrila chain building in the northern areas at Chilas, Skardu, Sost and Fairy Meadows. The above hotels are all comfortable but expensive (between US$20 and US$80 a night). The best hotels are usually fully booked all the time, so ensure that you make advance reservations.

The Pakistan Tourist Development Corporation runs motels and guest houses at the most popular tourist resorts and places of interest. These are at Besham and Gilgit (on the Karakoram Highway), Miandam and Kalam (in Swat), Balakot and Naran (in the Kaghan Valley), Chitral town, Skardu, Taxila, Moenjodaro and Keenjar Lake. They cost about US$15 to $30 a night, but the staff is usually extremely helpful (especially at Gilgit).

Every town has a wide range of locally-run hotels which vary greatly in price and standard (anything from US$1 to US$40 a night). Many are cheap by Western standards and give adequate accommodation. Some are exceptionally good value, but it is usually worth checking the condition of the room and the sanitary facilities before signing in.

It is the custom in Pakistan to provide only a bottom sheet and a well-used blanket in local hotels. It is advisable to carry your own sheet and pillow case (or a sleeping bag liner), towel and soap. In winter, or in the mountains, you will need a sleeping bag.

In local hotels you should order any food you want for the next 24 hours as soon as you arrive. However it is often more satisfactory to go out and find a food stall or local restaurant than to eat in the hotel.

At the bottom end of the scale are the *mussafar khanas* —local inns where a *charpoi* (rope bed) is provided (without bedding) in a communal dormitory or outside. These local inns and the really cheap hotels will usually not accept foreigners except in very remote areas where there is nothing else.

There are youth hostels at Lahore and Taxila and YMCA hostels at the major cities of Karachi, Lahore, Peshawar and Abbottabad; at Bhurban and Khanpur (in the Murree hills); Balakot, Sharan, Naran and Bat Kundi (in the Kaghan Valley); and Ketas (in the Salt Range). There are also YWCA hostels at Karachi and Lahore.

Railway Retiring Rooms are a leftover from British days. These are rooms with beds for passengers holding air-conditioned or first-class tickets. They are good value at between Rs 20 and Rs 40 and are available at Karachi (City and Cantonment), Lahore (City and Cantonment), Multan Cantonment, Rawalpindi Cantonment, Peshawar Cantonment, Sargodha, Taxila, Bahawalpur and Quetta.

Camping: Islamabad has the only official camp site in Pakistan, but it is often possible to camp in the garden of small hotels, rest houses or youth hostels and to use their facilities. You are not allowed to camp by the roadside, in tribal areas, or in some parts of the northern valleys. Camping in the open can be difficult as the locals are very curious and in some areas hostile.

Showers: Major railway stations usually have free shower rooms. In most towns and villages, the barber shops also provide *hammams*: usually a bucket of water (hot in winter) in a cubicle.

WHAT TO EAT

The best Pakistani food is delicious, lightly curried and with plenty of variety. Chicken, mutton and beef are on the menu in most restaurants, served with lentils *(dhal),* vegetables *(subzi)* and yogurt *(dahi),* and scooped up with *chapatis* or *naan* (two types of unleavened bread usually made with wheat flour). Lahore is famous for its Mughal cuisine, Karachi for its seafood and Peshawar for its kebabs, *naan* and green tea. Pakistani curries are usually not as hot as Indian, and many dishes have no chillies at all, though they are well seasoned with other spices. Chinese restaurants of varying quality are available in the main cities, and the international class hotels serve European dishes. All food and restaurant prices are very moderate by international standards.

Visitors should be sensible about what they eat. It is easy to avoid an upset stomach by taking a few simple precautions. Seasoned travelers in Asia will have developed some immunities, but new arrivals should avoid eating anything that has not been freshly cooked, especially salads, sliced tomatoes, even onion rings. Remember: boil it, bake it, peel it or forget it.

It is perfectly safe to eat at roadside stalls, but make sure that the food comes out of a boiling pot on to a clean dry plate. *Chapatis* and *dhal* is a good, high protein, cheap meal available everywhere. As a general rule, eat where the crowds are. The most popular stalls have the best, and freshest, food.

Buffet meals, even in first-class hotels, are sometimes a problem. Food kept warm for long periods may be contaminated.

NATIONWIDE

Tuesdays and Wednesdays are meatless days in most areas, when restaurants serve only chicken and fish. This is an attempt to save on meat consumption.

Fruit is particularly good in Pakistan. It is wise to peel all fruit with a clean knife before eating it. You can buy good folding knives in the bazaar. Cut fruit, mixed fruit juices and ice cream sold in the bazaar spell danger to all but the most seasoned of travelers in Asia.

Drink: Avoid drinking water that has not been boiled or purified. Avoid ice everywhere, even in major hotels, as it is not made with boiled water. Tea is usually a safe drink. It is the custom in Pakistan to boil milk before serving it, so it is safe to take milk in tea. Be sure the tea is poured into a clean, un-cracked, dry cup. International class hotels claim that their water is drinkable; it is wise not to risk it unless you know you have built up some immunities. Bottled drinks are safe and are available in all major towns and many smaller ones.

CITIES

KARACHI

Climate: Karachi is at its best during the winter months from mid-November to mid-March when the daytime temperature is between 60 F to 80 F (15 C and 20 C). In summer the temperature hovers around 100 F to 115 F (35 C to 45 C). In the monsoon season, during June, July and August, it is very humid, although there is little rain.

Shopping: Good buys in Karachi are new Pakistani carpets and old tribal rugs from Baluchistan, Afghanistan and Iran, leather, furs, jewelry (both antique and modern), cotton bedspreads, antique and modern brass and copper, embroidered table linen and handicrafts. Most carpet shops are on **Abdullah Haroon Road.** Keep to the hotel lobbies and shopping plazas for leather, furs and modern jewelry. The best antique jewelry is in the **Sarafa Bazaar** north of Boulton Road. For the rest try the **Saddar Bazaar** area, especially **Zainab Market**. Two recommended handicraft shops in Zainab are **Marvi Handicrafts** and **Village Handicrafts.** **Zainab Market** also sells very good, extremely cheap cotton shirts, ready made *shalwar-kameez*, general export rejects and T-shirts saying: "I caught crabs in Karachi." Bargain hard everywhere. Try the following:

Iridescence
10 A-7 Amir Khursro Road, off Karsaz Road, opposite the American school. Tel: 436987. Latest Pakistani fashions and modern Western dress. Block printing on the premises.

Haveli
10 C-1 Gizri Lane, DHS IV, Tel: 537514, 542237. Saris, traditional *shalwar-kameez* and western clothes.

Chaman
43 B-4 Block IV, PECHS. Tel: 430430. F-31 Block IV, Kehkashan, Clifton. Tel: 532515, 533334. Hand-printed fabrics and traditional Pakistani ready-to-wear.

Cleos
Hilltop Shopping Center 4 D-2 Gizri Boulevard, DHS IV. Modern *shalwar-kameez* and some Western clothing.

Fusun
9 A-1 Khayaban-e-Shujaat, DHS V. Tel: 536085. By appointment only. Western export clothing.

Koel
36-1 Khayaban-e-Hafiz, DHS V. Hand-block printed and embroidered traditional Pakistani clothing, cushion covers, table linen, wall hangings, silver jewelry. Block printing and hand embroidery on the premises.

Sehr
Opposite back entrance of Metropole Hotel. Tel: 514404. Export clothing and *shalwar-kameez*.

Nicky Malik
C178-2 PECHS Main Tariq Road, above International Furnishers. Tel: 442233. Smart western clothes.

Aliya Iqbal
16-1-2 3rd Zamzama Street, Clifton. Western couture clothes.

Hotels: Below is a sample hotel listing, divided into two price categories (Expensive and Moderate).

Expensive:

Sheraton
Club Road. Tel: 521021.

Holiday Inn
Abdullah Haroon Road. Tel: 522011, 520111.

Pearl Continental
Dr Ziauddin Ahmed Road. Tel: 515021.

Avari Towers
Fatima Jinnah Road. Tel: 525261.

Taj Mahal
Shahrah-e-Faisal. Tel: 520211.

Midway House
Stargate Road, near airport. Tel: 480371.

Moderate:

Beach Luxury
Maulvi Tamizuddin Khan Road. Tel: 551031.

Metropole
Club Road. Tel: 512051.

Mehran
Shahrah-e-Faisal. Tel: 515051, 515061, 514739.

Al-Farooq
off Zaibun Nisa Street. Tel: 22811, 511031.

Bristol
10 Sunnyside Road. Tel: 511980.

Columbus
Clifton Road. Tel: 511311.

Gulf
Dr. Daud Pota Road, Saddar. Tel: 515834.

Hostellerie de France
Main Drigh Road. Tel: 49501, 48101.

Imperial
Maulvi Tamizuddin Khan Road. Tel: 551051.

The Inn
Stargate Road, near airport. Tel: 412011.

Jebees
Abdullah Haroon Road. Tel: 512011.

National City
Sarmad Road. Tel: 513850.

North Western
26 Beaumont Road. Tel: 510843.

Palace
Dr. Ziauddin Ahmed Road. Tel: 511010.

Royal City
Sarmad Road. Tel: 512803.

Eating Out: Karachi now has hundreds of good restaurants, especially in Clifton shopping centers and along the airport Road. **Beach Luxury Hotel, Casbah Restaurant,** outside. Excellent grilled seafood and good atmosphere. Tel: 551031.

Pearl Continental Hotel, Chandni Lounge on ninth floor. International food and seafood. Tel: 515021.

Pioneer
Abdullah Haroon Road. Good vegetarian food on Tuesdays and Wednesdays.

Red Carpet
Seabreeze Center, Boat Basin, Clifton. Barbecue and curries.

Seagull
Seabreeze Center, Boat Basin, Clifton. Tel: 531244.

Dolphin
Boat View Arcade, Khayaban-i-Saadi, Clifton. Tel: 537429, 533874.

Shenzan Kohsar
Hill Park. Tel: 428628. Good Pakistani food.

The Village
Merewether Road. Tel: 512880. Barbecue.

Bundu Khan
M A Jinnah (Bundar) Road. Chicken *tikka* and *parathas*.

Star of Pakistan
Boulton Market. Tel: 225219.

LAHORE

Climate: October to March is the best time to visit Lahore. It is only 698 feet (213 meters) above sea level, and unlike Karachi, has no sea breeze, so is hotter than either Karachi or Islamabad, and can get extremely hot in summer.

Shopping: Good buys in Lahore are modern Pakistani carpets, antique brass, silk and cotton cloth and embroidered table linen. Try the shops in the hotel lobbies, **Faletti's** arcade, around Charing Cross and along the Mall. **Mozang Bazaar,** south of Charing Cross, is the best place to look for cloth. Bargain hard everywhere.

Tourist Information Center, PTDC Faletti's Hotel, Egerton Road. Tel: 303660, 303623-4.

Hotels

Expensive:

Hilton International
Shahrah-e-Quaid-e-Azam, (The Mall). Tel: 310281-10, 69971. International class, all facilities.

Pearl Continental
Shahrah-e-Quaid-e-Azam, (The Mall). Tel: 67831, 69931. International class, all facilities.

Moderate:

International
Upper Mall. Tel: 870281-7, 880196-8.

Faletti's
Egerton Road. Tel: 303660-10. A once gracious old building with arcades and a garden. More atmosphere than the big hotels.

Ambassador
7, Davis Road. Tel: 301861-

8, 302890. All facilities.

Amer:
46, Lower Mall. Tel 320101-3, 65072-3.

Indus
56, The Mall. Tel: 302850, 302856-8.

Country Club Motel
105-A, The Mall. Tel: 311361-2.

Orient
74, McLeod Road. Tel: 306794-6, 320261.

Lahore
Kashmire Building, McLeod Road. Tel: 320257-69, 320250.

Menora
41, McLeod Road. Tel: 224028-9, 224031.

Uganda
45, McLeod Road. Tel: 56077, 310553.

Shalimar
Liberty Market, Gulberg. Tel: 870331-3.

Liberty
44, Commercial Zone, Liberty Market. Tel: 870561.

Mughal
3-K ,Main Building, Gulberg. Tel: 882211.

Asia
Near Railway Station. Tel: 57429, 57997, 68685.

Parkway
Near Railway Station. Tel: 54507, 57259, 58553, 69838.

Shabistan
McLeod Road, Near Railway Station. Tel: 56744.

Eating Out: Restaurant food in Lahore is probably the best in Pakistan. Some of the best known restaurants are:

Gulberg Kabana
Main Boulevard, Gulberg. Tel: 871062, 872255. Pakistani food, quail especially good.

Kabeesh
Main Boulevard, Gulberg. Tel: 873218. Pakistani food.

Tung Fung
Main Boulevard, Gulberg. Tel: 87561. Chinese.

Saloos
Wapda House, The Mall. Tel: 325257.

Lords
The Mall. Tel: 312235.

Shezan Oriental
The Mall. Tel: 54450.

Kabana
Davis Road. Tel: 305489.

Kabana
Fortress Stadium, Cantt. Tel: 370550.

Tolenton Kabana
The Mall.

Cathay Restaurant
Opposite American Express on the Mall. Chinese.

Mozang Bazaar for chicken *tikka*.

Gamal Mandi area near old city is good for fried fish.

Lakshmi Chowk for local dishes of every kind.

Abbott Road wayside stalls serve cheap meals.

ISLAMABAD

Climate: Islamabad, at 1,700 feet (518 meters) above sea level, is at its best from October to March when the days are crisp and cool and the nights are cold. The hottest months are May and June before the monsoon, but even then the climate is not usually opressive, and you can always escape to the hills. In one hour's drive you can be up at 7,400 feet (2,250 meters).

Shopping: Islamabad's best buys are antique carpets, brass and copper, antique and modern jewelry and leather goods. **Melody, Super Market** and **Jinnah Market** offer the biggest choice during the week, but the **Juma Bazaar,** on Fridays only, is the most interesting for tourists and offers good bargains in everything. The Afghan refugees have the best carpets and antique jewelry. Bargain hard everywhere, and visit the following shops:

Threadlines Gallery
Super Market. A government-sponsored handicraft shop which has some excellent pieces at most reasonable prices.

Behbud Boutique
Super Market, G-6. Profits go to charity. Good selection of ready-made dresses, shalwar-kameez, table linen, and some traditional embroidery and tribal jewelry. Very reasonable prices.

Afghan Handicrafts and **Maharaja Handicrafts** in Super Market.

Fancy Handicrafts and **Kraftman** in Jinnah Market.

Chiltan Handicrafts, Pakistan Handicrafts and **Asian Arts and Crafts** in the Blue Area.

Erums and Behbud in Super Market. Good selection of ready-made shirts, trousers and *shalwar-kameez*.

Creation, Adam and Eve, and Guys and Dolls in Jinnah Market. Ready-made clothes, as above.

Bookshops:
Vanguard and Book Fair in Jinnah Market; **Mr Books** and **Lok Virsa** in Super Market; **London Book Shop** in Kosar Market; **Old Bookshop** (secondhand books) in Melody Market.
Carpets:
Pak Persian and **Qureshi's Carpets** in Melody Market; **Baluch Carpets, Lahore Carpet House, Shiraz Carpets, Nabeel Carpets** and others in the Blue Area.

Hotels

Expensive:

Holiday Inn
Aga Khan Road, F-5/1. Tel: 826121-35. International class, all facilities.

Moderate:

Islamabad Hotel
Municipal Road, G-6/2. Tel: 827311-31. Air-conditioned, all facilities.

Ambassador
Khayaban-e-Suhrawardy. Tel: 824011-6.

Eating Out:

Tabbak
13, West Blue Area. Tel: 812535. Pakistani, Chinese and English.

Kim Mun
Jinnah Market. Chinese.

White House
Super Market. Tel: 828213. Pakistani and continental.

Orient Express
Round Market, F-7/3, Pakistani and continental.

Kashmirwalah's
Daman-e-Koh.

Kao Wah
Aabpara Market, Khayaban Suhrawardy. Tel: 829898. Chinese.

Golden Dragon
Round Market F-7/3. Tel: 827333. Chinese.

RAWALPINDI

Climate: Rawalpindi is nine miles (15 km) from Islamabad and shares the same climate.

Shopping: Musical instruments, sports equipment, Kashmir shawls, antique silver jewelry, brass and copper and leather goods are all good buys in Rawalpindi. The markets are concentrated in two areas, around **Raja Bazaar** in the old city, and in **Saddar Bazaar** in the Cantonment. Everything can be found in the old city, if you have the patience to hunt for it. Shopping in Saddar Bazaar, the area off the Mall along Kashmir Road and Massey Gate, is easier.

Leather Goods: Shamas Din, on Massey Gate sells boots, shoes, suitcases, saddles and poufs.

Bookshops: English Book House and **Pak American Bookshop** on Kashmir Road.

Carpets, Brass and Antiques: Canning Road behind Flashman's, and on The Mall in front. They are also in the lobby of the **Pearl Continental Hotel.** Another good brass shop, **Shaukat Ali,** 170 D-Block, Satellite Town, tel: 842813, has a large selection of good quality ready-polished brass and copper.

Tailors: Men's tailors are on **Haider Road** and ladies' tailors in **Kamran Market** off Kashmir Road. Tel: 66648.

Hotels

Expensive:

Pearl Continental
The Mall. Tel: 66011-21, 62700-10. International class, all facilities.

Moderate:

Shalimar
Off the Mall. Tel: 62901-21. All facilities.

Flashman's
PTDC, The Mall. Tel: 64811-17. All facilities.

Kashmir Wala's Tourist Inn
The Mall. Tel: 68081-85. Recommended.

Silver Grill
The Mall. Tel: 64719, 64729.

Marhaba
Kashmir Road. Tel: 66021-2, 65178.

Parkland
Bank Road. Tel: 66080.

Potohar
Murree Road. Tel: 74398, 74366.

Shangrila
Murree Road. Tel: 74501.

United
Sand Hill, Gulnoor, National City and Park, all on Murree Road.

Eating Out: Besides the restaurants in the chief hotels, most of the best known restaurants are along the Mall or just off it. **Shezan** on Kashmir Road, **Kamran, Super and Shalimar** on Bank Road, **Chung Wah** on Murree Road. The best inexpensive restaurants are in the **Saddar Bazaar** area and

around **Raja Bazaar.**

Useful Information:

PTDC and Tourist Information Center
Flashman's Hotel, The Mall. Tel: 64811-2.

PIA
The Mall. Tel: 67011.

American Express
Murree Road. Tel: 65617.

General Post Office
Kashmir Road. Tel: 65691.

Telegraph and Telephone Office
The Mall. Tel: 65854, 65809.

PESHAWAR

Climate: Peshawar is at its best from November to March when the temperature ranges between 39 F to 78 F (3 C and 25 C). In summer it can be extremely hot with temperatures up to around 113 F (45 C).

Shopping: The best buys in the old city are brass and copper, Gardner Russian China, antique silver, old coins, military buttons and buckles and Astrakhan hats made of newborn lamb skin. **Saddar Bazaar** is well known for its Afghan carpets and wooden furniture with brass inlay work, besides the usual brass and copper. European-style smoked meat and sausages are available at **Brzybrowski's** in the Jamrud Industrial Estate, Tel: 50647.

Useful Information:
PTDC Information Center at Dean's Hotel; **TIC** at airport; Banks and GPO on Saddar Bazaar; Telephone and Telegraph Office on the Mall.

Hotels

Expensive:

Pearl Continental
Khyber Road. Tel: 76361-9. International class, all expected facilities.

Moderate:

Dean's
Islamia Road. Tel: 76481-4. PTDC Hotel, old-style building, some charm, verandahs and pretty garden.

Green's
Saddar Road. Tel: 76035-7. Comfortable.

Jan's
Islamia Road. Tel: 76939, 72056, 73009.

Eating Out: Pearl Continental, Dean's, Jan's and **Green's** all serve European and Pakistani food. The street food in Peshawar is as famous as some of the best in Pakistan. Try the stalls along **Khyber Bazaar** and **Qissa Khawani** where you can eat well and cheaply. In and around **Saddar Bazaar** are more cheap eating places.

Salatin's
Cinema Road. Tel: 73779, 73770. Best Pakistani food in Peshawar and famous for its Pathan atmosphere.

Nanking and Hong Kong restaurants
Both on the Mall. Both serve good Chinese food.

GILGIT

Climate: The Northern Areas are at their best in April, when the fruit trees are in bloom, and October, when the fall colors are at their brightest. Summer is the time for trekkers and climbers: the higher passes are only open from July to September. In winter the temperatures drop below freezing, though Gilgit town gets very little snow.

Shopping: Chinese porcelain, silks, embroidered table linen and irregular pearls are the best buys in Gilgit. The biggest selection is at the Chinese emporia near the Airport Chowk. G.M. Baig's in Jamat Khana Bazaar has a selection of antiques, books and maps of the Northern Areas. PTDC Information Center is at Chinar Inn.

Hotels

Moderate:

Serena Lodge
Jutial, Gilgit. Tel: 2330/1.

Chinar Inn
PTDC, Chinar Bagh. Tel: 2562.

Hunza Inn
Chinar Bagh. Tel: 2814.

Park
Airport Road. Tel: 2679.

HUNZA

Climate: Central Hunza, at 8,000 feet (2,500 meters) is cooler than Gilgit in summer, and snow bound in winter, and at its best in April and May, September and October.

Shopping: Nuts, fresh and dried fruit, and a few local embroideries and woven goods are available from roadside stalls.

Hotels

Moderate:

Central Hunza
Karimabad/Aliabad, two hours from Gilgit.

Serena Lodge
Karimabad, book through Serena, Karachi. Tel: 537506-9, Telex SERENA PK.

Moderate:

Shangrila
Sost, open in 1988. Book Rawalpindi 73006, 72948, or Karachi 520703, 520810, 520261-5.

Silk Route Lodge, Gulmit. Camping allowed.

SRI LANKA: SWEET SERENDIB

Shimmering in the blue expanse of the Indian Ocean, measuring just 270 miles (432 km) long and 140 miles (224 km) wide, is the island of Sri Lanka, *Taprobane* to the ancient Greeks and *Serendib* to the old Arab traders.

The most fascinating aspect of this island is the diversity that is packed into this 25,000-square-mile (65,000-square-km) land mass, of which one-tenth is still wild country. Perhaps no other country this small could show such cultural, climatic and environmental diversity, linked by a long and well-preserved history.

The variation among the Sinhalese people, the major ethnic group, is remarkable. Their attire, eating habits, interpretation of folklore and even the subtleties of language change from the low country to the hills, the dry to the wet zone and sometimes from village to village. Among the other groups are the Tamils, originally from India, the Moors who came as Arab traders, the Burghers, descending from the Portuguese and the Dutch and the Malays who came as soldiers from Malaysia. The Bhoras, the Parsis and the Sindhis all have their roots in India and towards Persia, while the aboriginal Veddhas are the oldest surviving people of this land and whose origins are lost in the mists of time.

The island's climate is sub-tropical and changes from one easily accessible region to another. A couple of hours drive from the warm, breezy, palm-fringed coastline brings you to the arid dry zone plains, where the temperature rises into the 90s, and where the great irrigation works and monuments of the ancient kingdoms can be seen. Also within easy reach is the steamy, green, riverine environment of the wet zone foothills, or even the mountains, where the mercury drops to the 30s and the surroundings are mist draped, stark and eerily beautiful. The weather is mainly governed by the productive southwest monsoon and the rain-drenched northeast monsoon.

For a small island, Sri Lanka's wildlife, both feathered and furred, is fantastic. Among the big game are elephants, leopards, bears and buffalos. Four main types of monkey and four species of deer are among the array of other smaller animals, which include reptiles and 425 different types of birds.

For centuries, travelers and explorers like Fa Hsien and Baker have written thousands of words extolling the beauty of this ancient land. Still, none could portray its absolute essence. Like one of its tasty curries and tangy teas, it cannot be described, it has to be experienced.

Preceding pages: Chubby wall dwarf at Kelaniya Temple; stilt fishing on the south coast. Left, here's looking at a local attraction.

The story of Sri Lanka's past, one of the longest written histories in the world, is contained in two great literary works, the *Mahawamsa* and the *Chulawamsa*, the 'greater' and the 'lesser' chronicles. But though these great works were firmly based on fact, particularly in the genealogical descriptions, their true significance was not established until 1826, when an English civil servant discovered the *pali* commentary in a temple at Mulgirigala off the southern coast of the island. Both these works were compiled by Buddhist monks, over many years, beginning in the sixth century by a monk named Mahanama under the orders of King Datusena.

The *Mahawamsa* identifies the beginning of the island's history to the landing of Prince Vijaya (the son of King Sinhabahu of India), with his retinue of 700 men, on the same day as the passing away of the Buddha. An ancient folk tale states that Sinhabahu was either brought up by a lion or was even the result of a direct union between the king of beasts and a woman. Thus, the island's people are named Sinhalese, *sinha* meaning lion.

What the *Mahawamsa* does not tell us of the indigenous people of Sri Lanka, the archaeologists are slowly discovering. It appears that *Homo Sapiens* first appeared in the island about 500,000 B.C. and Stone Age culture, about 10,000 B.C. From skeletal and other fossils found in the Balangoda region a Stone Age culture known as 'Balangoda culture' has been identified. 'Balangoda culture' made an initial impact about 5,000 B.C. and survived until about 500 B.C.

A shell cave uncovered at Kitulgala first yielded artifacts suggesting that the domestication of plants here began as early as 15,000 B.C. to 10,000 B.C. A recent discovery of a skeleton at the same spot, judged to be 13,000 years old, seems to confirm this. Further findings at Mantai, the ancient port of the island on the northwest coast, indicate that Sri Lanka had traded with the West long before the advent of Vijaya. The oldest ethnic group on the island is a fast-disappearing Stone Age tribe called the Veddhas, and they are more Australoid than Aryan.

The written history of the island begins in the arid, north central plains. Early settlements sprang up along the river banks and then spread across the land. Anuradhapura, founded by King Pandukhabaya in the fourth century B.C., was the first capital.

Persistent droughts in the plains led the Sinhalese people to develop one of the great irrigation systems of the ancient world. By the third century B.C., Sri Lankan engineers had invented the *bisokotuwa* (valve pit), a forerunner to the

modern surge chamber. This enabled engineers to regulate the flow of water from artificial lakes. Other feats of hydraulic engineering include the Nachchaduwa *wewa* (535 A.D.), Kala *wewa* (459 A.D.), Minneriya *wewa* (276 A.D.) and the Parakrama Samudra (1153 A.D.).

Buddhist Beginnings: In the third century B.C., during the reign of King Devanampiyatissa of Anuradhapura, Buddhism was introduced to Sri Lanka. It received royal patronage, and from this time, Buddhism became the greatest preoccupation of the Sinhalese monarchs. They built great monuments and buildings that ranked sec-

ond only to the great pyramids of Egypt. Even today, the 400-foot (121-meter) Jetavanarama, one of the three giant *dagobas* (reliquaries) in Anuradhapura, could be the largest monument in the Buddhist world.

Even though Buddhism took a strong grip on the country, the very same caste system which the Buddha had condemned also slowly grew until it eventually formed the basis of social stratification in the island. Though it was Indian in origin, the caste system in Sri Lanka took its own characteristics. The system is still extant in the rural areas but is fading out in the urban areas.

Time and again during the Anuradhapura period, adventurous soldiers from South India, tempted by the flourishing civilization, invaded the island and usurped the throne. In the recorded history of Lanka are 14 Chola and Pandya invasions. One such was a Chola general named Elara, who usurped the throne in the second century B.C. and ruled Anuradhapura for 44 years, earning himself a reputation for running and maintaining a just and impartial administration. Up to this time, the kings of Anuradhapura, though totalitarian in rule, were tolerant of local autonomy. Rarely was the entire island ruled by one monarch. The Ruhuna, in the south of the island, was ruled by King Kavantissa. In 161 B.C. his son Prince Dutugemunu, marched northwards and gradually pushed back Elara's forces, which

V. During the 53 years that the Cholas ruled the island as a province of South India, they took the capital to Polonnaruwa in the east, because it provided a more strategic position in defending an invasion from the Ruhuna. Despite this, the indigenous King Vijayabahu I mounted a long campaign against Polonnaruwa and the foreign invaders finally capitulated in 1070.

Vijayabahu ruled for 40 years, during which he started the reconstruction of the capital and restored Buddhism to prominence. The kingdom of Polonnaruwa lasted two centuries. Among the dozen or so rulers were two strong monarchs,

had spread far south. Dutugemunu met and killed Elara in single combat, then was made the king of Sri Lanka, bringing the entire nation under one banner for the first time. This system remained until the country finally fell to the British in 1815.

The kingdom of Anuradhapura endured for 1,400 years until the 10th century, except for 18 years in the fifth century when it was moved to the rock fortress, Sigiriya, by the rebel King Kasyapa.

In 1017, the Cholas invaded the island and captured the last king of Anuradhapura, Mahinda

Left, Buddhist priest. Right, temple painting of royalty at rest.

Parkramabahu I, also known as the Great, a contemporary of Thomas Becket of England, and Nissankamalla. Under their rule in the 11th and 12th centuries, Polonnaruwa reached the height of Sinhalese glory.

After Nissankamala's death, schisms among the Sinhalese themselves so weakened the nation that the Cholas once again captured the island.

Under the rule of Maga, a pirate from Kalinga, the island suffered some of the greatest damage to its ancient monuments and artifacts. After his death in 1255, the Sinhalese began to migrate to the island's wet zone in search of security and a new economic base.

Colonial Rule: Temporary but significant capitals were set up at Dambadeniya, Kurunegala, Panduvas Nuwara, Yapahuwa, Gampola,

Dedigama and Sitawaka. It was during the succeeding period that the Kandyan kingdom slowly developed, and by the time of Senerath I (1604-1635), the Portuguese had invaded the island. The Portuguese held on until the Dutch arrived and with the assistance of the Kandyan kingdom drove them out in 1658. The Dutch remained on the island, monopolizing the cinnamon trade, until the advent of the British in 1796. During this period, the Kandyan kingdom retained its independence until in 1815, the year of Napoleon's Waterloo, it finally fell to the British.

Britain had the greatest impact on Sri Lankan society in modern times. Today's economic base has been developed from the time of British rule. Export of tea, introduced by the British in 1867, constitutes the island's primary foreign exchange earner. The other two major exchange earners are

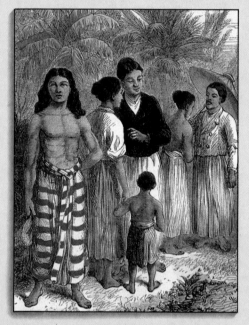

tourism and the inward remittances made by Sri Lankans working abroad.

One of the most significant events during British rule was the introduction of universal suffrage in 1931, when all men and women over 21 were permitted to vote. This move prompted the re-emergence of Buddhist nationalism, and progress was also made in the area of social welfare. One of the great achievements of that period was a comprehensive restoration program of the irrigation works of the dry zone and the resettlement to that zone of peasant 'colonists' from other parts of the country. The architect of this move was the dynamic Minister of Agriculture, Don Stephen Senanayake, under whose leadership the final phase in the transfer of power from British to Sri Lankan hands began, and who later became the

first prime minister of independent Sri Lanka.

World War II came to Sri Lanka on Easter Sunday in 1942, when Japanese planes bombed the capital and other ports. During the week, more than 1,000 Allied troops and Sri Lankan civilians lost their lives defending the island. But the defense was successful and is considered by some analysts as a crucial defeat for the Japanese.

Independence: On February 4, 1948, the nation gained independence. Since then, Sri Lanka has had seven prime ministers and one caretaker prime minister in nine governments. Among them was Sirimavo Bandaranaike, the world's first woman prime minister. She was the widow of S.W.R.D. Bandaranaike, the premier who was assassinated in 1959. Mrs. Bandaranaike dominated island politics for nearly two decades. Her government and subsequent governments took on a socialist bent. However, her continuing shift to the left led to the eventual downfall of her Sri Lanka Freedom Party.

Following an unsuccessful armed insurrection in 1971 by a group of ultra left youths, the government implemented a series of radical economic and social changes. It was during this set up, in 1972 that the island's name was officially changed from Ceylon to Sri Lanka.

In 1977, the United National Party, under the dynamic leadership of J.R. Jayawardene, a seasoned right-wing politician, came to power with an unprecedented majority. His government immediately embarked on a policy based on free enterprise that changed the face of the nation. On February 4, 1978, Jayawardene became Sri Lanka's first Executive President.

An election pledge by the leader of the main Tamil political party, promising a separate, autonomous state for the Tamil people in the north and east, sparked the emergence of politically motivated 'urban guerilla'-type Tamil terror groups. For four years, government forces and these groups waged war in the north and east, a conflict which threatened to cripple the economy of the country.

Then in July 1987, in an unprecedented but widely welcomed move, President Jayawardene and Premier Rajiv Gandhi of India negotiated a treaty granting the Tamil people a degree of autonomy. All parties concerned, some under protest, accepted the terms of the treaty, apart from radical Marxist elements.

The nation has remained calm during the difficult period, and despite periodic flareups, there is hope that the conflict in the problem areas will come to an end, and Sri Lankans are once again looking ahead with optimism.

Left, Sinhalese at Galle. Right, Kandyan chief in formal attire, early 1900s.

COLOMBO AND THE ROAD TO KANDY

Sri Lanka's ancient maritime capital is a fascinating place, full of contradictions: highrise buildings blend with squat colonial architecture, and western dress is worn just as easily as the traditional *saree* and *sarong*. The mellifluous notes of the Buddhist *pirit* are heard along with the haunting chant of a *muezzin* calling the faithful to prayer, while speeding cars flash past slow and creaky bullock carts.

The history of **Colombo** goes back to about the fourth century A.D. when Arab traders used it as a port to export cinnamon, and the seat of monarchy was in Anuradhapura in the north central plains. These Arab traders were still in Colombo when the Portuguese arrived in the 16th century, followed by the Dutch and the British. By the time the island gained independence, Colombo had become the hub of commercial activity. This centered around the **Fort**, the area encompassed by an old Portuguese fort, later reconstructed by the Dutch, and in an area called **Pettah**, just adjoining the Fort.

Downtown Colombo is a walkers' city. Any visitor checking in at one of the numerous hotels in and around Fort, braving the heat which averages about 82 F (28 C), can take in all the sights in a morning.

At the southern entrance to the Fort is the famous **Galle Face Green**. At either end are two equally famous buildings: the internationally-renowned **Galle Face Hotel** and the former Parliamentary building, which now houses the **Presidential Secretariat.**

Passing this edifice and the **Galadari Hotel** marks the entrance to the Fort. Immediately, you are in the shadow of the island's tallest building, the headquarters of the **Bank of Ceylon**. Ironically, next to it and now dwarfed by it is **Ceylinco House**, Sri Lanka's first highrise building. Opposite these are the giant **Intercontinental Hotel** and the **Central Bank of Ceylon**. Further on is perhaps the Fort's best known landmark, the **Lighthouse Clock Tower**. Now non-functional, the tower was built in 1857 and the clock installed in 1914. Until a new lighthouse was erected close to the shore along **Marine Drive** in the 1950s, this acted as a beacon to ships and a timepiece for strollers in the Fort.

A few paces to the north, past the imposing architecture of the **Chartered Bank**, is

Highrises in the Fort area.

the gleaming white of the **General Post Office**. Opposite this, with sentries in full ceremonial dress standing at each gate and surrounded by well-kept lawns and foliage, is the sprawling **President's House**. Built by the last Dutch governor of the island, J.G. Van Angelbeek, in the 18th century, the house became the official residence of British governors.

Standing by the east entrance to the house and looking towards Pettah is the imposing **statue** of Governor Sir Edward Barnes, who was responsible for the construction of the Colombo-to-Kandy road. All trunk road mileage in the island is measured from this statue. To the left of the statue are the heavily-guarded gates to the courtyard of the **Ministry of Defence**.

A stroll down **Sir Baron Jayatilleka Mawatha** brings you to Colombo's oldest (1844) department store, **Cargills**, and two blocks further along the sheltered sidewalks is **Laksala**, a government-sponsored emporium of traditional and modern Sri Lankan art and handicrafts.

A short trishaw ride away is the Pettah area, a word derived from the Tamil *pettai*, meaning 'outside' and in Sinhalese it is called *pitta kotuwa*, 'outside the fort'.

At the entrance to the Pettah is another old clock tower and to the right of it is **Front Street**, with its toy shops on one side and tailors and radio stalls on the other. The major shopping area is down **Main Street**, which ends at the **Old Town Hall**, now a market, and next to it, the historical **Kaymans Gate**. This is a 16th-century stone belfry and perhaps the oldest Christian structure on the island.

The **Dutch Period Museum** on **Second Cross Street** is a must for the visitor. It is the last vestige of an 18th-century Dutch residential community and was once the Old Post Office. Before leaving the Pettah area, drop in at the **Fort Railway Station**, which houses a collection of old railway equipment. Nearby is the **World Market**, an old-world bazaar where bargaining is the order of the day.

Cinnamon Gardens: Perhaps the greenest area in Colombo is the **Cinnamon Gardens** district, where almost all the streets are lined with giant trees and houses all have large flower gardens. In the past the entire district was covered with this tasty spice, but today it is known as 'Colombo 7' and has become the elite residential area in the city.

Situated in this district are most of the foreign embassies, some government of-

fices and **Colombo University**. In addition, Colombo 7 has some of the most important buildings on the island, beginning with the **National Museum**. This was established in 1877 by Governor Sir William Gregory and today its Sri Lankan and natural history sections are a must for the visitor.

Not far from the museum is the **Public Library** and the **War Memorial** to servicemen killed in the world wars. Both these are situated in **Viharamahadevi Park**, the prime amusement park in Colombo and named after the mother of Dutugemunu, one of Sri Lanka's greatest monarchs (Anuradhapura, 161 B.C.). Her statue can be seen amidst the lush vegetation. At the other end of the park is the **Town Hall**, the main municipal building in the city. Its tall pillars and dome bring to mind many state capitol buildings in America.

Two other important and imposing buildings in Colombo 7 are the **Independence Memorial Hall** and the **Bandaranaike Memorial International Conference Hall**. Both these buildings are a few minutes stroll from each other. The former is made in the classic style of a medieval Kandyan audience hall and it was here that the Duke of Gloucester, on behalf of the King of England, formally opened Sri Lanka's (then Ceylon) first Parliament on February 4, 1948. The latter is a huge octagonal building, a gift from the People's Republic of China. The main audience hall can sit 1,500 persons, making it one of the finest convention facilities in South Asia.

If time permits, take the seven-mile (11-km) drive from Fort to have a look at the **Parliamentary Complex** at **Sri Jayawardenapura Kotte**, the new administrative capital of the island. Surrounded by the waters of **Lake Diyawinna Oya**, the complex, designed by a leading Sri Lankan architect, is a classic study in simple oriental beauty.

The Road to Kandy: An important center of Buddhism, and the first stop along the Colombo-to-Kandy road would be the **Kelaniya Raja Maha Vihara temple** in a northeastern suburb of Colombo.

The Kelaniya temple has a special place in the hearts of local Buddhists, as it is one of the places the Buddha visited during his lifetime. The 'paddy-heap'-shaped *dagoba*, attributed to King Yattala Tissa (third century B.C.), marks the spot on which the Enlightened One sat on a gem-studded throne and preached to the Naga people at the request of their king. The Buddha's visit to the island was to settle a dispute between

Former post office now the Dutch Period Museum.

the Yakkas and the Nagas, the two predominant tribes at that time.

The Kelaniya temple holds an annual *perahera* (procession) whose pageantry and spectacle is second only to the Esala *perahera* in Kandy. This is held on the full moon day in January which is the Sinhalese month of *'Duruthu'*.

The modern *vihara* or image house built earlier this century has three Buddha images and a host of frescoes and paintings depicting the history of Kelaniya, Buddhist stories and episodes from the life of the Buddha. But by far the most memorable works of art in Kelaniya are the dwarfs that line the walls of the courtyard of the temple.

The growing town of **Kelaniya** is famous for its traditional Sinhalese pottery. A few miles past **Kadawatte**, along about a mile of road, are a series of roadside pineapple stalls. These delicious fruits are piled up in huts and their delightful odor signals their presence long before they are reached.

A few miles off the main road at **Attanagalla** is the **Attanagalla vihara**, built in the third century A.D. This is supposed to be the island's oldest vatadage, a curious architectural concept of a circular pillared structure enclosing a *dagoba*. Also on the temple grounds is a large 13th-century *dagoba*.

Just before the town of **Nittambuwa**, now back on the main highway, is the **tomb** of former Prime Minister S.W.R.D. Bandaranaike, who was assassinated in 1959.

A 15-minute drive away is the little village of **Batalinya** where signs proclaim *'Cadjugama'*, meaning 'village of cashews'. This is a little courtyard by the side of the road with about 50 makeshift stalls. Pretty, gaily-clad girls in traditional cloth and jacket (*redda* and *hette*) sell tasty cashews and refreshing king coconuts. It is a curious fact that cashew, being a nut that thrives under the most arid conditions, is not found growing anywhere around the village, which is in the wet zone.

A half-mile away from here is the village of **Weweldeniya** (Wewel-cane) which, as the name implies, is famous for its basketware and weaving. All sorts of cane work, from bizzare animal figures to comfortable and superbly designed pieces of furniture, are found in these stalls. But because cane is an increasingly rare commodity, the prices can be exorbitant.

Passing the jostling crowds on the road at the busy town at **Warakapola**, now exactly halfway to the hill capital of Kandy, one comes to **Ambepussa**, where the road forks, with one branch leading to Kurunegala and

otic fruit
ll on the
ad to
ndy.

Trincomalee and the other to Kandy. Located here is a charming **rest house** set in lush green surroundings, the ideal place to break journey for a cool drink or a hot cup of tea.

Nelundeniya marks the first leg of the climb to Kandy, flattening out in the town of **Kegalla**. Just past this busy town, turn left to visit the interesting **Elephant Orphanage** at **Pinawella**.

The orphanage, run by the Zoological Gardens of Colombo, is a fascinating place. Orphaned wild elephant calves from the jungle, some rescued from mud pits into which they had accidently fallen or abandoned by the herd are brought here by Department of Wildlife officials. The elephants are carefully nurtured, brought up and trained into adulthood. At this point they are either sold or gifted to temples for work or ceremonial purposes. Recently, a young cow elephant named Kumari (princess) gave birth to a calf here, the first-ever fully recorded birth of an elephant in captivity on the island.

About a mile-and-a-half from Pinawella, the climb commences again and soon on the left is a peak called **Utuwankanda**, which was the hiding place of Sri Lanka's most famous bandit, Saradiel, known as the Robin Hood of Sri Lanka. He was finally captured and executed by the British in 1860.

Beyond **Mawanella**, known for its spice gardens, is the **Kadugannawa Pass**, where the scenery is fabulous. The right side of the hill drops away into the valley and the rolling country stretches away as far as the eye can see. In the distance is the flattopped **Bible Rock**, rising 2,618 feet (793 meters) from the valley below.

The last major town before reaching Kandy is **Kadugannawa**. Here stands a 125-foot (38-meter) **monument** to S.F. Dawson, the British engineer who completed the Colombo-to-Kandy road in 1827. Asia's first mail coach service was inaugarated along this route in 1832.

A quick 12-mile (19-km) drive from Kadugannawa is the hill capital, Kandy, nestling amid lush greenery at an elevation of 1,600 feet (485 meters).

City in the Hills: **Kandy** is derived from the Sinhalese word *kandy*, meaning 'hills' and some bard has described it as the "place where river, sky and mountain meet." It was the capital of Sri Lanka from 1590 to 1815, when the island finally capitulated to the British and the last king Sri Wickrama Rajasingha was taken prisoner. It is a very

Kandy town and lake, circa 1864.

pretty city, set amid lush green surroundings, nestling at an elevation of 1,600 feet (485 meters).

Kandy is the home of the **Dalada Maligawa**, or Temple of the Sacred Tooth Relic of the Buddha, where all visitors should start their tour of the city. The relic was brought to Kandy in 1590, when King Narendra Sinha built a two-storey shrine for it. Improvements were made periodically, until the octagonal **Pathrippuwa** was added in the early-19th century.

By the side of the temple, adjacent to the modern **Court House**, is the **Queen's Palace**, now being restored by the Cultural Triangle project. Behind the temple is the **Audience Hall**, with its intricately carved pillars, and further north is the **King's Palace**, also in the process of being restored. Cross the moat here and you will come to the *devalas* (shrines) of the three deities, Natha, Pattini and Vishnu.

A pleasant way to spend some time is to walk around picturesque **Kandy Lake**, completed in 1807. Afterwards, drive up to **Castle Hill Park** and get a panoramic view of the city. The **Municipal Market**, west of the lake, is famous for Sri Lankan fruits and is worth a visit. Bargaining is a must at the souvenir stalls.

In and Around Kandy: A morning hike in **Udawattakele Sanctuary**, home of exotic birds, monkeys and fascinating flora, just behind the temple, and a visit to **Peradeniya Gardens** in the afternoon, followed by a boat ride along the **Mahaweli River**, is a richly rewarding experience. The 206-mile-(330-km-) long Mahaweli is the longest river in Sri Lanka. It rises high in the Hill Country and flows across two-thirds of the island's length and breadth to the sea near Trincomalee. More than 40 tributaries augment its course. South of the gardens is the University of Peradeniya's spacious green campus, by the banks of the Mahaweli.

Take a drive outside Kandy to see the historic temples, including **Degaldoruwa Cave Temple**, built in 1344 and Dravidian in style, the typically Kandyan **Lankatilaka Vihara**, built the same year, and the beautiful woodcarvings of the **Embekke Kataragama Devala**, attributed to King Wickramabahu II (1357-1374).

Finally, don't leave Kandy without seeing the bathing elephants at **Katugastota**. The best time to watch is during the late afternoon. At the foot of the main bridge heading north, *mahouts* lead their great beasts to the river to cool off after a day's work.

utting the
ght foot
rward at
e
erahera.

THE KANDY PERAHERA

The Tooth Relic of the Buddha has always had a special place in the hearts of Sri Lankan Buddhists. In fact, it has been the symbol of sovereignty since it was first brought to the island in the fourth century A.D.

King Megavanna of Anuradhapura (301 A.D.-331 A.D.) decreed that the Relic should be brought out from its enshrined place so that public homage could be rendered in a *perahera* (procession) once a year. Today, this once-simple ceremony has grown into one of the most splendid sights in Sri Lanka.

The beginnings of the proper Kandy Perahera go back to the 18th century, when King Kirthi Sri Rajasinghe ruled the island from Kandy. Siamese monks, whom he had invited to help in restoring the island's degenerating Theravada orthodoxy, pointed out their disappointment at the predominant religious activity of Kandy's Hindu *devalas* (temples) in a Buddhist capital. The monarch ordered that an annual procession of the Tooth Relic be instituted and that the four Hindu *devalas* be incorporated in this

open homage. The tradition lives to this day.

The *perahera* is led by four *devalas*, belonging to the deities Natha, identified with Maitreya, the Buddha-to-be, Vishnu, to whom special care of the welfare of Buddhism is entrusted, Skanda, the powerful God of War in the Hindu pantheon and Pattini, the female deity of health and chastity. Each is followed by a train of gaily-caparisoned elephants.

A magnificent tusked bull elephant, adorned with colorful cloth and lined with tiny electric bulbs, leads the column from the Dalada Maligawa (Temple of the Tooth). On his back he carries an illuminated howdah with the golden *Karanduwa*, a replica of the *dagoba*-shaped casket in which the Sacred Tooth is enshrined (The genuine Relic is no longer carried). The majestic elephant is followed by dozens of other elephants and behind them comes the Diyawadana Nilame, the chief trustee of the temple and holder of the highest lay office in the island, followed by other officials and assorted dancers, acrobats, drummers and schoolchildren.

For six nights, when the procession is known as Kumbal Perahera, the festival simmers, before reaching a boil on the seventh night, when the Randoli Perahera begins. The *randolis* (golden palanquins), bearing the deities' consorts, join the *devala* ranks, each borne immediately behind the elephants carrying the emblems which represent the respective deities. The circuits gradually increase in length and the trappings in grandeur, until after five nights of the Randoli, the Perahera reaches its colorful best. At this climactic stage, the Randoli may include 100 or more elephants.

The Perahera ends the next day, when the water cutting ceremony, a symbolic purification of the Kataragama deity's sword, is enacted. The water in the river at Getambe, a Kandy suburb, is parted with a circular sweep of the sacred sword and a clay pot from each of the *devalas* is filled with the water thus demarcated. These pots are preserved until the next year's Esala Festival. If any of the pots run dry before then, it is considered a sign of impending misfortune. The final *perahera* is held at noon, the only time a procession is held in daylight.

Almost all Buddhist temples in Sri Lanka have their own *peraheras* once a year. Participation is generally confined to the villagers of the little hamlets in which they are situated. Small processions weaving through the paddy fields are a fine sight, and make colorful subjects for photographers.

Caparisoned elephants play a vital role at the perahera.

ALONG THE SOUTH COAST

Sri Lanka's south coast offers a wealth of variety, from forests and beaches to parks and pilgrimage centers. Heading south from Colombo, the first stop along this 150-mile- (241-km-) long trunk road will be the **Dehiwela Zoo**, reputed to be the best in South Asia. A comprehensive visit will take the entire morning, and on the way back, stop by at **Mount Lavinia Beach** and the **Mount Lavinia Hotel**.

The **Gangatilaka Vihara** in **Kalutara** is the next historic landmark. The huge new *dagoba* is built on the site of an ancient temple and is hollow inside with a gallery of fine paintings. The *bo* tree shrine in front has a till, to which drivers traditionally make offerings to ensure a successful journey. Kalutara is also known for its delicious mangosteen fruits and fine basket-weaving.

The popular beach resorts begin from **Beruwala** and continue up to Hikkaduwa. In between are a multitude of excellent swimming spots and an equally generous number of wonderfully scenic sites.

At **Bentota** are a series of luxury hotels, with ample shopping, cultural displays and exhibitions. Some excellent local seafood is available here. From here, visit the 12th-century **Galapata Vihara** and **'Brief'** the sprawling, beautifully landscaped home of well-known artist Bevis Bawa.

Next stop is **Kosgoda**, known for its **turtle hatchery**, established by the Hasselblad Estate and operated by the Wild Life Protection Society of Sri Lanka.

Ambalangoda, the next major town, is noted for its ritual masks and 'devil dancing' (exorcism rituals). The town is also famous for its woodcarving and puppetry.

Hikkaduwa is the most famous beach resort on the island, catering to all tastes and pockets. The mile strip of road through the town is lined with a mass of shops selling batiks, swimwear and assorted curios, eating houses and low-budget rest houses. The beach here is superb and the colorful reef is snorkling paradise. For those who don't like to wet their feet, most hotels have glass-bottom boats at reasonable prices.

The most important town on the south coast is **Galle**, which at one time served as a major port. The oldest landmark is a large **fort** built by the Portuguese and later added to by the Dutch. Other than walking around the ramparts and eating large quantities of delicious seafood, drop in at the

Closenburgh Guest House, overlooking the beautiful bay of that name, then go on to **Buona Vista** for a panoramic view of the entire area.

The Wild Places: Visitors to Sri Lanka should allow some time for visiting at least one of its National Parks to experience the rich and varied fauna and flora.

Yala, also called the **Ruhuna National Park**, is situated at the corner of the south coast and consists mainly of open thorn bush country and rocky outcrops reminiscent of the African bush. It is famous for its elephants and also for leopard and bear. Large herds of deer and other small game can also be seen.

Accommodation is available in two luxury hotels outside and in six lodges inside the park. The best time to visit is between mid-October and July.

Lying on the northwest coast, the scenic **Wilpattu National Park** also includes leopards and bears among its inhabitants. Much more deeply forested than Yala, two of its main topographical features are the red soil and the shallow basins called *villus* (lakes). Deer and other small game are plentiful while elephants can also be seen during the dry season. The best chance to spot bears would be in late May to June.

KINGDOMS IN THE PLAINS

For almost 2,000 years the monarchs of ancient Lanka ruled the nation from their capitals in the north central plains in the dry zone. Here, they developed and mastered the art of hydraulic engineering, unsurpassed anywhere else in the contemporary world, a skill clearly reflected in the 11,200 man-made lakes (*wewa*) still extant in the plains and the amazing Jaya Ganga irrigation canal connecting two *wewas*, Kala Wewa and Tissa Wewa, where the gradient for the 17-mile (27-km) course is only six inches per mile. Here, they built monuments in the form of *dagobas* to the glory of their great faith, Buddhism, buildings that ranked second only to the pyramids of Egypt. They developed an aesthetic sense that made the architects of that bygone day utilize every boulder, stone and tree in their designs, landscape architecture of the highest order. Here, they built their great cities, once bustling, later abandoned and buried for centuries in the jungle, then found again and now being restored. Among them was the city that, in its heyday, historians and archaeologists describe as the greatest city of all.

Number One: According to ancient chronicles, **Anuradhapura** was a settlement long before it became a great city. In the fourth century B.C., Pandukabhaya, living in exile in the historic mountain of Ritigala, gathered an army and defeated his uncle, then founded the city of Anuradhapura and became its first king.

Except for a brief period, Anuradhapura remained the capital of Sri Lanka for 1,400 years and was ruled by about 125 kings. During this period, its influence extended from China to the court of Rome. Trade relations existed with the better part of the world. Periodically, it was conquered by the Cholans and Pandyans from India and ruled until recaptured by a Sinhalese ruler.

Anuradhapura today is one of the great, if not the greatest, Buddhist center in the world. For pilgrims, there are eight particularly sacred places at which they are obliged to worship. These are the Sri Maha Bodhi, the Ruwanveli Seya, the Thuparama Dagoba, the Jetavanarama Dagoba, the Abhayagiri Dagoba, the Lankarama Dagoba, the Mirisaweti Dagoba and the Isurumuniya Vihara.

The most famous edifice in the city is the **Ruwanveli Seya Dagoba**, built by King

Preceding pages: Granite Buddhas of the Gal Vihara. Dagoba and columns Anuradhapura

Dutugemunu in 144 B.C. The current *dagoba* is in fact a 1933 restoration of the ancient one, which was only a mound of earth when rediscovered by the British.

Nearby, reflecting the gleaming white of Ruwanveli, are the waters of **Basawakulam Wewa**, the first such *wewa* in Anuradhapura, constructed by pre-Buddhist King Pandukabhaya in the fourth century B.C.

A short and interesting stroll south, along a beautifully paved walk, leads to a forest of scattered granite columns. These are the remnants of the great **Loha Prasada** or Brazen Palace, a nine-storey building with 1,000 rooms, used by monks as a living quarters and library.

Just before the Brazen Palace is the most sacred place in the Buddhist world, the **Sri Maha Bodhi**. Now a giant bough, it was brought as a tiny sapling from the very *ficus religiosa*, or *bo* in Sinhalese, under which the Buddha attained enlightenment. It was a gift from Emperor Asoka of India, brought by his own daughter Theri Sangamitta to King Devanampiyatissa in 288 B.C. Today, this is the oldest historically documented tree in the world, and the importance of this tree is so great that in 1950, when a blight attacked it, the Smithsonian Institute sent a

botanical expert to treat the plant, with success.

East of the Sri Maha Bodhi is the gigantic **Jetavanarama**, the largest *dagoba* in the world. It originally stood over 400 feet (121 meters) tall, with a diameter of 370 feet (112 meters) and occupying an area of eight acres (3.2 hectares). Built by King Mahasena in 300 A.D., the Cultural Triangle is now in the process of restoring and conserving it.

A short walk north of Ruwanveli is the first *dagoba* in Sri Lanka, the **Thuparama**. A dwarf compared to the others, it is believed to enshrine the collarbone of the Buddha and was built by King Devanampiyatissa in 307 B.C.

A pleasant drive north from here is the third giant, **Abhayagiri**. Originally standing at a height of 370 feet (112 meters) with a diameter of 360 feet (109 meters), it was constructed by King Gajabahu in the second century A.D. in a monastic complex founded by the great King Vattagamini Abhaya in 88 B.C.

The grandeur of Anuradhapura is not in its size but in the intricate details of its ruins. In the vast Abhayagiri monastic complex which once housed 5,000 monks, are many interesting monuments for the visitor to see. Foremost among them would be the **Sa-**

madhi Statue, depicting the Buddha in deep meditation. Then there is the **guardstone** at the entrance to the **Ratna Prasada** (Gem Palace) and slightly northeast, the beautiful **moonstone**, considered the finest in the country. The **Kuttam Pokuna** or Twin Ponds were built in the third century A.D. as bathing ponds for monks, but they are in fact not identical.

Among the finest buildings in Anuradhapura are a series of hermitages known as the **Western Monasteries**. They lie west of the main citadel. As you drive towards them, turn left just before leaving the Abhayagiri complex and have a look at the **Eth Pokuna**. This is a larger-than-Olympic-size pool, featuring a beautifully structured line.

At the Western Monasteries are some fine examples of landscape architecture. These buildings, dating from the sixth to ninth centuries, were occupied by monks who practiced an austere and severe way of life. The main components of these buildings were the meditation hall and the veranda. Only the urinal stones of the monks were highly decorated, for which no satisfactory explanation has been given.

The road further west leads to the beautiful **Tissa Wewa**, a bund built by King Devanampiyatissa in the third century B.C. It is still the city's main water source. Drive down halfway along the bund, then turn left at the main road and visit the **Isurumuniya Rock Temple**, attributed to the same king. Featured here are some magnificent bas-reliefs of elephants playing in the water-lilies and the equally famous '**lovers**', a sixth-century Gupta-style carving.

Visitors with time to spare in this ancient city should also try to see the **Palace of Vijayabahu I**, the **Nakka Vihara**, a square brick *dagoba* of the late Anuradhapura period and the **Dakkina Dagoba**, believed to have been built over the cremated ashes of King Dutugemunu. Then take a stroll in the **Royal Pleasure Gardens**, known as Ran Masu Uyana, where legend has it the son of Dutugemunu met and fell in love with a beautiful but low caste Chandala girl, marrying her nevertheless and sacrificing accession to his father's throne.

Tours from Anuradhapura: Mihintale is a rocky hill east of Anuradhapura where in 247 B.C., King Devanampiyatissa converted to Buddhism, thus giving royal patronage to the faith. The climb along the rock-cut stone steps can be strenuous but is worth the effort. Among the other sights in the complex are the second-century **Kan-**

Two alluring Sigiriya Maidens.

taka **Chaitiya**, the Lion Bath, the sixth-century **Bhojana Salawa** or Eating Hall, the first-century **Maha Seya** and the numerous caves that housed the monks of that complex. The **Kaludiya Pokuna**, a secluded pool southwest of the complex, was the center of the monastic community.

A full day trip from Anuradhapura, **Kala Wewa** is a large and scenic *wewa* built by King Datusena in the fourth century. Drive slowly or walk along the shady bund and then visit the **Aukana Buddha** statue a mile-and-a-half away. At 41 feet (12.4 meters), it is the second tallest Buddha statue on the island and is in near-pristine condition. Built by the same king, it faces the sluice of the Kala Wewa, its right hand lifted in the *abhaya mudra* gesture, blessing the waters leaving to irrigate the fields.

The best time to visit Anuradhapura and Mihintale is June, particularly on the full moon day (*Poson Poya*) when the advent of Buddhism to the island is commemorated.

Lion Rock: Sigiriya is a giant flat-topped rock rising 600 feet (182 meters) from the plains. For 18 years (478 A.D.-496 A.D.) during the Anuradhapura period, the rock and many square miles around it served as the capital of Sri Lanka.

The ancient chronicle of the island says that Kasyapa, a son of King Datusena, murdered his father and usurped the throne. His half-brother Moggallana, the rightful heir, was exiled to India. Fearing retaliation, Kasyapa took his capital to Sigiriya. Moggallana returned 18 years later, defeated Kasyapa and moved the capital back to Anuradhapura.

There are diverse views among students of Sigiriya as to the accuracy of this legend. However, there are no dissenters to the opinion that this must have been one of the loveliest royal cities ever to grace the face of this earth.

It has been archaeologically established that most of the stupendous artistic, architectural and engineering achievements at Sigiriya are from the Kasyapan era. Additions were made later when it became a monastery and then a military outpost.

At the western approach to the rock are the **Water Gardens**, a series of beautifully landscaped ponds and terraced walls. Also here are the **Fountains**, which are gravity fed from two moats on either side. All that its modern discoverers had to do was to clean the conduits leading to the limestone openings, and the Fountains came to life after almost 1,500 years.

Halfway up the Sigiriya rock is the

▸ft, the ▯kana ▯ddha, ▯d right, ▯ws of ▯ Lion ▸rrace.

pocket containing the world famous frescoes of seductive, bare-breasted **Sigiriya Maidens**. Continuing up the **Gallery** walkway is the **Mirror Wall**, its lime plaster polished like glass and on it Sri Lanka's oldest graffiti, most of which are in praise of the maidens.

The Gallery ends at the **Lion Terrace**, which features the gigantic paws of a lion. The giant head with the open jaws, which gave Sigiriya its name (*sinha* = lion; *giriya* = throat) has long since collapsed, but the foundation up the face of the rock is clearly defined. Climb between the clawed paws to reach the steep stairway and the windblown railing that leads to the top.

The entire three acres at the summit was occupied by Kasyapa's **Summer Palace**, the remnants of which are clearly visible. Three beautiful pools are still extant, as is a magnificent **divan**, carved from naked rock. On the way down, look at the fine rock-cut **Council Chamber** and **Cistern Rock** and admire the roofline of the **Cobra Hood Cave**, where there are second-century inscriptions and fragments of ancient paintings.

Medieval Kingdom: It has not been firmly established as to why the capital was shifted from Anuradhapura to **Polonna-ruwa**. Some believe it was due to its more strategic position while others attribute it to an outbreak of malaria at Anuradhapura. Whatever the reason, Polonnaruwa was first made the capital by the conquering 11th-century Cholas from India, and remained so until the 13th century. Among the dozen rulers in its brief history were two of Sri Lanka's great monarchs, Parakramabahu I, who organized the island's first navy, and Nissankamalla.

The grandeur of Polonnaruwa is no jaded second to Anuradhapura. Except for a few sites, almost all the major ruins of Polonna-ruwa are confined to one large complex, the **Citadel**. Just outside is the beautiful **Rest House** on the bund of the giant **Parakrama Samudra**, the 5,600-acre (2,240-hectare) *wewa* constructed by Parakramabahu I.

A stone's throw away are the **baths** of King Nissankamalla and just beyond them are his palace and the **Audience Hall**. Next is the **Council Chamber**, which is one of the most interesting ruins on the island. On each pillar is carved the designation of the official who sat beside it. On this basis, historians have been able to establish the seating arrangements in the court of the Sinhalese kings.

Cross the **Habarana Road** and enter the

Painted cave ceiling at Dambulla near Sigiriya.

Citadel. On the right are the massive remains of the **Vejayanta Prasada**, the original seven-storey palace of Parakramabahu. Lying opposite is the great king's **Council Chamber** and below it, the **Kumara Pokuna**, the royal bath, featuring an intricate geometric design.

Driving or bicycling is the best way to see Polonnaruwa. Due west, past the 13th-century **Shiva Devala**, is the **Quadrangle**, a group of 12 buildings in the heart of the ancient city. The main building here is the open circular shrine, the **Vatadage**, built before the establishment of the capital. Opposite to it is the **Hatadage**, the Temple of the Tooth. Lying outside it is the 26-foot-long **Gal Potha** or 'Stone Book', describing Nissankamalla's invasion of India and his 'foreign policy'. Beyond this is the **Chapter House** and next to it is the amazing **Sathmahal Prasada**, or Seven-Storey Building. Reminiscent of the Khmer architecture of Cambodia, its origins and functions have still not been established. To the west is the **Atadage**, the original Temple of the Tooth, and to the south is a lovely pavilion, the **Lata Mandapaya**, with an image of a *bodhisattva* standing in the center. In the southwest corner is the magnificent image house, the **Thuparama**.

Back on the road, turn into the grounds of the **Pabulu Vehera**, a small brick *dagoba* supposedly built by Parakramabahu's wife Rupavati. At the end of the road is an 11th-century **Shiva Devala**, built by a Chola conqueror. On the main track again one comes to the majestic **Rankot Vehera**, at 180 feet (55 meters) the tallest *dagoba* in Polonnaruwa, built by King Nissankamalla.

Half a mile along the track and to the right is the beautiful **Gal Vihara**, once known as Uttararama, 'the northern shrine' and attributed to Parakramabahu I. Here are four Buddha statues in different poses, cut out from a single granite wall. They are undoubted masterpieces of Sri Lankan art. The first is in a Samadi pose, in deep meditation, and described by experts as one of the finest in the world. The second is within a cave and protected by a wire mesh. The third, a standing statue, is 23 feet (seven meters) high and is in a rare cross-armed pose. It was once thought to be Buddha's chief disciple Ananda. The last statue, 46 feet (14 meters) long, shows the Buddha reclining in his final moments. Note the slight depression in the pillow and the intricate carvings on the soles of his feet.

Cross the road and enter the **Alahana Pirivena** complex and ancient hospital site. The **Kiri Vehera** *dagoba* is thought to have been a gift of one of Parakramabahu's wives while the magnificent **Lankatilaka** image house features a huge headless statue of the Buddha. Southwards on a hillock is the sprawling **Baddhasima Pasada**, a convocation hall and below it, the 11th-century hospital site complete with its stone immersion bath.

Before leaving Polonnaruwa, travel along the bund of the *wewa* and view the **statue** of the 'Sage'. Its identity has still not been convincingly established but is believed to be that of the great Parakramabahu himself. About 300 feet (100 meters) to the south of it is the **Potgul Vehera**, thought to be a lecture chamber as the acoustics within are perfect.

About 25 miles (40 km) northeast of Polonnaruwa, a large wildlife refuge surrounds the **Somawathie Chaitiya**. Here, there are a monastery, a *dagoba* and other ruins.

Southeast of Polonnaruwa, the rock spire of **Dimbulagala**, also known as Gunner's Quoin, rises from the scrub jungle. From earliest Buddhist times, this has been a hermitage for meditating monks. About 500 rock caves are cut into the mountain; they have been occupied almost continuously since the third century B.C.

...onstone ...tail at ...lonna-...wa.

DESTINATION SRI LANKA

GETTING THERE

By Air: Most visitors to Sri Lanka arrive by air at the Katunayake International Airport (Colombo). It is located 21 miles (34 km) north of Colombo city. There is no other major airport on the island.

By Sea: Cruise ships are no longer the main means of transportation to Sri Lanka, but a number of cruise lines still call at its ports. If interested in cruising to Sri Lanka, contact several travel agents and make arrangements through the one which has schedules and itineraries most appealing to you.

Visas: Nationals of the following countries coming to Sri Lanka as tourists do not require entry visas for a period of 30 days (A valid passport, however, has to be presented): Australia, Austria, Britain and its colonies, Bangladesh, Belgium, Bahrain, Canada, Denmark, Eire, Federal Republic of Germany, Finland, France, Indonesia, Israel, Italy, Japan, South Korea, Kuwait, Luxembourg, Malaysia, Maldives, Netherlands, New Zealand, Norway, Oman, Pakistan, Philippines, Qatar, Singapore, Sweden, Switzerland, Saudi Arabia, Spain,Thailand, the United States, United Arab Emirates and Yugoslavia.

Visas should be obtained through a Sri Lankan consular office, or through a British consular office if there are no Sri Lankan offices in your country. If you need to extend your stay in Sri Lanka while there, you must apply for a visa extension in Colombo. Go to the Department of Immigration and Emmigration, Unit 6, Galle Buck Road, Colombo 1. Tel: 29851, 21509. Conditions for extensions are a return or onward ticket and sufficient money for maintenance in the island at US$15 per day.

Health: Health officials no longer require certificates of immunization unless you have passed through an infected area within 14 days of your arrival. Immunization against cholera, however, is strongly recommended for personal safety. Anti-malarial medications (prescribed by your doctor), such as chloroquine, should be started at least one week prior to arrival and continued for two weeks after your departure. Though all waterways and lakes in the island are safe for bathing, water should always be boiled before drinking. Water purification tablets, such as Puritabs, should also be used.

Money: Upon arrival in Sri Lanka, visitors are required to declare all foreign currency in their possession at the Official Exchange Control Form D which is attached to the landing card. This card is required to exchange foreign currency to Sri Lankan rupees. This form has to be surrendered to emmigration officials when you leave the country and it is also required to re-exchange any unspent rupees.

The exchange rates fluctuate with the world market. New rates are printed daily in the press. In late 1987, foreign currency rates quoted were Rs 29.71 to the US dollar, Rs 48.19 to one Pound Sterling, Rs 16.23 to one Deutsche Mark, Rs 4.83 to one French Franc, and Rs 20.70 to 100 Japanese Yen.

Customs : Upon arrival, visitors must declare all currency on the official exchange form. Any gems of Sri Lankan origin, set or unset, must also be recorded on this form.

Visitors are allowed to bring in the following duty free:
1) 200 cigarettes or 50 cigars or 12 ounces tobacco or any combination thereof provided the total weight does not exceed 12 ounces.
2) 1.5 liters of hard spirit and 2 liters of wine and a small amount of perfume.
3) Reasonable amount of sports equipment.
4) Personal photographic equipment, radios, recorders and typewriters.
5) Reasonable amounts of film for personal use.
6) Sri Lanka prohibits the importation of narcotics, pornography, firearms and ammunition.

Departure: When leaving Sri Lanka, baggage will be

INSIDE SRI LANKA

checked by customs on departure. You may take up to six pounds (3.1 kg) tea duty free. A duty of Rs 6.45 will be levied on each additional pound. You can buy more duty free goods once you enter the departure lounge.

Gems may be exported provided they were purchased with funds declared on the foreign exchange card. You will need to show your receipts for both purchases and money exchanges. To export gems received as gifts, permits from the Controller of Exchange, Central Bank, Colombo, and the Controller of Imports and Exports, National Mutual Building, Chatham Street, Colombo 1 are required.

The export of antiques (articles more than 50 years old) is banned. So is the export of wild animals, birds and reptiles or parts thereof, unless accompanied with proper documentation and licenses.

Any unspent rupees should be reconverted to foreign currency at a commercial bank or at the exchange counter at the lobby of the airport.

An embarkation tax is levied when departing from Sri Lanka: Katunayake Airport—Rs 200, Passenger Jetty (Colombo)—US$1.70.

GETTING ACQUAINTED

Climate: For a relatively small country, Sri Lanka's climate is remarkably varied. From dry desert-like areas to verdant rain forests, from sunny ocean beaches to misty mountain tops, Sri Lanka has it all. And since Sri Lanka is definitely in the monsoonal tropics, it has dry and wet seasons, which take place simultaneously on opposite sides of the island.

This pearl-shaped island of 25,332 square miles (65,863 square km) is subjected to two monsoons, the northeast and the southwest. The northeast monsoon, usually in December and January, brings rain to the dry northern and eastern parts of the island. The central hill region and the southern and western coasts receive most of their rain with the arrival of the southwest monsoon in May, usually lasting through July. Even during the monsoon season, most days are warm and sunny with rain generally falling in the afternoons and in the evenings.

In Colombo, the average annual temperature is 80 F (27 C). In Kandy, at an altitude of 1,600 feet (485 meters), the temperature falls to an average of 68 F (20 C). At Nuwara Eliya, nestled high in the hills at 6,200 feet (1,800 meters), the temperature averages 61 F (16 C) and can become quite chilly in the night. On rare occasions there has been frost.

The highest temperatures are usually reached between March and June, while November to January are considered to be the coolest months. In Sri Lanka the difference between the 'hot' and 'cold' season is only a matter of a few degrees. However, the ocean remains a constant 80 F (27 C) all year long. During October and November, there is an 'inter-monsoon' season when rain and thunderstorms can appear anywhere. But don't let this keep you away: Sri Lankan rains are usually delightful. One moment it is hot and stuffy, then suddenly the sky opens up and drops buckets of cool, refreshing rain. The plants release the most aromatic perfumes, the roads are filled with a myriad of miniature lakes, and best of all, the mosquitoes disappear. Just as suddenly, the rain stops and the sun is shining once again.

What to Wear: In Sri Lankan heat, light cotton clothing is the most comfortable and practical. For women, shorts are not considered proper anywhere but the beach. A skirt (with a T-shirt or blouse) is always appropriate and actually much cooler than shorts. A light cotton dress is also recommended, but leave your nylon stockings at home: they are too hot, and nobody wears them anyway. Western men can sometimes get away with wearing shorts, as

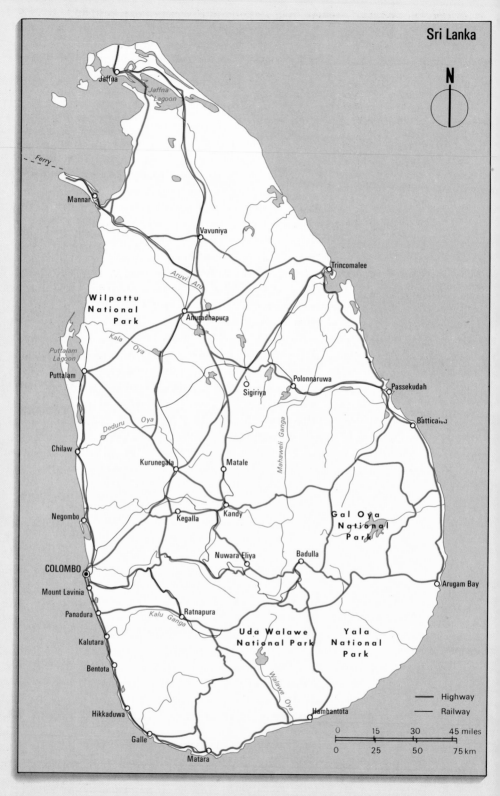

Sri Lanka

N

Jaffna
Jaffna
Lagoon

Ferry

Mannar

Vavuniya

Trincomalee

Aruvi Aru

Wilpattu
National
Park

Anuradhapura

Kala

Oya

Puttalam
Lagoon

Puttalam

Polonnaruwa

Passekudah

Sigiriya

Deduru

Oya

Batticaloa

Chilaw

Kurunegala

Matale

Mahaweli Ganga

Gal Oya
National
Park

Negombo

Kegalla

Kandy

COLOMBO

Nuwara Eliya

Badulla

Arugam Bay

Mount Lavinia

Panadura

Ratnapura

Kalu Ganga

Kalutara

Uda Walawe
National Park

Yala
National
Park

Bentota

Walawe Oya

Hikkaduwa

Hambantota

Galle

Matara

Highway
Railway

0   15   30   45 miles

0   25   50   75 km

308

local boys often wear them (although not adult men). It is best to wear light slacks and a cool, comfortable shirt.

Etiquette: Common courtesy is as important in Sri Lanka as it is worldwide. Sri Lanka has a long history and is home to four of the world's main religions, namely Buddhism, Hinduism, Christianity and Islam. In many instances, superstition, religion and tradition have merged to create important customs.

When entering temples and highly venerated holy areas, shoes and hats must be removed. Remember, in Sri Lanka, "once a temple always a temple." Even if it has been reduced to rubble, it is still sacred and calls for respect.

When you encounter Buddhist monks and wish to show respect, raise both hands in a prayer fashion to just below your chin. Do not shake hands: a monk shouldn't be touched. If you wish to present a gift to a monk it should be offered with both hands, showing that it was given freely and without obligation. Remember that a monk is not allowed to touch money. When giving money, it should be placed in the temple offering box and never handed to anyone.

In many parts of the world, shaking the head from side to side implies "no," while nodding the head up and down means "yes." Sri Lankans have another head movement, the "wobble" or "waggle," which is a cross between a nod and a shake. While amusing and confusing to foreigners, it indicates agreement or approval or a simple "yes."

One of the most awkward situations for foreigners to handle is when they are approached by beggars. Begging has long been a part of life in Asia and is generally accepted. Buddhist monks must denounce all possessions and beg for a living. Lay people "earn merit" by providing for the monks as well as by giving to the needy, and this has made begging a tradition.

It has also become an unholy profession, one of the most irksome aspects to visitors in Sri Lanka. Professional beggars haunt places of interest, busy streets and favorite tourist shops. You can certainly refuse them with a clear conscience, because you are already indirectly donating to them. The government charges foreigners high admission fees to zoos, gardens and archaeological sites in addition to a hotel tax to help pay for its social services. It is not recommended that you give to beggars.

Electricity: Sri Lanka uses 220-240 volts, 50 cycles, alternating current. Most outlets are three-pronged. No matter where you are, the electricity has a habit of going off. Most hotels provide candles in the room as a matter of course. Having a good flashlight would be useful.

Photography: Sri Lanka is a photographer's delight, especially if you have brought enough film with you.. Film, if it can be found, is usualy very expensive and its freshness is doubtful. Black-and-white film can be processed locally, but color film should be developed at home.

Permits are required at a number of sites before you can take photographs. If you are going to the ancient cities of Anuradhapura, Sigiriya and Polonnaruwa, you can save. time and money by buying an all-round "Cultural Triangle" ticket in Colombo, which includes permits for photograph-taking and admission to all archaeological sites, monuments and museums, as well as entry for vehicles. Single permits are usually available at the sites.

All permits are issued with the provision that unless in a respectful posture, no human figure should be featured in your photos. This simply means that posing is not allowed in front of holy monuments or paintings.

Tourist Information: Tourist Information Centers run in Colombo are located at 321 Galle Road, Col. 3. Tel: 573175. TIC's offer their services free of charge. Kandy TIC: Kandyan Arts Association Building. 72, Victoria Drive, Kandy. Airport TIC: Lobby of the Airport.

Reservations in National Parks: Dept. of Wildlife Conservation. Transworks House, Lower Chatham Street. Col. 1. Tel: 32698. Wildlife & Nature Protection Society of Sri Lanka,

Chaitiya Road. Col 1. Tel: 25248.

Archaeological Sites:

Entrance fees to the "Cultural Triangle are as follows: Anuradhapura: Rs 112. Sigiriya: Rs 112. Polonnaruwa: RS112. Kandy: Rs 84. Inclusive tickets for all sites (which includes Dambulla and Nalanda): Rs 336.

TRANSPORT

Air: Two inland air services are available for charter. Upali Travels Ltd., 34, Galle Face. Colombo 3. Tel: 20465, 29399. Air Taxi Ltd., Thomas Cook Overseas Ltd. Sir Baron Jayatilleke Mawatha. Colombo 1. Tel: 545971, 540978.

Airport Service: An airport coach service is operated for Airport and Aviation Services (Sri Lanaka) Ltd. by Mack Transport Ltd. Coaches cover all flights in and out. Fare: Rs 100 one way. Starting point: Hotel Lanka Oberoi. Pickup points: Taj Samudra Hotel and Mackinnon Bldg. Bookings and Inquiries: 11A, York Street, Colombo 1. Tel: 29888, 29881: Walkers Tours counter at Hotel Lanka Oberoi, Tel: 21171, 20001.

Rail: The Sri Lanka Government Railway provides an efficient service to places of interest, such as Kandy, Anuradhapura, Polonnaruwa, Galle, Hikkaduwa, Bentota and a host of other places, starting from Colombo. In addition, day tours with special air-conditioned Hitachi trains operate to Kandy and Hikkaduwa. The inter-city Express Service is available to and from Colombo/Kandy. Also available are special tours by restored vintage steam train. Information from: Railway Tourist Office. Fort Railway Station Colombo. Tel: 35838.

Bus: The Sri Lanka Transport Board maintains an island-wide bus service. Rates are among the cheapest in the world. Express services are available to all principal towns every half hour and regular service every 15 minutes, from the central bus stand, Pettah. A fast intercity express also operates between Colombo/Kandy. Information: Central Bus Stand, Olcott Mawatha, Colombo 11. Tel: 28081. Private bus services also operate luxury coaches. Information from Tourist Information Centers.

Self-Drive Vehicles: Self-drive cars are available from various firms, including: Hertz, represented by Quickshaws Ltd., Kalinga Place. Colombo 5, Tel: 831335. Inter-rent and Dollar-rent-a-Car: Mercantile Tours Ltd., (Cey) Ltd., 51, Janadhipathi Mawatha, Colombo 1. Tel: 28707, 28708. Avis: Mack Transport Ltd., Mackinnon Bldg, 11A, York Street, Colombo 1. Tel: 29881-9. Abans Tours, 498, Galle Road, Colombo 3. Tel: 274160, 573738.

Car Hire: Most local tour and travel agents can supply cars with drivers and can organize tours. Information on these tours are available at hotel reception desks, Tourist Information Counters and in the daily press.

WHERE TO STAY

Sri Lanka has a wide variety of accommodations available to travelers, from international class luxury hotels to modest guesthouses, dormitories and rooms in private homes. Not every town has a first-class hotel, but most communities can provide a pleasant place to stay.

Prices vary greatly throughout the country. In Columbo and some of the major resorts, expect to pay US$60 and up per night for a first-class double. Moderate hotels run between US$30 and US$60 per night. For inexpensive hotels, prices can start from about US$13. Outside of the major tourist areas, most hotels are considered inexpensive. Below is a listing of hotels (All prices quoted are for double rooms).

Ahungala:

Triton Hotel
Tel: 09-27228, 27218. Rs 1200.

Anuradhapura:

Miridiya Hotel
Rowing Club Road. Tel:
025-2112, 2519. Rs 430.

Nuwara wewa Rest House
New Town. Tel: 025-2565.
Colombo 583133. Rs 500.

Tissa wewa Rest House
Old Town. Tel: 025-2299.
Colombo 583188. Rs 480.

Bentota:

Bentota Beach Hotel
Tel: 034-75176-8, 75215.
Rs 480.

Hotel Ceysands
Tel: 034-75073-4. Colombo
20862, 21101-10, 27206. Rs
440.

Lihiniya Surf Hotel
Tel: 034-75126-9. Rs 780.

Beruwela:

Barberyn Reef Hotel
Tel: 034-75582. Rs 470.

Beach Hotel Bayroo
Tel: 0347-5297. Rs 890.

Neptune Hotel
Tel: 034-75218/9. Rs 820.

Colombo:

**Ceylon Hotel Interconti-
nental**
48, Janadhipathi Mawatha.
Fort. Tel: 21221 (20 lines).
Rs 2510.

Ceylinco Hotel
69, Janadhipathi Mawatha.
Fort. Tel: 20431-3.

Galle Face Hotel
2, Kollupitiya Road, Col. 3.
Tel: 541010-16. From Rs
1750.

Holiday Inn
30, Sir Mohammed Macan
Markar Mawatha, Col. 3.
Tel: 22001-9. Rs 1750.

Hotel Lanka Oberoi
77, Steuart Place, Col. 3. Tel:
20001, 21171. Rs 2700.

**Ramada Renaissance Ho-
tel**
115, Sir Chittampalam Gar-
diner Mawatha, Col. 2. Tel:
544200-09. Rs 2500.

Galadari Meridien Hotel
64, Lotus Road. Tel:
544544. Rs 1500.

Taj Samudra Hotel
25, Galle Face Centre Road,
Col. 3. Tel: 548816. Rs
2400.

Hotel Taprobane
2, York Street, Col. 1. Tel:
20391-3. Rs 650.

Galle:

New Oriental Hotel
10, Church Street. Tel: 09-
2059. Rs 340.

Closenberg
Closenberg Road, Magalle.
Tel: 09-3073.

Hikkaduwa:

Hotel Blue Corals
332, Galle Road, Tel: 09-
22679. Rs 450.

Coral Gardens Hotel
Tel: 09-23023. Rs 1000.

Kalutara:

Tangerine Beach Hotel
25th Milepost, Kalutara.
Tel: 034-22295. Rs 1150.

Hotel Meriviere
St. Sabastiens Road. Tel:
042-2339. Rs 440.

Kandy:

The Citadel
124, Srimath Kuda Ratwatte
Mawatha. Tel: 08-32085
(Colombo: 20862). Rs 690.

Mahaweli Reach Hotel
35, Siyambalagastenne
Road. Tel: 08-32062. Rs
560.

Queens Hotel
Dalada Veediya. Tel: 08-
22121. Rs 1800.

Katunayake (Airport):

Airport Garden Hotel
Negombo Road, Seduwa.
Tel: 030-3771/9. Rs 1800.

Mount Lavinia:

Mount Lavinia Hotel
Hotel Road. Tel: 71-5221.
Rs 500.

Polonnaruwa
Hotel Seruwa. Tel: 027-
2441. Rs 340.

Polonnaruwa Rest House
Tel: 027-2299 (Colombo:
23501-04).

BANGLADESH: HIDDEN CHARM

Arriving at Zia International Airport in Dhaka, visitors are greeted by a large poster with the words, "See Bangladesh before the Tourist." There lies a challenge that should not be ignored. It is a challenge, certainly, because being a tourist in Bangladesh is often not easy, as there is little other than goodwill in the way of tourist facilities in this beautiful country of hidden charms. But once you dispel the misconceived images—brought on by the media—of poverty and crowds, which do exist; and of seasonal floods and monsoons, then Bangladesh can be appreciated as one of the great unspoiled travel experiences.

A fiery red sunset over a sea of brilliant green paddy fields—the image has been adopted as the national flag of Bangladesh—evokes a beautiful agrarian setting for which Bangladesh is little known. Equally evocative is an armada of triple-sail boats, creating a patchwork quilt of color as they take advantage of a fair wind. The bustling ports, colorful bazaars and fascinating country fairs all add to the country's cultural mosaic.

Today, Bangladesh occupies what was formerly East Bengal, which has been aptly described as the crossroads of culture—indeed, history has shown it to play an important cultural role in the region's development. Sadly, due to the exigencies of a monsoon climate, much of this history— the mosques temples, palaces and even cities—has quietly disappeared under the unforgiving waters of an ever-changing delta landscape.

The surviving monuments may not be as spectacular as some of those in neighboring countries, but they are certainly not lacking in importance. During a 2,000-year history of floods, religious wars and earthquakes, many illustrious dynasties have left their mark in the shape of magnificent cities and monuments, the desolate remains of which are still visible in places throughout the country. The art and literature immortalized by the famous artist and writer, Rabindranath Taggore, record the beauty of these landscapes and their people.

Bangladesh is a Muslim country and Islam pervades every corner of the land—the regular calls to prayer are particularly noticeable at dawn and dusk, as a cacophony of amplified sounds echo across the city or countryside, followed by the sight of the faithful who prostrate themselves towards Mecca, whether it is on board a boat or plane, in a mosque or in open fields. Nevertheless, religious tolerance ensures that Hindu, Buddhist and Christian communities still flourish. All this and more will give visitors the chance to experience in Bangladesh an environment and culture that both surprises and delights.

Preceding pages: Terra-cotta detail from 18th-century Kantanagar Temple. Left, well-laden country boats are a common sight.

COUNTRY IN THE PLAINS

Background: Bangladesh emerged as an independent Asian country in 1971 by breaking away from Pakistan after the horrors of an incredibly savage civil war. The new country, formerly East Pakistan, and East Bengal (before the partition of India), is located on the northeast of the Indian subcontinent, lying across the Tropic of Cancer at about 90° longitude. Except for a 174-mile (278-km) stretch of common eastern border with Burma, Bangladesh is surrounded by 2,300 miles (3,680 km) of frontier with India. A highly indented coastline defines its southern land mass and a population in excess of 100 million people crowds onto an area of about 55,600 square miles (144,560 square km), about the same size as Wisconsin.

About 90 percent of Bangladesh consists of low-lying plains, mostly only a few feet above sea level, about 25 percent of which flood during the monsoon. The capital city of Dhaka is less than 25 feet above sea level. The areas not susceptible to flooding in the rural areas become inhabited islands which are only accessible by boat.

Bangladesh is the largest delta in the world, formed by the mighty rivers of the Bramhaputra, the Padma and the Meghna which, together with their countless tributaries, sweep across the vast deltaic basin in a bewildering network of channels and streams. Acting as arteries, they are largely responsible for shaping the destiny of the land and its people. The rivers, formed by the melting snows of the Himalayas, forge their downward courses through the delta and disgorge enormous volumes of fertilizing silt on the land before spilling into the Bay of Bengal. This gift from the rivers enriches the land with life-giving fertility and helps to sustain a teeming population. Rivers are constantly shifting their beds and in this process many settlements and historic buildings have been engulfed by the constant yielding of the river's banks. As a result, the mighty Padma has been named the *Kirtinasha*, literally translated as the Destroyer of Monuments.

The Himalayan ramparts effectively barred all communications with Bangladesh's northern neighbors of China and Tibet, whilst her east and west frontiers were protected by dense hill forests, fast flowing rivers or the sea. Due to these natural barriers and her remoteness from Delhi, Bengal drifted in isolation for many centuries.

Thanks to her natural fertility, her climate and her fabled riches, Bengal has always attracted new settlers, traders and conquerors, mostly from the west. The delta became a vast melting pot of a variety of ethnic groups that mingled together to

from a hybrid race with a dominant non-Aryan strain.

With the advent of Islam in the early-13th century and the influx of Muslim traders, missionaries, fortune seekers and conquerors, a new element consisting of Arabs, Turks, Persians, the Mughals and even the Abyssinians added to an already diverse population. The Muslims ruled the country for about 600 years and intermixed freely among the local people, creating a country which is now a Muslim majority state. There is a marked Mongoloid element in the people along the border areas, especially in the hilly north,

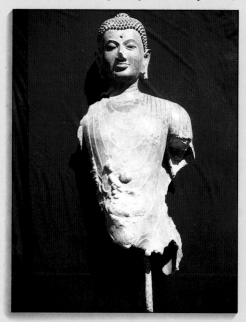

northeast and southeast areas consisting of the Kochs Hajos, the Garos, the Khasia Chakmas and the Maghs, who are associated particularly with Sylhet, Mymensingh and the Chittagong Hill Tracts where they settled from the 17th century onwards.

Early Days: The early history of Bengal is at its best legendary, and it is only possible to pick up the threads of recorded history from the fourth century B.C. With Alexander the Great's arrival in the Punjab in 326 B.C., a mighty empire in the Ganges Delta, known as the Gangaridae, was preparing to resist the Greek invaders with an army of 4,000 trained war elephants. News of this formidable foe deterred Alexander who, with his exhausted warriors withdrew to Babylon, having been routed by the Mauryan emperor Chandra

Gupta.

In the third century B.C., evidence found at the archaeological site of Mahasthan established that the Bangladesh of today formed part of the great Mauryan Empire known as Pundravardhana Bhukti. Events during the next six centuries in Bengal are difficult to decipher but it is certain that the smaller kingdoms of the area were perpetually at war with each other. It was only around 300 A.D. that the great Gupta Dynasty was founded by Chandra Gupta in Magadha, South Bihar, from where the greater part of northern India, including Bengal, was ruled till the

elected a *Kshatriya* (warrior) chief named Gopala from Varendra as king and with his enthronement began the famous Pala Dynasty of Bengal. It would last for over four centuries, bringing with it a period of prosperity and stable government previously unheard of.

Dharmapala, who succeeded his father Gopala, is considered the real founder of greatness in the Pala House as, by conquest, he made himself the master of most of northern India. Like all other members of his family, he was a devout Buddhist and patronized many Buddhist institutions throughout his empire, of which the Vik-

seventh century A.D.

In the early-seventh century, Sasanka, the first independent king of Bengal, rose from a humble position to take the throne due to the collapse of the Gupta Empire and a spate of foreign invasions. After his death, his far-flung empire passed to Bhaskaravarmana, the king of Kamarupa, in Assam. The history of Bengal becomes somewhat obscure again during the following century. This was a period of political chaos in Bengal, due probably to the lack of leadership. In order to introduce a settled government, the people

Left, early Buddhist sculpture. Above, waterways form a vast network across the deltaic basin.

ramsila Monastery in Bihar and the gigantic Somapura Vihara, later to be known as Paharpur, are the best examples. He also established diplomatic relations with the Indonesian kingdom of Srivijaya which then controlled the greater part of the archipelago. Dharmapala was succeeded by his son Devapala who went on to extend the massive empire he had inherited by embracing the whole of northern India from Assam to the confines of Kashmir and from the Himalayas to the Vindya mountains in the south. Devapala was succeeded by a series of imbecile brother kings who lost the kingdom to the mighty Senas from south India. The records of Sena rule are somewhat scanty but the family was famous for their support of the arts. They ruled until the latter part of the 12th century.

The Islamization of Bengal is thought to have coincided with the dramatic conquest of Ikhtiyaruddin Muhammad Khajli in 1204 A.D. However, Arab merchants are said to have established a few colonies in the coastal region of Chittagong in the eighth and ninth centuries after they had already captured the spice trade of the East and dominated the sea traffic in the Indian Ocean.

The Muslim conquest of Bengal was not the result of a premeditated plan by the overlords of Delhi, but the outcome of the independent adventures of Muhammad Khajli, who set out to seek his fortunes in distant lands. After overrunning Bihar in 1199, he launched a surprise attack on the Hindu kingdom of Bengal which was under the rule of a decrepit Lakshmana Sena. With only 19 troopers, Khajli took the poorly fortified tempo-

The Portuguese were the first Europeans to establish a colony in Dhaka in 1616 on land granted by the Mughal governor, Shaista Khan, in return for their support against the troublesome Magh ruler of Chittagong. They were soon joined by other Europeans. However, the greatest impact was undoubtedly caused by the arrival of the British from the East India Company, thanks to Robert Clive, who started as a clerk in the East India Company and rose through the ranks and by his military successes became the effective governor of Bengal. He was appointed to lead the relief of Calcutta and with his 3,000 trained troops and cannon, Clive won a decisive battle against the Bengalis at Plassey, routing an opposing army estimated at 50,000.

Rocky Road to Independence: Being one of India's most densely populated states,

rary capital of Naudia and went on to conquer the main city of Gauda with his full army. Northwest Bengal thus passed dramatically into the hands of the Muslim invaders and heralded a long and prosperous rule. The emperor Jehangir eventually consolidated the Mughal rule to make Bengal one of the richest provinces of the Empire until the death in 1707 of Aurangzeb, the last of the great Mughals.

The decline of Muslim rule in India coincided with the emergence of the Marhatta power under Sivaji in the Deccan Plateau and the more formidable alien powers of the West: the British, French, Dutch and Portuguese who initially came to India for commercial gain but who eventually ruled the country with economic chains rather than the sword.

Bengal's religious dichotomy already held the seeds of future violence. Unlike the rest of India, it was predominantly a Muslim population. Despite their religious differences, there were also internal economic differences, a rapid population growth causing administrative difficulties, and problems in communication, resulting in the stagnation of East Bengal. This led Lord Curzon, the governor-general of India at that time, to partition Bengal in 1905 for the first time by uniting Assam and Chittagong with 15 districts of East Bengal to form a new province with Dhaka as its capital. This partition met with violent opposition from the Bengali Hindus, who saw it as a threat against the renascent Bengali nationalism and it was annulled in 1911. However, the new Muslim League continued to press for Muslim autonomy and in 1947, first mooted the idea of the formation of Pakistan.

The struggle for independence after World War II had been bitter, especially in Bengal where the situation was complicated by the violent enmity between Hindus and Muslims. It was under pressure from the Muslim leader Muhammad Ali Jinnah that the Viceroy, Lord Mountbatten, decided to partition the subcontinent. In August 1947 the State of Pakistan was born, complicating an already volatile situation by having two territories separated by over 2,000 miles (3,200 km).

Differences in race, culture and tradition were not compensated by a common religious bond and attempts at unification by making Urdu the national language in 1952 exploded into rioting, causing the deaths of 12 students at the hands of

government and announced the establishment of the world's 139th nation.

By the end of 1974, a state of emergency was declared and Sheik Mujib declared himself president. His term was short-lived as he was overthrown in a military coup and assassinated on August 15, 1975. In November 1976, after a particularly unstable period, Ziaur Rahman, the head of the army staff, took over as chief martial law administrator and in April 1977, he became president, at the same time forming the Bangladesh Nationalist's Party. The party won by a two-thirds majority in the parliamentary elections of 1979, the president's own position having been consolidated by an overwhelming victory in the 1978 presidential poll.

An attempted coup by an army general on May 30, 1981 resulted in the assassination of President

the Pakistani police and forcing democracy to give way to martial law. East Pakistan, under Sheik Mujibur Rahman and his Awami League Party, sought internal self-government and, in elections held in 1971, won a clear parliamentary majority. This unwelcome result precipitated the War of Independence when Sheik Mujib declared East Pakistan to be an independent Bangladesh.

The ensuing war was one of the shortest and bloodiest of modern times, lasting for only nine months and coming to an end on December16, 1971, when Sheik Mujib took over the reins of

18th-century colonial buildings, left, are long gone; modern-day Bangladesh is reflected in new government offices, above.

Zia and left Bangladesh in a political vacuum as he had no obvious successor. Under the vice-presidency of Abdus Sattar, who assumed the office of acting president, Bangladesh tried to settle back into the state of calm created by President Zia, but increasing concern about the government led Lieutenant General Hussain Mohammad Ershad to take over the leadership of the country after a bloodless coup on the eve of March 24, 1982, and to become the chief martial law administrator with a pledge to return the country to parliamentary rule within two years. It took General Ershad more than the projected two years to fulfil his pledge but eventually, elections took place in 1985 and martial law was replaced by democratic rule as General Ershad was elected president.

DHAKA

Dhaka (or Dacca as it was previously spelled) is a relatively young capital for Bengal. But it has always been the capital for Bangladesh. Prior to 1608, Sonargaon had been the capital of the region, but following the shifting of the major river courses and the collapse of the sultanate, Dhaka replaced it as the capital and remained so until 1704 when the capital was moved to Murishabad. Dhaka was first settled as early as the fourth century and the evolution of the city can be divided into four specific periods: the Pre-Mughal stage, dominated by Hindu and Buddhist influences from the south, and the flowering of a civilization; the Muslim period of the Mughal Empire, which was a period of establishment; the period of the British Raj, responsible for the development of international trading; and the most recent period of autonomy and independence when Bangladesh was born. Under the control of the Mughals, Dhaka was considerably enhanced with the construction of mosques, palaces, caravanserais, forts and gardens, which attracted foreign traders. Later, a further architectural extravagance developed with the importation of Christian churches, British Raj palaces and other public buildings, many of which are still standing.

A tour of Dhaka is best begun at the **Lalbagh Fort** at the edge of **Old Dhaka** and, for the intrepid explorer, it is possible to see most of the following areas on foot.

Lalbagh Fort or Fort Aurangabad, located in the southwest corner of the old city overlooking the **Buriganga River**, is the most imposing, albeit sadly incomplete, Mughal building in Dhaka. As its original name implies, its construction was begun in 1678 by Prince Azam the third son of Emperor Aurangzeb but he was unable to finish it during his short 12-month tenure and Nawab Shaista Khan, his successor, took up the work. The story goes that the premature death of Shaista Khan's favorite daughter, popularly known as Bibi Pari, caused total suspension of building activities in the fort as he considered it inauspicious to continue. Among the surviving structures are a long fortification wall with semi-octagonal bastions, on the southern side, with a three-storey gateway in the southeast corner. There are high defence

Boatyard on the Buriganga River.

320

walls running along the western side and two other gateways in the north wall. Within the walls there is a small three-domed **mosque** on the western boundary, the **Mausoleum of Bibi Pari**, and the **audience hall** and **Hammam** of the complex in the center. Beyond the mausoleum was the residence of Shaista Khan.

After visiting Lalbagh, the adventurous can take the road leading southeast along the Buriganga (at one time the river lapped the southern boundary walls of the fort — it has moved several hundred yards further south now) and follow **Waterworks Road** until it reaches the hub of the old city—**Chowk Bazaar**. The stretch of highly twisting road is of great interest as here you can still breath the atmosphere of 19th-century Dhaka. The streets are narrow and tortuous and lined with tall, decrepit and precariously poised old houses accommodating, at ground floor level, wholesale shops selling all sorts of merchandise. The seething crowd of pedestrians is hounded by a constant stream of indiscriminate cycle-rickshaws, pushcarts, and occasionally by a hackney-carriage. You are just as likely to be confronted by an ambling bullock cart as you are by the latest Mercedes Benz as it hustles its way at a snail's pace through the crowd, reminiscent of the Nawabs on their caparisoned elephants.

Chowk Bazaar will bring you to the second collection of important buildings. **Bara Katra**, built in 1644 by Mir Abul Qasem, is one of the most important early structures erected in Dhaka. Little survives of this magnificent edifice which had a river frontage of over 200 feet (60 meters). Originally, the building was planned on a grand scale following the traditional pattern of the caravanserai of central Asia, embellished with imperial Mughal features. A further 200 yards (182 meters) to the east of Bara Katra is **Chota Katra**, a smaller version built by Shaista Khan in 1663.

Further to the south along the river is the most spectacular of all the British Raj buildings—the **Ashan Manzil** or the Nawab's Palace, as it is often called. This stately palace close to **Wise Ghat** was built in 1872 on the site of an old French factory and named after Nawab Ashanullah Bahadur. A silver model of the original design survives in the National Museum. The palace was badly damaged in 1888 by a tornado but reconstructed with considerable alteration.

A striking monument of the Christian influence can be seen in **Armintola** along **Church Road**. The Church of the Holy

Sepulchre or as it is more commonly known—the **Armenian Church**—built by the Armenian colony in 1791, is worth visiting as a haven of peace in its bustling surroundings.

Returning along **Islamapur Road** you will locate the **Sitara** (Star) **Mosque**, which derives its name from its glittering star-patterned mosaic of broken china. It dates originally from the 18th century but during the earlier part of this century, it was redecorated by a zealous businessman in a style popular among Bengalis of that time.

The next area of interest is focused around **Curzon Hall** in **Ramna**, most of which belongs to the early-20th century and the British Raj period. In the wake of the first partition in 1905, a group of architecturally homogeneous buildings appeared in Dhaka, illustrating a happy blend of European and Mughal tastes. Curzon Hall is the earliest example of such buildings, exhibiting a fine Victorian brick edifice with Mughal trimmings of cusped arches, fretted screens, and kiosk-like turrets. It was founded as a town hall by Lord Curzon in 1904 but has now been taken over as a university faculty. Almost opposite is the imposing **Old High Court** building which was originally to be the governor's residence, dating from about 1905. This follows the neoclassical style prevalent in Europe at that time.

Of the many Mughal mosques to be seen in Dhaka, perhaps the most attractive is the **Sat Gumbad** (Seven-domed) **Mosque** located on the northwestern corner of Dhaka City in **Jafarabad**. It illustrates a fine example of the provincial Mughal style of the 17th century. Probably erected by Shaista Khan, the mosque stands in a beautiful setting on a high bank overlooking the flood plain of the Buriganga. It has three domes over the main prayer hall and a further four corner domes over octagonal towers.

Dhaka's skyline as seen from miles beyond is fast becoming that of a cosmopolitan metropolis, now that highrise buildings vie for supremacy in the commercial area around **Motijheel** and **Dhaka Stadium**. The city may well be proud of her **Kamalpur Railway Station** which is a stylish concrete building of 'Gothick' inspiration. Closer to the commercial area and near the Stadium is the **Baitul Mukarram Mosque**, which is the largest mosque in the city. Its design, which was inspired by the Kaaba in Mecca, consists of a large prayer hall extending onto a vast verandah used especially during the Eid festivals. Beneath the

Rickshaw jam in downtown Old Dhaka

complex there is a large and thriving modern shopping center.

Recently, a new **National Museum** has been opened to house an assorted collection representative of the country's history, culture, art and fauna, all housed in a building of distinctly odd proportions. Its collection does not match up to some of the other site museums found in the country.

Dhaka's most surprising new building is the new **Parliament Building** in modern Dhaka at **Sher-E-Bangla Nagar**. A colossal complex of geometrical inspiration in natural concrete and brick, it was conceived by the American architect Louis Kahn. It is certainly a building that does not go unnoticed, standing out strongly on the skyline in sharp contrast to its surroundings and yet akin to the basic architectural forms of the country. The contrast in materials and the clever use of moats as reflecting pools creates a strong sense of curiosity in everyone who sees it.

No visit to Dhaka is complete without a journey to the old capital — the fabled Sonargaon which lingers in reality as only a memory of the halcyon days of pre Mughal supremacy. Located about 16 miles (26 km) from the center of Dhaka, formerly between the Sitalakhya and Meghna rivers, the few scattered ruins of this once-prosperous 'Golden Town' are to be found in an extensive fertile tract of land. The old city, identified as being located in present-day **Painam Village**, is virtually forgotten as only a few straggling remains of ancient earthworks, bridges, moats and monuments appear through the shady foliage of encroaching jungle.

This amazing neoclassical streetscape was only constructed within the last hundred years by a group of wealthy Hindu merchants. Close by there is the Sardar Bari, a large mansion of the same period overlooking two ponds which is now the **National Folk Art Museum**.

A half-hour walk in a northeasterly direction through typical farmland will lead to the small but enchanting **Goaldi Mosque**, standing amidst the paddy fields. This is the earliest mosque of the district, dating from 1519, during the heyday of the old capital.

When returning to Dhaka, visit the old medieval river fort of **Hajiganj,** which is one of a pair, the other being the **Sonakanda Fort** across the river. They were placed to control the invading Portuguese pirates who chose to sneak up the rivers into Dhaka. You can still see the protective ramparts and parapets pierced with holes for musketry.

[margin caption:] ...ear- ...eserted ...ain street ... Sonar- ...aon, ...bandoned ...arly this ...entury.

RAJSHAHI DIVISION

The **Division of Rajshahi** in the north-western corner of Bangladesh is bordered on the east by the mighty **Jamuna River** and the **Padma/Ganges River** on the south, and shares a disputed border with India to the north and west, making access to **Gaud**, one of the most interesting archaeological sites in all of Bengal, almost impossible. During partition, the ancient capital of Gaud was split through the middle and now part of it lies in Bangladesh and part in India.

Rajshahi Division has an impressive collection of historic sites which are spread over a wide area and are best reached by private vehicle.

Rajshahi is a university town, the center of the silk industry, as well as being an important cultural center. Formerly it was also quite famous as a focal point for the indigo trade with the **Baro Kuthi** building still standing as witness to the supposed countless atrocities related to this disreputable trade. The **Varendra Research Museum** is an essential starting point as it contains an impressive collection of arti-

facts related to the area. The building itself is a blend of Hindu and Buddhist styles of the eighth and ninth centuries with the pre-vailing British influence of the 1920s. Inside is one of the finest collections of black stone sculptures in the country.

Eighteen miles (29 km) east of Rajshahi town, in the village of **Puthia**, is a fascinating but little-known group of medieval Hindu temples. Besides the imposing **Maharani's Palace**—Puthia was formerly a large estate—there is an interesting variety of temples. At the entrance to the village is a large white stucco temple dedicated to Shiva, following a typical north Indian design and dating from 1823. To the left of the main facade of the palace is the **Govinda Temple**, dedicated to the Hindu god Krishna, which follows a typical Hindu temple shape prevalent in Bengal at the time. It is decorated with delicate terra-cotta panels depicting scenes from the *Radha Krishna* and other Hindu epics. At the back of the palace is another delightful Bangla-style **miniature temple**, which is in the shape of a Bengali bamboo hut but built of brick and adorned with some exquisite terra-cotta designs.

Across a large tank to the right of the palace are a further pair of temples exhibit-

Preceding pages: "Take me home, country road." Below, people power: ploughing the paddy fields.

ing a variation of styles. One, the **Jagaddhatri Temple** dedicated to the Hindu goddess Durga, is a combination of the Bangla style and the Chau-chala style, or hut-shaped roof with four slopes. The other temple alongside is also of the Chau-chala style. Both temples are liberally decorated with terra-cotta designs.

To continue the tour of Rajshahi, it is best to drive via **Bogra** to visit the Mahasthan and Paharpur sites. On the way, you will witness some fascinating local fishing methods—fish being the staple diet of the Bangladeshi—whether by casting or laying a net, by spear, or by trapping the unsuspecting fish in an upturned basket. You will see large expanses of sugarcane or cotton, which are 'dry crops' and of course an abundance of paddy fields as well as jute, which is grown throughout Bangladesh.

The archaeological site of **Mahasthan**, dating from the third century B.C., which is about eight miles (13 km) north of Bogra, represents the earliest city site in the whole of Bengal. It is an impressive fortified city covering about 2.3 million square feet (210,000 square meters), most of which is still buried beneath farmland. The citadel is encircled on three sides by artificial moats and by the **Karatoya River** on the fourth.

Other ruins fan out within a semicircle radius of about five miles (eight km), making it one of the most important of all ancient sites in the region. It is worth walking up onto the platform of the citadel, which stands above the surrounding countryside, to see the extent of the site and to take a closer look at some of the recently exposed rampart walls. Outside and beyond the citadel on the right of the road is another interesting site where the remains of a brick Hindu temple, the **Govinda Bhita**, have been exposed. They stand on the bend of the Karayatoya, which was said to have been the widest river in Bengal; today it is just a backwater. Opposite is the fine **Mahasthan Site Museum**, filled with finds from local archaeological excavations.

About four miles (six km) west of Mahasthan are the ruins of **Vasu Bihar**, an early Buddhist monastic site recorded by the famous Chinese pilgrim Hiuen Tsang in the seventh century. Recent excavations have shown several changes during its 500-year history.

By far the most spectacular Buddhist site to be discovered is the gigantic temple and monastery of **Paharpur**, dating from the eighth century A.D. Paharpur is about 35 miles (56 km) northwest of Mahasthan via

the busy market town of **Jaipurhat**. Access from Jaipurhat is along a rutted cart track that is sometimes passable in an ordinary car. Paharpur has been identified from a series of inscribed clay seals as the Somapura Vihara from the great Pala Dynasty. It is the biggest single *vihara* (image house) south of the Himalayas, measuring approximately 900 feet (273 meters) along each side and enclosed by an outer wall with 177 monastic cells built into it. In the center of the 22-acre (nine-hectare) courtyard are the ruins of a mighty temple which rises to a height of 72 feet (22 meters)—an unusual hillock giving the local village of Paharpur its name (*pahar* meaning 'hill'). The temple is cruciform in plan, built in high quality brick with thousands of terra-cotta plaques depicting the art form of that period, whether it be religious or secular, human or animal, mythological or purely an artist's whim.

Following the Buddhist creed and ritual, the monastery was built in the wilderness—but not too far from a town to enable the inmates to beg from the nearby town—alongside a river which ran along the southern side. Today, the remains of the bathing and toilet facilities beyond the outside wall can also be seen in the southeastern corner.

The temple was planned with two circumambulatories, lined with the terra-cotta plaques, which were enclosed walkways enabling the faithful to circumambulate in a clockwise direction and, at the upper level, within the cruciform projections, pay homage to the main Buddhist divinities.

Inside the courtyard there are the remains of several ancillary buildings and it is possible to make out the refectory, a miniature version of the main temple and a large well which the locals believe provides waters with great healing powers.

During recent exploratory excavations, an important archaeological find of a large bronze Buddha dating from the Gupta period was accidentally discovered in one of the monks cells. It is considered to be one of the most splendid specimens of mature Pala art of the ninth century, cast using the 'wax loss' process.

Paharpur's later history is uncertain but it seems to have been abandoned in the 12th century A.D., probably due to flooding. Today the site is under water during the monsoon.

In 1979, the government joined forces with the United Nations and UNESCO to prepare a conservation program to safeguard this priceless site. There is a small site museum close to the monastic complex containing, amongst other finds, some interesting stone images which are representative of over 55 *in situ* pieces hidden below present ground level at the base of the temple.

A few hundred yards from the monastery, on the eastern side, are the ruins of **Satyapir Bhita**, a Buddhist temple complex apparently dedicated to Tara, the female consort of the Dhyani Buddha.

A long day's trip to the north end of Bangladesh, about 12 miles (19 km) beyond **Dinajpur**, is the beautiful Hindu temple of **Kantanagar**, which was built in 1752 by Maharaja Pran Nath of Dinajpur. This temple, which is famed for its fine terracotta work, was originally a nine-tower structure crowned with four richly ornamental towers at two levels, with a central spire over the third. It was badly damaged in an earthquake at the end of the 19th century, but it is still possible to make out the bases of the towers. Nevertheless, the temple rightly claims to be one of the best examples of its type in brick and terra-cotta built by Bengali artisans. Dedicated to the Hindu divinity Krishna, the structure stands on a stone plinth, in sharp contrast to the warm red of the terra-cotta, which depicts in the spandrels over the archway scenes from the *Ramayana* and the *Mahabharata*.

Defaced Buddhist panel at Paharpur

WATERWAYS

As Bangladesh is the largest delta in the world, it is not surprising that boats are one of the most common forms of transport. The rivers range from the mighty Jamuna, which often has a width of over three miles and a powerful current and where the sturdy triple-sail transport or country boats ply, to the docile backwaters and flood plains where anything that floats, from elegant crescent-shaped fishing boats to rafts made by lashing plantain stems together, will serve as a ferry across the dyke or river to the village or hut.

There are boats for every activity. The simple but maneuverable fishing boat with its demountable mast and two sails—the topmost is dropped to reduce speed—has a crew of two and is steered with an oar lashed to the boat's side. If the wind drops it can be sculled or float along on the current, if it is running in the right direction.

At the other extreme are the large cargo boats, beamy and deep, loaded to the gunwales with jute and leaving only a few inches of freeboard. Powered by three mighty sails, it is an unbelievably beautiful sight to witness an armada of up to 40 boats sailing towards you on a free wind with their colorful sails billowing before them. Colors from russet to blue, old *sarees* or even grain bags stitched together form an interchanging patchwork quilt against the bluish gray waters of the Jamuna.

The boats are dependent on a following wind. The length of river that they run under sail in a few days may take weeks of sweated labor to retrace. The only power against the wind is that of the oar—galley-style, three or four pairs of oarsmen will row the boat in long sweeps as they walk the massive oars to and fro. Alternatively, manpower will haul the boat along the towpath—four men harnessed to long ropes fixed to the mast head, will struggle up the towpath dragging the boat against the current and the wind, while the owner lazily steers the craft from on board. Some enterprising skippers have now contrived a method of harnessing their diesel-run water pumps to a propeller and installing them into the old hulls, no doubt to the delight of their crews.

Every year on the Buriganga River, there are spectacular boat races, featuring low, sleek, canoe-like craft powered in unison by 21 paddlers. This colorful event takes place in March.

The sea-going vessels are a totally different shape to those of the river craft. They have powerful, high-set bows with a strong entry to enable them to carve their way through the stormy waters of the Bay of Bengal. They have a demountable mast set on the main deck and on the stern an overhanging poop deck to protect the vessel from running seas.

The rivers are alive with ferries of all shapes and sizes.Large flat-bottomed boats from Scandinavia, ferrying heavy lorries and buses, with a few cars crammed into the remaining narrow interstices, manage to get up to 50 vehicles onto one ferry. Passenger ferries, also bursting at the seams, powered by noisy diesel engines, run a kind of water-bus service between villages up and down the rivers, loading and unloading people, animals, produce and fish.

Other than for modern-day ferries, boat styles have changed little over the centuries, as evidenced from examples recorded in the centuries-old terra-cotta panels on several of the Hindu temples. Their delicate crescent shapes often seem to mirror the curvilinear cornices that are so typical of the Bangla dwelling, and which was later adapted to the cornices of temples and mosques.

Hugging the coastline on the Jamuna River.

KHULNA DIVISION

The **Division of Khulna** is considerably influenced by the tributaries of the Ganges, which find their way into the Bay of Bengal through a vast maze of waterways, making two-thirds of Khulna marshland or dense jungle consisting of mangrove swamps, an absolute haven for wildlife. The great tidal forest of the **Sundarbans**, as this lower area is called, an ideal habitat for the Royal Bengal tiger, stretches along the indented coastline of the Bay of Bengal for about 170 miles (276 km) and in places penetrates up to 80 miles (128 km) inland from the sea. The heavy mangrove forest floor of the Sunarbans is intersected by shark-infested rivers with their bewildering maze of ever-shifting tidal tributaries.

In this inhospitable region, the affluent township known in history as **Khalifata-bad** was laid out by a little-known warrior saint Ulugh Khan Jahan, in the mid-15th century, at the present location of **Bager-hat**, the "abode of the tigers." Khan Jahan came from Delhi to settle a Muslim colony in this swampland in the early-15th century

and was no doubt the earliest torchbearer of Islam in the south. Legend has it that he constructed about 360 mosques and as many freshwater tanks, as well as palaces, mausolea and other public buildings in a very short space of time. He also constructed a network of roads linking important centers in Bengal with his city.

Today, most of these buildings have been swallowed up by the rivers and jungles, although a few spectacular ruins can still be traced, half-hidden in the luxuriant coconut groves and tall palm trees.

Only a handful of the mosques still stand, examples of Tughlaq architecture of stark simplicity imported from Delhi—simple brick structures with tapering corner towers projecting like the bastions of a fortress, a form not usually associated with a house of prayer.

Of the surviving mosques, the **Shait Gumbad Mosque** is the most magnificent, and certainly the largest brick mosque surviving in Bangladesh. Its name, meaning '60 domes', is misleading as in reality, it is roofed over with 77 small domes supported by a forest of slender columns covering a large prayer hall and giving it the appearance of a medieval church crypt. At sunrise when the rays of the sun penetrate the east-

The Shait Gumbad Mosque has more than 60 domes.

ern entrances, the interior comes to life. There is little adornment to this building other than the carved stone decoration to the central *mihrab* at the western end of the prayer hall. The exterior facades, with slightly 'battered' walls, have discernible curving cornices—a concession to the local style. There is access to the corner turrets from where the faithful were formally called to prayer. Behind the mosque is a large freshwater tank known as **Ghora Dighi**, adding to the serene ambience of this beautiful rural setting.

Close to the Shait Gumbad are another three mosques, all very similar in style and design. Just across the new highway is the **Singar Mosque** and on the west bank of the Ghora Dhigi is the **Bibi Begni**, while the **Chunakhola Mosque** is surrounded by paddy fields. All of them are single-domed structures with massive brick walls and attached circular corner turrets.

The **Mausoleum of Khan Jahan**, the warrior saint himself, is located along a small road not far from the previous group of mosques. It is an important pilgrimage center for all Muslims. The mausoleum and adjacent mosque are perched on the edge of another enormous tank known as **Thakur Dighi**, home to some benign marsh mugger

crocodiles. The saint's sepulchre follows the typical style of a single-domed brick structure with corner turrets. In the center on a raised platform is the saint's sarcophagus, which is built of stone and beautifully engraved with verses of the *Quran*, as well as the date of his demise on October 25, 1459.

The mound on which the mosque and mausoleum are set was raised by the excavated earth of the 1.67-million-square-foot (150,000-square-meter) lake. A broad flight of steps leads down to the large expanse of water where a colony of crocodiles lives. Two notable characters, Kala Pahar and Dhola Pahar (meaning 'black and white mountain'), are fed daily with offerings of live chicken by the *mutwalli* (caretaker) of the tomb—a custom not usually associated with Islamic practices.

In the vicinity there are several other mosques in varying stages of decay. At the northwest corner there is a fine domed brick mosque with stone columns supporting the roof and, at the road intersection, there is the mighty **Ronvijoypur Mosque**, which boasts the largest dome in Bangladesh, spanning over 35 feet (11 meters). The walls are massive, measuring over nine feet (three meters) thick, with simple but small arched openings on three sides, producing little light to the somber interior.

Although **Khulna** has little to offer in the way of history, it is a thriving industrial and shipping center. There are some amazing industrial relics to be found—mammoth steam engines abandoned along the tracks, dejected steel hulks of passenger ferries or coasters floundering on the river banks, all mingling with the intense activities of a bustling river port.

One of the most interesting ways of reaching Khulna and subsequently the Bagerhat monuments is to travel there by boat from Dhaka on the 'Rocket Service', a relic of the British Raj. The boats are vintage paddle steamers with accommodation ranging from steerage to First Class. The trip takes anything from 20 hours to 24 hours, depending on the state of the rivers, and is a wonderful way of exploring the Sundarbans, seeing the river life and reminiscing on what travel in India must have been like at the beginning of the century.

It is also possible to hire a boat or join a trip through the Sundarbans from Khulna to **Heron Point**, where there is a guest bungalow and plenty of wildlife to be seen. You may get the chance to see the Royal Bengal tiger, which grows to enormous size in the Suhndarbans and whose propensity for eating humans is legend.

Multi-
arched
interior of
Shait
Gumbad.

CHITTAGONG DIVISION

Chittagong Division, the second most developed division of the four in the country, shares its northern border with Assam—the tea-growing area—and, to the east, with Burma. It has the distinction of being Bangladesh's only hilly region with hills ranging from about 800 feet (242 meters) in the north to about 200 feet (60 meters) in the southern ranges. The narrow coastal strip is crowded in by hills to the east, which is the only region where the land is not fragmented by river deltas.

In the northeastern district of **Comilla**, there are archaeological sites second only in importance to those at Mahasthan. If you are driving to Chittagong and Cox's Bazar, the **Mainamati** sites are about 60 miles (100 km) southeast of Dhaka. Although there is an extensive range of over 50 very important Buddhist sites uncovered along the north-south Lalmai-Mainamati range of hills, many of them are located in a military zone, making access to them almost impossible. The **Mainamati Archaeological Museum** and some of the accessible sites

are about six miles (10 km) west of Comilla town. Mainamati echoes the memory of the celebrated King Govinda Chandra's mother who was so popular in local legends and folk ballads, whilst *lalmai* or 'red hill' refers to the red color of the soil. Most of the sites contain various types of Buddhist structures dating from between the eighth and 12th centuries, consisting of monasteries, temples and *stupas*, which have produced a rich collection of archaeological remains.

Close to the site museum is **Salban Vihara**, a Buddhist monastery which had 115 cells built around a spacious courtyard with a cruciform temple in the middle. Deep excavations have revealed as many as six rebuilding phases, four of which have intelligible plan forms. In the early periods it was very similar to Paharpur, being built of brick and with scores of terra-cotta plaques adorning the circumambulatories. The monastery was probably constructed at the beginning of the eighth century by Bhava Deva, the fourth ruler of the Deva Dynasty.

About three miles (five km) north of Salban Vihara, is a unique group of Buddhist brick monuments known as the **Kutila Mura**. They consist of three *stupas*, possibly representing the Buddhist trinity or three jewels—Buddha, Dharma and

The Tea Gardens in Sylhet.

Sangha. The **Charpatra Mura** is about two miles to the northwest, and several of its important finds can be seen in the museum. The largest of the ridge sites—the **Ananda Vihara**, another Buddhist monastery, is only about a half-mile away. It probably derives its name from Anandadeva, the third and greatest ruler of the early Deva Dynasty. All these sites are out of bounds unless prior permission is received from the army.

Fortunately, the museum is well stocked with the various finds made at these sites. There is a large collection of bronze images of the Buddha, Bodhisattva and Tara. There is also an interesting solid cast bronze *stupa* measuring 10 inches high, giving an interesting insight into the original shapes of the ruined *stupas*.

Sadly, no terra-cotta plaques are to be found in situ on the Salban Vihara. However, several were collected during the excavations and are on display. They are fine examples of an animated rural art form with a host of different subjects ranging from birds and animals to humans and semi-divine beings depicting the local folklore and mythology.

This ensemble of Buddhist sites reflects an unmistakably high standard of material civilization achieved by the people of southeast Bengal between the seventh and 12th centuries.

Sylhet is in the northern part of Chittagong Division, located in a gentle sloping upland valley between the Khasia, Jaintia and Tripura hills, bordering on Assam. Gentle slopes, rich light soil, a congenial climate and abundant rainfall have made Sylhet one of the largest tea-producing areas in the world. These conditions have also provided rich tropical forests where big game—tiger, panther and wild boar—abound. Tribal life is strong and folk dancing, like the famous Manipuri dance, is still performed by the local tribes.

Sylhet town has a strong British influence which is reflected in its colonial-style architecture. The tea gardens are clustered around **Srimangal** to the south and at the **Bangladesh Tea Research Institute** you can follow all the stages of tea cultivation and processing.

Of interest to archaeologists are the megalithic monuments of **Jaintiapur**, the former residence of the Khasi kings. These are located about 26 miles (42 km) east of the town on the Tamabil road. The megaliths or menhirs, standing eight feet in height, are all that remain of the Jaintia

kingdom. The crude megaliths, now blackened with age, bear important historical and social significance but their real purpose has yet to be ascertained, although some locals believe them to be death memorials.

The busy port of **Chittagong** has long associations with seafaring traders and is strongly linked with the colorful spice trade between Europe and the East. Today, it is a large and thriving city set amid beautiful natural surroundings, studded with green-clad knolls, coconut palms, mosques and minarets against a background of the **Bay of Bengal**. The city is located on the **Karnapuli River**. As a seaport it has always been a great center for trade, especially after the Portuguese overran the city in the 16th century. There is also a strong British influence in some of the colonial administrative buildings. The **Circuit House** is one of the most attractive buildings left by the British and has been the scene of a number of historic and bloody events, the last being the assassination of President Ziaur Rahman on May 30, 1981.

The most notable of the numerous mosques around Chittagong are the **Jami Mosque**, built by Shaista Khan's son to commemorate the reconquest of Chittagong in 1666, and the **Qadam Mubarak Mosque** in the **Rahmatganj** area of Chittagong, built in 1719 by Muhammad Yasin and one of the few mosques of the area that retains its original features. Of particular interest is the *qudam mubarak* or 'foot-print' of the Prophet.

The lush tropical vegetation and unique concentration of tribal cultures has made the **Chittagong Hill Tracts** a potentially fascinating tourist destination in Bangladesh. Ironically, it is the most troubled region in the country and has therefore been made a restricted area, permitting tourists to visit only Rangamati and Kaptai.

Rangamati, the headquarters of the Chittagong Hill Tracts, is a favorite holiday resort because of its location on an isthmus projecting into **Kaptai Lake**. You can enjoy swimming, boating, sunbathing and exploring the small islands off the peninsulas. Each year in mid-April there is a colorful Buddhist water festival. For those interested in some ethnic shopping, the tribal woven fabrics are of excellent quality with simple but bright and beautiful patterns.

There are innumerable boat trips that you can make on the 170-square-mile (426-square-km) lake, the most feasible being to **Kaptai**, where the site for a hydroelectric project is located.

Buddhist reliquaries dominate the hills above Cox's Bazaar.

About three miles (five km) beyond Kaptai is **Chitmorong**, a Buddhist village where one of the many Buddhist monasteries exhibits a strong Burmese influence.

Perhaps the best-known tourist destination in Bangladesh is **Cox's Bazaar** and the beaches around it. **Inani Beach**, south of Cox's, claims to be the longest in the world. The town derives its name from Captain Hiram Cox, who in 1798 was commissioned to settle the region with Arkanese immigrants fleeing from Burma. Cox's Bazaar developed with the influence of the new refugee Magh settlers who erected a series of picturesque white plastered pagodas or *stupas* on the low hilltops above the town. In true Burmese fashion, they also built the 19th-century *khyangs* or monasteries, which can be seen at **Ramu** and in Cox's Bazaar itself.

The **Bara Khyang** of **Lama Bazaar**, near Ramu, consists of three separate buildings, one of which houses interesting reliquaries and Burmese handicrafts as well as the largest bronze statue of the Buddha in Bangladesh, cast at the end of the last century. These buildings characterize an imported style typical of the buildings along the Burmese border—timber framed with multi-tiered pitched roofs and extremely decorative fretted carvings. The interiors are generally simple spaces with a forest of columns supporting the complicated roofs above.

There is a similar compound in Cox's Bazaar known as the **Aggameda Khyang**, which nestles at the foot of a hill. The main prayer hall is raised off the ground on a series of round columns. Unlike at Lama Bazaar, there is an active Buddhist community of monks performing their daily worship. Scattered around the compound are a fine collection of Buddhist images, mostly of Burmese origin.

Later, the region was the favorite haunt of Mogh pirates and brigands who, with the Portuguese, used to ravage the Bay of Bengal in the 17th century. The Moghs have remained, maintaining their tribal ways through their handicrafts, their hand-made cheroots and their decorative shell work. In Cox's Bazaar it is still possible to see the shy and unassuming Mogh craftsmen at work.

To get away from it all there are the beaches, usually fairly well-populated with local tourists for the first few hundred yards. But beyond this are more than 70 miles (112 km) of silver-gold sand and surf, enough to satisfy even the most incurable beach bum.

rmese luence evident this hill be.

DESTINATION BANGLADESH

GETTING THERE

By Air: There are at least 14 different international airlines that have regular services into Zia International Airport, a smart and efficient group of terminal buildings where, if you are delayed, at least you can take advantage of the facilities. There are direct flights to all neighboring capitals, especially Bangkok, five times a week, Singapore and Kuala Lumpur once a week, with onward connections to the East. Getting to Dhaka from Europe, there are regular flights from London and Amsterdam connecting with other European Capitals. From the US it is possible to connect via Delhi, Calcutta or Bangkok to Dhaka going east, or via Hongkong or Singapore going west. From Australia, the simplest way is via Bangkok, or also via Hongkong and Singapore. There are daily flights to Kathmandu and regular flights to Bangkok and Rangoon. Dhaka is a popular transit point for Burma, Thailand and Nepal, due to Biman's (the national carrier's) competitive fares.

Overland: There are two main crossing points from India for international travelers; Benapol on the route from Calcutta and Jaintiapur on the route from Shillong in the north. There is no crossing in the northwest leading the short distance to east Nepal, or crossings into Burma. Import of vehicles with a Carnet de Passage is permitted provided the vehicle is registered in its home country and is re-exported within the specified time.

Visas: Visa regulations are continually changing. It is therefore advisable to check the latest position at your local embassy or high commission. The situation to date is that no visa is required for a Commonwealth country—EXCEPT India, the U.K. and Australia—No visa is required for 15 days if a return air ticket is held for citizens of Australia, Belgium, Canada, Denmark, Finland, France, Germany, Holland, Indonesia, Italy, Luxembourg, Malaysia, Nepal, Norway, Portugal, Singapore, Spain, Sweden, Thailand, and the US. It is possible, in cases of emergency, to obtain a 72-hour entry permit, at your point of entry, within which time a visa can be obtained from The Director of Immigration and Passports in Dhaka.

Health: It is recommended that you have a valid International Certificate of Vaccination for cholera and typhoid which can be taken as TABC protecting you against typhoid, para-typhoid A and B and cholera. Yellow Fever inoculations are essential for those traveling from or via Central Africa or Northern South America.

Medically, Bangladesh is considered to be one of Asia's higher risk areas and therefore it is recommended that you take precautions before, during and after your visit.

Most of the diseases you are likely to fall prey to are water borne. It is recommended therefore, that you only drink treated water and try to avoid eating uncooked food or unpeeled fruit.

There is a risk of contracting malaria as mosquitoes are rife in Bangladesh, especially during the winter months. Visitors should therefore take anti-malarial tablets regularly before, during and after your stay if you are likely to be exposed to mosquito attack. It is best to consult your doctor on the best tablets for this area.

To allay your fears on the medical side, it is recommended that you take out a good comprehensive medical insurance. Rest assured, there are excellent and highly qualified doctors, although the facilities and back up are still lacking.

Money: Bangladesh currency is called Taka and the exchange rate is approximately 33 Taka to the US Dollar. There are seven denominations of notes: Tk1, Tk 5, Tk 10, Tk 20, Tk 50, Tk 100 and Tk 500. The taka is subdivided into 100 Poisha and there are coins of 1, 2, 5, 10, 25, and 50 poisha as well as a 1 Taka coin. When describing large sums of money, as elsewhere in Asia, the terms 1 Lakh equalling

336

INSIDE BANGLADESH

100,000 Taka and 1 Crore equalling 10,000,000 Taka are commonly used.

Banking has become quite sophisticated in Dhaka especially if you use Grindlays Bank, and the Chartered Bank, which have branches throughout Dhaka and quick and efficient links with most banks throughout the world. There is also an American Express Bank in the Commercial District of Motijheel. Travelers checks can be changed at the airport and at all leading international hotels and banks. However if you are traveling in the countryside you are advised to change the money you will need in the major cities before you leave.

Customs: Tourists are permitted to bring into Bangladesh free of duty, clothing and other personal effects exclusively meant for their own use. You must declare on the Currency Declaration Forms provided at the airport, if they are available, all jewelry, electronic goods, watches, cameras and especially videos. You should also declare any money, whether traveler's checks or currency over US$1,000, but there is no restriction on the amount you can carry with you. You can also take in with you a reasonable amount of alcohol and tobacco.

Departure: If you are traveling on internal flights you will need to pay two taxes which have to be paid at different booths. For international departures at the airport, you may pay a 200 Taka Airport Tax. At customs you may be required to hand back the Currency Declaration Form and show, if asked, the articles you originally declared on entry. You should not take more than 100 Taka local currency with you out of the country.

GETTING ACQUAINTED

Time: Bangladesh is six hours ahead of GMT. From Bangkok you will have to set your watch back one hour.

Climate: Bangladesh has three main seasons—the Cold Season from mid-November to the end of February; the Hot Season from March until the end of May, when the monsoon lowers the temperatures and brings in the Wet Season. The climate during the Cold Season is dry, pleasant and fresh with clear blue skies. The days are balmy and sunny with a chill in the air, especially in the northern regions. The countryside is green and the hills in Sylhet are at their best.

The Hot Season is relatively pleasant to start with, especially in the north and in the Hill Tracts. However temperatures rise rapidly from mid-April. As the monsoon approaches the humidity which is less bearable than the heat, rises to unbearable levels when even the locals long for the relief brought by the monsoon.

The monsoon is usually expected to arrive in Bangladesh on June 15 but can be three weeks earlier or later. By the end of June the monsoons will be well established over the whole country, to die away around the middle of October. Although the rains can be trying and flooding makes travel within the country difficult, the scenic beauty is an unforgettable experience, producing the most awe-inspiring sunsets. Cyclones hit Bangladesh on an average of about 16 times a decade and mostly affect the coastal areas. These tropical cyclones build up in the Bay of Bengal, lash the coast between Calcutta and Cox's Bazaar before slowly diminishing in strength as they come inland.

In the Cold Season, temperatures range from 21 C (70 F) in the day to 10 C (50 F) at night, with humidity at about 70 percent. During the Hot Season temperatures rise to an average of 35 C (95 F) in the day and 29 C (85 F) at night, with humidity at about 95 percent. During the monsoon the temperatures fluctuate due to the cooling influence of the rains.

What to Wear: Light and loose fitting cotton garments are recommended for all seasons, with a woollen sweater or cardigan for use during the winter months. To avoid embarrassing stares or religious wrath, do not wear

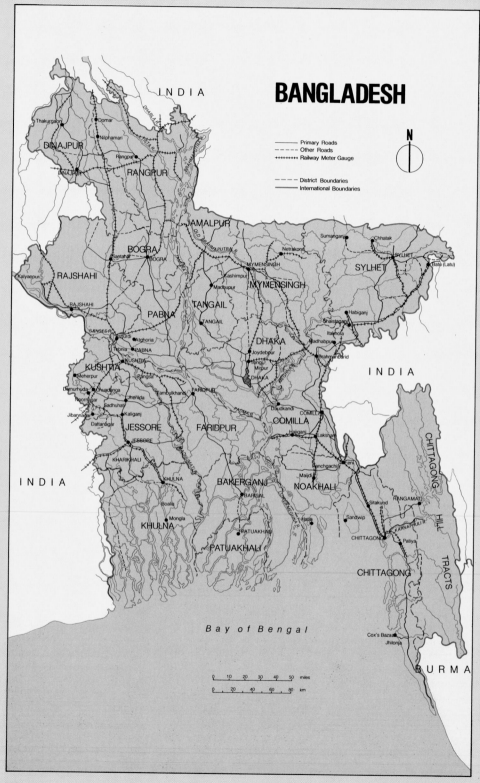

BANGLADESH

Primary Roads
Other Roads
Railway Meter Gauge

District Boundaries
International Boundaries

N

INDIA

Thakurgaon
Domar
Nilphamari
DINAJPUR
DINAJPUR
Rangpur
RANGPUR

Kalyaopur
RAJSHAHI
RAJSHAHI
Santahar
BOGRA
BOGRA

JAMALPUR
Sumanganj
Chhatak
SYLHET
Bala (Latu)
Netrakona
MYMENSINGH
SYLHET

Kashimpur
Madhupur
MYMENSINGH
Habiganj
Shaistaganj
Itakhola

PABNA
TANGAIL
Madhabpur
Brahmanbarid

GANGES R.
Surdi
Atghoria
Tebria
PABNA
DHAKA
Joydebpur
Mirpur
DHAKA

KUSHTIA
Meherpur
KUSHTIA

Damurhuda
Chuadanga
Pangsa
FARIDPUR
Noorhagar
Sadhuhati
Jhenida
Tambulkhandi
Daudkandi
COMILLA
Jibannagar
Kaliganj
Dattanagar

JESSORE
FARIDPUR
COMILLA
Haliganj
Lakshan

JESSORE

INDIA

KHARIKHALI
Panchgachia
Feni

KHULNA
BAKERGANJ
NOAKHALI
Maijdi
Boalia
BARISAL
Sitakund
RANGAMATI

Mongla
Hatia
Sandwip

KHULNA
PATUAKHALI
CHITTAGONG
Paliya

PATUAKHALI
CHITTAGONG
RAMGATI

INDIA

CHITTAGONG

HILL

TRACTS

Bay of Bengal

Cox's Bazaa
Jhilonja

BURMA

0 10 20 30 40 50 miles
0   20   40   60   80 km

338

shorts beyond the confines of your hotels except at the beach, and women are best dressed in long flowing dresses or skirts with respectable shirts/blouses with sleeves. It is wise also to wear a sun hat as the heat from the sun can be relentless. An umbrella is also reckoned to be a valued traveling companion against both the rain and the sun. If you are planning to visit the mosques it is wise to wear slip-on shoes as they must be removed before entering the mosque or even in the precincts of the mosque.

Survival Bangla: The language of Bangladesh is officially referred to as 'Bangla' or 'Bangala' and is Sanskrit based, with a degree of similarity to Hindi. English used to be more common than it is now, due to the upsurge of nationalism. However, it is still widely used and understood but there are no sign posts in English and recently all shop signs have reverted to Bangla (with an English translation below if required). The standard Bangla greeting among Muslims is *Assullam Walaikum,* or "Peace be unto you," with the reply being *Walaikum Salam—'"* Unto you also peace." Other words and phrases that you may find useful:

Thank You
Dhonnobad
Goodbye
Khudahafiz
How are You?
Kaemon achen

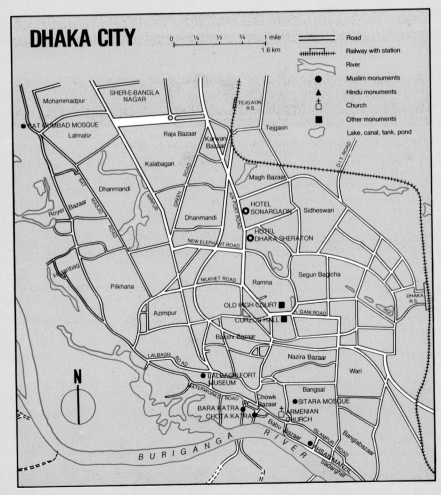

DHAKA CITY

0   ¼   ½   ¾   1 mile
1.6 km

Road
Railway with station
River
● Muslim monuments
▲ Hindu monuments
⌂ Church
■ Other monuments
Lake, canal, tank, pond

Mohammadpur
SHER-E-BANGLA NAGAR
TEJGAON R.S.
● SAT GUMBAD MOSQUE
Lalmatia
Raja Bazaar
Karwan Bazaar
Tejgaon
SAT MASJID ROAD
Kalabagan
GREEN ROAD
MIRPUR ROAD
AIRPORT ROAD
D.T. ROAD
Dhanmandi
Magh Bazaar
Royer Bazaar
Dhanmandi
NEW ELEPHANT ROAD
HOTEL ● SONARGAON
Sidheswari
HOTEL ● DHAKA SHERATON
Hazaribag
NILKHET ROAD
Ramna
Segun Bagicha
Pilkhana
Azimpur
OLD HIGH COURT ■
CURZON HALL ■
A. GANI ROAD
DHAKA R.S.
Bakshi Bazaar
LALBAGH ROAD
Nazira Bazaar
Wari
N
● LALBAGH FORT MUSEUM
WATERWORKS ROAD
Bangsal
Chowk Bazaar
● SITARA MOSQUE
BARA KATRA
CHOTA KATRA
✝ ARMENIAN CHURCH
Babu Bazaar
ISLAMPUR ROAD
Banglabazaar
● AHSAN MANZIL
Sadarghat
B U R I G A N G A   R I V E R

I am well
Nhalo achi
See you again
Abardekha hobe
How Much?
Dam Koto?
Where are you going?
Kothai Jaben
What is the time
Koto Baje
What do you want?
Ki Chai?
Is it available?
Eta Ki Pawa Jai
Not Available
Pawa Jaina
Yes
Hañ
No
Na
Good
Bharo
Bad
Kharap
Enough
Bas/Jathesto
Open
Khola
Close
Bondo
Far
Dur
Near
Kache
New
Nuttan
Old
Purana
Quick
Taratari
Slow
Ashte-ashte
Hot
Goram
Cold
Handa
More
Aro
Nice
Sundar

Business Hours: Friday is the weekend holiday and business organizations take Thursday afternoon as well. Embassies all seem to have slightly different working hours but all take both Friday and Saturday as weekend holidays.

Banking hours are from 9 a.m. to 1 p.m. Saturday to Wednesday and 9 a.m. to 12 noon on Thursday. Government office hours are 7:30 a.m. to 2 p.m. from Saturday to Thursday, whereas the business fraternity work from 9:30 a.m. to 5:30 p.m.

Shops are open from 10 a.m. from Saturdays to Thursdays until late in the evening and the New Market stays open on Fridays but closes on Mondays and Tuesdays.

Religion: The Muslim religion affects all aspects of life in Bangladesh even though the state is officially secular. Islam, the newest of the universal religions, originated in the sixth century A.D. when the prophet Mohammad, who lived in Mecca was called upon to recite God's word—the *Quran*—and bring it to his people. Mecca is the center of Islam and Islam is all pervading. It governs a Muslim's daily existence— his social, political and religious life and the *Quran* is the word of God. The most crucial observances of a Muslim are known as the Five Pillars of Islam which govern the life of a good Muslim.

He must acknowledge the unity of God and, to quote from the *Quran*: "There is no God but Allah and Mohammad is the messenger of God."

He must pray five times daily, facing Mecca and on Friday go to the mosque.

Give alms as an offering to Allah and an act of piety.

Observe the fast of *Ramadan* when no food or drink must be taken between sunrise and sunset.

Undertake *'Haj''*—the pilgrimage to Mecca—once in a lifetime.

Mosques are not sanctified ground but meeting places for like-minded believers. Islam forbids the decorating of any religious building with either human or animal images—only floral or geometric decoration is permitted.

Festivals: The Buddhist and Hindu festivals common in adjacent countries are celebrated by the various religious communities in a small way throughout Bangladesh. The main Muslim and national holidays are listed below:-

Bengali New Year: Pahela Baishakh falls on April 14 and is a public holiday commemorating the introduction of the Bengali era in 1556 by the Mughal emperor Akbar.

Eid-e-Miladunabi: The Prophet was born and died on the same day of the month (12th Raibul Awal) in mid-December. The day is a national holiday and meetings are held and food is distributed to the poor.

Independence Day: March 26 is the biggest state festival which is celebrated

ON THE MOVE

with due pomp and circumstance. The great boat race is held on the Buriganga River and buildings and streets are illuminated.

Martyr's Day: Shahid Dibosh: February 21 commemorates the death of students who protested against the introduction of Urdu as the national language which was understood as a symbol for the state's recognition of Bengali culture.

Eid ul-Fitr: "The rejoicing of piety and giving of alms" is the biggest Muslim festival of the year and is celebrated at the end of *Ramadan*. Prayer takes place in the open early in the morning before which time the family heads must have contributed to the poor so that they can also enjoy the celebrations.

Eid ul-Azha: "The rejoicing of Sacrifice" is the second of the big Muslim festivals falling in September and marks the annual pilgrimage or *Haj*. Prayer takes place in the open after which the family will sacrifice according to their means, an animal in recnogition of Hazrat Ibrahim's preparedness for the supreme sacrifice to Allah. The sacrifice is distributed among relatives and the poor.

Muharram: a day of ceremonial mourning to commemorate the tragic martyrdom of an important Muslim saint, Immam Hussain in 680 A.D. in Iraq.

Durga Puja—is the most important and spectacular Hindu festival celebrated throughout Bangladesh in October and dedicated to the goddess Durga. It lasts over ten days and in the final stages the idol is immersed in the River Buriganga amidst great ceremony.

TRANSPORT

Internal transport, even by air, is generally very cheap, so cheap that everyone uses it. So try to book well in advance to avoid disappointment. Public transport is usually very crowded and all vehicles were built for people with an average height of about five feet (1.5 meters).

Air: Biman, the national carrier, links all major towns and cities with Dhaka, with fairly regular flights mostly serviced by a small Fokker jet. There are airports at Chittagong, Jessore, Sylhet Saidpur, Cox's Bazaar and Ishurdi, all of which are connected directly from Dhaka.

River: This is the traditional means of transport in a country that has 5,000 miles (8,000 km) of navigable waterways. Water transport is mainly operated by Bangladesh Inland Waterways Transport Corporation (BIWTC), which also runs the large car ferries. One of the most interesting river trips is on the service known as the 'Rocket' from Dhaka to Khulna. The vessels running this route are original paddle steamers. Tickets and timetables are available from the BIWTC offices.

City Transport: Traveling around the city is not as easy as you will find in other Asian countries as taxis are few and far between. Alternatives are the boneshaking "Baby-taxi," which is a motorized three-wheeler for which bargaining is necessary to arrive at a reasonable price. For short trips around town the most common form of local transport, the ever-present cycle rickshaw powered by human endeavor, is readily available. Fares have to be negotiated, an interesting task as it is unlikely that a rickshaw *wallah* will speak English. However, a trip to old Dhaka by rickshaw is an experience worth paying a little extra for.

Taxi/Car Rental: There are taxi and car rental services available, mostly run by Parjatan Tourist Information Centers. The large hotels also have their own rental fleet, or have a Hertz or other car rental office.

WHAT TO DO

There is little regular Western-style entertainment or nightlife in Bangladesh, although the two international hotels stage special sponsored events and have regular discotheques in the evenings. However, Bengal being the home of the classical performing arts, there is always some Bengali production being performed, ranging from sitar concerts to classical dance and traditional theater. The cinema is very popular throughout Bangladesh and the screening of the ever popular Hindi movies, as well as locally-made films takes place throughout the country. The films nearly always follow the same standard and popular theme where good eventually overcomes evil, with plenty of song and dance thrown in.

Sports: For the sportsman, there is a surprisingly varied assortment of different activities available. There is an excellent 18-hole golf course in Dhaka which is beautifully landscaped with good club facilities. Visitors are welcome. Tennis and squash can be played in main hotels where there is a 'marker' who will give you a game if you are without an opponent. There are also excellent swimming pools at the same venues.

Shopping: Souvenirs in Bangladesh include jewelry, garments, brasswork, leatherwork, ceramics, jute products, artwork and terra-cota work. Special items of particular interest are the famous pink pearls, fine muslin, *jamdani* and silk *saris;* intricately patterned jute carpets at exceptionally reasonable prices; and for the curio hunter there is a mass of brass and bronze work ranging from old ships' compasses to beautiful simple brass bowls and dies for casting gold ornaments in. There are several handicraft shops to be found in and around the main hotels. Any antique which is an object of cultural value over 100 years old must have the stamp of approval of the Department of Archaeology before it can be exported. The Department is strict and seldom will clear a genuine piece. If you have any doubt it is best to get their approval. They will readily approve pieces that are not antiques to assist you with customs clearance.

WHERE TO STAY

As a result of people on business visiting Bangladesh, there are several hotels catering for all pockets. In Dhaka there are two international class hotels providing excellent accommodation and facilities. Elsewhere in Bangladesh there is limited accommodation mostly run by the Parjatan Tourist Corporation, especially in areas classified as tourist destinations. A few privately-owned middle level hotels are now being opened and it is sometimes possible to rent some of the government- or Corporation-owned rest houses. All hotel bills must be paid in hard currency or traveler's checks. Bills for food, drink etc. paid for immediately can, however, be settled in Taka.

Hotels

Dhaka:

The Sonargaon Hotel (Five-star)
Kawran Bazaar, Dhaka. 327 Rooms.
Tel: 315071-95. Highly Recommended.

The Dhaka Sheraton (Five-star)
Minto Road, Dhaka. 280 Rooms.
Tel: 252911-19. Highly Recommended.

Purbani International (Three-star)
Motijheel, Dhaka. 175 Rooms.
Tel: 25081-86. Acceptable.

Hotel Sunderbhans (Three-star)
Kawran Bazaar, Dhaka. 125 Rooms.
Acceptable.

Chittagong:

Hotel Agrabad (International Standard)
Agrabad, Chittagong. 101 Rooms.

FOOD DIGEST

Tel: 87001. Acceptable.

Hotel Shaikat (Parjatan Tourist Board)
Motel Road Cox's Bazaar. 24 Rooms.
Tel: 275.Reasonable.

Motel Probal (Parjatan Tourist Board)
Motel Road, Cox's Bazaar. 36 Rooms.
Tel: 211. Reasonable.

Hotel Sayeman (Two-Star)
Forest Colony Road, Cox's Bazaar. 50 Rooms.
Tel: 231. Acceptable.

Bogra:

Parjatan Motel (Parjatan Tourist Board)
Banani Road, Bogra. 17 Rooms.
Tel: 5044. Acceptable.

Khulna:
Rupsa International
North Jessore Road, Khulna. 30 Rooms.
Tel: 61563. Acceptable.

Selim Motel (Parjatan Tourist Board)
Shamshur Rahman Road, Khulna. 11 Rooms.
Tel: 20191. Spartan.

Rajshahi:
Parjatan Motel (Parjatan Tourist Board)
Abdul Masjid Road, Rajshahi. 50 Rooms.

Sylhet:
Hilltown Hotel ('Deluxe')
Telehaor, Sylhet. 56 Rooms.
Tel: 8262-64. Reasonable.

WHAT TO EAT

The food of Bangladesh, like the rest of the sub-continent, is influenced by the regional variations of its history. As an outpost of the Mughal empire it retains part of its heritage through its cuisine. *Kebabs* and *Koftas* of all kinds are available. There is also an abundance of excellent seafood. The Bangladeshis produce some wonderful curried dishes using the abundant varieties of fish and crustacia available. Snacks consisting of samosas, a batter-covered triangle containing meat or vegetables; *puri*, a stuffed pancake, and spicy omelettes are available everywhere. Bangladeshis have a very sweet tooth and there are many different sweet-meats to tempt you. Regional specialities, such as the delicious but very sweet yoghurt *misti dohi* from Bogra, are worth sampling.

Being an Islamic country, Bangladesh is a country of soft drinks. Even in the most remote outposts you will be able to find a coke. However, one of mother nature's more refreshing drinks is the green coconut, a guaranteed sterile drink, full of goodness and good for distressed stomachs. In Dhaka, other than the main hotel restaurants where there is a wide variety of cuisines available, there are a host of Chinese Restaurants serving western style Chinese dishes at a very reasonable price. There is a Thai restaurant and a Korean restaurant next door to one another at the western end of Gulshan Avenue. Recently, an authentic Chinese restaurant has opened on the Old Airport Road near the railway crossing, under joint Chinese and Bangladeshi ownership. The best local food is available at the Purbani Hotel in Motijheel.

ART/PHOTO CREDITS

INDEX

A